THE BEHAVIORAL NEUROSCIENCE OF ADOLESCENCE

A Norton Professional Book

THE BEHAVIORAL NEUROSCIENCE OF ADOLESCENCE

LINDA PATIA SPEAR

W. W. Norton
New York • London

For information about permission to reproduce selections from this book, write to
Permissions, W. W. Norton & Company, Inc., 500 Fifth Avenue, New York, NY 10110

For information about special discounts for bulk purchases, please contact W. W.
Norton Special Sales at specialsales@wwnorton.com or 800-233-4830

Manufacturing by Courier Westford
Production manager: Leeann Graham

Library of Congress Cataloging-in-Publication Data

Spear, Linda P.
  The behavioral neuroscience of adolescence / Linda Patia Spear. — 1st ed.
      p.   cm.
  Includes bibliographical references and index.
  ISBN 978-0-393-70542-3 (hardcover)
  1. Adolescent psychology.   2. Developmental neurophysiology.   3. Developmental
psychobiology.   I. Title.
BF724.S595 2010
155.5—dc22   2009022680

ISBN: 978-0-393-70542-3

W. W. Norton & Company, Inc., 500 Fifth Avenue, New York, N.Y. 10110
www.wwnorton.com

W. W. Norton & Company Ltd., Castle House, 75/76 Wells Street, London W1T 3QT

1 2 3 4 5 6 7 8 9 0

To the major blessings of my life:
Skip, Mandy, and Jen
and the next generation of emerging adolescents—
Kyra, Nate, Reed, Calvin, and Lily

Contents

• •

Preface

●●

The building of the brain was long thought to be essentially complete well before adolescence, with "raging hormones" blamed for any untoward adolescent behaviors. Recent research discoveries, however, have uncovered remarkable developmental transformations in the adolescent brain—knowledge that is revolutionizing our understanding of why adolescents behave the way they do. This book explores the neuroscience of the adolescent brain and considers how this developmental remodeling contributes to adolescent-typical ways of thinking and behaving. The strategy is to consider the complex and dynamically changing adolescent brain within a framework set by genetic heritage and early experiences, and modified by ongoing influences of pubertal hormones and adolescent life events. Thus, the chapters that follow represent a multidisciplinary excursion into past experiences, inherited characteristics, physiological and hormonal states, and current life stressors, and explore how these factors interact with the dynamics of the adolescent brain to influence normative adolescent function, as well as individual differences among adolescents in their vulnerability to or resilience regarding the emergence of adolescent-limited or more persistent difficulties.

The research-based focus of this book was designed to be accessible not only to professionals and students of behavioral neuroscience, but also to interested individuals without scientific training in neuroscience, genetics, endocrinology, or developmental processes. To accomplish this, the chapters of Part 1 begin with introductory and basic background information on these topics, although escalating rapidly thereafter to consider issues of theory and interpretation designed to be of broader general interest. Building upon the fundamentals presented in Part 1, a multidisciplinary perspective is used in the chapters of Part 2 to explore how the marked developmental alterations in the adolescent brain, along with hormonal, environmental, and gene expression changes of adolescence, influence the development of cognitive skills and self-control, alter social behavior, increase propensity for risk-taking and alcohol/drug use, and contribute to the emergence of drug abuse, depression, and other psychological disorders among the most vulnerable adolescents.

An important theme that resonates throughout this book is that the biological roots of adolescence are deeply embedded in our evolutionary past—that is, adolescents of a diversity of mammalian species share numerous commonalities with human adolescents in the hormonal and brain changes of adolescence, the genetics of development, and in certain adolescent-characteristic behavioral strategies as well. Among the implications is that some of the seemingly counterproductive behaviors occasionally exhibited by adolescents today may reflect in part behaviors of adaptive significance during our evolutionary past. The evolutionary conserved nature of adolescence supports judicious use of basic animal models of adolescence to explore aspects of adolescent brain development, physiology, and neurobehavioral function that are difficult to study in human adolescents, given the constraints necessary when conducting research in developing humans. Thus, the approach taken throughout this presentation is to complement findings from human imaging studies with data derived from basic science studies when exploring brain/behavioral interrelationships during adolescence.

Research examining the adolescent brain is escalating rapidly, and hence any summary of the state of work in this area, by necessity, provides but a static snapshot of this rapidly developing field. Such an interim summary of the current state of understanding of adolescent brain function, however, can be valuable not only for codifying emerging findings, but also for highlighting ongoing controversies, underexplored areas, and intriguing puzzles that remain, with an eye toward future work. The intent of this presentation has been to do both.

One particularly crucial and intriguing question about adolescence is whether the changes occurring in the adolescent brain reflect a time of particular vulnerabilities, or opportunities, or both. That is, do high levels of drug use, multiple life stressors, or other challenges disrupt normal processes of brain maturation during adolescence, thereby exerting a long-lasting impact on brain function that is not evident following similar experiences in adulthood? Or does the remodeling of the adolescent brain represent an enhanced opportunity for the developing brain to recover from the consequences of a difficult adolescence? And perhaps even more intriguingly, do highly practiced and frequently experienced activities during adolescence serve to "tailor-make" a brain that at maturity reflects these adolescent proclivities and interests? Hints to the answers to these questions, and how these adaptations may be moderated by individual differences in genetic heritage and in life experiences, are beginning to appear and represent another reoccurring theme in the pages to follow.

Acknowledgments

● ●

It is hard to know where to begin to thank those that have helped me through this project. First and foremost, my husband, Skip, deserves a "major award" for his incredible patience, humor, support, and encouragement throughout this project. In this project, like so many other activities, I have benefited considerably from his research expertise, wise counsel, and prodigious knowledge of developmental psychobiology (not to mention his ability to spell even the most obscure word). I am also immensely grateful for his knack in helping me find some semblance of balance across the diverse pieces of my life.

I owe a particularly large debt of gratitude to Dr. Ellen Witt at the National Institute on Alcohol Abuse and Alcoholism (NIAAA) for all of her encouragement and support during the early years when there was little interest in studying the behavioral neuroscience of adolescence; from the beginning, she has been a tireless advocate for adolescent research, particularly when seeking the roots of alcohol abuse and dependence. I am also thankful to my graduate mentor, Dr. Robert L. Isaacson, who strove to help me think more creatively and write more clearly, with mixed success on both counts. My graduate students—and the ideas, creativity, enthusiasm, and data they generate—remain major sources of inspiration. These include current students Rachel Anderson, Maggie Broadwater, Melissa Morales, Liane Ramirez, Courtney Vetter-O'Hagen, Amanda Willey, and Carrie Wilmouth, as well as former trainees whose work continues to inspire, including Drs. Marisa Silveri, Tammi Doremus-Fitzwater, Cheryl Kirstein, Rob Ristuccia, and Charles Heyser, among many others. Special thanks go to my close collaborator and long-term research colleague, Dr. Elena Varlinskaya, who has provided strong support and has sharpened my thinking on every level. I also owe a debt of gratitude to my office assistant, Suzanne Rodriguez, who has provided critical help on this and so many other projects, and shown remarkable patience throughout. Also greatly appreciated are the valuable comments, encouraging feedback, and wise counsel of Kristen Holt-Browning at Norton—thanks much for gently shepherding me through this process.

Although I write as a cloistered activity, I do so in the company of the data, wisdom, and creativity of all whose work I have cited throughout these pages. My sincerest thanks to all of you for your exceptional work and thought-provoking insights that continue to inform and inspire me. Hopefully, I have acknowledged your ideas and represented your work fairly; if upon any occasion I did not, I apologize. When I started to list colleagues who have influenced my thinking about adolescence through discussions during meetings, symposia, study section breaks, dinners, taxi rides and extended flight delays over the years, the list quickly became unmanageably long. So I am using this as an excuse not to attempt to list everyone here (thereby avoiding inadvertently leaving out someone critical). Should any of you read these pages, please know that I am highly appreciative of your thoughts and wisdom. Last, but definitely not least, I am indebted to NIAAA and the National Institute on Drug Abuse for their past and ongoing support of the research in my laboratory.

Quick Reference

• •

Acronym	*Term*
A	adenosine
ACC	anterior cingulate cortex
ACTH	adrenocorticotropic hormone
ADHD	attentional-deficit/hyperactivity disorder
ANS	autonomic nervous system
BDNF	brain-derived neurotrophic factor
BLA	basolateral nucleus of the amygdala
BNST	bed nucleus of the stria terminalis
BOLD	blood-oxygen-level-dependent
C	cytosine
CeA	central nucleus of the amygdala
CB	cannabinoid
CD	conduct disorder
CNV	contingent negative variation
COMT	catechol-O-methyl-transferase
CORT	corticosteroids
COS	child-onset schizophrenia
CPP	conditioned place preference

CRH	corticotrophin releasing hormone
CTA	conditioned taste aversions
DRD1	D1 subtype of DA receptor
DRD2	D2 subtype of DA receptor
DRD4	D4 subtype of DA receptor
DA	dopamine
dlPFC	dorsolateral prefrontal cortex
DNA	deoxyribonucleic acid
DTI	diffusion tensor imaging
DZ	dizygotic (fraternal) twins
EEG	electroencephalogram
ERN	error-related negativity
ERPs	event-related potentials
FA	fractional anisotrophy
fMRI	functional MRI
FSH	follicle-stimulating hormone
G	guanine
GABA	gamma-aminobutyric acid
GnRH	gonadotropin releasing hormone
GPR54	G protein-coupled receptor which binds the peptide kisspeptin
GSR	galvanic skin response
G×E	gene–environment
HPA	hypothalamic–pituitary–adrenal
HPG	hypothalamic–pituitary–gonadal
HR	heart rate
5–HT	serotonin (5-hydroxytryptamine)
IQ	intelligence quotient
LG	licking–grooming
LH	luteinizing hormone
MAO-A	monoamine oxidase A
MRI	magnetic resonance imaging
mRNA	messenger ribonucleic acid
MRS	magnetic resonance spectroscopy

MZ	monozygotic (identical) twins
NAc	nucleus accumbens
NE	norepinephrine
NgR	nogo receptors
NMDA	N-methyl-D-aspartic acid
NRG1	neuroregulin
ODD	oppositional defiant disorder
OFC	orbitofrontal cortex
OPRM1	mu opiate receptor
P	postnatal day
PET	positron emission tomography
PFC	prefrontal cortex
PNS	parasympathethic nervous system
"P rats"	"preferring" rats (rats selectively bred to prefer alcohol)
RNA	ribonucleic acid
rRNA	ribosomal RNA
ROI	region of interest
SN	substantia nigra
SNS	sympathetic nervous system
SSRIs	selective serotonin-reuptake inhibitors
T	thymidine
TCAs	tricyclic antidepressants
THC	delta-9-tetrahydrocannabinol
vmPFC	ventromedial PFC
VTA	ventral tegmental area

THE BEHAVIORAL NEUROSCIENCE OF ADOLESCENCE

· ·

PART I

The Basics of Development: Evolutionary, Genetic, Hormonal, Neural, and Sociocultural Factors

CHAPTER ONE

Adolescence as a Unique Developmental Stage

• •

"While adolescents as we know them—kept in the natal home under the authority of parents, attending school, and bedeviled by a bewildering array of occupational choices—are a modern phenomenon, adolescence as a social stage with its own activities and behaviors, expectations and rewards, is well recorded in the history and literature of earlier times."

—Schlegel & Barry (1991, p. 2)

Adolescence is a time of transitions: from childhood to adulthood, from dependence to (relative) independence, from a nonsexual state to sexual maturity. To successfully negotiate these transitions, the adolescent must effectively function within this time of inherent change and uncertainty, while also preparing to take on future adult roles and responsibilities. The central thesis of this book is that many adolescent-typical ways of thinking, feeling, and behaving are a result of normal developmental changes in the adolescent brain and ultimately serve to address the immediate and future-directed needs of the adolescent. Although it has long been recognized that brain development and differentiation are lifelong processes, much of the traditional focus has been on early developmental stages, especially the period of particularly rapid brain growth and

3

differentiation that begins well before birth and continues into infancy as the infant begins to interact with the world. Yet, over the past decade or so, attention has turned to another period of particularly dramatic developmental change in the brain: adolescence. Precipitated initially by basic science studies conducted in laboratory animals documenting the often marked remodeling of the brain during adolescence at cellular, molecular, and anatomical levels, this focus escalated rapidly with advances in noninvasive brain imaging technology, allowing researchers to examine developmental changes in brain structure and activity in normal children and adolescents.

These glimpses into the changing brain of the adolescent are transforming our understanding of the causes, contributors, and consequences of adolescent-typical ways of behaving and thinking. Such adolescence-associated alterations in the brain likely evolved to support the adolescent through this developmental transition while also serving to promote development of the cognitive competencies, knowledge base, emotional regulation, and social relationships necessary for effective adult functioning. Indeed, certain of the characteristic behavioral features and neural changes of adolescence are seen during the transition from dependence to independence in other mammalian species as well, suggesting that these brain changes, and the behaviors they support, have ancient biological roots deeply embedded in our evolutionary past.

The road from life as a child to that of an adult can be a bumpy one, with mortality rates higher during this otherwise unusually healthy time of life than at younger or older ages— mortality rates that, as we shall see, are driven largely by unfortunate consequences of adolescent behaviors. Notable individual differences characterize how adolescents fare in negotiating the transitions of adolescence, and in the developmental trajectories they display toward, and away from, problematic behaviors. Indeed, adolescence is the time of greatest risk for the emergence of psychological disorders, ranging from a marked rise in the incidence of depression, anxiety, and conduct disorders beginning in early- to midadolescence, to the increased incidence of schizophrenia that emerges during the late-adolescent to adult transition. Alcohol and drug use is also frequently initiated at this age, with the highest rates of alcohol abuse and dependence seen during mid- to late adolescence and the transition into young adulthood. Exciting advances in our understanding of the adolescent brain are beginning to provide important pieces of the puzzle as to why different youth are particularly vulnerable or resistant to the emergence of such disorders during the transitions of adolescence.

THE TIMING OF ADOLESCENCE: ADOLESCENCE VERSUS PUBERTY

Adolescence and *puberty* are not synonymous terms. Adolescence consists of the entire transition from childhood to adulthood, whereas puberty refers to the more restricted time interval associated with the hormonal and physiological changes of sexual maturation. Although the onset of adolescence is sometimes synchronized with the appearance of pubertal-associated biological changes (e.g., Petersen, 1998), the timing of puberty within the adolescent period has been shown to vary notably among adolescents (e.g., Dubas, 1991). Indeed, there are no set biomarkers for the onset or offset of adolescence, with youth often becoming progressively more "adolescent-like" in their behavior and thinking around the beginning of the second decade of life, and gradually subsiding in their adolescent-typical characteristics a decade or more later. Yet, although prototypic adolescence is considered by some to subsume the second decade of life (e.g., Petersen et al., 1996), others include ages up to 25 years or more as late adolescence (e.g., Baumrind, 1987) or "emerging adulthood" (Arnett, 2004).

5

The task of characterizing the time course of adolescence and puberty is also complicated by evidence that this timing is influenced by environmental conditions (e.g., Enright et al., 1987), nutritional status (delayed with lower body fat; Frisch, 1984), and sex (with females typically entering and moving through adolescence more quickly than males; Savin-Williams & Weisfeld, 1989). Sociocultural values also dramatically influence how adolescence is viewed as a developmental stage and how it is expressed and managed. Even the biology of adolescent transitions—for example, the timing of puberty—is sensitive to cultural practices. Thus, as background for exploring the behavioral, cognitive, and social neuroscience of adolescence in later chapters, the critical impact of culture on adolescence is briefly considered here.

CULTURAL INFLUENCES ON THE EXPRESSION OF ADOLESCENCE

In traditional, nonindustrial cultures, children and adolescents are expected to work, taking care of younger children and helping in procuring food; in such societies, adolescents often begin to work full-time by 10–12 years of age and assume adult workloads by 14–16 years of age (e.g., see Weisfeld & Janisse, 2004). It has sometimes been argued that in complex societies where substantial education and training are required prior to assuming adult occupational status, the period of adolescence has been prolonged to provide adequate time for such training. And when unemployment is high, the time taken to achieve a salary sufficient for independence and support of a spouse, home, and children may be relatively delayed, a point to which we will return later. As a result, some college graduates may gravitate back to living at home or with a group of roommates, often extending adolescent-typical behaviors such as all-night partying, binge drinking, and "hooking up" (sexual encounters outside of romantic relationships). This extension of "adolescence" has been called "emerging adulthood," "guyland," and the like (e.g., Arnett, 2004; Kimmel, 2008). On the other hand, provoked perhaps partly by highly publicized and glamorized pregnancies of teenage media stars, pregnancy and mother-hood have become seeming status symbols among some groups of young teen girls. Pregnancy may also serve as a means by which girls living in difficult family circumstances attempt to curtail an abusive childhood, declare their reproductive matu-rity, and improve their social circumstances via formation of a new family unit (e.g., Smith, 1996).

Adolescence is not, however, merely a creation of modern society. As we shall see in later chapters, certain characteristic features of adolescence, including an increased focus on peer-directed social relationships (along with rising conflicts with parents) and elevations in risk-taking and sensation-seeking behaviors are seen not only in human adolescents but in those undergoing the developmental transition from dependence to independence in other species as well. Moreover, as alluded to in the quote that opened this chapter, adolescence and adoles-cents have long been favored subjects in the classic literature—an obvious example being Shakespeare's Romeo and Juliet.

How adolescent-typical behaviors, expectations, and emo-tions are interpreted, however, is strongly dependent on the overall sociocultural environment. In many modern societies, a certain proportion of adolescents are more or less expected to be delinquents; yet adolescents engaging in similar behav-iors may not be viewed as delinquent in other cultures. Schle-gel and Barry (1991) give a number of such examples from their anthropological studies of adolescence. For instance, among certain sociocultural groups (e.g., Asian immigrants living in Chinatowns in large cities in the United States), ag-gressive behavior instigated by male adolescents toward po-tentially violent intruders may have helped to protect the social group from harm. Likewise, among the Mbuti people, a hunter-

7

gatherer group indigenous to the Congo region of Africa, adolescents often served as "enforcers," sanctioned to punish adults whose behavior did not meet societal expectations by mocking and ridiculing them and vandalizing their property. In cultures where even relatively extreme adolescent behaviors can be co-opted to support cultural norms and values, adolescence is likely to represent a less tumultuous transition than in cultures where those behaviors are viewed as inappropriate and disruptive to others.

Cultures have also differed in whether the pubertal transition to adulthood is accompanied by a formal initiation ceremony and by the nature of that symbolic transition, if it is conducted. This initiation often began with an initial separation of prepubertal youth (around 8–10 years of age) from their parents and opposite-sexed peers for several years, during which select elders taught the emerging adolescents sex-specific skills necessary for functioning as adults. In boys, this transition may have required successful completion of one or more challenging and often hazardous ordeals. The ending of this transitional phase several years later (at about 12–15 years) was often marked by a ritual that symbolized the initiates' incorporation into adult society and, especially for females, formally recognized their reproductive fertility (Weisfeld, 1979). Initiation rites were sometimes painful, accompanied by genital mutilation (in females), tattooing, scarification (skin cuts to induce scars), or insertion of objects into the ear lobes or nose; body painting or the wearing of special costumes and masks are less painful rituals that have been used by some cultures.

Cultures also have differed dramatically in how the emerging sexuality of adolescence is managed. For instance, among certain tribes in Melanesia, for a transient period during adolescence boys were expected to engage in homosexual acts. Among the Muria, a tribe found in the hills of India, adolescent males and females lived together in adolescent-only houses where they were encouraged to trade sleeping partners frequently. In contrast, among dowry-exchanging cultures, a high premium was characteristically placed on virginity at marriage, with both adolescent girls and boys typically discouraged from engaging in any type of sexual relationship prior to marriage (Schlegel, 1995).

Sociocultural practices influence not only how adolescents are viewed and managed, but also the biology of adolescence as well. Consider, for instance, cultural influences on the timing of the physiological and hormonal changes associated with puberty. In polygamous societies, where adult males typically have multiple offspring with different wives and thus seemingly have less contact with each child, girls tend to go through puberty earlier than in monogamous societies (Bean, 1983). While there are undoubtedly more differences between polygamous and monogamous societies than father–child contact time, lower paternal investment has been linked to accelerated pubertal maturation in girls even within monogamous cultures. For example, a study conducted in Canada found that girls who experienced paternal absence prior to 10 years of age matured about 6 months earlier than girls from intact homes (Surbey, 1990). It remains to be determined, however, as to whether this finding reflects father absence per se, or some other factor such as heritable differences (with early-maturing mothers perhaps being more prone to early pregnancy and single parenthood; see Surbey, 1990) or stress effects (with family conflict accelerating onset of puberty; e.g., Kim & Smith, 1998; see Weisfeld, 1999, for further discussion). Indeed, there is evidence that culture-specific exposure to stressors, including pubertal rite practices involving genital mutilation or scarification, can influence pubertal timing, with adolescents from cultures using these practices progressing through puberty more quickly than cultures without such initiation ordeals (Surbey, 1998). Thus, as illustrated by these examples, although the study of adolescence is often dichotomized into sociocultural versus biological approaches, these distinctions are not completely separable, given, for instance, notable cultural influences on the biological progression of puberty.

ECONOMIC INFLUENCES ON PERCEPTION OF ADOLESCENCE

How adolescents are viewed and managed varies not only across cultures but within cultures over time. One likely relevant variable that fluctuates with time is economic. Enright and colleagues (1987) used a historical approach to examine how adolescence was viewed during two periods of notable economic depression in the United States (the post-Industrial Revolution depressions of the 1890s and 1930s), relative to two alternating intervals of unusually rapid economic expansion (World Wars I [1917–1919] and II [1941–1945]). Although there are undoubtedly other differences between periods of war and intervals of peace that could influence attribution of differences across these time windows, their analyses revealed marked disparities in how adolescence was viewed between times of economic depression versus expansion. During times when the economy was depressed, unemployment rates high, and jobs few, adolescents typically were viewed as immature, slow to develop, psychologically stressed, and in need of protracted education and support. In contrast, during times of economic expansion when labor needs were great, adolescence was perceived as a relatively brief developmental stage, with adolescents viewed as psychologically competent, relatively mature, and with adult-like capacities for work. At these times of greater labor demands, child labor and education laws were often tempered or abandoned (Enright et al., 1987). This historical perspective argues that the adolescent population provides a means by which size of the workforce can be adjusted to meet labor demands, with adolescents mobilized into labor

10

when needs are high, but encouraged to prolong education and delay entry into the workforce when the economy is depressed and unemployment rates are high.

Weirdly enough, a somewhat similar relationship between economics/labor needs and the speed of transition from immaturity to maturity is also seen in honey bees. Immature honey bees typically work in the hive, taking care of the brood, whereas mature bees serve as foragers, bringing back nectar and pollen to the hive. This maturational change from immature to mature worker status involves changes in gene activation and brain structure and chemistry—changes that can be slowed down or sped up by the economics within the hive (Whitefield et al., 2003). That is, in the absence of mature bees—when labor needs are high—many immature bees undergo the transition to maturity early, truncating the length of their immature status. In contrast, when foragers are abundant and labor needs are low, the transition to mature worker status is often delayed. Thus, varying the timing of the transition from immaturity to maturity may be one strategy used by broadly different social groups to flexibly adjust the size of the workforce to changing labor needs.

SUMMARY AND CLOSING COMMENTS

As illustrated by the examples given in this chapter, behaviors typical of adolescence are seen across cultures, although there are sometimes marked differences among cultural groups in how these behaviors are viewed and managed. Even the more tumultuous of adolescent behaviors, viewed as disruptive or delinquent in many cultures, may be channeled into culturally endorsed activities serving useful societal functions in certain cultures. Alternative views of adolescents as competent, mature, and suited for work versus immature, slowly developing, and in need of extended education may wax and wane over

11

time, driven in part by economic conditions and labor demands. Sociocultural practices influence not only how adolescence is viewed within that society, but also the biology of adolescence—notably, the timing of the physiological transformations of puberty.

Recognition of the critical role of socioeconomic and cultural influences on the pace, perception, and management of adolescence does not diminish the significant impact of neural, hormonal, and other physiological changes on the developing adolescent. Indeed, recent advances in the neuroscience of adolescence have revealed marked alterations in adolescent brain that are transforming our understanding of adolescent-typical ways of thinking, feeling, and behaving.

The chapters that follow first explore the explosion of research in genetics and how that is helping to inform (and challenge) our understanding of adolescent-typical transformations (Chapter 2). Puberty and the reinstatement of gonadal hormonal release during adolescence are then discussed (Chapter 3), before considering the dramatic transformations that occur in the brain of the adolescent (Chapter 4). With this material as a background, later chapters discuss the behavioral neuroscience of cognitive skills (Chapter 5); impulsivity, risk, and the emergence of self-control (Chapter 6); social behavior and emotions (Chapter 7); alcohol and drug use and abuse (Chapter 8); the emergence of psychological disorders in adolescence (Chapter 9), and finally close with a consideration of whether the neural transformations of adolescence represent a time of particular vulnerabilities and opportunities for the developing adolescent (Chapter 10).

CHAPTER TWO

The Genetics and Evolution of Adolescence

•••

This chapter focuses on two intersecting topics. First, adolescence is viewed within a broad evolutionary approach, to explore the extent to which remnants of the evolutionary past are embedded in the brain and evident in the behavior of today's adolescents, and considering in turn the relevance and limitations of basic research using animal models for the study of adolescence. Then we examine the currency through which hereditary information is passed along: genetics. This will help set the stage for discussions in later chapters of genetic contributions to the behavioral and neural diversity of adolescents, and of the question of why some adolescents who live in difficult circumstances develop problems with drug abuse or psychological disorders, whereas others facing the same difficulties thrive.

ADOLESCENCE FROM AN EVOLUTIONARY PERSPECTIVE

"immature animals . . . frequently inhabit environments that are . . . different from those of the adult. Consequently, each of these stages may have required the evolution of specific morphological, biochemical, physiological and behavioral mechanisms which are different from the adult, and which may require modification, suppression or even destruction before the adult stage can be obtained."

—Oppenheim (1981, p. 74)

As described in this quote by Oppenheim, physiological and behavioral needs of developing organisms change as they pass through different developmental stages, requiring age-specific adaptations (i.e., "ontogenetic adaptations") of the growing organism to meet these needs. According to this view, developing organisms are not simply immature and incomplete adults; rather, they reflect adaptations to the particular developmental niches they encounter as they mature. An exaggerated and unequivocal form of ontogenetic adaptation is *metamorphosis*—the process by which the form of the developing organism changes so drastically that pre- and postmetamorphosis forms sometimes were mistaken for different species. A classic example is the metamorphosis from tadpole to frog, a transition from swimming in ponds to hopping on land that requires dramatic physiological changes and a notable restructuring of the nervous system to support the behavioral transformations necessary for functioning in the new environment. Albeit less dramatic, adolescence likewise involves complex developmental changes that include the physiological transformations of puberty, notable restructuring and adjustments of the brain, along with expression of characteristic age-specific behaviors.

This developmental transition from a condition of immaturity and dependence to the emergence of a sexually mature and (relatively) independent state defines adolescence, and it is a transition that can be identified widely across mammalian species, as noted previously. During the adolescent period, developing organisms across a variety of species undergo puberty and are faced with the common challenges of surviving this often stressful transition while attaining the cognitive, social, and emotional regulatory skills necessary for independence from parents and for attracting a suitable mating partner (or partners). As we shall see, commonalities are seen among adolescents across a diversity of mammalian species in the physiological and brain changes they undergo, and in certain basic behavioral strategies they display. These characteristics seemingly have proved sufficiently adaptive for navigating adolescence to have been maintained ("conserved") by common evolutionary pressures. Even the typical sex difference in timing of puberty, with females maturing earlier than males, is widespread across mammalian species and birds (Weisfeld, 1979).

Among the common behavioral proclivities seen in human adolescents and their counterparts in other species is an increasing focus on, and time spent interacting socially with, peers, along with a transient increase in fighting with parents in some species (e.g., Csikszentmihalyi et al., 1977; Primus & Kellogg, 1989; Steinberg, 1989). Indeed, basic science studies have found that peer-directed interactions are deemed especially rewarding during adolescence (Douglas et al., 2004) and that these interactions help participants develop new social skills and support (Galef, 1977; Harris, 1995) which may ease the transition to independence away from the family. In many species, social interactions with peers help guide choice-related behavior such as food selection, and provide the opportunity to practice and model adult-typical behavior patterns, including the emergence of sexual behaviors (see Spear, 2007b, for discussion).

Another common behavior among mammalian adolescents, perhaps especially adolescent males, is an increase in a group of related behaviors termed novelty-seeking, risk-taking, and sensation-seeking (Adriani et al., 1998; Trimpop et al., 1999). Even in studies using a simple animal model of adolescence, novelty has been shown to be particularly rewarding for adolescent males, more so than their adult counterparts (Douglas et al., 2003). From an evolutionary perspective, risk-taking has been hypothesized to serve a number of adaptive functions, such as providing opportunities to explore adult behaviors and privileges (Silbereisen & Reitzle, 1992) and to face and conquer challenges (Csikszentmihalyi & Larson, 1978). There is evidence that risk-taking may increase the probability of reproductive success in males from a variety of species, including humans (Wilson & Daly, 1985), and may provide "developmentally appropriate experimentation" (Shedler & Block, 1990).

Adolescent-associated increases in peer-directed interactions and in the seeking of novel and exciting stimuli may increase the impetus for groups of adolescents to explore new and broader areas away from the home. This expansion of interest to more distant and unfamiliar regions may have been of particular importance evolutionarily in that such behaviors could help instigate emigration by groups of adolescent peers away from their home territory. Emigrating away from the home—and hence from sexually active adults to whom/which they are genetically related—around the time of sexual maturation appears to be a strategy commonly used by mammalian species to avoid inbreeding—that is, the lower viability and other damaging effects often seen in offspring derived from the mating of closely related individuals (e.g., father–daughter, brother–sister) due to the greater expression of recessive genes in these offspring (Bixler, 1992; Moore, 1992). Indeed, in most mammalian species, including our human ancestors (e.g., Schlegel & Barry, 1991), male adolescents (or less frequently, female adolescents or adolescents of both sexes) emigrate from their natal area around the time that they begin to become sexually mature, a venture often taken in association with peers (e.g., Keane, 1990). Because of the high cost of inbreeding for the resulting offspring, behaviors facilitating emigration, such

as risk-taking, are likely to have been under considerable selection pressure during evolution. Yet, even in modern human
societies where there are strong cultural traditions against inbreeding, which seemingly would diminish pressure for emigrating, adolescent risk-taking still thrives. Indeed, a majority
of adolescents engage in some risk-taking behaviors, including
drunk driving, sex without protection against disease or pregnancy, use of illicit drugs, fighting, theft, other illegal acts, and
so on (Irwin, 1989). Risk-taking may persist among human adolescents partly because of its other potential adaptive consequences (as discussed earlier).

Yet, the evolutionary persistence of risk-taking in adolescence is not innocuous, with such risk-taking often well earn-
ing the designation of *risk*. Indeed, risk-taking to excess or with
bad timing is often disadvantageous if not life-threatening,
with death rates notably higher than at younger or older ages
among adolescents across a broad variety of species, including
humans (e.g., Irwin & Millstein, 1992; Crockett & Pope, 1993).
This increase in mortality occurs despite adolescence being
one of the otherwise healthiest of life stages and is due largely
to misfortunes arising from risk-taking behaviors (e.g., Muuss
& Porton, 1998), with the three highest causes of mortality
among adolescents in the United States being accidents, homicides, and suicides (Irwin et al., 2002).

Other functional commonalities are seen across adolescents of a variety of species, including similarities in cognitive
development and in age-related transitions in restorative behaviors such as eating and sleeping (see Spear, 2000a, for review). For instance, the adolescent-typical shift in sleep
patterns to going to bed later and waking later than at younger
ages is seen not only in human adolescents (e.g., see Dahl &
Lewis, 2002) but also adolescents of other species (Alföldi et
al., 1990). Along with the considerable growth spurt characteristic of adolescence is a notable enhancement in food consump-

tion that is generally seen in human adolescents (aside from cultural trends for thinness and dieting among females in some cultures), as well as adolescents of other species (Nance, 1983; Post & Kemper, 1993; Blackwelder & Golub, 1996). Adolescent rodents (Brunell & Spear, 2005; Doremus et al., 2005), like human adolescents (e.g., Johnston et al., 2003), even drink more alcohol per occasion than their adult counterparts. Taken together, these types of findings suggest that certain fundamental adolescent behavior patterns have deep evolutionary roots and have been highly conserved during evolution across species.

Along with these characteristically conserved adolescent behavior patterns are numerous across-species similarities in the sculpting of the adolescent brain, with alterations similar to those seen in human adolescents evident during the adolescent transition in mammalian species ranging from rodents to nonhuman primates. These often dramatic brain transformations, which are discussed in detail beginning in Chapter 4, may have been subject to a variety of evolutionary pressures. In addition to serving as the substrate for emergence of the adult brain, adolescent brains must also support age-typical behavioral and cognitive functions and precipitate the hormonal and physiological changes of puberty (see Spear, 2007a, for review).

Of course, although certain neural, hormonal, behavioral, and physiological similarities can be identified between human adolescents and their counterparts in other species, these other species do not display anywhere near the complexity of neurobehavioral function evident during adolescence (or any other time of life, for that matter). Nevertheless, such across-species commonalities provide opportunities to use simple animal models of adolescence to address certain questions that are challenging or ethically inappropriate to examine in developing humans. For instance, it is generally ethically inappropriate to administer alcohol and other drugs of abuse to adolescents to determine whether their brains respond differently to these drugs, and whether there are lasting effects of such adolescent exposures. Thus, much of what is known about the intricacies of brain development, including the sculpting of the brain during adolescence, has been obtained from anatomical and neurochemical studies in laboratory animals, using levels of analysis well beyond those that can be examined with imaging or other non-invasive procedures in humans.

The appropriateness of any simple animal model depends on the question under examination. Certainly there are many areas of adolescent functioning in humans that are not amenable to examination using animal models—to give but a few examples: issues regarding self-esteem, parenting styles, and cultural differences in the perception of adolescence. The adolescent period is also very abbreviated in short-lived species (e.g., lasting only about two weeks [from about postnatal days (P) 28–42] in rats), limiting the length of training and testing periods, and constraining the types of testing that can be conducted. Yet, in some instances, animal models can be used to probe adolescent brain function and behavior, particularly when exploring adolescent behaviors that have been highly conserved across species. For instance, laboratory animals, including adolescent rats (e.g., Doremus et al., 2005; Kerstetter & Kantak, 2007), generally voluntarily self-administer and find the same drugs rewarding that humans do (e.g., cocaine, alcohol, nicotine, heroin; see Koob & LeMoal, 2006). Indeed, much of what is known about brain substrates of the reinforcing effects of drugs and other rewarding stimuli has been obtained in rodent studies (for review, see Koob & LeMoal, 2006), supporting the use of simple rodent models of adolescence for examining neural and environmental factors that contribute to the frequent initiation of drug use during adolescence and to the escalation of use among the more vulnerable.

GENETICS

Now that hereditary influences on adolescence have been viewed from the long-term perspective of evolution, we turn to considering the currency through which hereditary information is passed—genes—to set the stage for later discussions of the exciting ways by which genetics research is transforming our understanding of adolescence.

The Basics: DNA, RNA, Proteins

Research in the area of molecular genetics has escalated rapidly, with the complete sequencing of the human genome during the past decade and the advent of new molecular genetic techniques for determining genetic variants across individuals. Before delving into key findings of the genetics revolution, a few basics of genetics are briefly highlighted as a refresher for those whose studies in basic biology may be but a dim memory.

All parts of the body, including the brain, are built from roughly identical sets of chemical instructions contained within a substance called deoxyribonucleic acid (DNA) that consists of a backbone supporting long strings of nucleotide bases. Information is coded by the ordering sequence of these nucleotide bases along the DNA—roughly analogous to beads on a necklace. There are only four different bases—adenosine (A), thymidine (T), cytosine (C), guanine (G)—but the ordering of these four bases along the DNA chain forms the genetic code by which hereditary information is passed along from parent to offspring, and from mother cell to daughter cell as the cells of the body are formed and differentiate. The code itself is based on information contained in each three-base sequence: for example, AAT, AAG, GAG, GAC, and so on. Generally speaking, each three-base "word" (called a *codon*) is read and translated into a particular amino acid; as successive codons are read and translated, a string of amino acids is built. Long strings of amino acids form proteins that serve structural roles in cells and function as enzymes to catalyze the chemical reactions in the body. Shorter strings of amino acids form peptides that serve many roles, including the communication of information within and between cells. Thus, the genetic code ultimately codes for proteins or precursors to peptides, with the long sequence of codons providing information for one such product called a *gene*.

Even slight differences in the nucleotide bases coding for a particular protein may change one or more of the specific amino acids in the chain. For example, GAA and CAA code for different amino acids. Small changes in the genetic code for a particular gene, called *genetic polymorphisms*, can disrupt or alter in other ways the functioning of the protein coded by that particular gene. Indeed, as is explored further in Chapters 8 and 9, there is increasing evidence that the incidence of various genetic polymorphisms differs among individuals with and without certain psychological disorders.

Although genetic polymorphisms may influence the propensity of individuals to express particular behaviors or psychological disorders, genes do not code for behaviors, only for proteins and peptides. Thus, there are no genetically determined behaviors. Instead, genetically-induced alterations in the amount or functioning of brain neurochemical systems alter brain structure and functioning, thereby influencing how an individual thinks, feels, and behaves. Sometimes many behaviors are influenced by one gene, particularly when that gene controls fundamental chemical processes used in many nerve cells throughout the brain. In other instances, one behavior can be influenced by many genes. Indeed, in studies of genetic contributions to behavioral disorders such as depression, anxiety, conduct disorder, substance abuse disorders, and so on, 25–50% or more of the variance in incidence of the disorder across individuals may be attributed to genetic factors, even though any specific gene found to be associated with a particular disorder typically only accounts individually for 5–6% or less of the variance in incidence of the disorder (Kendler & Prescott, 2006). And, although rapid progress is being made in determining the genetic heritability of different psychological disorders, most of the genes involved (and their functions) still remain to be identified.

DNA is normally packaged into 26 pairs of chromosomes in humans—with one member of each chromosome pair donated by the father, and the other provided by the mother. Each chromosome is typically closely associated with, and surrounded by, chemicals called *histones* that serve to modulate the degree of accessibility of specific genes for transcription. The process of gene transcription into proteins involves a number of steps. First, a copy of the portion of DNA containing the gene to be transcribed is made, using a type of material similar in structure to DNA, called *ribonucleic acid* (RNA). RNA copied from the DNA template—that is, "messenger RNA (mRNA)"—is then "read" and translated into the string of amino acids by another type of RNA (ribosomal RNA [rRNA]). This process of transcribing and translating genes into proteins or peptides is exquisitely complex and highly regulated. As discussed later, the DNA itself or the histones around it can be chemically modified to make areas containing particular genes more or less accessible for transcription. Even when the DNA coding a particular gene is available for transcription, activation by particular "promoters" or "regulatory sequences" may be required before transcription of that gene can be initiated. Once the working mRNA copy of the gene is made, it can be "edited" by splicing out certain portions of the mRNA, with different splicing options leading to diverse peptide or protein products. Recent research has revealed that many of the component steps that influence gene accessibility are highly sensitive to modulation via environmental experiences—a process termed *epigenetic regulation*. As we shall see, epigenetic regulation is a critical means by which the environment can influence gene transcription, with lasting effects that may persist throughout the lifetime (and even, in some cases, passed on to the next generation).

Developmental Neurogenetics

Different waves of genes are activated at different points during development to control specific aspects of brain development occurring at those times. For instance, in a study that examined which of 11,000 genes in the mouse hippocampus were being transcribed ("expressed") at different times during development, about 2,000 genes were found to change their expression (Mody et al., 2001). Some clusters of genes, particularly those involved in regulating the formation of new nerve cells (neurons), constructing cellular components, and modulating transcription of other genes and translation into proteins, were expressed most strongly during the embryonic period, declining in activity thereafter. Other genes, such as those involved in differentiation of neurons and the formation of connections (synapses) between them, were most active shortly after birth and during infancy. In contrast, and of particular relevance for our interests here, other clusters of genes reached their highest expression during adolescence; functions of these genes included regulation of synaptic function, communication (signal transduction) at the synapse, and control of metabolic activities necessary to fuel the brain. Even more dramatic developmental changes in gene expression across three brain regions and multiple prenatal and postnatal ages were reported by Stead and colleagues (2006), with > 97% of the (about) 10,000 genes examined showing some developmental change in expression; in this study, although the most dramatic expression changes were seen during infancy, gene expression profiles again showed clear developmental changes through adolescence. Thus, part of the reason that the brain of the adolescent differs from other-age brains is that the genetic information being tapped by the adolescent brain is different from the portions of the genome being used by the brain at other ages.

The genes that are essential for controlling early development have been highly conserved during evolution, with, for instance, 99% of these early genes being the same (homologous) between fish and humans (Amsterdam et al., 2004). Activation of these early genes in the nervous system appears to produce a basic "scaffold" of connections among neurons that is largely prescribed genetically, with the later selective enlargement, refinement, and modification of these connections in part influenced by experience (e.g., Sur & Rubenstein, 2005). The topic to which we now turn—the issue of genetic interactions with the environment to produce particular outcomes— is an important theme to researchers and developmentalists.

Genes, the Environment, and Epigenetic Regulation

Traditionally, there has been substantial interest in determining whether particular behavioral, cognitive, or physiological characteristics (i.e., phenotypic traits) are due to genetic make-up (genotype) or to environmental influences. This focus on "genes versus the environment" implies a dichotomy that does not exist. It is rather like asking which part of a car is more important to get from point A to point B: the engine or the wheels. The actions of genes are expressed within, and influenced by, multiple environmental contexts. At the molecular level, the context includes the chemical environment within and among cells; for the fetus, the environment includes effects induced by the stresses, drugs, and nutrients to which the mom-to-be is exposed; for the child and adolescent, environmental influences extend to parental care and monitoring, and interactions with peers, teachers, law enforcement, the community, and so on.

Given the now general recognition that genes and environments are inexorably interrelated, the focus has turned from "genes versus the environment" to the study of gene–environment (G×E) interactions. Exploring such interactions is critical when addressing issues such as why some individuals show remarkable resilience when growing up under difficult circumstances that seemingly overwhelm others. To take a fictitious example, individuals living under supportive and relatively unstressful circumstances who have a genetic polymorphism that slows their capacity to recover from the effects of stress hormones might not differ from others having a more active form of that gene. However, when exposed to a chronically stressful and chaotic environment, those with the polymorphism that slows their recovery from stress might well suffer adverse consequences from these life circumstances that are not evident among those with the more active variant of that gene. Thus, genes can influence sensitivity to environmental consequences. This relationship is not one-sided, however; the environment likewise exerts important influences on which genes are expressed via processes such as epigenetic regulation.

All cells in the body contain basically the same DNA, but not all cells do the same thing. This difference in function requires some specificity in which portions of the genome are activated in different types of cells. That is, selective expression and repression of different portions of the genome allows cells to take on their unique characteristics and pass these on when they divide into "daughter cells." Such differentiation emerges gradually during development. Early on, when the fertilized egg has divided enough to become a ball of cells, all cells may retain the capacity to become any part of the body; as development continues, cells become specialized to form a particular part of the body (e.g., nervous system); with further development specialization increases, forming, for example, a nerve cell (neuron) that uses a particular type of chemical for communication, forms connections with specific types of neurons, and so on. Epigenetic regulation plays a critical a role in this differentiation process, helping to "lock" cells into progressively more specialized states as development proceeds. These epigenetic messages typically are passed across cell divisions, stamping in this differentiated state to the daughter cells as well.

Epigenetic regulation is primarily exerted by chemically altering the DNA via the addition of methyl groups to one of the nucleotide bases (cytosine). The presence of methyl groups in regions coding a particular gene makes it more difficult to transcribe that gene. Histones around the DNA in regions to be repressed may also become methylated, causing the histones to condense around the DNA, further decreasing the accessibility of that portion of the DNA for transcription. Other chemical reactions conversely loosen the grip of the histones around a portion of the DNA coding a particular gene(s), or remove methyl groups from the DNA in those coding regions, thereby increasing access of the gene(s) for transcription (see Szyf et al., 2007, for review).

What is of particular interest here is that the process of epigenetic regulation—the turning off and on of different portions of the genome—is exquisitely sensitive to environmental influences. Early on, the environmental influences consist of the microenvironment around a given cell, driven largely by chemical and electrical signals given off by other cells that are in direct contact or nearby. As the organism develops, the external environment also begins to play a role in epigenetic regulation of the brain via environmentally induced alterations in hormone levels and regional brain activities.

One striking example derived from basic research is the epigenetic programming of stress reactivity via maternal behavior. Mother rats (called *dams*) differ in the amount of attention they direct to their infant rat pups, with some dams licking and grooming their offspring a lot, and other dams providing less of this tactile stimulation to their pups. As adults, offspring of high-licking–grooming (LG) dams are less fearful than offspring of low-LG dams and show a more moderated hormonal response to stressors. These differences are not genetic; if offspring of low-LG dams are fostered to high-LG dams, they act like normal adult offspring of high-LG mothers (i.e., they are low in fear and show moderated stress responses in adulthood). The converse is seen when offspring of high-LG dams are reared by low-LG dams. The critical period for this maternal care-mediated effect is the first postnatal week. Intriguingly, these lasting effects of early mothering appear to be mediated, at least in part, by epigenetic regulation of the promoter region of a gene that codes for a stress hormone receptor. The "story" goes as follows: Between the late prenatal and early postnatal period, the promoter region for this gene becomes highly methylated. Methylation remains high in this region in offspring reared by low-LG dams, suppressing transcription of this promoter region and its associated gene, with the result that levels of this stress hormone receptor remain low in the offspring throughout life, decreasing their ability to cope effectively with stressors. In contrast, maternal stimulation by high-LG dams precipitates a dramatic decline in methylation in this promoter region of their offspring, evident by the sixth day postnatally, thereby allowing expression of the gene for this receptor that is important in modulating stress hormone responses. During the first postnatal week, administration of a drug that disrupts methylation in low-LG offspring converts their hormonal stress response to that seen in high-

LG offspring. Thus, beneficial effects of early maternal care can be mimicked, at least in part, by altering epigenetic regulation (see Weaver et al., 2004, for details of these studies).

As illustrated by these basic science studies, one of the ways that prior environmental experiences can have long-term effects on offspring behavior and physiological function is via epigenetic programming. In this case, variations in maternal behavior influence patterns of DNA methylation, altering gene expression and exerting permanent effects on offspring physiological functioning. To the extent that variations in life experiences during development are predictive of environmental conditions likely to be faced in the future, environmentally induced alterations in epigenetic regulation may serve adaptive functions in preparing the organism for its future. Evidence also suggests that although most prevalent early in life, epigenetic influences continue to be exerted to some extent even into adulthood, providing a way for the environment to shape the phenotype (i.e., particular behavioral or physiological outcomes) throughout life (Whitelaw & Whitelaw, 2006).

Methods for Exploring Genetic (and Environmental) Influences on Behavior

There are a number of ways to estimate the relative genetic and environmental contributions to the development of particular behavioral and cognitive functions. Basic science studies have used a variety of approaches to examine how different developmental experiences alter gene regulation and expression, and how genes influence phenotypes. These include selective breeding of a particular trait, relating genetic differences to variations in behavior across inbred lines of animals that differ genetically and in the behavior of interest, blocking or stimulating expression of particular target genes, and other biogenetic approaches. In studies with humans, relative genetic and environmental contributions have been explored through strategies such as family and twin studies, and through the study of genetic polymorphisms.

Twin Studies

Basically, the greater the genetic influence on a particular trait, the more that trait should cluster in families, with those individuals who are most strongly related having the greatest trait similarity. Twin studies have proved especially valuable for exploring the relative impact of genetic and environmental influences on a particular trait. These types of studies use the difference in genetic relatedness of identical versus fraternal twins to model and statistically disentangle the relative contribution of genetics versus environmental factors. Identical (monozygotic [MZ]) twins are derived from the same fertilized egg, and hence have the same genes, whereas fraternal (dizygotic [DZ]) twins, although sharing the same prenatal environment, are derived from different fertilized eggs and hence are genetically no more related to each other than any other nontwin brother or sister. Assuming that the twins are raised together, their environmental experiences can be separated into two types: shared and nonshared (i.e., individual-specific). Shared environmental experiences are those associated with the family and other aspects of the twins' common environment, including parental rearing styles, socioeconomic status, and school and neighborhood experiences. Not all family experiences are necessarily shared, though. For example, occasionally only one twin is exposed to sexual abuse by a parent. The latter would be an example of an individual-specific experience. Such individualized, nonshared experiences between twins typically increase with age, as they develop different friendships and interests, and as they leave home and engage in different types of postsecondary education and jobs.

In analyses of twin data, if MZ twins are found to be significantly more alike than DZ twins on a particular measure, genetic factors are thought to play a particularly important role, and this measure is thought to have high "heritability." If MZ and DZ twins are similar on the measured response (and more similar on this measure than pairs of unrelated individuals), shared environmental rather than genetic factors would be thought to contribute to the similarity. In instances when MZ twins differ from each other (i.e., are discordant) on the target measure, it would suggest that nonshared (individual-specific) experiences are of particular importance. As discussed in Chapters 8 and 9, the results of such studies evaluating twins have played an important role in our understanding of genetic contributions to the emergence of drug abuse and other psychological disorders during adolescence. An extensive discussion of the twin approach and data obtained using this strategy to explore the relative impact of genetic and environmental influences on the development of drug abuse and psychopathology can be found in Kendler and Prescott (2006).

Gene "Knock-Outs," Genetic Polymorphisms, and Microarrays

Genetic "knock-outs" are popular and powerful tools used in basic science to explore functional consequences of particular genes. A genetic knock-out is an engineered mutation in a particular gene such that animals (often mice) with mutated copies of the gene are unable to make ("express") the normal protein product of that gene. Although this approach to relate particular genes to their functions has revealed valuable information, this technique is not immune to problems. In typical knock-out studies, animals are without the target gene throughout development and into adulthood, so the consequences observed may more reflect how the brain develops in (and compensates to) the absence of that gene rather than the normal function of that gene. This concern has led to the development of "conditional knock-outs" wherein a chemical trigger is used to induce expression of the mutation after the early developmental period. Researchers have also sometimes found very different functional consequences when the same gene was "knocked out" in different strains of mice (e.g., Bailey et al., 2006) that, like different breeds of dogs, differ genetically in ways that influence their appearance, baseline levels of anxiety, overall levels of activity, and so on. Despite these issues of interpretation, however, knock-out studies have proved very valuable in revealing phenotypic associations with specific genes.

One strategy frequently used for examining potential relationships between genes and behavior in humans is to conduct a genetic association study to determine whether a particular variant of a gene differs between groups of individuals that vary on some dimension (e.g., such as whether or not they are dependent on alcohol). One way to do this is to search for genetic polymorphisms—slight variations in the DNA sequence for a particular gene that are seen across individuals within a given population. These polymorphisms frequently consist of a repeat or a deletion of a portion of the DNA sequence and, if occurring in critical coding regions or (perhaps even more importantly) regulatory sequences for a particular gene, they may alter the relative efficiency or activity of the receptor, enzyme, or other protein product coded by that gene, ultimately influencing behavior. To give but one example, there are many variations in the DNA sequence of the gene coding a specific subtype of receptor, called the *dopamine* (DA) *D4 receptor* (DRD4), used for sensing chemical communication between neurons. One polymorphism involves a repeat of a particular 120 base portion of the DNA sequence for this receptor, such that some individuals have the 120 base form, whereas others have the 240 variant. The longer (240 base pair) variant of this "120/240 polymorphism" is more common in individuals with attention-deficit/hyperactivity disorder (ADHD) than in those without the disorder, suggesting that this genetic variant may serve as one risk factor for ADHD (McCracken et al., 2000). As we shall see in later chapters, a number of genetic polymorphisms are emerging as potential risk factors influencing vulnerability to a variety of psychological disorders. In this work, evidence is emerging that the specific gene variants influencing risks for particular disorders may vary during development (Dick et al., 2006).

Microarrays have proved to be an extremely valuable tool to examine expression of hundreds or thousands of genes at a time in humans and other animals. This method uses probes to the mRNAs transcribed from these genes or even to the final protein product of these genes (an approach called "proteomics") to determine which genes have been transcribed recently. These methods allow changes in expression of large numbers of genes to be examined simultaneously.

Heritability Increases during Adolescence

A number of studies has found data consistent with the provocative suggestion that heritability of a variety of behavioral phenotypes increases through adolescence and into young adulthood. Rising heritability estimates during this age span have been reported for such diverse phenotypes as amount of exercise, participation in sports, parental interactions, social attitudes, vocabulary knowledge, eating habits, and IQ, with these heritability estimates slowing down or declining at later ages (see Bergen et al., 2007, for review and analysis). For instance, in a study comparing the cognitive development of 1- to 16-year-old adopted children and their biological and adoptive parents, evidence of an increasing genetic influence was seen with age, an effect particularly pronounced for general cognitive function and verbal skills (Plomin et al., 1997). That is, by adolescence, adopted youth showed more of a resemblance to their *biological* parents than the parents who had raised them, data interpreted by the authors to suggest that "genes that stably affect cognitive abilities in adulthood do not all come into play until adolescence" (Plomin et al., 1997, p. 447). That is not to say, however, that environmental influences have no impact on intelligence in adolescence. For instance, in a study examining IQs of brothers, increasing similarities in the ages between pairs of brothers was associated with increases in the similarity of their IQ scores; given that siblings closer in age are likely to share more environmental similarities than siblings more distant in age, these data were interpreted to support a role for family environmental factors in determination of IQ among late adolescent males (Sundet et al., 2008).

A variety of possible explanations have been advanced for the seemingly counterintuitive finding that genetic influences become stronger during adolescence. One possibility is that biological changes during adolescence trigger changes in gene expression that ultimately increase the overall genetic influence on behavioral and cognitive function. Data cited in support of this notion include a study examining heritability of eating disorders in prepubertal and pubertal female twin pairs. Genetic influences were found to be account for notably more variance (> 50%) in eating behaviors among pubertal twins than prepubertal twin pairs (about 0% of the variance), with heritability estimates of "pubertal 11-year-old twins more closely resembl[ing] those of 17-year-old twins than prepubertal twins *of their same age*" (Klump et al., 2003, p. 290). From these data, the researchers posited that pubertal increases in ovarian hormones such as estrogen and progesterone may trigger expression of genes that ultimately play a role in modulation of eating patterns, thereby increasing heritability of eating-related disorders in postpubertal females.

Other potential mechanisms postulated to contribute to heritability increases during adolescence include the cumulative long-term effects of a single set of genes expressed throughout development, or the emergence of new sources of environmental variance at adolescence, thereby presumably allowing for the expression of greater genetic diversity (e.g., see Eaves et al., 1986; Bergen et al., 2007). It is also possible that the increasing heritability seen commonly during adolescence in twin and adoption studies may be partly a function of the methods used to distinguish between genetic and environmental sources of behavioral variance (e.g., see Sundet et al., 2008, for discussion). The bottom line is that increases in heritability have been documented during adolescence across a broad variety of behaviors. Why this might occur remains a puzzle, challenging the creativity of researchers to develop testable hypotheses to explain this reliable but seemingly counterintuitive finding.

SUMMARY AND CLOSING COMMENTS

When viewed through the lens of evolutionary history, adolescence emerges as a developmental transition having deep evolutionary roots, with certain neurobehavioral and physiological characteristics that have been conserved across a variety of mammalian species, including humans. The conserved nature of such adolescent-typical characteristics leads credence to basic science studies using animal models of adolescence to study adolescent brain development, physiology, and neurobehavioral function. Indeed, as we shall see in later chapters, studies using animal models in combination with recent advantages in human brain imaging have yielded substantial converging data on brain/behavior interrelationships during adolescence.

The revolution in genetics likewise provides valuable tools for exploring the genetics of adolescence. Gene expression changes during adolescence fuel the remodeling of the adolescent brain and contribute to the pattern of hormonal, behavioral, and physiological transformations seen at this ontogenetic stage. New developments in the study of molecular genetics have also provided new insights regarding roles of genetics and epigenetic regulation in the individual differences seen among adolescents in their vulnerabilities for the development of psychological disorders, drug abuse, and other adverse outcomes, as are discussed in later chapters. Burgeoning work in this area is transforming our understanding of genetic vulnerabilities and the relationship between genes, environmentally induced genetic regulation, and the vulnerabilities and resiliencies of adolescents.

CHAPTER THREE

Sex Differences, Puberty, and the Hormonal Reawakening of Adolescence

••

The most obvious biological transformation of adolescence is puberty—that is, the sex-specific hormonal and physiological changes that lead to sexual maturation. Puberty is associated with a considerable increase in hormones released from the gonads, including androgens such as testosterone released from the testes in males and estrogen (and progesterone) released at particular stages of the egg maturation process in the ovaries of females. Although these hormonal increases are largely sex-specific, both of these types of sex hormones are present to some extent in mature individuals of both sexes. These so-called "raging hormones" of puberty traditionally have been blamed for adolescent peculiarities in behavior and thinking by parents and the mass media, although, as we shall see, in many cases these hormones seem to have been falsely accused. Rises in gonadal "sex" hormones, however, have been linked to a growing interest in sexually related stimuli during adolescence, as well as to increases in sexual motivation and sexual behaviors. Males and females also differ in a number of behaviors not related to sexual activities per se, and in certain cognitive strategies as well; many of these differences become more pronounced during adolescence, although evidence for their triggering via hormonal action is often less clear. Male and female brains are different, and there is increasing evidence that pubertal rises in sex hormones may help sculpt the remodeling of the adolescent brain in ways that are appropriate for each sex. But a big piece of the story about how male and female brains are produced occurs much earlier—during the fetal period—so that is where we begin.

First, a cautionary note: When thinking about sex differences in brain, behavior, or cognitive function, it is easy to begin to stereotype and overstress differences between males and females. Yet, although the brains (and behavior) of males and females differ on average, we are, after all, subgroups of the same species, with attributes that overlap considerably. To take a simple example, although men are more interested football, on average, than women, some women are at the top of their fantasy football league whereas some men couldn't tell you in what city the Eagles are based. It is also important to emphasize that just because biological factors contribute to sex differences (as well as differences in sexual orientation), these differences are by no means an inalterable biological heritage. Psychosocial influences dramatically influence how individuals perceive themselves in a multitude of respects, including the assumption of particular sex roles and identification as a sexual human being.

SEXUAL DIFFERENTIATION OF THE BRAIN

Males and females differ genetically. The genetic blueprint, DNA, is clustered into 23 pairs of chromosomes in humans, one of each pair derived from their father and the other from the mother. Both chromosomes in each pair are normally the same in size for 22 of these chromosome pairs, whether they were maternally or paternally derived. The 23rd chromosome pair, however, differs markedly between males and females. This pair consists of two X chromosomes in normal genetic females, whereas males have only one X chromosome, which is paired with a much smaller Y chromosome. Despite its relatively diminutive size, the Y chromosome somehow coordinates the developmental process to induce the essentials of maleness physiologically throughout the organism, ranging from the appearance of the sex organs to the characteristics of the brain and resulting thoughts and behavior. In contrast, the presence of two X chromosomes supports differentiation of sex organ physiology, brain, and behavior in a female-typical pattern. Traditional dogma is that genetic differences between males and females lead to alterations in the early hormonal environment that, in turn, drive sex-appropriate differentiation of the body and brain. Indeed, as discussed below, there is ample evidence that levels of sex hormones play an important role in the process of sexual differentiation. This does not seem to be the whole story, however. Even before the fetal gonads have developed enough to release hormones, male and female brains differ in what genes they express (Dewing et al., 2003) and in certain cellular characteristics (Beyer et al., 1991; see Pilgrim & Reisert, 1992). Thus, although hormones still get the lion's share of the credit, some sexual differentiation of the brain appears to be hormone-independent.

The structure and function of male and female brains are similar but not identical. Male brains are slightly larger than the brains of females, even when brain size is considered relative to body weight. Within the brain, the size of particular regions varies between males and females, with some areas larger in males and others in females. Such size differentials may be driven either by differences in the number of nerve cells (neurons), the size of those neurons, or their connectivity. Along with sex differences in neurocircuitry are differences in the level of functional activity of neurotransmitter systems that communicate information between neurons (see Pilgrim & Reisert, 1992). Although some of these sexually dimorphic brain regions have been associated with particular behavioral differences between the sexes, especially in animal studies (e.g., Sisk & Zehr, 2005; Schulz et al., 2009), many of the links between sex differences in the brain and typical behavioral differences between the sexes remain speculative. Male and female brains also differ in terms of the number of receptor sites available to bind testosterone and estrogen, binding differences that are seen not only in sexually dimorphic regions but also in other brain areas as well. It is via hormonal interaction with these receptors that the ongoing presence of sex hormones influences brain function in the sexually mature individual. Indeed, expression of certain sex differences in behavior requires the ongoing presence (i.e., "activational" effects) of gonadal hormones, a topic to which we turn later.

Much of what is known about how these sex differences arise has been gleaned, by necessity, from studies using animal models. In research conducted in laboratory animals, levels of various hormones can be experimentally manipulated at specific times during development by injecting the hormone of interest, or by castrating males or removing the ovaries in females, and so on. Obviously, it is not possible to do such manipulations in humans. Instead, to explore the role of hormones in sexual differentiation in humans, researchers have had to rely on examining the behavior of individuals with genetic mutations or clinical syndromes that involve abnormally high or low levels of sex hormones. Although it is more difficult to determine whether altered hormone levels are actually driving observed behavioral changes from such "experiments of nature" (see Gorski, 2002), in general the findings from these case studies are reminiscent of research conducted in laboratory animals in supporting the importance of the early hormone environment for induction of sex-typical differentiation.

Much of the differentiation of the brain in female- versus male-specific ways is driven by the gonadal hormone environment during a critical developmental window prior to birth and into the early postnatal period. During this critical period, brain development is channeled along a male-typical differentiation path by the action of gonadal hormones. In contrast, when gonadal hormone levels are low or absent during this critical period, brain development proceeds in a female-like pattern. In other words, the brain is inherently female and will proceed along the female "default" path unless diverted via gonadal hormones to differentiate in a masculine direction. A similar phenomenon occurs in the reproductive system itself, with initial undifferentiated precursors developing into testes and a penis when stimulated by the presence of androgens during a critical period, but into ovaries, uterus, and clitoris in the absence of significant gonadal hormone stimulation during that critical developmental window (see Gorski, 2002, for review).

Paradoxically, not only testosterone but also estrogen may serve to steer brain differentiation into a male-typical direction. Testosterone and estrogen are similar chemically, and testosterone can be converted into estrogen in the brain. In at least some species, the estrogen so produced plays an essential role in male-typical differentiation. Evidence for this role has been obtained in studies showing that early exposure to estrogen masculinizes and defeminizes behavior of females in studies conducted in laboratory animals, whereas perinatal administration of drugs that block estrogen receptors (but not androgen receptors) is effective in suppressing brain masculinization (see Ward & Ward, 1985, for review). In humans, however, androgens such as testosterone may play a more active role in channeling development of the brain in a male-typical direction. For instance, genetic males with a mutation in their DNA that blocks functioning of their androgen receptors are unable to detect the presence of testosterone and other androgens in their bodies. Although genetically male and having internalized testes, individuals with this "androgen insensitivity syndrome" look like typical females, generally view themselves as heterosexual females, and even consider themselves to be particularly feminine (Batch et al., 1992). In contrast, genetic females who are exposed to elevated androgen levels due to a clinical syndrome called "congenital adrenal hyperplasia" are often behaviorally masculinized to some extent in that they tend to be tomboys and to play with toys classically preferred by boys (e.g., Berenbaum & Hines, 1992).

From studies in laboratory animals and examination of case studies involving individuals with genetic mutations or other "experiments of nature," there is ample evidence that, during various critical periods before and around the time of birth, different components of the developing brain are channeled into male- versus female-typical differentiation patterns by "organizational" effects induced by the presence of high versus low levels of gonadal hormones, respectively. At this time, levels of gonadal hormones are normally low in girls but high in boys, with testosterone levels in 4-month-old infant boys rivaling those of adult males. Levels of sex hormones then decline markedly thereafter where they remain low in both boys and girls throughout the childhood/juvenile period until release of these hormones is reactivated at puberty (see Grumbach, 2002).

NEURODEVELOPMENT OF SEXUAL ORIENTATION

Among the broad diversity of sex-relevant behaviors that may be influenced by the early hormonal environment is sexual orientation—that is, sexual interests and preferences directed toward others of one's own sex (homosexuality), toward individuals of the other sex (heterosexuality), or a combination of the two (bisexuality). The issue of what "causes" homosexuality is a particularly controversial one, seemingly in part because of the stance taken on this subject by some religions.

There is scientific evidence for a biological component to homosexuality, in that the brains of homosexual and heterosexual males differ in their morphology in several areas of the hypothalamus—a brain region that, among other activities, forms part of the network that controls hormone release throughout the body (Swaab & Hofman, 1990; LeVay, 1991). Whether there are likewise differences between the brains of heterosexual and homosexual women has been little explored to date. Yet, it is likely that early emerging biological factors also influence the sexual orientation of women, given evidence that the prenatal environment can influence sexual orientation of both women and men (though the nature of those influences sometimes is gender-specific). Prenatal influences are just one piece of the picture, though. A number of factors contribute to the emergence of a particular sexual orientation, and various hypotheses have been advanced as to which of these factors are most critical in the emergence of homosexuality.

The hormonal environment of the fetus may be critical not only for sexual differentiation of the brain but in the development of sexual orientation as well. For instance, incidence of bisexuality and lesbianism is elevated in girls who are exposed to elevated levels of androgens associated with congenital adrenal hyperplasia (Dittmann et al., 1992). These girls, however, are exposed to elevated levels of androgens throughout life, so it is difficult to determine when this hormonal influence is exerted. Females whose mothers were given the synthetic, estrogen-like compound diestrostibestrol during the 1940–1960s to avoid miscarriage, however, have also been reported to be more likely to have a same-sex sexual orientation (Meyer-Bahlburg et al., 1995). In this case, hormone exposure was restricted to the prenatal period, suggesting that the hormonal environment prior to birth may play a role in influencing the emergence of sexual orientation later in life. The data are mixed in males, with indirect evidence that some homosexual males may have been exposed to relatively low levels of androgens prenatally, whereas others may have had elevated levels of early androgen exposure (see Rahman, 2005, for discussion).

Other prenatal circumstances may exert influences on sexual orientation as well. A number of studies has reported that maternal stress during pregnancy increases the probability of homosexuality in male offspring (Ellis et al., 1988; Bailey & Pillard, 1991; Ellis & Cole-Harding, 2001). For instance, Ellis and Cole-Harding (2001) found that mothers of homosexual men were significantly more likely to have had stressful experiences during those pregnancies, particularly during the first trimester, than mothers of heterosexual men. These researchers found a different pattern in female offspring, with maternal stressors during pregnancy *not* influencing their probability of homosexuality, although mothers of lesbians were found to have smoked significantly more cigarettes during pregnancy than mothers of heterosexual women. These effects on sexual orientation, although slight, are reminiscent of the substantial evidence that prenatal exposure to drugs or stressors can exert a broad diversity of long-lasting influences on offspring neurobehavioral functioning (e.g., see Spear, 1997; Austin et al., 2005; Glantz & Chambers, 2006, for review).

Sexual orientation tends to "run" in families, to some extent. For example, homosexual men and women have more homosexual brothers and sisters than would be expected by chance (e.g., Bailey & Bell, 1993). There are a number of ways by which the family could exert effects on the sexual preference of offspring. Genetic influences are a possibility and can be examined using a number of strategies, including twin studies. The twin study design uses the strategy that, to the extent that a trait is genetically based, genetically "identical" (MZ) twins should be more likely to be the same on that trait than fraternal (DZ) twins or other nontwin siblings. Twin studies have revealed a substantial genetic influence on sexual preferences (e.g., Bailey & Pillard, 1991; Kendler et al., 2000). For instance, in a national sample of twin and nontwin sibling pairs, 31.6% of MZ twins were found to be concordant for homosexuality—that is, if one twin was homosexual, there was almost a one in three probability that the other member of the twin pair would show this sexual orientation as well. This concordance rate is higher than the 21.4% concordance rate seen in same-sex DZ twins and nontwin sibling pairs (Kendler et al., 2000). Studies like this one, showing a modestly elevated probability of homosexuality in MZ twins of homosexual individuals than in same-sex DZ twins or nontwin siblings of those individuals, support the conclusion that there is a genetic component to the emergence of sexual orientation. Exactly which genes contribute to the development of sexual orientation, however, is currently a matter of controversy. Studies investigating potential genetic contributors to homosexual orientation have revealed a number of candidates, although little consensus has emerged thus far as to which of these candidate genes are most likely involved (see Swaab, 2004, for review). As with most complex behavioral/cognitive characteristics, multiple genes likely contribute.

There is convincing evidence that the more older brothers a boy has, the greater the probability that he will have a same-sex sexual orientation (Blanchard, 2004). Indeed, it has been estimated that the sexual orientation of one in seven homosexual men is a result of this "fraternal birth-order effect" (Cantor et al., 2002). This effect of birth order is not evident in women, with no difference between lesbian and heterosexual women in the number of older sisters they have (Bogaert, 1997). It is not known conclusively why birth order has this effect in males. One possibility is immunological. The thinking is that the immune system of some pregnant women detects male-specific antigens in their male fetus and begins to mount an immune response by making antibodies against those male-typical antigens. The more times these women carry male fetuses, the more they are exposed to male antigens, and hence the greater the accumulation of these antibodies. The hypothesis, then, is that as these anti-male antibodies build up over pregnancies, they interfere somehow with hormonally induced sexual differentiation of the brain, hindering development of a masculinized brain and associated behavior and increasing the probability of a same-sex sexual orientation (e.g., Blanchard & Bogaert, 1996). Although intriguing, this hypothesis has been criticized on a number of grounds (see James, 2006) and has not yet been supported by data linking levels of male-typical antibodies during pregnancy and later sexual preferences of male offspring. It is nevertheless the case that the birthweights of homosexual males with older brothers are significantly lower than those of heterosexual males with an equivalent number of older male siblings (Blanchard et al., 2002)—findings consistent with an immunological interpretation of this birth-order effect.

Social context, particularly within the family, also has been suggested to play a critical role in the emergence of sexual orientation. For instance, it is possible that growing up around someone who is homosexual might predispose a child to develop a homosexual orientation. This possibility has been raised as a concern by some groups with regard to children reared by lesbian or gay parents. The possibility was examined by Andersson et al. (2002) in an analysis that thoroughly evaluated the results of 23 studies comparing children raised by homosexual parents (mostly lesbian mothers) with those reared by heterosexual parents. They found that children reared by homosexual parents did not differ from those reared by heterosexual parents in gender identity, sexual preference, gender role behavior, or behavior adjustment.

Although the bulk of the evidence to date leads to the conclusion that rearing by homosexual parents does not influence sexual orientation, there are other routes by which the postnatal environment could contribute to the emergence of a same-sex sexual orientation. One possible contributor is early sexual abuse. Indeed, in many (but not all) studies, males who are homosexual were found to be more likely to report that they had been sexually abused in childhood than heterosexual males (see James, 2006, for review and references). However, as is always the case when examining correlational data, it is not possible to determine whether the relationship between early sexual abuse and homosexuality is causal. On the one hand, it is possible that early sexual abuse by a same-sex individual could increase the probability of homosexuality in adulthood. Alternatively, early sexual abuse and homosexuality could be correlated because there is something about the behavior or social environment of young boys who are likely to develop a same-sex sexual orientation that makes them more likely to be targeted for such abuse.

Taken together, the data support the conclusion that there are multiple paths to the development of same-sex sexual orientation: genetic influences; maternal stress during pregnancy; chemicals such as hormones, antibodies, and drugs in the prenatal environment; as well as early life experiences.

PUBERTY, HORMONES, AND THE EMERGENCE OF SEX DIFFERENCES

When observing young children, it is obvious that there are sex differences in behavior during infancy and childhood, despite low levels of gonadal hormones at this time. Even as babies and toddlers, boys and girls differ in interests, temperament, and play behavior (e.g., Martin et al., 1997; Pellegrini, 2006). These behavioral differences are fostered not only by sex differences in brain structure induced by "organizational" influences of hormones early in life, but also by cultural and social influences, including differences in the expectations others have for them and the way they are treated (e.g., see Bussey & Bandura, 1999). Other sex differences do not emerge until adolescence or later; although the sexually dimorphic brain substrates underlying these behaviors may be laid down early in life, they remain latent until awakened by the rise in sex hormones that begins at puberty. Sex differences that require the presence of gonadal hormones for those differences to be expressed are said to be dependent on "activational" effects of these hormones.

Research in laboratory animals has revealed that the distinction between early, long-lasting "organizational" effects of hormones on the brain versus later, transient "activational" influences of hormones is far from absolute. For one thing, administration of testosterone or estrogen to juveniles well before puberty is sometimes not effective in activating particular sex-typical behaviors, although those behaviors are readily activated by the same hormone exposure following puberty (Romeo et al., 2002). Thus, there seems to be something about the changes that occur during puberty that are necessary for hormonal activation of certain sex-typical behaviors. This is one example of the mounting evidence that challenges the traditional dogma that organizational influences of sex hormones are exerted only during the period before and shortly after birth. Indeed, many studies have now shown that the pubertal period itself serves as a second critical period for sexual differentiation, during which rising levels of sex hormones serve to further differentiate the brain in sex-appropriate ways. For instance, based on their work studying the effects of hormone manipulations at different points in development in male hamsters, Cheryl Sisk and colleagues concluded that two developmental periods are critical for male-typical sexual differentiation: (1) the perinatal period, during which the presence of gonadal hormones induces basic sexual differentiation of the brain; and (2) the pubertal period, during which rising levels of gonadal hormones produce the final maturational changes in the brain needed for adult-typical sexual behaviors (e.g., Sisk et al., 2003; Schulz et al., 2009).

Studies have just begun, however, to determine which brain regions are influenced by pubertal rises in gonadal hormones. In a recent landmark study, MRI was used to examine sex differences in gray matter volume of different brain regions in 8–15-year-olds of both sexes (Neufang et al., 2009). Individuals were characterized by Tanner stage (an index of sexual maturation based on various physical indicators—e.g., pubertal hair, breast development) and blood levels of gonadal hormones. Stage of pubertal development was found to be significantly associated with sex differences in gray matter volume of the amygdala (larger in boys than girls) and hippocampus (larger in girls than boys), with levels of gonadal hormones explaining 13–15% of the variance in gray matter volume in these regions. In contrast, pubertal status did not exert a significant impact on gray matter volume in another sexually dimorphic brain region (where volume is greater in girls than boys): the striatum. Although causal conclusions cannot be conclusively determined from such cross-sectional studies, these findings are exciting and of critical importance in linking the pubertal process and pubertal hormones to expression of sex differences in the anatomy of the adolescent brain.

THE NOT-SO "RAGING HORMONES" OF ADOLESCENCE

Pubertal rises in sex hormones may not only contribute to sexual differentiation of the brain, but may also exert more immediate effects to activate certain sex-typical adolescent behaviors, a topic to which we now turn. There has been much speculation as to the link between the dramatic rise in hormone levels at puberty and the emergence of particular adolescent moods and behaviors, including sexual activity per se. Humans are unlike many other mammalian species in that they are not completely dependent on gonadal hormones for stimulation of sexual activity. For instance, although experiences of women during the decline in hormone release associated with menopause are complex and influenced by a multitude of factors (Mishra & Kuhn, 2005), some women report improved sexual function post-menopause (e.g., Shifren & Avis, 2007). Nevertheless, although estrogen and testosterone may not be necessarily required for sexual function, they exert considerable influences on sexual motivation in humans (Wallen, 2001). Indeed, pubertal increases in these hormones contribute to the rising sexual interest and sex drive of adolescents (Steinberg & Belsky, 1996). Among 7th and 8th graders, 17% report that they have been sexually active, with percentages increasing to 49% for 9–12th graders (Resnick et al., 1997). Among sexually active young women in grades 9–12, 20% report that they became pregnant one or more times (Resnick et al., 1997), an incidence rate that undoubtedly would have been even higher if there were not a period of relative infertility following puberty (Short, 1976).

Puberty and its associated rise in sex hormones may be associated not only with increases in sexual activity and interest, but also with developmental changes in other behaviors as well. Among the behaviors hypothesized to be influenced by pubertal maturation are adolescent-typical alterations in arousal, motivation, and emotion, with chronological age postulated to be more associated with cognitive maturational processes (e.g., Steinberg, 2005). Indeed, in some studies comparing adolescents at different stages of pubertal development, progress through puberty was found to be associated with a variety of adolescent-typical behavior patterns, including increased conflicts with parents (Steinberg, 1988), later onset of sleep (Carskadon et al., 1993), and increased risk-taking behaviors, including alcohol and drug use (Harrell et al., 1998; Wilson et al., 1994). Yet, significant relationships between pubertal status and adolescent behaviors are not always seen. For instance, in a study using meta-analysis, a statistical approach that analyzes the combined results of many separate published studies, pubertal status was found to have little impact on amount of parent–child conflict, whereas such conflict was significantly related to chronological age, declining across age from early to late adolescence (Laursen et al., 1998). Likewise, in work examining adolescent changes in sleep, the normal development of sleep stage components was not significantly influenced by pubertal stage, but rather was predicted by age and sex (Feinberg et al., 2006). Part of the variability in findings across studies may be related to the strategies used when attempting to disentangle general age-related maturational changes from the consequences of puberty, per se—distinctions often difficult to make, given that pubertal status is so strongly correlated with age.

When examining the association between hormones and mood/behavior during adolescence, it is important to consider not only associated pubertal rises in gonadal hormones, but increases in other hormones as well. Notable among these other hormones are those released from the adrenal gland, such as the stress hormone cortisol and androgen-like steroids such as dehydroepiandrosterone (see Goodyer et al., 2003). The magnitude of the associations between particular hormones and target behaviors or moods is often surprisingly weak, however. For instance, when examining contributors to negative affect, levels of gonadal hormones were found to account for only about 4% of the variability seen among adolescents in amount of negative affect, whereas 8–18% of this variability was attributed to social factors (Brooks-Gunn et al., 1994). Things do not get much better when stage of pubertal maturation is the focus rather than gonadal hormone levels, per se. For instance, stage of pubertal maturation was found to account for only about 5% of the variability in adolescent/parent relationships (Steinberg, 1988).

So there is a considerable contrast between the folklore of the "raging hormones" of adolescence and research showing modest contributions, at best, of pubertal stage and hormones to the neurobehavioral function and mood of adolescents. The truth may lie in-between. It is possible that associations between puberty (or pubertal-associated hormone changes) and adolescent-typical behaviors may be stronger than often revealed in the studies to date. Because hormone levels fluctuate within individuals over days (and often hours), any given sample may or may not be representative of the overall hormonal milieu of that individual (Worthman, 1999). In addition, there may be a lag between the time when levels of a hormone increase and its behavioral impact, further complicating detection of relationships between hormones and behavior (see Buchanan et al., 1992). It is also likely that assessments focusing on a single hormone may be overly simplistic. Because cells of the brain and body are bathed by multiple hormones and other modulators, examinations designed to detect more complex, multihormonal influences may reveal stronger associations between hormones and behavior than those focused more narrowly on a single or a few hormones (Angold, 2003). Finally, adolescent behaviors occur in particular contexts, and it is likely that these contexts may moderate hormonal influences on behavior. For instance, in a study examining risk-taking in 6- to 18-year-olds, little direct relationship emerged between testosterone level and risk-taking when the entire sample population was examined. When only those children and adolescents from family settings characterized by lower-quality parent–child relationships were examined, however, evidence for testosterone-related risk-taking was revealed (Booth et al., 2003a).

So, the evidence to date suggests that hormonal increases associated with puberty fuel a rising interest in sexual stimuli and sexual motivation, and may also influence, albeit modestly, mood and certain other behaviors of the adolescent. Expression of other adolescent-typical behaviors and cognitive strategies, however, seem largely independent of puberty and associated hormonal changes and appear to reflect neural alterations whose unfolding is based on chronological age or some maturational index other than puberty (see Chapter 4 for more discussion).

TRIGGERS OF PUBERTY

Something must trigger the rapid rise in gonadal hormone release that occurs early in puberty and that initiates the development of secondary sexual characteristics (e.g., breast development, pubertal hair growth) and other physiological changes of puberty. Release of sex hormones from the gonads is the end point in a hormonal cascade that begins in the brain, a cascade collectively referred to as the hypothalamic–pituitary–gonadal (HPG) axis. Gonadotropin releasing hormone (GnRH), produced in the hypothalamus, travels to the pituitary gland, where it induces release of other hormones (follicle-stimulating hormone [FSH] and luteinizing hormone [LH]) into the bloodstream. These hormones, in turn, induce testosterone release from the testes in males, and stimulate growth and release of egg follicles in females and associated release of hormones such as estrogen and progesterone. Given this hormonal cascade, when seeking triggers of puberty, it is not surprising that many researchers have turned to the hypothalamus and possible changes occurring there.

And indeed, there are changes in the hypothalamus around the time of puberty. As mentioned earlier, the HPG axis is very active prior to birth, producing high levels of gonadal hormones in males at the time of initial sexual differentiation during the prenatal and early postnatal period. Following this period of precocial activity, though, activity of the HPG axis is suppressed throughout childhood, due in large part to active suppression ("inhibitory tone") of GnRH release at the level of the hypothalamus. Puberty is largely associated with a weakening of this inhibitory tone. As well, there are increases in excitatory influences on GnRH release that likely reflect inputs from other brain regions. As a result of weakening inhibitory influences and greater excitatory input, GnRH release is reinstated.

But how does the brain know that it is time to trigger puberty? Researchers are a lot closer to understanding triggers of pubertal onset with the recent discovery of an important "gatekeeper" of puberty. This gatekeeper consists of a group of peptides called "kisspeptins" and their associated receptor in the brain, known as GPR54. The discovery of the importance of kisspeptins in puberty is a great example of serendipity. Kisspeptin was first of interest in the field of cancer research due to its expression in slowly developing cancer cells. Associated with research to determine the role of kisspeptin in tumor development and cancer, mice with genetic knock-outs of the kisspeptin receptor, GPR54, were generated. These mice failed to mature sexually and did not go through puberty, data suggesting that kisspeptin may play a role in puberty—an entirely unexpected outcome. Likewise, a rare human condition characterized by a failure to mature sexually (hypogonadotropic hypogonadism) was also associated with a failure to express

GPR54 due to mutation in the gene coding this receptor. Further work has shown that in normal animals, administration of kisspeptin increases release of GnRH, LH, and FSH, and, when administered to prepubertal mice, is sufficient to precipitate the onset of puberty (Navarro et al., 2004). Indeed, normally there are developmental increases in the hypothalamic expression of genes for GPR54 and kisspeptin at the time of puberty, as would be expected if kisspeptin and GPR54 were playing a critical role in the timing of puberty. As noted in numerous excellent reviews (e.g., Kaiser & Kuohung, 2005; Tena-Sempere, 2006), together such findings make a compelling case for the importance of kisspeptins and their receptor, GPR54, in the restoration of the HPG axis at puberty.

Regardless of whether kisspeptins or some other to-be-discovered substance serves as the ultimate gatekeeper for triggering puberty, what drives the timing of puberty? And perhaps even more fundamentally, what are the physical requirements that a developing organism needs to have in place in order for puberty to occur? To take the latter first, size is a major consideration, particularly for females, but also for males to some extent. Body weight and percentage of body fat have been strongly linked to the timing of puberty in a variety of species. Puberty is delayed in individuals who are protein malnourished or who have anorexia, as well as in individuals engaged in sports activities such as ballet, gymnastics, and wrestling, which involve extensive energy expenditure and where lighter weight is an advantage (see Roemmich et al., 2001). In contrast, elevated body weights are reliably associated with earlier puberty in girls (e.g., Karlberg, 2002). For boys, in contrast, the relationship between body weight and pubertal timing is less clear, with reports that elevated body weights are associated with earlier (see Karlberg, 2002), later (Wang, 2002), or little alteration (Slyper, 2006) in pubertal timing.

The relationship between body size and puberty may be particularly strong among girls, given that body size/composition provides evidence as to when the body contains sufficient energy stores to support a pregnancy and several months of lactation (Frisch, 1991). Information regarding available energy stores is provided, at least in part, by leptin, a hormone released by fat cells that signals the brain about available energy stores. Rises in leptin levels reflect the increase in body mass that precedes puberty and are greater in obese individuals (Shalitin & Phillip, 2003). Rising leptin levels, or attainment of a particular body mass per se, does not appear to be sufficient to trigger puberty alone, but rather appears to serve as a necessary precursor that must be in place before puberty can proceed (Grumbach, 2002; Mann & Plant, 2002). Many nerve cells containing kisspeptin express receptors sensitive to leptin; hence it may be via activation of these kisspeptin neurons that leptin influences the onset of puberty (e.g., see Tena-Sempere, 2006, for review and references).

Factors other than body size also influence the timing of puberty. Sex differences are obvious, with girls, on average, entering and progressing through puberty earlier than boys. The magnitude of the timing difference between the sexes depends on what signs of puberty are examined, with measures such as breast budding or onset of menstruation (menarche) in girls obviously not applicable to boys, for whom growth of penis and testes or "break" in voice can be used, although some measures such as pubic hair growth can be examined in both (see Karlberg, 2002). There is also a substantial genetic component to puberty, with identical twins, for example, showing more closely synchronized timing of pubertal events than fraternal twins (see Karlberg, 2002, for review and references). Size at birth is also critical, although in this case, low birth size (in particular, long and thin babies) has been reliably associated with earlier puberty in girls (Adair, 2001), whereas both delayed (Delemarre-van de Waal et al., 2002) and earlier puberty (Karlberg, 2002) have been reported in low birth-weight boys. The elements in the prenatal environment that might predispose for early puberty are not yet clear. This association between birth size and early puberty in girls is still evident when statistically controlling for a variety of maternal factors (e.g., age, socioeconomic status, number of prior pregnancies) as well as the rate of "catch-up" growth following birth (see Adair, 2001). It has been hypothesized that this birth size effect may represent a type of "fetal programming" that may influence (i.e., "program") the timing of puberty many years later (see Karlberg, 2002), perhaps by exerting long-term influences on the function of leptin and other hormone systems (e.g., Harigaya et al., 1992).

Puberty is occurring earlier these days in Europe and the United States (e.g., de Muinck Keizer-Schrama & Mull, 2001; Parent et al., 2003). Over the past 100 years, the age at the time of onset of menstruation has declined 6–12 months, to around 12.5 years (de Muinck Keizer-Schrama & Mul, 2001). The factors contributing to the decline in the age of pubertal onset are largely unknown, although there is no shortage of speculations. Dietary factors are a major suspect—not only improved nutrition but also the ready availability of "junk" foods that may foster the emergence of obesity in childhood. Improved health care and other advantages of the rise in the middle class over the past century may also have contributed. Indeed, higher socioeconomic status (SES) is correlated with earlier age at menarche (Adair, 2001), although, again, what it is about higher SES that contributes to this association is unclear. Rises in environmental contaminants have also been added to the suspect list, given that some of these environmental chemicals serve as endocrine disrupters, potentially altering hormonal levels (see Parent et al., 2003, for discussion).

THE IMPORTANCE OF TIMING: THE ISSUE OF
EARLY VERSUS LATE PUBERTY

Kids differ widely in their pubertal timing, with onsets of puberty varying by 4 years or more among individuals within a given population. In middle school this difference is particularly obvious, with shapely, mature-appearing girls sitting next to girls that still bear childlike appearances, and both groups towering over many boys of their age. Whether one enters puberty early or late can have a considerable impact on social and psychological functioning, although the consequences of early versus late pubertal timing are notably different for boys and girls.

Early puberty is associated with an increase in a variety of adverse outcomes in girls, including greater levels of psychological distress (Ge et al., 1996), as well as earlier use of alcohol and other drugs, greater levels of risky drinking in high school, earlier and risky sexual behavior, as well as increased delinquency and antisocial behavior during adolescence (Waylen & Wolke, 2004; Deardorff et al., 2005; Bratbert et al., 2007). Many of these effects could be due to these more mature-looking girls becoming involved with older males and gaining access to opportunities (e.g., alcohol, drugs, adult movies) that are largely unavailable to their younger-appearing counterparts (see Waylen & Wolke, 2004). These associations with early puberty in girls appear to be largely "adolescent-limited," with no notable consequences of pubertal timing on later psychosocial function among adult women, although the average education level reached by women undergoing early puberty was found to be lower than other women (Johansson & Ritzén, 2005).

As was the case in girls, early puberty in boys is likewise associated with earlier substance use, sexual activity, and delinquency (e.g., Flannery et al., 1993; Tschann et al., 1994;

Bratbert et al., 2007). Aside from these associations, though, the effects of early puberty largely appear to be advantageous for boys. Because boys who enter puberty early are bigger and more mature looking than their slower-to-mature peers, they have an advantage in a variety of sports. Perhaps in part as a consequence, early-maturing boys tend to be of relatively high status within their social group and to have high self-esteem (see Waylen & Wolke, 2004). Late puberty also seems to have consequences for boys; these boys are more likely to engage in antisocial behaviors, perhaps because they are trying to seek status by engaging in risky behaviors that might be viewed as "cool" by others (Waylen & Wokle, 2004). Thus, for males, those who mature "off-time"—both early as well as late—show more delinquent behavior than those who undergo puberty with more typical timing (Williams & Dunlop, 1999).

Some of the associations seen with early puberty may not reflect consequences of pubertal timing, per se. Rather, early puberty may be an outcome of particular environmental situations that might independently increase vulnerability of the adolescent for developing drug abuse or antisocial behaviors and expressing other risky behaviors. For instance, negative parenting, low parental involvement, absence of the biological father, and/or the presence of an unrelated male adult in the household have been associated with early puberty in girls and, to some extent, in females of other species as well (e.g., Surbey, 1998; Belsky et al., 2007). These environmental experiences may not only predict earlier puberty, but also perhaps contribute to other outcomes associated with advanced pubertal timing.

SUMMARY AND CLOSING COMMENTS

The process of sexual differentiation of the brain begins early during the prenatal period, but is not completed then. After a hiatus during childhood, sex hormones appear to exert a second organizational period during adolescence to further differentiate the brain in a sex-typical manner. The timing of puberty and the rise in sex hormones then stimulate increased sexual interest and motivation in adolescents and may influence other behaviors and moods as well. Although parents and other adults have blamed the "raging hormones" of adolescence for many of the annoying aspects of this time period, evidence to date suggests that hormonal influences, per se, are often modest at best. Adolescent-typical alterations in behavior, mood, and cognitive function, whether stimulated by gonadal hormones or not, are presumably mediated in large part by developmental changes in the brain of the adolescent. It is to this topic that we turn in the next chapter.

CHAPTER FOUR

The Brain, Its Development, and the Neuroscience of Adolescence

••••••••••••••••••••••••••••••••••••••

A big part of the story as to why adolescents behave the way they do involves the changes that are going on in their brains— transformations that are in some ways as dramatic as, and often reminiscent of, processes guiding early development of the brain during the prenatal and infant periods. In the chapters to follow, the focus will often be on these striking brain transformations, when considering factors contributing to adolescent-characteristic behaviors and the increased incidence of certain problem behaviors among some adolescents. This chapter first offers a brief primer on brain structure and function, before highlighting several key principles of brain development. A broad overview of the major transformations occurring in the adolescent brain are then presented, along with a review of major technical advances that have led to the recent surge of studies exploring the adolescent brain, and their successes and limitations.

BASICS OF BRAIN STRUCTURE AND FUNCTION

The brain is a 3-pound conglomerate of some 100 billion nerve cells (neurons) and even more support cells (glia). The brain accomplishes its many goals—such as sensing, moving, thinking, feeling, monitoring, and controlling body systems—via communication among cells within the brain and receiving and supplying information to other regions of the body via the spinal cord and peripheral nervous system.

Neurons

Nerve cells, often called *neurons*, are specialized for receiving, analyzing, and transmitting information, often over long distances. They consist of a cell body region with special branch-like appendages, called *dendrites,* that extend off the cell body, as well as an often very long appendage, called the *axon,* through which information is passed along to its most distal part, the axon terminal (see Figure 4.1).

Neurons primarily receive information in the region of the cell body and dendrites. On the cell surface of the neuron in these regions are different types of specialized sites (*receptors*) that recognize particular chemicals. These chemicals include substances called *neurotransmitters*, which are released from other neurons, as well as certain hormones that reach the brain through the bloodstream after being released from distal sites. Other hormones cross cellular membranes, gaining access to the inside of neurons and interacting with receptors there to influence DNA transcription.

Thus, communication between neurons is chemical, with neurotransmitter release from one neuron interacting with receptors on other neurons to induce changes in those neurons. Much of this chemical communication occurs via release and diffusion of the neurotransmitter across a short distance, from the sending to the receiving neuron, at specialized junctions between the neurons called *synapses* (see Figure 4.1). The nature of the change induced by interaction of a neurotransmitter with its associated receptors varies not only with the neurotransmitter being released, but also with the specific characteristics of its associated receptor(s) as well. There is of-

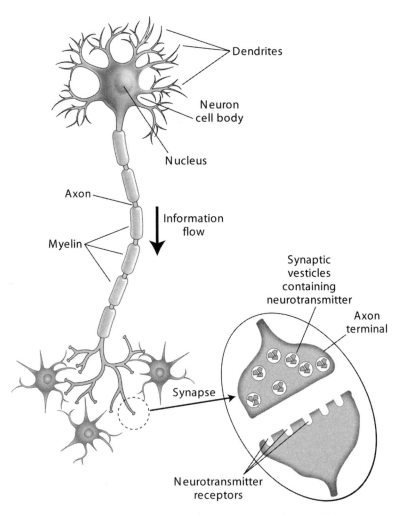

Figure 4.1. Major components of a neuron and one of its synapses with another neuron.

ten a variety of different subtypes of receptors for a given neurotransmitter that vary in how they react neurochemically to stimulation, and hence in the effect that they have on the neurons upon which they are located. This diversity of receptors for a particular neurotransmitter provides substantial diversity in the types of messages that can be passed along by that neurotransmitter. For instance, one major distinction among receptor subtypes is whether they are *ionotrophic* or *metabotrophic*. The former refers to a receptor that, when activated, directly alters excitability of the neuron upon which it is located by altering the flow of electrically charged ions into or out of the neuron. In contrast, when metabotrophic receptors are activated, they not only alter the excitability of the cell, but they also trigger "signal transduction" mechanisms—that is, a cascade of chemical alterations that can ultimately influence which genes are transcribed from the DNA within the neuron, resulting in the production of new proteins that can influence structure and function of that neuron.

Through activation of such receptors, a neuron on the receiving side of such input (i.e., the *postsynaptic* neuron) may receive concurrent input from a variety of neurotransmitters and hormones. Activation of some of these receptors will increase excitability of that neuron, whereas activation of others will suppress neuronal excitability, whether or not longer-lasting influences are also exerted via altering DNA transcription. At any point in time, if the net effect of these excitatory and inhibitory inputs induces a sufficiently large excitatory electrical response to exceed a particular threshold, an electrical signal will be produced in the post-synaptic neuron that is passed along its axon to reach the axon terminals; if this threshold is not exceeded, then this signal will not be produced. Once the electrical signal reaches the axon terminals, it stimulates neurotransmitter release at these synapses, thereby passing information along to their postsynaptic neurons (see Figure 4.1).

Transmission of an electrical impulse (*action potential*) along the length of an axon often occurs over relatively long distances. Consider, for example, the distance traveled by electrical impulses passing down axons of motor neurons that project from cell bodies in the spinal cord to axon terminals in the muscles of the foot—a considerable distance (even if not considering pro basketball players). The process of transmitting an action potential down an axon occurs via movement of ions across the membrane of the axon that proceeds in a wave along the axon, a process that is accelerated considerably when the axon is insulated via a fatty substance called *myelin*. Myelin is produced by a particular type of glia support cell that encases the axon with layers of insulating material separated by small gaps (see Figure 4.1). This allows the electrical impulse to jump from gap to gap, considerably speeding information flow along the axon and decreasing the amount of energy needed for the axon to recover normal ion balance following passage of an action potential. Thus, two neurons with axons of the same length will transmit information at different rates if one is myelinated and the other is not. For instance, when you touch a hot stove, myelinated axons in a sensorimotor reflex circuit induce rapid hand withdrawal—often before you are consciously aware of the burning sensation transmitted to the brain by unmyelinated axons in the pain system.

Major Structures of the Brain

The brain is like the rest of the head in its bilateral organization—with the left side being roughly a mirror image of the right. Like eyes on the face, structures located off the midline have a representation on each side, whereas midline structures (again, to use the facial analogy, like the nose or mouth) are singular but with similar representations on each side of the midline. Sensory information gains access to the nervous system, and motor instructions are carried to the muscles, via the spinal cord and cranial nerves. This information typically is channeled into and out of the brain through large myelinated tracts that run through the brainstem and midbrain regions that form the base of the brain (see Figure 4.2a). Interestingly, when passing through the midbrain/brainstem, pathways carrying information to and from the left side of the body typically cross over to connect with higher brain areas on the right side of the brain, whereas information from the right side of the body goes to left cortical regions. That is why, for instance, individuals with a stroke that impairs movement on the left side of the body are likely to have sustained damage to the right side of their brain.

Brainstem and midbrain regions serve as much more than a freeway for the passage of tracts to and from the brain. They also contain regions in which cell bodies of neurons are clustered into groups (*nuclei*) that are critical for regulating alertness and arousal, along with such basic physiological functions as breathing, temperature regulation, and fluid balance. Other important functions of the brainstem are attributed to an extension called the *cerebellum*, a large, intricately folded structure located at the lower back of the skull (see Figures 4.2a, 4.2b). This region is critical for skilled motor movements and balance and also plays a role in cognitive functions via connections with other brain regions. The brainstem and midbrain also include regions containing the cell bodies of neurons that send axons forward into the brain (i.e., into the forebrain), where they release neurotransmitters that have been shown to modulate functioning in these forebrain regions. Prominent forebrain-projecting neurotransmitter systems include norepinephrine and serotonin, as well as the dopamine (DA) system. Amphetamine, methamphetamine, and cocaine exert their stimulant effects largely via interactions with norepinephrine and DA systems, whereas antidepressants such as Prozac and other selective serotonin reuptake inhibitors (SSRIs) largely exert their effects through interactions with the serotonin system. DA cell bodies in the substantia nigra (SN) and ventral tegmental area (VTA) project to the forebrain, where they play important roles in motor behaviors and in motivating reward-related behaviors and drug/alcohol use. These DA projection

65

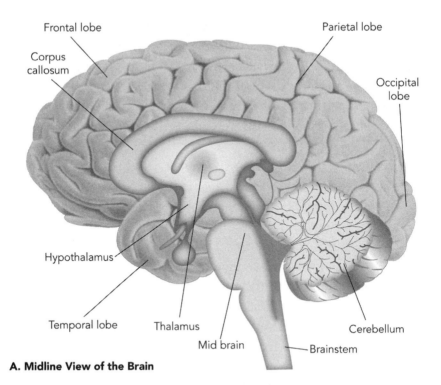

Frontal lobe

Parietal lobe

Corpus callosum

Occipital lobe

Hypothalamus

Temporal lobe

Thalamus

Mid brain

Brainstem

Cerebellum

A. Midline View of the Brain

Figure 4.2a. The medial surface of the right half of the brain. The front of the brain (e.g., frontal lobe of the cortex) is on the left, with the back of the brain (e.g., cerebellum and occipital lobe) on the right.

systems show notable developmental changes during adolescence and hence receive particular attention in later chapters.

These forebrain-projecting neurotransmitters, with their cell bodies localized in brainstem/midbrain areas and axons that have widespread forebrain projections, contrast with others that show different localization patterns. For instance, the predominant excitatory neurotransmitter in brain, glutamate, stimulates neurons via interconnections coming from and going to a wide variety of brain regions. That is, cell bodies of neurons that utilize glutamate as a neurotransmitter are located in numerous brain regions and typically send their axons to

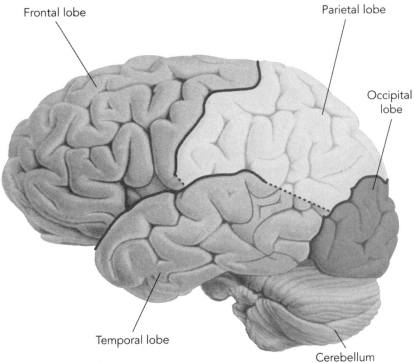

Frontal lobe

Parietal lobe

Occipital lobe

Temporal lobe

Cerebellum

B. Outside View of Brain

Figure 4.2b. An external view of the left half of the brain. The front of the brain (e.g., frontal lobe of the cortex) is on the left, with the back of the brain (e.g., cerebellum and occipital lobe) on the right.

other brain regions with which they are functionally connected, stimulating certain neurons in those regions when they themselves are activated. In contrast, the predominant inhibitory neurotransmitter in the brain, gamma-aminobutyric acid (GABA), typically is released by small neurons, called *interneurons*, that serve to inhibit nearby neurons within a given brain region.

Returning to the major structures of the brain, perched on top of the brainstem and extending forward to fill the rest of the brain cavity is the realm of the forebrain. Particularly prominent in the forebrain are neocortical regions. Most developed and extensive in humans, these cortical areas completely cover the outer brain surface (see Figure 4.2b). Tucked underneath these cortical regions are a number of other critical brain regions, including limbic regions, the basal ganglia, and the diencephalon. The thalamus and hypothalamus comprise the diencephalon (see Figure 4.2a). The *hypothalamus* is located at the bottom of the forebrain where (as discussed in the previous chapter) it plays an important role in the regulation of hormone release from the pituitary gland. Above the hypothalamus is the *thalamus*, a brain region that, among other functions, serves as a relay station for information to and from the neocortex—sending sensory information to the cortex and receiving instructions in return that serve to filter this input.

The basal ganglia are important in motor control. Primary subregions include the *dorsal striatum*, through which most input to the basal ganglia is received (including DA input from the SN), the ventral striatum (a critical component of the limbic system that will be discussed later), and the *globus pallidus*, which serves as a major output portion of the basal ganglia. Damage to the DA system projecting to the striatum can result in difficulties initiating voluntary movements, such as is seen in Parkinson's disease. Fortunately, however, symptoms of Parkinson's disease typically do not emerge until DA levels in this striatal projection have been reduced to about 5% of normal—a testimony to the remarkable capacity of the brain to compensate for deficiencies.

The *limbic system* is involved in a number of functions that include the processing of emotions and emotion-based behavior, as well as facilitating learning and memory. Among the significant components of the limbic system are the hippocampus, septal area, amygdala, and related areas included within the "extended amygdala," such as the bed nucleus of the stria terminalis (BNST) and, importantly, the shell portion of the

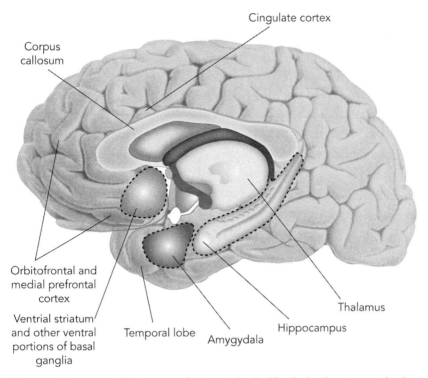

Figure 4.3. A medial view of the right half of the brain, with the brainstem, midbrain and cerebellum removed. Structures bounded by dashed lines—i.e., the hippocampus, amygdala, and ventral striatum—are located deep below the overlying cortical surface.

nucleus accumbens (a brain region also called the *ventral striatum*). These regions are tucked underneath neocortical regions (as indicated by the dotted line outlines in Figure 4.3). The *hippocampus*, in conjunction with other limbic and nonlimbic areas, plays a particularly critical role in learning and memory. The *amygdala* consists of a variety of disparate subregions that work in conjunction with other limbic and nonlimbic areas to influence emotional and affective responding. For instance, neurons in the central nucleus of the amygdala (CeA) are critical for the emergence of conditioned fear responses, such as developing a fear of a particular garden (or gardens more generally) after being startled by several snakes there. In contrast, the BNST is more critical for responding to sustained threats in the environment (Walker et al., 2003).

Although many limbic regions receive DA projections from the VTA, the DA projection to the nucleus accumbens shell is particularly pronounced and forms the cornerstone of the so-called *mesolimbic DA system*. The nucleus accumbens (NAc), with its DA input, is involved in the attribution of motivational value to reward-related stimuli and in directing behaviors toward those rewards (e.g., see Kalivas et al., 1993; Berridge & Robinson, 1998). The mesolimbic DA system is normally activated by natural rewards such as social stimuli, food, novelty, sex, and so on, and is thought to become "hijacked" by repeated use of alcohol and other drugs of abuse to produce the excessive wanting/craving characteristic of substance addictions (Volkow et al., 2002a).

Several deeper and evolutionarily older cortical regions are intimately interconnected with subcortical limbic structures. These regions—the *orbitofrontal cortex* (OFC), medial portions of the *prefrontal cortex* (PFC), and the *cingulate cortex*—together with the hippocampus and portions of the amygdala, form a border (*limbus* in Latin) around non-cortical regions of the brain (see Figure 4.3) and were the first structures identified as part of the limbic system.

Neocortical regions are located in two hemispheres (one on the left, one on the right). When looking at an exterior view of the neocortex (see Figure 4.2b), one obvious characteristic is that the surface is very convoluted and consists of numerous hills (*gyri*) and valleys (*sulci*), with a majority of the actual cortical surface hidden in the folds of the sulci in humans. Although some other species have as convoluted a cortex as humans (e.g., dophins), nonhuman primates have notably fewer gyri and sulci, cats and dogs even fewer, whereas rodents have an almost smooth cortex. Such folds allow for increases in

cortical surface area without having to have corresponding en-
largements in head/skull size. Indeed, relative amount of
cortical mass is directly related to the amount of cortical fold-
ing, with the neocortex comprising the greatest percentage of
the total brain mass in humans relative to nonhuman primates,
which in turn have a larger percentage of their brain devoted
to the neocortex than do cats and dogs, and rodents trailing at
the end of this dimension among mammals.

The cortex can be divided into four lobes: occipital, temporal, parietal, and frontal (Figure 4.2b). Although the lobes are
defined anatomically and are highly interconnected with each
other and other brain regions, to some extent each plays a different functional role. The occipital lobe is critical for the processing of visual information, whereas auditory information is
processed within areas of the temporal lobe. Portions of the
parietal cortex receive somatosensory information—that is,
touch, temperature, pain, movement, and limb location (pro-
prioception). The frontal lobe is critical for the execution and
control of motor functions and consists of two primary subar-
eas. One area encompasses primary motor regions that are located just in front of the parietal lobe, and whose neurons send
their axons down through the brain to synapse on motor neurons in the spinal cord. In front of this motor area and extending down into the cortical midline at the centermost part of
each cortical hemisphere (see Figure 4.3) is the other major
subarea of the frontal lobe: the PFC and related regions such
as the OFC and anterior portions of the cingulate cortex (ACC).
Activity in these regions appears to be critical for higher-level
functions such as goal-directed planning, temporal integration, self-control, and emotional regulation. Research groups
differ somewhat in the strategies they use for dividing the frontal cortex into subregions and in the names ascribed to particular subregions. For instance, some researchers view the
medial OFC as part of the ventromedial PFC, whereas others

consider this portion of the OFC distinct from the PFC. These "potato/po-tah-to" issues sometimes add challenges to interpreting findings across studies.

Each of the cortical lobes includes areas not only devoted to the sensory and motor functions discussed above, but also *association regions* that receive inputs from more than one sensory system and that have more complex, integrative functions. For instance, although the primary visual cortex in the occipital lobe is critical for vision, association areas in the parietal and temporal lobes also play an important role in the processing of visual stimuli. Additional complexity is added by the fact that some brain functions are lateralized. For instance, areas for the understanding language (Wernicke's area in the temporal lobe) and producing speech (Broca's area in the frontal lobe) are largely lateralized to the left hemisphere, particularly in right-handed individuals. Remembering that sensory and motor input and outputs to the neocortex are largely crossed, so that sensory information from the right side of the body activates the left neocortex, and vice versa, it thus would be more likely that a stroke that disrupts both language and sensorimotor functions would impact sensory and motor behavior on the right side of the body than on the left.

Normally, however, the two cerebral hemispheres are in close communication, with input initially received in one hemisphere normally being transferred to the other hemisphere via neurons with axons that connect the two hemispheres. These axons are often large, fast-communicating, myelinated, and bundled together into large tracts that connect the two hemispheres. The largest of these is the *corpus callosum*, a massive connection of myelinated axons (see Figures 4.2a, 4.3). Myelin, because it contains substantial amounts of fatty-like insulation, looks white in unstained brain tissue. Hence tracts such as the corpus callosum, where myelinated axons are collected, are called *white matter*. In contrast, brain structures such as those discussed above primarily consist of cell bodies of neurons and their support cells (glia); although some axonal fibers may pass through these regions, they are not collected into tract-like bundles. Because cell bodies do not contain as much fatty material as does myelin, these regions appear gray in color when looking at unstained brain tissue. The ratio of white–gray matter is often used as a general index of brain development, given that myelination occurs later in development than the formation of most neuronal populations.

A substantial amount of work has provided a wealth of knowledge about the importance of different brain regions in various behaviors and cognitive function. Yet, although certain functions (e.g., motor control, memory, fear conditioning, inhibitory control) have been sometimes associated, very generally, with particular regions, it is critical to recognize that no brain region functions in isolation. The brain is a series of networks, each interconnecting functionally related regions. Activity in one brain region influences activity elsewhere in the network. Indeed, it has been argued that studies of brain development may not be well served by trying to determine when a particular brain region comes "online," but instead should focus on assessing maturation in terms of developmental changes in the region's pattern of functional connections with other brain regions (e.g., Johnson, 2001). This point is important to keep in mind as we discuss, in future chapters, the relationship between adolescent brain development and specific adolescent-typical ways of behaving and thinking.

BRAIN DEVELOPMENT

If there is anything more mind-boggling than considering the sheer complexity of the 100 billion neurons of the adult brain, each with thousands of connections to other neurons, it is to contemplate how this complexity developed from a single fertilized egg. This incredible story of the construction of the brain during the prenatal period is a fascinating and lengthy tale (e.g., Rao & Jacobson, 2005), the details of which are well beyond the scope of interest here. Yet, the significance of developmental transformations that occur in the adolescent brain can best be understood within a broader developmental context. Thus, we begin by very briefly highlighting some of the major principles of how the brain is formed and molded early in development, to set the stage for discussions of the brain transformations of adolescence.

• *Development of the brain is subject to strong genetic influences, a genetic blueprint that contains general plans of action rather than detailed instructions for point-to-point connections.* There is not nearly enough information contained in our DNA to specify in detail which neurons should be connected with what other neurons. Instead, genes largely specify plans of action—strategies that can be used by developing neurons and their processes to eventually result in appropriate connectivity. Variations seen across individuals in brain region volume and other characteristics are driven strongly by genetic factors, although the relative strength of these genetic influences often changes with age. Interestingly, stronger heritability is generally seen in association areas of the cortex that in other cortical regions, with primary sensory and motor regions of the cortex being particularly strongly influenced by environmental factors (see Lenroot & Giedd, 2008, for review).

• *Cells of the nervous system are produced in central locations and typically have to migrate to reach their target locations elsewhere in the brain.* Centralized production and distribution networks are an efficient way not only for industries to provide goods to consumers, but also for creating the nervous system as well. Cells that serve as precursors for neurons and their supporting glia cells surround fluid-filled spaces in the brain called *ventricles* (or, in the spinal cord, the spinal canal). There, as each precursor cell divides, it produces two cells, both of which can either stay near the ventricles to serve as precursor cells for further divisions or migrate away from the ventricles and differentiate into neurons or glia cells. By processes that are still incompletely understood, as cells migrate through the developing brain their "fate" is established—becoming destined, for example, to terminate migration in the ventral striatum and differentiate into a GABA interneuron there.

• *Chemical and mechanical cues in the immediate cellular environment serve to guide neurons and their processes.* Neurons and glia use chemical and mechanical cues available to them in their immediate environment to guide their migration and let them know when they get to an appropriate target destination. Likewise, physical and chemical cues also often guide dendrites and axons as they grow and establish appropriate connections with other neurons. For instance, axons growing toward target regions avoid "reinventing the wheel" whenever possible—that is, they adhere to, and grow along, axonal tracts laid by other axons where available, then leave that support system as they approach their target region, either by being drawn to chemical attractors or repelled by repulsive factors (see Sanes et al., 2000, for review). Once the appropriate target location is reached, synaptic connections are established between the growing axon and the target neuron (or muscle, in the case of neurons of the motor system that innervate muscle tissue). Similar chemical cues are used to guide the growth and branching of dendritic trees.

• *Specificity in synaptic connections is established by a process of overproduction and pruning.* Many more synaptic connections are made than are kept. The strategy used by the nervous system is for axons, once they have grown to their general target region, to produce synaptic connections promiscuously. Then, only those connections that are most appropriate (e.g., that capture a previously under-innervated target or reach some threshold of functional activity) are maintained, while the rest are lost (e.g., see Rakic et al., 1994). This process of exuberant overproduction and subsequent decline seems wasteful, and it is—energy is required to produce synapses and to maintain them until their demise. Thus, there must be some considerable adaptive benefit to override this essentially wasteful process whereby only about 60% of the synapses produced are ultimately retained (see Huttenlocher & Dabholkar, 1997). One critical benefit is that by pruning away the most unfruitful connections and leaving the most suitable intact, appropriate connectivity would be attained without requiring the massive number of genes that would be necessary to specify precise neuron-to-neuron connectivity genetically.

Synaptic overproduction and pruning are also likely to be one of a number of means by which brain connectivity is adjusted to match the particular environment in which the organism finds itself. The visual system provides a good example of this functional malleability. Studies have shown that adult cats that are reared in an environment with many horizontal lines during a critical developmental period have more neurons in their visual cortex that respond to horizontal lines than vertical lines (e.g., Blakemore, 1974). As another example, normally in the visual cortex, about as many neurons respond to stimuli from one eye as from the other; in contrast, if vision is disrupted in one eye during a critical period early in life (such as might occur if one is born with poor vision in one eye or a "lazy eye," such that the other eye is used preferentially), few neurons respond to the bad eye. This decline is long-lasting, with many neurons of the visual cortex permanently losing the capacity to respond to stimuli from the affected eye, even if vision is corrected later in life (Wiesel & Hubel, 1965).

• *Death is a normal part of development, with many more neurons produced early in life than will be maintained.* Not only are many synapses lost during development of the nervous system, but many neurons die as well—up to 80% in some brain regions (Oppenheim, 1991). This cell death is driven largely by activation of "death genes" that induce an orderly and tidy process of demise that is not disruptive to neurons around them. This is in contrast to injury-induced cell death, wherein dying cells often "leak" toxic components onto other neurons, stressing them as well. This process of overproduction and death is not unique to the developing nervous system, although the amount of cell death that occurs during development in other body regions is generally much less than in the nervous system.

Even more energetically costly than synaptic pruning, programmed cell death is thought to exert a number of beneficial functions during nervous system development. Cell death serves to eliminate neurons whose axons don't find the appropriate target area. Most axons find appropriate targets, though, so cell death due to this cause is rare. Instead, the major function of programmed cell death seemingly is to match sizes of neuronal projection regions to their target cell regions, and vice versa. Thus, if the size of a postsynaptic target is increased, more neurons that send axons to that area will survive, whereas if the target is decreased, fewer neurons projecting to that area will survive. In at least some cases, whether or not a neuron survives seems to be dependent on whether it receives enough of a chemical survival factor (*neurotrophin*) to keep it alive. That is, target sites produce a limited amount of a neurotrophic factor, which is taken up by the axons of the neurons projecting to that target. Those projecting neurons that take up enough neurotrophin survive; those that do not, die.

Overproduction and death of neurons is thought to play an important role in brain plasticity. For instance, a larger peripheral target (e.g., bigger muscles) would support more neurons in the regions projecting to that target (i.e., motor neurons);

the larger number of neurons in that region (in this example, more motor neurons) would support more neurons in regions that project to those neurons, and so on. By this "wave" of transsynaptic influences, the relative size of different subregions of the brain can be matched to the size of interrelated brain regions in a coordinated effort to maximize benefits to the organism. Via this process of matching inputs to outputs, different brain regions could be selectively elaborated over the course of evolution.

• *The emerging brain is "developmentally programmed" to correspond to the characteristics of the environment in which the growing organism finds itself.* Via processes that include synaptic pruning and programmed cell death, among others, the brain that develops is adjusted to correspond to the surrounding early environment. One of the best studied examples of this process is the plasticity in the visual system mentioned earlier, whereby sensitivity of mature neurons to particular visual stimuli is set by the visual experiences of the organism during a critical period early in life. It is gradually becoming recognized that sensitivity of the adult brain is altered not only by early visual experiences, but also by other types of early experiences, and that such "developmental programming" also extends to physiological systems other than the brain.

Among the early experiences thought to exert developmental programming effects are nutrition and stressors. Early undernutrition is thought to influence a number of adult health outcomes, with low birthweight (or thinness at birth) associated with a greater probability of developing obesity, diabetes, and coronary heart disease (Godfrey & Barker, 2000). It has been hypothesized that the lack of adequate nutrition during gestation and lactation alters development in a variety of brain, hormonal, and metabolic systems to induce expression of a "thrifty phenotype" designed to maximize available nutrients throughout life (see Gaspar de Moura & Passos, 2005). Although the metabolic alterations associated with this phenotype may be adaptive if the person is faced with chronic nutritional inadequacy, when food is readily available, these metabolic alterations promote development of obesity and other adverse health outcomes (e.g., Oken & Gillman, 2003).

Exposure to stressors during the prenatal or early postnatal period may likewise exert long-lasting influences on later stress responsiveness through developmental programming. In animal studies, prenatal stressors or extended periods of maternal separation early in life have been shown to increase later anxiety as well as to accentuate later hormonal and behavioral responses to stressors (Vallée et al., 1997; Meaney, 2001). Such accentuated responses may help the organism to remain vigilant in uncertain and potentially dangerous situations and to respond robustly when confronted with a potentially life-threatening stressful situation. However, such elevated stress reactivity may also enhance reactivity to the mild stressors of daily life, increasing vulnerability to stress-associated illnesses (Ladd et al., 2000). And when the early stressful experiences are intense, such as those associated with early child abuse, brain development in a variety of regions is affected, not only increasing alertness to danger, but predisposing the individual to respond aggressively even to perceived minor threats (Teicher, 2002).

Other early experiences, in contrast, may exert protective effects, lowering the behavioral and hormonal response to later stressors and speeding the poststress recovery process (Liu et al., 1997; Vallée et al., 1997). One type of protective factor was discussed earlier: maternal care and the tactile stimulation it provides. As outlined in Chapter 2, in a simple animal model using rats, offspring of high LG mothers (who spent a lot of time licking and grooming their pups) exhibit more moderated stress responses than offspring of low LG mothers (e.g., Liu et al., 1997). Similar benefits of tactile stimulation have been reported in human infants, with neonates in intensive care units showing greater weight gain, shorter hospitalization stays, and improved test performance on the Brazelton when given explicit tactile stimulation (15-minute massages, three times/day; see Field, 1998; Field et al., 2007, for review).

• *An important way by which the brain is developmentally programmed by the environment is via genetic silencing of certain genes (epigenetic regulation).* Long-lasting effects of early nutrition, stressors, and maternal care are mediated in part via relatively permanent alterations in which genes are available for transcription through the process of epigenetic regulation. As discussed in Chapter 2, the process of silencing a gene does not alter the nature of the DNA code, but rather makes the DNA inaccessible for transcription, either via adding methyl groups to portions of the DNA to obstruct transcription of those regions or via altering the structural supports (histones) to those areas of the DNA, blocking their accessibility (see Szyf et al., 2007, for review). Thus, via processes of epigenetic regulation, early life experiences can exert long-term influences on which genes are capable of being expressed without permanently altering what information is carried in the genetic code (Langley-Evans, 2007; Meaney et al., 2007; Szyf et al., 2007).

• *Brain development is a lifelong process.* Although most neurons of the brain are generated, migrate to their final locations, and begin to establish their connectivity prenatally, brain differentiation and growth continue at a rapid pace during the first few postnatal years as well. Even thereafter, the brain is not static, but continues to dynamically change into midadulthood or later, with further changes associated with the aging process (Sowell et al., 2003). Even the process of neuronal formation is not limited to the early developmental period; indeed, the formation of some new neurons occurs in certain brain regions throughout life (Eriksson et al., 1998).

Within this extended developmental time frame, the adolescent period stands out as a time of particularly dramatic remodeling and sculpting of the brain.

GENERAL FEATURES OF ADOLESCENT BRAIN DEVELOPMENT

Although adult brain weight is reached by about 10–12 years of age (see Paus et al., 2001), the brain continues to undergo considerable developmental change through adolescence. Cerebral volume peaks at 10.5 years in girls and 14.5 years in boys, with developmental declines in gray matter volume after these peaks are reached (Lenroot et al., 2007). Indeed, although some of the changes occurring in the adolescent brain are progressive, a good part of this developmental remodeling is regressive, involving not only declines in the volume of brain regions but also the loss of connections. Along with this streamlining, the brain becomes more efficient and energy conserving. A few of the major changes in the brain that occur during adolescence are highlighted below.

• *Many adolescent-typical brain changes are regressive, with the elimination of a substantial number of synapses during adolescence.* Synaptic pruning is not only characteristic of the pre- and early postnatal period, but undergoes a resurgence during adolescence as well, with almost half of the synaptic connections in some brain regions eliminated at this relatively late point on the road to maturity. It is not clear why so many synapses are lost during adolescence. However, more synapses are not necessarily better. For example, some forms of mental retardation are associated with greater numbers of synapses (Goldman-Rakic et al., 1983). It seems improbable that the culling of synapses during adolescence merely reflects developmentally delayed elimination of nonfunctional synapses, given the high cost of maintaining synapses—why utilize all the energy necessary to maintain nonfunctional synapses for a decade or more before their elimination? Rather, this synapse elimination may reflect, in part, a fine-tuning of neural connectivity to allow the emergence of mature patterns of brain effort (Zehr et al., 2006). Indeed, the synaptic pruning that occurs during adolescence is not random, and is often more pronounced with particular types of input (e.g., synapses releasing the excitatory neurotransmitter glutamate) and in particular brain regions (e.g., more pronounced in cortical than subcortical regions [e.g., Rakic et al., 1994] and in prefrontal and as-

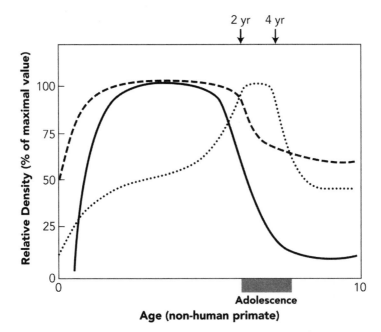

Figure 4.4. Age-related changes in various inputs to layer 3 pyramidal neurons in primate dlPFC, with data represented as % maximal value for each measure (regardless of the developmental age at which this maximal value was reached). The dashed line represents excitatory input (indexed via density of protrusions [spines] on pyramidal cell dendrites where excitatory synapses are located). The solid line represents inhibitory input (indexed via number of chandelier [inhibitory] interneuron axon terminals). DA input to this region is represented by the dotted line. Adapted from Lewis (1997).

sociation areas than other cortical regions [Giedd et al., 1999a]). One example focusing on developmental transitions within a portion of the dorsolateral PFC (dlPFC) in the non-human primate brain is shown in Figure 4.4. As illustrated here, dramatic developmental declines in markers of both excitatory and inhibitory synaptic input (represented by dashed lines and solid lines, respectively) are seen during adolescence, whereas a measure indexing DA synaptic input to this region (represented by the dotted line) rises to reach a plateau during adolescence at levels higher than seen earlier or later in life (see Lewis, 1997).

Synaptic pruning during adolescence could provide a relatively delayed opportunity for the brain to be sculpted by the environment, although whether adolescence indeed represents a transient reinstatement of the plasticity characteristic of early development has yet to be investigated systematically. In this context, though, it is interesting that work with genetically manipulated mice has shown that the axons of adolescent animals are very dynamic, growing and retracting in response to the cellular environment in a manner of minutes, whereas axonal growth/retraction is rare in adults (Gan et al., 2003). We will return to the intriguing issue of synaptic pruning and environmental plasticity during adolescence in Chapter 10.

• *Speed of information flow in brain is increased during adolescence via myelination of selected pathways.* Axon myelination is a protracted process that begins during the early postnatal period and continues into midadulthood (e.g., Benes et al., 1994; Inder & Huppi, 2000). Myelination is not a birthright of all axons, however: Most axons, in fact, are never myelinated (see Markham & Greenough, 2004). Those that are tend to be relatively large axons located in tracts that extend between different brain regions or across the midline to connect the left and right hemispheres. Myelin typically emerges earliest in the back of the brain (e.g., the brainstem) and gradually extends, over time, into tracts located more frontally. Sensory tracts are generally myelinated before those conveying motor information, with both of these types of projections maturing before tracts involving areas of association cortex (e.g., Jacobson, 1963; Yakovlev & Lecours, 1967). The largest fiber tract in the brain is the corpus callosum, which consists of masses of axons that largely serve to interconnect equivalent areas in the left and right hemispheres. Although clearly evident even in infancy, the size of the corpus callosum continues to increase into young adulthood as more and more callosal axons become myelinated. Intriguingly, the portion of the corpus callosum at the back of the brain (*splenium*) is the slowest to attain adult-typical size, whereas the front (*genu*) of the callosum develops adult-typical size early (Giedd et al., 1999a); this seems counterintuitive in that it is the genu that bilaterally interconnects the prefrontal cortex, a region that undergoes particularly prolonged developmental alterations. In addition to developmental increases in myelination, and hence in the volume of brain allocated to white matter, more recent advances in imaging technology (diffusion tensor imaging) have shown that measures of axonal fiber organization likewise increase in various white matter systems throughout adolescence (Barnea-Goraly et al., 2005; Ashtari et al., 2007).

Myelination speeds information flow. As axons become myelinated, the messages they provide arrive more rapidly—maybe even 50–100 milliseconds earlier—than they did before they were myelinated. More rapidly arriving impulses have been speculated to be more influential by virtue of being more likely to drive responses to stimuli than inputs arriving later (see Markham & Greenough, 2004). Hence, via myelination, the impact of axons traveling longer distances across cortical regions could be increased when pitted with smaller, typically unmyelinated interconnections within brain areas. Selective myelination may also serve to coordinate timing of inputs, despite differences in axonal lengths (see Fields, 2008). For instance, inputs from a variety of different sensory systems, after synapsing in the thalamus, are relayed to the appropriate sensory cortex. The distance axons have to travel from the thalamus to reach the appropriate cortical region varies considerably across sensory systems, however, so without some means to differentially regulate conduction speed, different types of sensory information about the same object would likely reach the cortex at different times. Via selective myelination to "eliminate the timing disadvantage of long-distance connections" (Salami et al., 2003, p. 6174), constant latencies of transmitting sensory information from the thalamus to the cortex are maintained regardless of sensory modality. Mature patterns of conduction velocity are reached in these thalamocortical projection systems during adolescence (Salami et al., 2003).

Influences between myelin and axon function are bidirectional: Not only does myelin speed axonal conduction, but axonal activity can, under some circumstances, stimulate myelin formation (Demerens et al., 1996). Glia cells responsible for myelinating axons contain receptors for some types of neurotransmitters and hence can potentially detect neurotransmitter release induced by electrically active axons in their vicinity (Stevens et al., 2002). In response to this stimulation, glia begin to myelinate those axons (Stevens et al., 2002)—assuming that the frequency of impulse activity is appropriate for stimulating myelination in that neural region (Zalc & Fields, 2000). Since neuronal activity is largely driven by input from the environment, these and other basic research findings support the suggestion that myelination is a dynamic process that is sensitive to environmental experiences, perhaps even into the adolescent period and beyond (see Fields, 2008).

Indeed, studies of environmental enrichment have found that raising groups of rats or primates in complex environments containing multiple objects to manipulate and crawl on or under exerts a number of long-lasting neural alterations. Among the effects observed were regionally specific alterations in myelination, with enriched animals having significantly more myelinated axons and a larger corpus callosum when compared with conspecifics reared in restricted environments (see Markham & Greenough, 2004, for review). Although little investigated, there are a few intriguing hints that similar environmental-dependent myelination may also be seen in humans (see Fields, 2008). For instance, the corpus callosum is smaller in neglected than non-neglected children (Teicher et al., 2004). As a second example, among professional pianists, the structural integrity of white matter in a variety of tracts in the brain was found to be correlated with practice time, with more correlations associated with amount of practice during childhood and adolescence than with the amount of practice as adults (Bengtsson et al., 2005). We will return to the intriguing issue of experience-dependent myelination in Chapter 10.

• *During adolescence, both progressive (increases in white matter) and regressive (decreases in gray matter) changes are seen in the brain, resulting in a shift in balance between white matter and gray matter.* As a consequence of the notable myelination of axons during the period leading into and through adolescence, the volume of white matter in the brain increases (Sowell et al., 1999). As illustrated in Figure 4.5 for frontal cortex, in contrast to these developmental increases in white matter volumes, declines in gray matter volumes are seen after peak volumes are reached. The timing of these developmental declines vary with brain region, and to some extent, sex (e.g., see Lenroot & Giedd, 2006), extending later in adolescence in the prefrontal cortex and other cortical association areas thought to subserve more advanced cognitive functions than in sensory and motor areas of the cortex (Gogtay et al., 2004; Lenroot & Giedd, 2006). These developmental regressions in the volume of gray matter may reflect, in part, declines in overall mass of

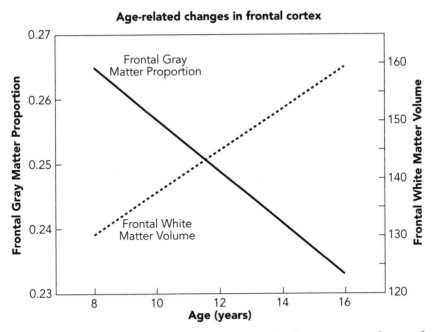

Figure 4.5. Age-related changes in gray and white matter volume of the frontal cortex. Data represent summary regression lines (collapsed across sex) of frontal white matter volume and of frontal gray matter volume relative to total brain volume. Adapted from Sowell et al. (2002).

cellular matter associated with synaptic pruning, and associated alterations in neuropil (number of dendritic processes and non-myelinated axons). Developmental declines in gray matter are also likely a consequence of developmental increases in white matter, given the finite amount of space available within the skull cavity (see Paus, 2005). Regardless of the cause, however, developmental declines in gray matter, when combined with developmental increases in white matter, result in considerable developmental increases in the ratio of white to gray matter during adolescence.

• *The timing of brain development is regionally dependent, with posterior regions (e.g., primary sensory and motor regions of the cortex and subcortical regions) generally developing before more anterior areas (e.g., PFC and other frontal regions).* Brain development does not occur simultaneously in all areas. Rather, more evolutionarily ancient areas—brainstem regions, hypothalamus, thalamus—generally tend to be more precocial in their developmental appearance than limbic regions and primary sensory and motor regions of the cortex. In turn, these latter regions tend to mature earlier than more recently evolved regions of prefrontal cortex and other frontal regions that have been evolutionarily most elaborated in primates, especially humans. For example, not only does the production of synapses occur earlier in the auditory cortex than in the PFC, but so does synaptic pruning, with pruning in the auditory cortex complete by 12 years, whereas it extends to midadolescence in the PFC (Huttenlocher & Dabholkar, 1997). A posterior-to-anterior shift is also generally seen in terms of myelination (Gogtay et al., 2004) and in terms of developmental peaks and subsequent declines in gray matter (Giedd et al., 1999a). Thus, brain maturation occurs heterogeneously, with brain regions located more posteriorly tending to be at more advanced developmental states than more anterior regions throughout the developmental process.

• *The adolescent brain becomes more efficient, streamlined, and cost-effective.* The brain requires the most energy to conduct its business from roughly 3–4 years of age through the remainder of childhood. During this time, levels of glucose and oxygen utilization and amount of blood flow to the brain are maintained at notably higher levels than seen in adults, with overall levels of energy utilization lower in adolescence than in childhood, and eventually reaching the relatively low levels typical of adults (e.g., Chugani, 1994, 1996) (see Figure 4.6). This overall decline in energy needs is detectable regionally, with different brain areas undergoing these declines at different times. For instance, relative blood flow was found to de-

Developmental changes in brain glucose utilization

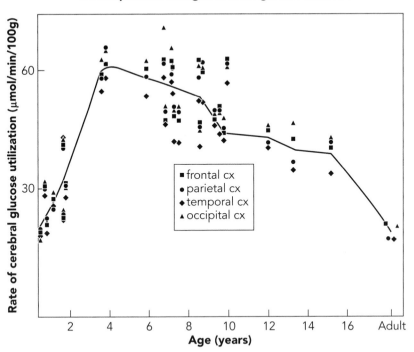

Figure 4.6. Metabolic rates of glucose utilization in samples of frontal cortex (squares), parietal cortex (circles), temporal cortex (diamonds), and occipital cortex (triangles) in individuals of different ages. A line representing a rough averaging of data points at each age is included to help visualize age-related metabolic patterns. Adapted from Chugani (1998).

cline significantly across the age span from 7 to 19 years in slowly maturing association areas of the cortex critical for the development of higher-order language skills, but not in the earlier maturing primary auditory cortex where basic speech stimuli are processed (Devous et al., 2006). Thus, it appears that as a brain region matures, its energy needs decline, lowering the demand for blood flow to that region.

There are a number of possible contributors to the maturation-associated decline in blood flow. Because synapses are costly to maintain, it is probable that synaptic pruning plays a critical role in the declining energy needs (and hence lower blood flow) of maturing brain regions. To the extent that maturation processes result in fewer neurons needing to be recruited for a given task, energy needs and blood flow would likewise be expected to decline (Devous et al., 2006). More globally, declines in overall cerebral blood flow are also likely associated in part with the rising proportion of axons surrounded by the energy-conserving insulation of myelin. By all of these means, as the adolescent brain becomes more efficient in terms of speed of information flow and more streamlined in its synaptic connectivity, it likewise becomes more cost-effective, requiring fewer energy resources than the younger brain.

METHODS OF STUDYING ADOLESCENT BRAIN DEVELOPMENT

In the last decade, there has been a revolution in the field of neurodevelopment. It is increasingly recognized that brain development is not the sole purview of the prenatal and early postnatal period; rather, the brain undergoes considerable transformation and developmental change during adolescence. The impetus for this change in thinking was driven, in part, by technological advances which have permitted researchers to noninvasively examine the structure and function of the brain in normal children and adolescents. The information provided by these new technologies has helped to transform our understanding of the biology underlying adolescent behavior, as detailed in the chapters to follow. These techniques are briefly described here, along with a consideration of their strengths and limitations, including some of the challenges when interpreting the data they generate. Areas of investigation that are still not amenable to investigation in human adolescents, but can be aptly modeled in laboratory animals, will also be considered briefly.

Human Electrophysiology

For centuries, the only view scientists had of the human brain and its development was gleaned from autopsy material. Things have changed dramatically, due largely to two major advances: one in electrophysiology and the other, brain imaging. Electrophysiological techniques provided the first window into the living brain via detection of electrical currents that reflect ongoing brain activity. Changes in current flow in the brain produce electrical activity that is sufficiently strong to pass through the skull and be detected with electrodes placed on the head. These electrical currents reflect the moment-to-moment sum of ongoing electrical activity in the brain and largely reflect the additive effects of ongoing postsynaptic potentials. This electrical activity can either be examined under various baseline conditions—the basic *electroencephalogram* (EEG)—or activity evoked in response to particular stimuli can be examined—termed *event related potentials* (ERPs). The traditional weakness of EEG/ERP studies has been the limited ability to relate electrical currents detected on the outside of the skull to activity in specific brain regions. Recent technological advances, however, have provided arrays with large numbers of detection electrodes and computer programs capable of deconstructing the data provided by these arrays to determine more precisely sources of the electrical activity. The advantage of EEG/ERP over imaging techniques (discussed next) is the high temporal resolution of electrophysiology, enabling researchers, in the case of ERP, for example, to examine precise timing of the brain processing associated with some initiating event. ERP data usually reflect a series of waves of alternating positivity and negativity emerging at characteristic times (i.e., with particular latencies) after the precipitating event. For instance, when performing a task, trials where the elicited response was incorrect are associated with an early error-related negativity

(ERN) followed by a longer-latency positive response. These different ERP components appear to be generated via different brain regions and develop at different times. For instance, the ACC has been strongly linked to generation of the ERN, with the ERN response maturing only slowly, reaching adult levels in late adolescence (in contrast to the positive response that matures well before adolescence) (Davies et al., 2004).

Human Imaging Techniques

Although ERPs and other electrophysiological recordings continue to generate valuable developmental data, these methods have been largely overshadowed by brain imaging techniques by which it is now possible to examine structure and functioning of the intact human brain. Early imaging approaches such as *positron emission tomography* (PET) necessitated the use of ionizing radiation, constraining experimental use of these techniques in infants, children, and adolescents, except for diagnostic purposes in cases of suspected brain dysfunction. Increased opportunities for imaging the developing brain emerged with the development of *magnetic resonance imaging* (MRI), along with rapid and ongoing improvements in scanning technology. Instead of using radiation, MRI relies on the properties of magnetic fields to organize alignment of substances within the field, and of substances so aligned to return to their natural state after perturbation, with this "relaxation time" varying with substance content and density. Gray matter, white matter, and fluid-contained spaces within the brain, called *ventricles*, all have different substance characteristics and varying densities, and hence can be distinguished through the use of *structural MRI* assessments (see Peterson, 2003; Bremner, 2005, for further discussion). Via assessment of these varying signal intensities with structural MRIs, many brain regions can be identified and their structural changes examined during development.

Functional MRI (fMRI) measures blood-oxygen-level-dependent (BOLD) signals, which are a reflection of changes in blood flow in particular brain regions during performance of a particular task relative to blood flow under baseline, control conditions. Blood flow in the brain changes with need, increasing in active areas to power postsynaptic activity and action potentials (more specifically, to restore normal ion balance following the message-conveying ion changes induced by these activities) (Attwell & Iadecola, 2002). Thus regions where neural activity is increased during task performance show elevations in blood flow that are detected by elevations in BOLD signals, relative to baseline conditions (e.g., Mukamel et al., 2005). Via this means, developmental differences in which brain regions are activated (or inhibited) by particular stimuli or tasks can be explored (e.g., see Peterson, 2003, for review). The time course for fMRI data collection is an order of magnitude longer than the moment-to-moment information provided via ERPs, although the spatial resolution of fMRIs is generally superior by at least an order of magnitude (see Banaschewski, 2007). Thus, the data provided by ERP and fMRI are different but complementary.

Another advancement in MRI technology, *diffusion tensor imaging* (DTI), is used to index neuronal connectivity—specifically, the integrity of white matter. DTI assesses the speed of water diffusion and its directionality, using the property of water to diffuse more rapidly in the same direction of axonal tracts rather than across them, particularly when they are covered with fatty sheaths of myelin (Inder & Huppi, 2000). The direction of water diffusion is quantified via calculation of fractional anisotrophy (FA), a variable that is used to quantify the "integrity" of the myelin. This FA index seems to be a more sensitive measure of subtle changes in white matter associated with aging, neurological disorders, and cognitive performance than white matter volume measures per se (McLaughlin et al., 2007).

Another technique—*MR spectroscopy* (MRS)—is essentially neurochemical imaging that uses magnetic resonance to measure the physical properties (spectra) of individual chemical substances in the brain. Although it would be exciting to be able to examine substances such as neurotransmitters and their second messengers in specific regions of the brain, few such substances can be distinguished at present, given that the spectra of many interesting substances are obscured by competing signals from water, fat, and other common brain substances (Inder & Huppi, 2000; Bremner, 2005)

With the development of these noninvasive techniques, research examining structure and functioning of the developing brain has mushroomed during the past decade. Much of this research is highlighted in the chapters to come as we explore common adolescent behaviors and their potential neural substrates. Although imaging data have helped to revolutionize our understanding of adolescence and the adolescent brain, it is important to recognize its limitations. Brain regions differing in size and location vary in how sensitively they can be imaged. MRI measures provide only an indirect measure of the structure and function of the brain and little information regarding the mechanisms underlying alterations in these properties seen developmentally, during task performance, or under pathological conditions (Casey et al., 2005). The smallest unit of analysis in structural MRIs is the voxel—a three-dimensional index of volume density of that particular area of tissue. Although voxel sizes vary along a number of dimensions (e.g., type of scanner, methodology used, scanning time), it can be estimated from studies using autopsy material that a typical voxel of 1 mm^3 (Ashburner & Friston, 2000) might represent some 45,000 neurons (Pakkenberg & Gundersen, 1997) and 450–500 million synapses (Scheff et al., 2001). Thus, even at the limits of spatial resolution (a single voxel), data observed represent summed information from thousands of neurons, millions of synaptic inputs likely utilizing many different neurotransmitter substances, axons passing through the region, blood vessels in the vicin-ity, and so on. It is a long way from seeing changes in MRI images to interpreting the neural sub-strates that underlie those changes.

Animal Models

Although exciting progress has been made in noninvasive imaging of the human brain and the technology continues to advance rapidly, there are still many questions about the brain of the adolescent that are difficult, if not impossible, to address in studies using humans. For instance, to quantify the amount of synaptic pruning, fixed tissue obtained from human autopsy material or more invasive animal studies is typically required. To explore the role of particular brain structures in behavioral and cognitive function during development in humans, although individuals of different ages with brain damage sustained in those areas can be examined, the number of affected youth is often small and damage at all ages typically extends beyond the target region of interest. Consider, for example, the deficits in cognitive functioning and affect regulation seen in adults, but less evident in children, following damage to the cerebellum (Schmahmann & Sherman, 1998). When researchers attempted to assess when this "cerebellar cognitive affective syndrome" emerged during development, the strongest conclusion that could be reached based on the limited number of cases available was that deficits characteristic of this syndrome were more apparent in older than younger individuals among the group of 3- to 16-year-olds with cerebellar damage that was examined (Levisohn et al., 2000).

Using laboratory animals, it is possible to look at the adolescent brain at a more microscopic level to see how it is changing along critical dimensions, such as synaptic number and structure, action and transduction of neurotransmitters and neuromodulators, and the characteristics of different hormone and neurotransmitter receptors. Thus, although imaging studies provide valuable information about changes in the relative size of different gray and white matter regions during adolescence, and in functional activation patterns of different brain regions under specific conditions, studies in laboratory animals are often necessary to determine the critical neurochemical, structural, and epigenetic substrates that drive these macroscopic changes in the adolescent brain.

Techniques available for study of the adolescent brain in laboratory animals include neuroanatomical studies in which number of synapses, neurons, supporting glia cells, myelinated versus unmyelinated axons, receptors for various neurotransmitters, and so on, can be visualized and quantified within very specific brain regions at specific points in development. Release of neurotransmitters and electrical activity of particular neurons can be explored via the insertion of probes into the brain. Such studies can be conducted either in intact animals or in animals with accelerated, delayed, or disrupted puberty; with a history of early enrichment or abuse; or following damage to particular brain regions, depending on the research questions of interest. Moreover, with the development of techniques for genetic manipulation of rodents (typically mice) to eliminate expression of a particular gene (genetic "knockouts") or to overexpress that gene (thereby increasing production of the product of that gene), the function of specific genes affecting myelin production, particular neurotransmitter receptors, chemical pathways activated by that neurotransmitter, or a myriad of other genes of interest can be explored.

SUMMARY AND CLOSING COMMENTS

The brain is an intriguingly complex organ that continues to change throughout life. Adolescence is a period of particularly dramatic changes which ultimately transform the immature brain into the more efficient, streamlined, and cost-effective brain characteristic of adulthood. As we have seen, these transformations of the adolescent brain are both progressive and regressive, with characteristics and timing that are highly regionally specific. Recent advances in the noninvasive imaging of the human brain, along with basic research findings in laboratory animals, are revolutionizing our understanding of the brain during adolescence, and its role in shaping adolescent-typical ways of functioning cognitively and behaviorally. It is to these topics that we now turn.

PART II

Adolescent Development
and the Brain

CHAPTER FIVE

Development of Cognitive Skills

••••••••••••••••••••••••••••••••••••••

Cognitive skills improve considerably during adolescence. Few 10-year-olds can handle learning calculus, yet by mid- to late adolescence, cognitive performance often rivals that of adults. In this chapter we first consider how adolescents differ cognitively from children, and when different aspects of their cognitive performance become mature. We also consider the challenging and sometimes controversial issue of what changes in the brain are associated with the maturation of cognitive capacities in adolescence.

ADVANCES IN COGNITIVE PERFORMANCE DURING ADOLESCENCE.

• *Adolescents not only know more than kids do, they also often think in ways that are more mature.* Among the improvements seen are increases in the ability to reason logically, both in terms of deductive reasoning (determining conclusions that follow logically from a set of known facts) as well as inductive reasoning (inferring possible conclusions from available evidence). Adolescents are also more likely than children to think abstractly, consider hypothetical situations, reflect on multiple facets of an issue, view answers as relative rather than absolute, and think introspectively about their own thoughts and emotions (see Steinberg, 2005). Over the years, psychologists have postulated that, as individuals develop, they go through an invariant series of cognitive stages, each characteristic of the thinking within a particular age range. The best-known example of this approach is the work of Piaget (1954). He considered a major accomplishment of adolescence to be the transition from the stage of concrete operations, prevalent in children 6–11 years of age and characterized by rational thinking that is based on tangible ("concrete") stimuli, to the formal operations stage, a cognitive approach based on abstract and hypothetical thinking.

Careful assessment of cognitive function among adolescents, however, has revealed little evidence of either a single set of cognitive skills that would be characteristic of the formal operations stage, or any indication of a step-like shift in cognitive function from stage to stage. For instance, a given adolescent may display some cognitive strategies consistent with the formal operations stage in certain instances, but these strategies may be interspersed with other occasions when the thinking displayed is, at best, consistent with the concrete operations stage (Keating, 2004). Steinberg (2005) nicely summarizes this literature by saying that "rather than talking about a stage of cognitive activity characteristic of adolescence, . . . it is more accurate to depict these advanced reasoning capabilities as skills that are employed by older children more often than by younger ones, by some adolescents more often than by others, and by individuals when they are in certain situations (especially, familiar situations) more often than when they are in other situations" (p. 73).

• *Among the important changes in cognitive function seen during adolescence are developmental increases in a variety of information-processing abilities.* Cognitive maturation during adolescence has been partitioned into a series of separable processes that contribute to developmental changes in the speed and accuracy of performing cognitive tasks. Different researchers vary, however, in which specific cognitive process- es they consider as fundamental, and in how they cluster these basic information-processing abilities into broader categories of cognitive function—categories that potentially could reflect similarities in their underlying neural substrates. On a theo- retical level at least, these efforts could be considerably en- hanced by analyzing the timing of emergence of different cognitive processes during development (e.g., Demetriou et al., 2002) and their relationship with ongoing functional altera- tions in the brain. As with overall cognitive development, such analyses are complicated considerably by many issues, includ- ing the fact that the expression of even specific cognitive skills is probabilistic during development and can be considerably influenced by task difficulty, test context, subject mood, and so on. Nevertheless, researchers generally agree that there are de- velopmental improvements through adolescence in a variety of information-processing abilities.

One component skill frequently mentioned as improving notably during adolescence is what has varyingly been called processing efficacy, processing speed, or fluid and speeded re- sponding (e.g., Welsh et al., 1991; Demetriou et al., 2002; Keat- ing, 2004). As the speed of processing task-relevant information increases, scores on timed tasks (e.g., standardized tests) im- prove (see Steinberg, 2005). Developmental increases in the speed by which information is processed are particularly char- acteristic of the initial transition into adolescence and the ear- ly- to midadolescent period, leveling off gradually thereafter (Kail, 1991).

Another frequently mentioned cognitive process that im- proves into adolescence is working memory. In fact, memory generally improves into adolescence—both long-term memory (the ability to remember things learned some time ago) as well as working memory (the ability to hold information in short-term storage, on the order of seconds or minutes). The latter type of memory is used, for instance, to remember a phone number from the time you look it up in the phone book until you pick up the phone and dial it. Working memory is critical not only for daily tasks but also for effective performance of more challenging cognitive tasks that require thinking about a number of concepts at one time. Although some elements of working memory emerge by 6 years of age, notable increases are seen in the functional capacity of working memory from early- to midadolescence (e.g., Gathercole et al., 2004; see also Demetriou et al., 2002; Luciana & Nelson, 2002; Conklin et al., 2007) or even late adolescence (i.e., 19 years of age; Luna et al., 2004), depending on the tasks used to index working memory. Developmental improvements in working memory permit successful performance of increasingly sophisticated cognitive tasks (e.g., Welsh et al., 1991).

During adolescence, developmental advancements are also seen in cognitive abilities varyingly referred to as problem solving, reasoning, and planning (Welsh et al., 1991; Demetriou et al., 2002; Keating, 2004). Without getting into the nuances of whether these terms reflect the same underlying processes or are separable, highly effective reasoning, problem-solving, and planning skills are among the slowest cognitive abilities to emerge developmentally. For instance, whereas even 6-year-olds demonstrate some planful behavior and reasoning, performance on more challenging cognitive tasks that require complex planning and problem-solving skills is substantially improved by 12 years of age, although performance even at this age does not yet approach adult levels (Welsh et al., 1991).

There is evidence that processing speed, working memory, and problem-solving/planning skills reflect separable abilities with distinct developmental time courses. For instance, Luna and colleagues (2004) found adult-typical processing speeds emerging, on average, by 15 years of age, whereas adult-typical performance on working memory tasks was only reached around the age of 19. Yet, although these component cognitive skills are separable and emerge according to their own developmental timeline, to some extent each ability is influenced by the state of development of the others. For instance, improvements in processing speed may mean that more information can be processed and held in working memory prior to the time the earliest-arriving information is forgotten. This ability would increase the amount of information that can be considered simultaneously, improving strategic thinking and performance on problem-solving tasks that require consideration of multiple factors. Thus, cognitive development can be viewed as a process of interactions among separable component abilities that each matures along its own time scale, with progress in one component necessary but not sufficient for improvements with another (Demetriou et al., 2002).

• *Adolescent improvement in cognitive processing is often over-simplistically characterized as the emergence of executive functions.* The discussion thus far has avoided one of the biggest "buzz terms" in cognitive development: *executive function.* Generally speaking, executive function can be viewed as "'higher-level' cognitive functions involved in the control and regulation of 'lower-level' cognitive processes and goal-directed, future-oriented behavior" (Alvarez & Emory, 2006, p. 17). Although some consensus is building for the notion that executive function reflects a set of higher-order control systems that serve to coordinate brain function, there is less agreement as to the component cognitive processes. Also controversial is the degree to which neural substrates underlying executive functions reside in, and are restricted to, the frontal cortex per se, a topic to which we turn later in this chapter.

When viewing executive function as a regulator of "lower-level" cognitive processes, it may be useful to first consider the lower-level functions that are subject to this regulatory control. Cognitive functions of this nature include sensory perception, basic learning tasks, short- and long-term memory, language and reading ability, and fine motor skills (Anderson et al., 2001; Alvarez & Emory, 2006). These basic cognitive functions are thought to be integrated, modulated, and controlled via a series of specific executive control functions (see Royall et al., 2002). Although complete consensus is lacking across investigators as to specific functional domains that comprise executive control, most agree that *selective attention* is one critical component, along with another domain (or group of related domains) varyingly referred to as *goal-setting/ rule discovery/planning/decision-making*. Two other cognitive components commonly considered within executive control functions are *response inhibition* and *working memory* (Royall et al., 2002; Alvarez & Emory, 2006; Blakemore & Choudhury, 2006). Others include domains such as *set shifting/cognitive flexibility* in their parsing of executive function (Anderson et al., 2001; Jurado & Rosselli, 2007; Davidson et al., 2006).

Two of these component executive functions are cognitive processes already discussed as showing developmental improvements through adolescence: working memory and problem-solving/planning (e.g., Demetriou et al., 2002). Attentional control (Anderson et al., 2001) and response inhibition (e.g., Leon-Carrion et al., 2004; Luna et al., 2004) likewise continue to improve developmentally into midadolescence. As one example, consider a visual–motor task called an "antisaccade" task, in which performance is strongly influenced by inhibitory control capacities. In this task, individuals visually fixating on a central stimulus are periodically exposed to a target in their right or left visual field and asked to respond not by looking at the target, by instead by rapidly diverting their gaze to the opposite side of the visual field (e.g., looking to the left when the object is presented to the right side). On this type of task, adolescents show improvements until about 14 years of age (e.g., Luna et al., 2004).

It is important to recognize, however, that aspects of executive function are clearly functional in children, and that for some component domains, improvements on tasks indexing particular executive functions may even be more marked during childhood than during adolescence. As one example, whereas Anderson and colleagues (2001) found developmental spurts in goal setting and attentional control capacity around 12 and 15 years of age, respectively, the rate of improvement during adolescence was modest relative to the rapid improvements in attentional capacity seen during childhood. Thus, it is overly simplistic to view adolescence as a time of emergence and maturation of executive functions. Not only do children show evidence of executive function, but (as discussed earlier) older adolescents and even adults on some occasions do not seem to function in ways indicative of efficient executive controls. Even when signs of executive function are seen among children, though, they may use different response strategies than those used by adolescents or by adults. For instance, children tend to show different speed/accuracy tradeoffs than older individuals: i.e., as task difficulty increases, Davidson and colleagues (2006) found that the accuracy of children decreased as they maintained response speed, whereas adolescents showed the adult-typical strategy of slowing down to maintain accuracy.

• *In addition to general developmental improvements in cognitive abilities during adolescence, there is evidence of transient developmental declines in performance on certain specific cognitive tasks.* Intriguingly, adolescent-typical changes in cognitive function are not always characterized by age-related enhancements in cognitive abilities; indeed, some transient developmental declines are seen on some tasks. For example, a number of older studies has shown that accuracy on a task involving face recognition improves during childhood (up to about 10–

11 years), takes a downward dip during early adolescence, and again improves thereafter (beginning around 14–16 years) (Carey et al., 1980). As a result, the ability of girls to recognize faces around the time of puberty was found to be poorer than among younger or older girls (Diamond et al., 1983). A similar transient developmental decline in performance was reported more recently by McGivern and colleagues (2002) in a matching-to-sample task that involved matching faces with emotional expressions to words describing those emotions. Reminiscent of performance on face recognition tasks, performance improved on this task until early adolescence (11–12 years), at which time decreases in performance were seen, with performance improving and stabilizing by midadolescence (around 15 years). Although the researchers of these studies have suggested that these changes are pubertally related, their studies were not designed to dissociate pubertal state from age, and hence the contribution of pubertal hormones to this developmental decline in performance on perception of facial and emotional stimuli is unknown.

It has long been known that adolescents in other species also show transient developmental declines in performance on a variety of cognitive tasks, particularly those that involve stressful circumstances. Very briefly, on complex tasks that involve learning how to avoid or rapidly escape foot shock, adolescent rats often have been found to exhibit impaired performance relative to animals at other ages (see Spear & Brake, 1983). In basic animal studies, adolescents have also been found to sometimes exhibit unusual responses to rewarding stimuli and reward contingencies—for instance, often showing less persistence than younger or older animals during extinction of a task where correct performance was reinforced only intermittently (Brake et al., 1980). On the other hand, as in human adolescents, developmental improvements are often seen through adolescence in performance of other tasks. These include tasks that use appetitive stimuli (e.g., food) and capitalize on the increased exploratory proclivities of adolescents (i.e., maze tasks) rather than using aversive (foot shock) stimuli to motivate conditioning (see Spear & Brake, 1983, for review). Thus, embedded within the general improvement of cognitive abilities during development are a few transient declines in performance on certain cognitive tasks that emerge during adolescence, even in simple animal models of adolescence in the rat. Tasks that seem to be particularly likely to show a performance downswing during adolescence are those requiring the processing of emotional, stressful, or anxiety-provoking stimuli, a topic to which we return in a later chapter.

IMAGING, BRAIN DEVELOPMENT, AND COGNITIVE FUNCTION

Functional imaging studies in adults have been extensively used to explore the neural substrates of cognition. In a review of much of the early literature in this area, Cabeza and Nyberg (2000) observed some regional specificity, with certain brain regions consistently activated by particular types of cognitive tasks, whereas other areas were broadly activated by a diversity of cognitive challenges. Often, it appeared that a given brain region was "not committed to specific functions, but may play a role in a variety of cognitive and other operations" (Cabeza & Nyberg, 2000, p. 35), with activation of this region during a particular cognitive situation correlated with activity in other interconnected regions to form functional networks. Thus, when considering changes in the brain that contribe to cognitive gains during adolescence, attention should be directed not only at maturation patterns of specific brain regions, but also toward approaches that emphasize activation within networks involving multiple, interconnected regions.

• *It is tricky to relate improvements in cognitive function to specific anatomical changes in the brain.* Many changes occur at roughly overlapping times during adolescence, including changes in the size of particular brain regions, gray–white matter ratios, and degree of myelination of particular groups of axons. When examining a large number of kids of different ages and maturational status, certain cognitive and brain measures may be highly correlated (e.g., two measures might be relatively high in some kids, relatively low in others). But correlations do not necessarily reflect functional relationships. To take a ridiculous example, foot size often increases considerably in early adolescence, as does cognitive ability, but a correlation between these two measures does not mean that improvement in cognitive skills is related to foot growth. Even if there is reason to believe that two correlated measures are likely to be functionally related, causal inferences cannot be drawn. Consider, for example, a data set showing that amount of myelination of a particular white matter tract is correlated with performance of a certain cognitive skill among a group of adolescents. From this correlation alone, it is not possible to determine whether it is the myelination of that tract that improves cognitive performance or whether it is the neural activation provided by skilled performance on that task that facilitates the myelination process (although this possibility is somewhat provocative, remember from Chapter 4 that under some circumstances, the amount of impulse activity in axons can indeed stimulate their myelination). There is also a third possibility: that some other, unmeasured maturational event (e.g., shift in balance of activity between two brain regions interconnected by that white matter tract) might facilitate expression of the target cognitive skill, as well as foster myelination of that tract.

In part for these reasons, there has been increasing emphasis on examining functional neuroanatomy during development, using fMRI to investigate which brain areas are activated during performance of the target task at different ages. Using this approach, rather than focusing on how absolute size or amount of myelination in particular brain regions correlates with cognitive performance across different individuals, the focus is on comparing changes in activation of various brain areas during performance of the target task with activation of those same regions during a control task (see Peterson, 2003). This approach has the considerable advantage of scanning the same individuals while performing target and control tasks; hence, via subtracting activation patterns on target and control tasks, activation patterns seen within specific regions of interest (ROI) that are associated with performance of the target cognitive task can be identified.

Data derived with fMRI, however, is only as good as the choice of control task. Brain activation during a particular target task reflects not only activation necessary to cognitively "solve" or perform the task, but also activation associated with the particular characteristics of the stimuli (e.g., color, brightness), task difficulty and the effort required to "stay on task" and avoid distractions, the motor response required and its timing, the number of incorrect responses and possible affective consequences of negative feedback, and so on (see Peterson, 2003). Ideally, the control task should be matched on all of these levels with the target task other than the essential cognitive component of the task—quite a tall order. Indeed, Peterson (2003) concludes that many fMRI studies have used nonoptimal controls, and that this weakness presents probably the greatest challenge to accurate interpretation of fMRI data.

Another challenge when using fMRI to examine task-related regional brain activation across age is that task performance itself typically improves with age. Under this circumstance, it is difficult to interpret age differences in brain activation. That is, if younger subjects activate different brain regions as they attempt to perform the task than do more mature subjects who perform the task more adeptly and accurately, do these activation differences reflect age differences or "greater effort or frustration, or some other epiphenomenon feature associated with poorer performance on the task?" (Peterson, 2003, p. 820). This is not a trivial issue, with about half or so of the regional brain activation seen during task performance in developmental studies related to performance differences (Brown et al., 2005). One strategy that has been used to address this performance issue is to vary task difficulty so that individuals of each age can be divided into subgroups based on their task performance. This method allows comparison of brain activation patterns between subgroups of individuals that are matched on performance but of different ages (e.g., Casey et al., 2005), thereby permitting brain regions whose activation is correlated with age versus performance to be distinguished in statistical analyses (e.g., Schlaggar et al., 2002). A more recent approach is to track performance of each subject individually, adjusting task difficulty on a trial-by-trial basis to equate performance across subjects and across age (Rubia et al., 2007). All of these approaches to address performance–age confounds still present interpretation challenges, among them the issue of causality—that is, whether observed neural changes are critical for task performance or whether they merely track performance or reflect activation in other regions. Varying task difficulty to equate task performance across age is also likely to create age differences on other dimensions such as interest in and motivation for the task, attentional demands, and so on.

Most developmental imaging studies to date have used a cross-sectional approach by which individuals of different ages are compared. Yet, given considerable individual differences in brain activation characteristics, some spurious age effects could emerge when using this design. That is, with the typical small sample of individuals examined in imaging studies, it is possible that observed differences across age groups could reflect individual differences in the participants making up each age group rather than true age effects. This issue can be circumvented by examining changes in individuals across time using a longitudinal design to infer age-related changes (Casey et al., 2005).

Through the use of structural and functional MRI in studies using cross-sectional and longitudinal designs, a variety of brain regions have been shown to exhibit different developmental trajectories, with, for example, regions involved in sensory and motor function maturing before other regions such as the PFC. There are also considerable age differences in the extent to which particular brain regions are activated during performance of different cognitive tasks. Before considering in more detail these age differences, let's first consider a fundamental question: Is more or less brain activation advantageous? When examining individuals who have some sort of cognitive impairment, regionally specific increases as well as decreases in activation of certain brain regions may be seen. Given that the target group is being studied because of their cognitive dysfunction, group differences in activation patterns— whether those alterations reflect increases or decreases from the activation pattern seen in the normal controls—are generally attributed to impaired cognitive function. Although these different patterns of brain activation may themselves be subject to several alternative explanations (see Price & Friston, 1999; Peterson, 2003), interpretation of regional differences in brain activation becomes even more intriguing when examining the developing brain. That is, as detailed later, when the adult brain is used as a referent point, both relative increases as well as decreases in activation patterns are seen in particular regions of the adolescent brain. Here it is even more critical to consider whether greater activation of a brain region during a particular task is advantageous. What about when activation in a region decreases during task performance?

• *Both increases and decreases in brain activation may be advantageous, complicating interpretation of developmental data.* To begin considering the implications of whether increases or decreases in brain activation are advantageous when performing a cognitive task, let's first consider what happens in the brain during forgetting. Although forgetting of desired memories is often frustrating, forgetting is essential to reduce overall memory burden—it would be incapacitating to remember forever all the details of everything one had experienced and learned. It has long been known that the forgetting of competing memories can enhance the ability to retrieve a particular target memory. In a recent study (Kuhl et al., 2007), such forgetting was also shown to increase brain efficiency, resulting in a "neural processing benefit." In that study, as individuals successfully retrieved a particular target memory, this retrieval was initially associated with activation of the dlPFC. However, as this memory was recalled over repeated trials, retrieval was associated with progressively less PFC engagement, with the extent of the decline in task-related PFC activation strongly correlated with the amount of forgetting of competing memories. That is, forgetting of competing memories was interpreted to increase brain efficiency by decreasing the amount of brain activation necessary to retrieve the target memories.

The amount of brain activation associated with task performance may also depend on the demands of the task—both the nature of the cognitive challenge as well as its difficulty. Indeed, different cognitive tasks are thought to challenge different brain regions. For instance, circuitry involving more ventral portions of the PFC (e.g., the OFC) is thought to play particularly important roles in executive function tasks involving an emotional component, including reversal learning tasks, whereas more lateral regions of the PFC (e.g., dlPFC) are likely to be recruited for more cognitive-based tasks such as those involving planning and spatial working memory (see Kodituwakku et al., 2001; Robbins, 2005).

In terms of task difficulty, when learning a simple task—for example, a basic sequence of finger movements—acquisition of the task is often associated with progressive decreases in brain activation within task-relevant sensorimotor regions of the cortex both in individuals who have had a lot of finger sequence training (pianists) as well as those who have not (nonpianists) (Landau & D'Esposito, 2006). When learning and performing more complex tasks, though, recruitment of higher-level association regions in frontal and other cortical areas may be necessary to maximally and flexibly meet task demands. For instance, when task difficulty was increased, both pianists and nonpianists showed recruitment of frontal and other cortical association regions (although the specific regions activated differed somewhat across groups). Interestingly, the extent of this brain activation was greater in pianists than in nonpianists, with the pianists also showing superior acquisition of the more complex task (Landau & D'Esposito, 2006). Reminiscent of the reduction in activation of sensorimotor regions during acquisition of a simple motor response, activation of association regions recruited when learning more complex motor tasks may also become less pronounced as acquisition proceeds (e.g., Toni et al., 1998).

In contrast, other regions critical for expression of the learned task may become progressively more active during learning. For instance, activation of a region termed the *supplementary motor area* has been found to be positively associated with performance of a trained sequence of motor movements (see Toni et al., 1998, for discussion). Similarly, in a study where brain activity related to reading was examined across individuals ranging in age from 6 to 22 years (Turkeltaub et al., 2003), reading skill accomplishments were associated with two types of neural changes: decreases in activity in "extrastriate" brain regions in the right hemisphere that are important for recognizing stimuli on a nonlexical (i.e., non-word-related) level, as well as increases in activity in language-critical regions of the left temporal cortex. Thus, greater competence and skill are sometimes associated with increased activation of certain areas during task performance, along with decreases in recruitment of other regions.

The picture that emerges is a complex one: While learning a task, a number of task-relevant regions of the brain are activated, whereas activity is suppressed in default regions. As the task is learned and performance becomes more rote, activation in some task-relevant regions may decline, whereas activity within focal regions critical for expression of the learning may be retained or even increased. When the task is more challenging, additional brain areas (especially cortical association areas, including portions of the PFC) may be recruited to meet the challenge, with activity in these regions sometimes declining as learning proceeds and the cognitive burden is lessened. Under other circumstances, greater recruitment of portions of the association cortex may be persistently linked with superior performance on challenging tasks, with, for instance, pianists showing greater recruitment of association regions during learning of complex motor sequences than nonpianists, and also showing superior task performance (Landau & D'Esposito, 2006).

On the other hand, there are numerous examples of individuals with impaired cognitive functioning (e.g., those with Alzheimer's disease or fetal alcohol syndrome) also showing greater recruitment, in the PFC and association regions of the temporal and parietal cortices, during cognitive challenges than nonimpaired individuals (e.g., Pariente et al., 2005; Fryer et al., 2007; Sowell et al., 2007). Similar increases in brain activation during challenging tasks are also seen in individuals with other types of neurological disorders—for example, multiple sclerosis (Mainero et al., 2004) and Tourette's syndrome (Marsh et al., 2007). In such instances, the greater recruitment ("hyperactivation") during task performance has been postulated to reflect compensatory responses generated in an attempt to offset cognitive deficits that may be associated with attenuated activation in other regions (e.g., Rajah & D'Esposito, 2005; Sowell et al., 2007). Alternatively, increases in functional activation during task performance, at least in the case of aging and Alzheimer's disease, have been suggested to possibly reflect reduced specialization of brain function ("dedifferentiation"), essentially producing greater noise in the system and obscuring task-relevant activities (Rajah & D'Esposito, 2005).

The notion that individuals with less effective cognitive function may activate more brain tissue in association areas such as the PFC when performing certain tasks than individuals with superior cognitive skills is consistent with a recent hypothesis of neural efficiency proposed by Rypma and colleagues (2006). In the study upon which this hypothesis was based, brain activation was examined during performance of a processing speed task where the goal was to correctly decode as many digit/symbol pairs as possible over a set time interval. The brain regions activated by faster- and slower-performing individuals on this non-executive function task differed somewhat, with slower individuals showing greater dorsal PFC activation in contrast to greater activation of parietal regions and ventral PFC among faster individuals. These activation patterns were interpreted to suggest that slower individuals required notable dorsal PFC control over other brain regions when attempting to optimize performance, whereas faster-performing individuals had more efficient connections across brain regions and did not necessitate as much "top-down" control from the dorsal PFC to maximize performance. It could also be speculated that expenditure of significant cognitive effort via activation of "top-down" control mechanisms, while perhaps serving to enhance performance of executive-function-type tasks, might functionally slow performance of simpler, speed-based tasks.

HOW DO CHANGES IN THE ADOLESCENT BRAIN RELATE TO IMPROVEMENTS IN COGNITIVE FUNCTIONS?

There has been a recent explosion of research findings regarding the relationship between cognitive development and maturational changes in the brain. Although some work has attempted to relate structural changes in the brain to the emergence of cognitive abilities (e.g., see Paus, 2005, for review), most studies have taken advantage of fMRI, and, to a lesser extent ERPs, to examine how brains at different ages respond when performing a cognitive task. With the subtraction method used with fMRIs, the focus is on how brain activation differs during performance of the target task relative to the control task, with the goal of minimizing any age differences in overall amount of brain activation globally precipitated by engagement in the tasks. Many developmental fMRI studies to date have focused on areas that show increased activity during task performance, rather than regions whose activity might be task-dependently suppressed. Given evidence that some cognitive processes are associated with regional deactivations (Cabeza & Nyberg, 2000) that reflect inhibition of "default" patterns of brain activation seen under basal conditions (Fair et al., 2009), ultimately it is likely to prove at least as informative to explore brain regions whose activity is suppressed during task performance, and how that suppression differs with age.

An examination of the flurry of recent fMRI studies investigating cognitive development reveals no overriding consensus as to the specific brain regions or neural networks linked with cognitive development during adolescence. This is not surprising, given differences across studies in the executive or other cognitive functions targeted for examination, the tasks used to examine those functions and the associated control task conditions, the stimuli and motor response systems necessary to perform the task, difficulty of the task, and the test procedures and methodology used. Nevertheless, some tentative principles are beginning to emerge.

• *Cognitive maturation during adolescence is not so much associated with developmentally delayed brain regions finally becoming functional, but rather with the emergence of functional networks supporting more efficient strategies for performing particular cognitive tasks.* A considerably oversimplified view of adolescent brain development popular in the media is that the late maturation of the PFC is responsible for the cognitive immaturities and other typical characteristics of the adolescent. Yet, it is not simply the case that the PFC is nonfunctional until adolescence. Indeed, as mentioned earlier, portions of the PFC and other frontal regions are active and play a role in the cognitive function of children and even infants (e.g., Diamond & Goldman-Rakic, 1989). Moreover, although there are clearly developmental changes occurring in the PFC throughout adolescence, which undoubtedly contribute to the maturation of cognitive functions during this stage, age differences in task-related brain activation are evident in many other brain regions as well. Simply stated, the same cognitive task often activates different brain regions in children, adolescents, and adults.

Thus, rather than viewing adolescent brain maturation merely as the last remnants of a series of brain regions sequentially maturing and coming "online," a more contemporary view of brain development is that it reflects a dynamic process of network organization, with different regions competing, influencing, and cooperating with each other over time during development, and in the process acquiring new (and often more efficient and able) roles in the modulation of cognitive abilities (see Johnson, 2001, for review). As we shall see, the net effect of these dynamic interactions during development may result in both regressive, "growing down" changes, whereby some brain regions activated in children performing the task may not be activated in adults, as well as progressive, "growing up" changes, in which top-down control systems recruited during task performance of more mature individuals may not be utilized earlier in life (Brown et al., 2005).

• *The brain regions activated during performance of cognitive tasks are often broader and more diffuse in younger than mature individuals.* Although we tend to focus on age differences, it is important to note that during performance of cognitive tasks, children, adolescents, and adults show equivalent activation throughout much of the brain, particularly when performance is matched across age (e.g., Schlaggar et al., 2002; Brown et al., 2005). When age differences are seen, in numerous instances children and young adolescents have been reported to show more task-related activation of brain tissue than adults—particularly in subcortical regions (Thomas et al., 2004), posterior areas (Rubia et al., 2006; Scherf et al., 2006), and regions located more ventrally (deeper) within task-relevant cortical and subcortical regions (Casey et al., 2002) . Greater activation in these regions in children and adolescents has been reported not only with tasks involving the processing of simple stimuli and stimulus–response tasks (e.g., Casey et al., 2002; Schlaggar et al., 2002; Thomas et al., 2004; Brown et al., 2005), but also with tasks tapping various executive functions (Rubia et al., 2006; Scherf et al., 2006). Performance under these circumstances is thought to reflect recruitment of earlier maturing brain regions to cope with task demands by an immature brain not yet able to fully engage later maturing cortical association regions, especially in frontal and parietal cortical regions (e.g., Rubia et al., 2006). For example, when examining fMRIs of children, adolescents, and adults performing a working memory task, children showed only limited activation of core regions thought to be critical for task performance (dlPFC and parietal regions), instead recruiting substantial areas of striatum and the insula region, with activation in task-relevant core regions diffusely increasing among adolescents and becoming more focal in adults (Scherf et al., 2006). Based on assessments involving a word generation task, Brown and colleagues (2005) concluded that the immature brain recruits more brain regions for task performance than adults, with developmental declines in activation within these regions as "higher-level control mechanisms" emerge. Indeed, as discussed next, early task-related activation broadly seen in ventral, posterior, and/or subcortical regions may decline developmentally with increases in activation in frontal and parietal regions.

• *Development of more efficient executive and other cognitive functions sometimes is viewed as a shift from more diffuse to more regionally specific activation, particularly in frontal regions.* Developmental increases in activation in frontal regions (including portions of the PFC, parietal cortex, and ACC) have been reported during performance of a variety of working memory and response inhibition tasks (e.g., Adleman et al., 2002; Klingberg et al., 2002; Kwon et al., 2002; Crone et al., 2006; Olesen et al., 2006; Scherf et al., 2006). For instance, in a working memory task, 8- to 12-year-olds showed poorer performance than adults and failed to show adult-typical, task-dependent activation in PFC (right hemisphere dlPFC) and parietal (bilateral superior parietal cortex) regions (Crone et al., 2006). Similarly, Rubia and colleagues (2006) examined adolescents and adults in a variety of tasks tapping cognitive control ability and found that developmental improvements in task performance were associated with attenuated activation of diffuse posterior brain regions, along with increases in activation of networks interconnecting frontal and parietal regions with other areas, including the striatum and portions of the temporal cortex. Thus, task-dependent activation of earlier maturing and inefficient neural systems may regress as more "top-down" frontal–parietal control mechanisms are progressively recruited during development (Brown et al., 2005).

• *Reports of both developmental increases as well as decreases in task-related PFC activation complicate simple notions of increasing frontal involvement during adolescent development.* Despite substantial evidence of increases in task-related activation of frontal regions during development, there are other instances where developmental declines in activation of frontal regions are evident during adolescence (e.g., Casey et al., 1997b, 2000, 2005a, 2005b; Booth et al., 2003b; Durston et al., 2006). As one example, Booth and colleagues (2003b) found that 9- to 12-year-olds showed greater activation in a network that included frontal and cingulate regions than did adults during a response inhibition task.

Interpretation of data involving greater task-related PFC activation among younger participants can be complicated if tasks are not equated for difficulty or the number of correct versus error trials across age: More effortful tasks may require greater recruitment of the PFC, and activation maps produced where error trials are included may be more diffuse than those excluding incorrect trials (see Rubia et al., 2007; Brown et al., 2005, for discussion). Moreover, the extent of task-related activation of the PFC may vary with the nature of the task (Cabeza & Nyberg, 2000) and the amount of training, with lower PFC activity, for example, associated with better performance on well-trained, autonomic tasks where less neural processing could lead to shorter reaction times and less time on task (see Klingberg et al., 2002).

Under some circumstances, developmental declines in the

overall amount of task-related activation in frontal regions are associated with the emergence of more restricted activation within certain discrete frontal regions—a notion reminiscent of the diffuse-to-more-focal developmental shift discussed earlier. One example of a developmental shift to more focal frontal activation was seen in a study examining response inhibition using a go/no-go task—that is, a task requiring participants to press a button to a variety of sequentially presented stimuli, while withholding the response when a particular nontarget stimulus appeared in the sequence. During performance of this go/no-go task, similar frontal regions were activated in children and young adolescents as in adults, although volume of activation in the dlPFC was greater in the younger group of participants than the adults (Casey et al., 1997b; 2000; Durston et al., 2006). Although these data could be interpreted to suggest that children and young adolescents require greater activation of the dlPFC to perform effectively, this possibility seems unlikely, given that amount of activation in this region of the PFC was uncorrelated with task performance (Durston et al., 2006). In contrast, activity within a restricted region of the ventral PFC showed both task- and age-related increases, and was more activated on trials in which subjects having difficulty performing the task were successful in withholding their response than on trials when they were unsuccessful (Durston et al., 2006). These results have been interpreted as an example of the developmental shift from diffuse to focal cortical activation, with PFC regions uncorrelated with task performance (i.e., dlPFC) being recruited less and PFC regions critical to task performance (i.e., ventral portions of the PFC) increasing in activation during development (Durston et al., 2006). Scherf and colleagues (2006) reached a similar conclusion based on their data examining working memory, postulating that developmental advances in cognition through adolescence are associated first with greater and more diffuse

123

activation of frontal and parietal regions from that seen in adulthood, followed by more discrete, task-related activation in specific PFC (and other frontal and parietal) regions that form part of the "performance-enhancing" neurocircuitry seen in the mature individual. Indeed, maturational changes in the PFC should be considered within a context of what is going on in other brain regions—a topic to which we now turn.

• *Different brain regions and neural networks may be recruited to perform a given task by developing individuals than by adults.* The study by Durston and colleagues (2006) just discussed is a good example of how children and adolescents activate different brain circuitry than do adults when solving the same cognitive tasks. Indeed, in studies showing greater overall task-related PFC activation in children and adolescents than in adults, somewhat different prefrontal regions generally were activated across age (Casey et al., 1997b, 2000; Luna et al., 2001, Rubia et al., 2000). Developmental differences in the involvement of particular brain regions may be task-dependent, with some evidence that a given task may activate brain regions in youth that may not be activated when the youth are tested with tasks requiring other cognitive skills (see Bunge & Wright, 2007, for discussion and references). Indeed, the functional role of a given brain region seemingly depends, in large part, on its moment-to-moment neural context—that is, the amount of coordinated activity within the various neural networks in which it participates (see Cabeza & Nyberg, 2000; McIntosh, 2000). These neural contexts change dynamically as separate networks gain strength, weaken, or incorporate different component structures (nodes) during development. For instance, in a study by Rubia and colleagues (2007) in which task difficulty was adjusted separately for each individual, developmental increases from childhood through adolescence and into adulthood were seen in coordinated functioning within neurocircuits involving frontal, striatal, and thalamic regions (a fronto–striato–thalamic network) and frontal and cerebellar regions (i.e., a fronto–cerebellar network). Similarly, Bunge and Wright (2007) have suggested that suboptimal response control in children and adolescents reflects insufficient recruitment of neurocircuitry interconnecting portions of the PFC with the thalamus, striatum, and cerebellum. Thus, brain development through adolescence may be characterized not so much by increases in task-associated activation of the PFC and other frontal regions, per se, but by an increased reliance on distributed brain regions that function in "collaborative" networks of activity with frontal regions such as the PFC (Luna & Sweeney, 2004).

• *Critical developmental advances during adolescence are seen in neural networks linking frontal–parietal regions with other brain regions.* A recent review has argued that functional fronto–parietal networks involving the dlPFC, the ACC, portions of the parietal lobe, and even portions of the temporal and occipital regions of the cortex are critical for determining intelligence levels and cognitive competence (Jung & Haier, 2007). Although the relationship between the strength of these networks and IQ remains controversial (as detailed in the commentaries associated with the Jung & Haier, 2007, review), many agree that connectivity linking frontal–parietal areas and other brain regions is important for cognitive function. Using several new strategies to estimate connectivity across neural regions, evidence is emerging that networks involving frontal and parietal regions undergo significant changes during adolescence that likely contribute to the maturation of working memory and cognitive control.

One technical approach has been to examine correlations of neuronal activation patterns across multiple brain regions under resting conditions and during performance of cognitive tasks, arguing that regions that closely mirror each other in their activity across time likely represent functionally related networks. In a study that used this approach to assess functional connectivity during a response inhibition task, adults generally showed greater activation in portions of the PFC than 10- to 17-year-olds when successfully inhibiting the task, but greater activation in the ACC on trials where responding was not inhibited successfully (Rubia et al., 2007). When activity was correlated across brain regions during performance of the inhibitory task, age-related increases in correlated activities were seen between frontal cortex and striatal, thalamic and cerebellar regions, leading the researchers to conclude that the emergence of inhibitory control during development is associated with the emergence of networks that interconnect frontal regions with subcortical regions and the cerebellum. In a study comparing correlations of activity across regions under resting conditions, Fair and colleagues identified a so-called "default network" whose activity is thought to support mental functions at rest, with activity in this network suppressed during cognitive challenges. Coordinated activity among these default regions is limited in children (7–9 years old), with notable developmental increases in the functional correlations among regions in this default network seen through adolescence (Fair et al., 2007, 2008). Developmental increases in connective strength are particularly notable between frontal–parietal regions and more distant brain regions. Based on their analyses, Fair and colleagues (2009) concluded that maturation of this default network is characterized by a gradual shift from a "local to distributed" organization as longer axonal pathways become myelinated, permitting more effective communication and stronger functional correlations among relatively distant regions.

In addition to measuring connectivity in terms of the coordination of activity among brain regions, some researchers have used myelination, specifically, white matter integrity, as a presumptive index of connective strength and cognitive efficacy (e.g., Rypma et al., 2006). Certainly myelinated axons transmit information more rapidly and efficiently, and such properties could support the emergence of coordinated activity among more distant brain regions. Indeed, in a study comparing maturation of working memory and white matter integrity through the use of DTI, development of working memory was found to be positively correlated with the integrity of the white matter interconnecting frontal and parietal cortical regions (Nagy et al., 2004). When white matter integrity indexed via FA values was compared with fMRI during a working memory task in 8- to 18-year-olds, FA values were found to be significantly correlated with task-related activation in a variety of frontal and parietal regions, as well as in certain subcortical (e.g., striatal) regions thought to be critical for development of working memory (Olesen et al., 2003). Thus, evidence for the importance of networks involving frontal and parietal regions in improvements in working memory during adolescence has emerged not only in terms of correlated task-related activity in these networks, but also in terms of the integrity of the white matter linking these regions.

• *ERP data support the protracted development of dlPFC and ACC through adolescence.* Electrical activity seen when measuring EEG responses to particular cognitive stimuli also shows evidence of continued development of the dlPFC and ACC through the adolescent period. One of the voltage-related waves of electrical activity in the EEG that is induced by exposure to cognitive stimuli is a negative wave termed the *contingent negative variation* (CNV) that is thought to reflect anticipation of an upcoming event. When the surface of the skull is covered by a cap of some 100+ electrodes, the timing and appearance of this negative wave can be examined as it moves across the skull, and the generator of the wave extrapolated. Using this approach, the generator of this CNV has been deduced to reside in the PFC—in particular, the dlPFC. A

127

strong CNV is elicited, for example, when adults are given a warning stimulus indicating an upcoming "go" trial on a go/ no-go task, with this negative wave increasing in intensity until the actual onset of the trial. The magnitude of this negative wave increases with age and does not reach adult levels until late adolescence—ERP evidence consistent with the suggestion that the dlPFC continues to mature through adolescence (Segalowitz & Davies, 2004).

Similar ERP evidence for late adolescent maturation of frontal regions is also derived from studies examining waveforms that emerge after a response is made. Following an incorrect response, a characteristic negative wave (ERN) emerges in the EEG of adults, sort of the brain equivalent of "oops." As mentioned in Chapter 4, this error-related response is thought to be generated by the ACC and doesn't reach maturity until late adolescence (Davies et al., 2004). Examination of other components of the complex pattern of waves elicited in anticipation of, and following responding on, a variety of cognitive tasks has yielded similar evidence for delayed emergence of mature patterns of frontal–parietal function into mid- to late adolescence (e.g., Lamm et al., 2006). Not all of the waveforms, however, show developmental changes, adding strength to the suggestion that the considerable changes seen in ERP production through adolescence are not a function of immature electrophysiological properties of the brain generally, but instead reflect maturational changes in frontal regions where these specific waves are generated (see Davies et al., 2004).

SUMMARY AND CLOSING COMMENTS

The explosive surge of developmental research examining brain activity during cognitive tasks has revealed maturational changes through adolescence in the activation of frontal–parietal regions and associated networks interconnecting these regions with other cortical as well as subcortical regions. This field of research is still in its infancy, however, and controversies remain. Is it more appropriate to view adolescent neural development as a transition from diffuse task-related activation to more focal activation, as the progressive emergence of neural networks recruiting more distant regions, or simply as age-related activation of different brain regions? Or perhaps a more accurate way to phrase the question: Under what specific circumstances does each type of developmental pattern emerge? Clearly, the brain regions activated during cognitive tasks differ somewhat with the nature of the cognitive task, differences that have been glossed over in this chapter, and consensus has not yet been reached on many of the details. Perhaps one of the most intriguing questions that has received little attention to date is the issue of whether immature cognitive-related neurocircuitry reflects constraints associated with anatomical/molecular immaturity of the child and adolescent's brain, or whether it represents cognitive inexperience that diminishes during the cognitive challenges and experiential education of adolescence. This distinction is critical and gets at the fundamental issue of whether the neural maturation occurring during adolescence provides a unique developmental window of vulnerability and opportunity to experientially "tune" cognitive (and other) neurocircuits within the brain of the developing adolescent. Is this appealing notion supported by the limited data currently available? We return to this question in Chapter 10.

CHAPTER SIX

Risk-Taking, Impulsiveness, and the Emergence of Self-Control

• •

"By definition, a transition period such as adolescence is disequilibrating and disrupting and thus replete with opportunities that are both dangerous and growth enhancing."
—Baumrind (1987, p. 98)

Adolescents are risk-takers. Relative to children and adults, adolescents exhibit a disproportionate amount of risk-taking and reckless behavior (e.g., Trimpop et al., 1999). This chapter explores why this is the case from a variety of perspectives, including consideration of the characteristics of the risk-prone brain.

ADOLESCENT RISK-TAKING: PREVALENCE AND COST–BENEFITS

Some degree of risk-taking is normative during adolescence: Over 50% of adolescents in the United States engage in risky behaviors, including drunk driving, sex without contraception, use of illegal drugs, and minor criminal activities (e.g., Arnett, 1992a), and most adolescents report at least moderate amounts of risk-taking under certain circumstances (Muuss & Porton,

1998). Such observations led one early researcher in the field to suggest that "actual rates of illegal behavior soar so high during adolescence that participation in delinquency appears to be a normal part of teen life" (Moffitt, 1993, p. 675). For some adolescents, risk-taking may intensify into a deviant lifestyle associated with continued criminality and exacerbation of problem behaviors that persist into adulthood (Lerner & Galambos, 1998). For most individuals, however, risk-taking is limited to adolescence and, unless resulting in some untoward negative consequences, is all but forgotten as they reach adulthood.

Risk-taking appears to be a highly conserved characteristic of adolescence, with adolescents of other species likewise seeking out novel and potentially risky aspects of their environment. For instance, even among rats and mice, adolescent animals typically approach novelty stimuli more quickly, exploring novel situations and stimuli more than other-age animals, and find novel stimuli to be more rewarding than do adults (e.g., Adriani et al., 1998; Douglas et al., 2003). These data obtained in laboratory studies are reminiscent of field studies showing that rats in the wild begin to leave the protective constraints from the burrow early in adolescence (P28), and by mid-adolescence (P34) have explored some distance from their home territory and been successful in acquiring food outside of the nest and interacting with conspecifics outside their family (Galef, 1981). Elevations in risk-taking in juvenile primates are frequently associated with the process of emigration that typically occurs during adolescence, with males (or, less commonly, females or animals of both sexes) migrating away from the natal territory (e.g., Pereira & Altmann, 1985). Although common among primates, the process of emigration is fraught with dangers and considerably elevates risk of mortality, a point to which we return shortly.

Adolescent Risk-Taking Exerts a High Cost

Risk-taking, by definition, is risky, and carries with it some potential for negative outcome. Given that most adolescents exhibit risk-taking under some circumstances, they are engaging in "acts that sometimes, even though relatively rarely, result in accidents and lead to tragic consequences" (Muuss & Porton, 1998, p. 423). Such negative consequences include incarceration, AIDS or other diseases that can be transmitted sexually, unintended pregnancy, alcohol or drug dependence, disruption in school attendance and a diminished likelihood for further education, as well as an increased probability of death due to mishap (Irwin, 1989). Indeed, despite the overall healthiness of adolescents, death rates increase 2–4 fold during adolescence, a rise in mortality rates particularly pronounced among males and seen not only in humans but in other species as well (e.g., Crockett & Pope, 1993; Irwin & Millstein, 1992). The cause of this elevated mortality is essentially behavioral, with accidents, homicides, and suicides collectively accounting for 75% and 72% of all deaths among 15- to 19-year-olds, and 20- to 24-year-olds, respectively (Heron & Smith, 2007).

Emigration in primates, the prototypic example of risk-taking, is also associated with dramatic increases in mortality rate. Such life-threatening risks include not only predation and within-species aggression, but also malnutrition and starvation as animals move into unfamiliar territory containing unfamiliar foodstuffs (see Crockett & Pope, 1993). In free-ranging populations of nonhuman primates, there is direct evidence of associations between risk-taking and mortality. Among Japanese macaques, death in males was found to be related largely to increases in risk-taking behaviors following sexual maturity (Fedigan & Zohar, 1997). Likewise, the probability of dying within a 4-year period encompassing the prepubertal-to-adult transition was elevated in male rhesus monkeys that had a biological characteristic (specifically, low concentrations of a metabolite of the neurotransmitter serotonin in fluid derived from their brains) associated with high levels of risk-taking and aggression (Higley et al., 1996a).

Why Has Adolescent Risk-Taking Been Preserved Despite Its High Costs?

Given the considerable mortality associated with risk-taking, one could question why this typically adolescent behavior would have been preserved across so many different species. Probably numerous factors, some species-specific, are involved. To begin to consider this issue, let's consider risk-taking from a cost–benefit perspective, using a simple example in fish. Once on their own, developing organisms of a variety of species typically must engage in some risky behavior to procure food. Among fish, the costs are considerable for being small, with small size generally equated with being easy prey. In an environment with many predators, fish that grow rapidly minimize the time that they are especially vulnerable to predators. But rapid growth requires a successful search for food and often involves considerable risk-taking as the young fish expose themselves to potential predators while hunting for food. When food supplies are scarce (and hence the alternative to risk-taking is starvation), levels of risk-taking among young fish is high (see Biro et al., 2005). Yet, high levels of risk taking are disadvantageous when predators are numerous. For instance, fish bred for high growth rates (domesticated "farm-raised" fish) take greater risks when searching for food and grow faster than wild fish. But in an environment with abundant predators (as is typically the case in the wild), the high levels of risk-taking among young domesticated fish lowers their survival relative to their more cautious wild-type counterparts (Biro et al., 2004). Thus, in fish, the amount of risk-taking by youth is a cost–benefit tradeoff, with increases in risk-taking increasing the probability of survival when food resources are low but decreasing survival in the presence of abundant predators. And, under the fairly common circumstances of both low food availability and high predation, young displaying relatively high levels of risk-taking as well as those being risk adverse fare less well, on average, when compared with moderate risk-takers. Thus, a trait that increases mortality when expressed at high levels nevertheless could be evolutionarily adaptive to the extent that moderate levels of expression of that trait are advantageous.

Indeed, the advantage of moderation is a rather common theme in the evolutionary and genetic literature. To give a sense of the genetic literature, consider sickle-cell disease. Individuals who have sickle cell *disease* inherit a gene from both of their parents that produces hemoglobin with a structural/chemical defect, resulting in chronic anemia, lowered oxygen-carrying capacity of the blood, and greater vulnerability to a variety of health problems. Individuals with sickle cell *trait* have only one copy of this gene, with the result that their hemoglobin is altered only slightly—not enough to induce anemia or lower blood oxygen capacity, but sufficient to increase their resistance to malaria, a disease caused by a blood-bound parasite common in some warm climates. Thus, the incidence of the sickle cell gene is relatively high among certain ethnic groups, despite the increased mortality associated with those with sickle cell disease, because of the adaptive benefit of protection against malaria among individuals carrying only one copy of the gene (i.e., those with sickle cell trait).

To the extent that adolescent risk-taking can be profitably viewed from a cost–benefit analysis, there may be advantages beyond the procurement of food. One benefit that has received considerable attention is that accruing to emigration. An increased impetus to seek out risky and novel stimuli would likely have facilitated emigration—a migration away from the natal group that is commonly seen among juveniles/adolescents of mammalian species, including primates and our human ancestors (e.g., Schlegel & Barry, 1991; Keane, 1990). Emigration of male adolescents, female adolescents, or both sexes around the time of sexual maturity would serve to remove sexually emergent individuals from the proximity of those with whom they are genetically related, thereby avoiding inbreeding and the lowered viability of resulting offspring due to greater expression of recessive genes (Bixler, 1992; Moore, 1992).

Yet, in modern human societies where cultural traditions largely protect against inbreeding and where the risk-taking of adolescents is rarely related to food procurement or emigration, adolescent risk-taking still persists. This may be in part because the impetus to engage in risk-taking could be long retained under relaxed selection pressure, as a remnant of our evolutionary past. Nevertheless, the persistence of risk-taking despite its potential costliness suggests that it likely continues to confer some beneficial consequences. Among the possible adaptive benefits attributed to risk-taking are increases in the probability of reproductive success in males of a variety of species, including humans (Wilson & Daly, 1985). According to this perspective, risk-taking behaviors "may be—or at least once were—means of securing physical resources, attracting mates, and denying mating opportunities to competitors" (Steinberg & Belsky, 1996, p. 117). Risk-taking has also been suggested to benefit adolescents by providing them with opportunities to explore adult behaviors and privileges (Silbereisen & Reitzle, 1992), to face and conquer challenges (Csikszentmihalyi & Larson, 1978), to master the developmental difficulties of adolescence (Silbereisen & Noack, 1988), and to increase status and peer affiliation within certain peer groups (e.g., Kaplan et al., 1987). Considering drug use as an example of risky behavior, Shedler and Block (1990) found that adolescents who showed moderate experimentation with drugs were more socially competent both in childhood and adolescence than either frequent users or drug abstainers, with frequent users characterized as alienated, distressed, and deficient in impulse control, and abstainers as anxious, overcontrolled, emotionally restricted, and lacking in social skills. From these data, they concluded that occasional risky drug use may reflect a manifestation of "developmentally appropriate experimentation"—again, the notion of potential advantages of moderation in risk-taking.

CONTRIBUTORS TO ADOLESCENT RISK-TAKING

Adolescents may be prone to display risky behaviors for a number of reasons. For starters, they differ from adults in the way they make decisions regarding risks—perhaps because of their decision-making processes, because their goals differ from adults, or because they view potential outcomes of risk-taking—in terms of benefits, costs, probability of occurring, and effectiveness of deterrents—differently than do adults. The risk-taking of adolescents may also be fostered by immature inhibitory control systems, leading adolescents to react impulsively under some circumstances, particularly in emotional situations when they are with peers and where logical decision-making abilities may be suppressed. Adolescents may also engage in risky behavior in part because they are seeking the stimulation of thrills and new experiences. And, as discussed later, each of these contributors to adolescent risk-taking may be influenced by adolescent-related changes in brain.

Risk-Taking as a Result of a Decision-Making Process

As discussed in the last chapter, improvements in cognitive skills and decision-making occur throughout childhood and continue in adolescence. Developmental improvements in cognitive reasoning and rational decision-making through adolescence could lead to the gradual decline in risk-taking with maturity, and indeed there is a long history of studying adolescent risk-taking from a decision-making perspective. In such research, improvements in judgment on decision-making tasks have been reported throughout adolescence, despite notable individual differences within each age group (see Cauffman & Steinberg, 2000, for review).

When viewing the relationship between risky behavior and decision-making processes in adolescence, some researchers have focused not so much on the process of decision-making per se, but rather on possible differences in the "data" that adolescents, as opposed to adults, feed into the decision-making process—for example, the costs–benefits identified with particular risks, the importance attributed to those benefits, the relative value conferred to immediate versus delayed consequences, and the probability attributed to possible negative outcomes. Adults particularly prone to take risks, for instance, have been reported to be more sensitive to rewarding stimuli but less sensitive to punishments (see Fishbein et al., 2005, for review). Indeed, adolescents who exhibit high levels of risk-taking see more benefits in the behavior than those who engage in less risk-taking (Benthin et al., 1993; Rolison & Scherman, 2003), and they also tend to view particular outcomes, such as increased peer acceptance, as being particularly important (e.g., see Romer & Hennessy, 2007). Galvan and colleagues (2007) concluded that decisions of adolescents to engage in risky behavior, like those of adults, were generally associated with anticipated positive consequences, whereas their risk-averse behavior, like that of children, was driven largely by anticipated negative consequences. Indeed, adolescents are aware of the potential costs of risk-taking, although findings vary as to how much their propensities to engage in, or avoid, risks is influenced by perceived costs (e.g., Benthin et al., 1993; Rolison & Scherman, 2002, 2003; see also Reyna & Farley, 2006). There is evidence that children and young adolescents who are prone to take risks are less sensitive generally to the outcomes of their risk-taking than are more risk-averse youth (Miller & Byrnes, 1997). Indeed, developmental increases in sensitivity to both positive and negative future consequences are seen throughout adolescence (Crone & van der Molen, 2004).

Reyna and Farley (2006) have argued that, even though overall reasoning ability continues to improve throughout adolescence, adolescents sometimes display stronger evidence of rational decision-making than adults when making decisions about risk. They base this counterintuitive conclusion on studies demonstrating age-related increases in "gist-based" cognitive processing, with "gists" being defined as generalized, partial, "fuzzy" mental representations that are generated quickly, without reasoned thinking. According to this perspective, mature individuals tend to respond quickly to the overall "gist" of risky situations, typically in risk-averse ways, whereas adolescents tend to generate and rationally weigh various costs and benefits of even clearly dangerous situations before responding. Thus, Reyna and Farley (2006) argue that although adolescents engage in more risk-taking behavior than adults, this propensity occurs *despite* their bias to engage more in rational decision-making processes when thinking about risks than mature individuals.

Indeed, for a variety of reasons it has been argued that trying to understand adolescent risk-taking as if it were simply the result of a rational, reasoned evaluation of options, possible outcomes, and costs and benefits has "yielded . . . little in the way of explaining the phenomenon" (Steinberg, 2004, p. 52). One major difficulty in trying to relate adolescent decision-making processes to actual risky behavior is that adolescents may think and reason about risky situations under typical classroom or laboratory testing conditions in ways that bear little resemblance to the risky choices they make in more affect-laden, high-arousing, and emotional "real-world" settings with their friends. The critical distinctions between decisions reached in these two types of settings have been labeled in a variety of different ways, including "cold" versus "hot" cognitions (e.g., Dahl, 2004) or "reasoned" versus "reactive" (Reyna & Farley, 2006) routes to risk-taking.

Risk-Taking as "Hot Cognitions"

As discussed above, adolescents often demonstrate excellent rational decision-making when thinking calmly and logically about risks (see Reyna & Farley, 2006). Their logic may be sublime, presenting relevant facts, reasoning logically, and mounting a moving argument to extend a curfew or gain some other privilege. Yet, in other instances, these same ostensibly logical adolescents may behave in ways that seem inconsistent with even the most rudimentary thought (see Steinberg, 2004). The capacity for rational decision-making does not necessarily translate into thinking logically under all circumstances. Indeed, under circumstances where affect is high—for example, in the excitement of being around friends in a stimulating context—rational decision-making may be suppressed, increasing the likelihood that adolescents will engage in risky behaviors. Under these circumstances, the excitement and emotions that are aroused may drive behavioral choices, with rational decision-making taking a backseat. Such "hot cognitions" may not take into consideration the costs–benefits of risks that the adolescent may weigh when making decisions about risks under conditions of low emotional involvement and arousal—that is, the "cold cognitions" typically displayed in home, school, or laboratory settings (Dahl, 2001). This difference presents a particular challenge for prevention work targeted at reducing the propensity of adolescents to engage in risk-taking. That is, knowledge learned in "cold cognition" settings may have little impact on behavioral choices induced in settings that promote "hot cognitions." And those individuals who are less able to regulate their emotional states (e.g., see Steinberg, 2004) or who are more arousable/excitable (Brown et al., 2006) may be particularly prone to exhibit risk-taking behavior in these settings. Such reactive risk-taking choices are more prevalent among adolescents than adults, and are particularly likely in social situations involving the presence of peers (see Gardner & Steinberg, 2005), with those youth who are most influenced by their peers showing the least impulse control (Grosbras et al., 2007). The issues of emotional stimuli and peer influences on risk-taking and their neural substrates are examined in more detail in the next chapter.

Risk-Taking as Sensation-Seeking

Risk-takers often view taking risks as "fun," exciting, and rein-forcing (Maggs et al., 1995; Romer & Hennessy, 2007) and may engage in risky behavior to attain the positive arousal pro-duced by sensations of novelty, complexity, or intensity of ex-perience (Zuckerman, 1992). For instance, most young smokers think little of risks when they begin smoking, but rather are enticed to begin smoking because they expect it will be fun and exciting (Slovic et al., 2004). Indeed, the most common reason given for trying a drug for the first time is to satisfy cu-riosity or to experience something new or different (Zuckerman, 1992). Likewise, the most common reason given by college stu-dents for their engaging in delinquent behaviors, including theft, vandalism, and use of illegal substances, was for "fun/ thrills" (Pfefferbaum & Wood, 1994).

Sensation-seeking is a complex trait associated with the desire for diverse, novel, complex, and intense experiences and the willingness to engage in risks to attain those experiences (e.g., Zuckerman, 1990). Sensation-seeking includes a number of dimensions: thrill and adventure-seeking (the desire to engage in activities involving speed and danger); disinhibition (desire for partying, sexual activities, social drinking); experience seeking (nonconforming lifestyle, seeking travel/new sensory experiences); and boredom susceptibility (aversion to routine, repetition, and dull people) (Zuckerman et al., 1978). Adolescents generally exhibit more sensation-seeking than individuals at other ages, with the dimensions of thrill/adventure-seeking and disinhibition being particularly pronounced among adolescents and declining notably thereafter (Zuckerman et al., 1978). Not surprisingly, those adolescents showing high levels of sensation-seeking engage in more risk-taking behavior than those lower in sensation-seeking (e.g., Greene et al., 2000; Rolison & Scherman, 2002). As might be expected if risk-taking reflects the seeking of diverse new experiences, adolescents who engage in one form of risk-taking often engage in others as well (e.g., Muuss & Porton, 1998). Indeed, high sensation-seekers not only take more risks, but also seek out high-intensity stimuli in other forms, including, for example, hard rock/heavy metal music (Arnett, 1992b).

As the perceived costs of risk-taking decline with age during adolescence (Irwin, 1993), the level of risk-taking necessary to attain an "adrenaline rush" of danger may rise, perhaps leading to an escalation of these behaviors in certain individuals—particularly those with poor prospects for attaining other kinds of reinforcers through school, work, athletics, and so on (Wilson & Daly, 1993). For most individuals, though, risk-taking declines with the transition from adolescence to adulthood, with little long-term cost unless their risky behaviors happened to lead to an unfortunate outcome.

For some adolescents, risk-taking may reflect not so much the seeking of positive reinforcers from novel and intense stimuli, but rather may serve as a means of reducing dysphoria or coping with stress (Jessor et al., 1996; McCord, 1990). In gen-

141

eral, adolescents report positive situations to be less pleasurable than both younger or older individuals, a "falling from grace" associated with a 50% decline in reports of feeling "very happy" between late childhood (5th grade) and early adolescence (7th grade) (Larson & Richards, 1994). Not only do adolescents rate comparable activities as less pleasurable than do adults (Larson & Richards, 1994), they are also less optimistically biased when compared with college students or adults (Millstein, 1993). Furthermore, adolescents exhibit an increase in negative affect, affect disturbances, and depressed mood relative to younger or older individuals (Larson & Asmussen, 1991; Rutter et al., 1976). Adolescents who are especially prone to exhibiting negative affect and a lack of positive feeling in response to common situations may be particularly likely to engage in risk-taking as a means to attain pleasurable sensations associated with dangerous and intense stimuli.

Brain regions undergoing particularly marked remodeling during adolescence include regions critical for modulating the reinforcing nature of natural stimuli, including novel and exciting (albeit potentially dangerous) stimuli, as well as alcohol and other drugs of potential abuse. The neural substrates of reward and their developmental alterations during adolescence are discussed further in Chapter 8.

Risk-Taking as Impulsiveness or Insufficient Inhibitory Control

Adolescents may also engage in risky behaviors because they tend to respond impulsively and display limited self-control. Impulsivity is characterized by the tendency to react spontaneously without thinking much beforehand as to the consequences of one's actions. High levels of impulsivity are related to greater engagement in delinquent behaviors during adolescence (Pfefferbaum & Wood, 1994). Yet, risk-taking seemingly involves more factors than impulsivity, per se, with some researchers reporting little direct correlation between levels of

impulsivity and amount of risk taking in adolescent populations (Galvan et al., 2006).

One way that impulsivity has been examined experimentally is to examine preferences for smaller immediate rewards
over more delayed but larger rewards—a phenomenon termed
delay discounting. In this test, greater impulsivity is indexed
via more rapid declines in the reward value of the larger reward with increasing delays. Among adults, greater delay discounting has been shown to be a risk factor for a variety of
addictive disorders, ranging from pathological gambling to
drug and alcohol abuse (Bickel et al., 1999; Alessi & Petry, 2003).
Adolescents generally display more delay discounting than do
adults, an age difference seen not only in humans (Green et al.,
1994) but even when using simple animal models of adolescence as well (Barreto et al., 2005). Moreover, those adolescents
who show greater delay discounting exhibit greater involvement with alcohol and other drugs (Wulfert et al., 2002).

Impulsively engaging in risky behaviors is often thought to
reflect limited self-control. As discussed in Chapter 5, inhibitory control is one of a series of executive control functions
that continues to mature into adolescence (e.g., Leon-Carrion
et al., 2004; Luna et al., 2004). For instance, in a task for which
individuals are asked to inhibit a prepotent response when
confronted with a stop signal, Williams and colleagues (1999)
found that the speed of inhibiting responding improved with
age through childhood and into midadolescence (13–17 years),
age-related changes in inhibitory control that were not simply
a function of general age-related differences in reaction times.
The capacity for inhibition has been suggested to be critical
for resisting interference. Using a variety of tasks sensitive to
interference, developmental improvements through childhood
and into adolescence have been reported (Dempster, 1992).
Thus, inhibitory self-control, when indexed in terms of the
ability to withhold prepotent responses and resist interference,

continues to improve well into adolescence. Immaturity in such inhibitory self-control mechanisms likely contributes to the propensity of some adolescents to impulsively engage in risky behaviors.

THE ADOLESCENT BRAIN, RISK-TAKING, IMPULSIVITY, AND SELF-CONTROL

Many of the questions we would like to ask about the neural substrates of adolescent risk-taking cannot be asked directly—such as what is (or perhaps more to the point, what is not) going on in brains of adolescents when they decide to pile into a car with friends who have been drinking and go for a "joy ride." It is difficult to model such situations within the constraints of an MRI scanner. Nevertheless, through the use of scanner-compatible decision-making tasks involving varying risks, imaging studies have revealed a number of brain regions whose activity is associated with levels of risk-taking, impulsive decisions, and self control, and where some differences in the extent of recruitment of these regions are evident between adolescents and adults.

Key among the brain areas implicated in adolescent risk-taking is the PFC, although the specific regions of the PFC engaged often vary across risk-taking tasks (see Vorhold et al., 2007, for discussion). Brain substrates particularly implicated in adolescent-related risk-taking include ventral regions such as the ventromedial PFC (vmPFC) and the ACC, along with other portions of the "emotional brain" such as cortical (insular) and subcortical (amygdalar) regions involved in the detection of bodily states. Other critical contributors to the propensity of adolescents to take risks are developmental changes that occur in reward-related neurocircuitry. Together, research in this rapidly evolving area is adding considerable richness and complexity to our understanding of the neural substrates of adolescent risk-taking.

Neural Substrates of Adolescent Decision-Making: A Focus on the PFC

Although activity in the dlPFC has most often been associated with response selection and working memory, this region has also been implicated in the successful inhibition of risky choices. For an example of data supporting this conclusion, we turn to findings obtained with a new technique that is able to stimulate or disrupt activity in particular cortical regions in humans by passing electrical currents into their brain from electrodes placed on the skull. Using this amazing technique, stimulation parameters sufficient to increase activity in the dlPFC of the right hemisphere or both hemispheres were found to suppress risk-taking (Fecteau et al., 2007a, 2007b). Conversely, risky behavior was elevated when activity of the dlPFC of the right hemisphere was suppressed by the current (Knoch et al., 2006). Although the locus of these effects may not be precisely restricted to the dlPFC, due to some spread of the current, these data suggest that the dlPFC may play a role in adaptive decision-making, with activity in this region potentially serving to constrain responding under risky conditions.

This conclusion is supported by fMRI findings as well. Indeed, when forced to make decisions under conditions of high risk (i.e., high probability of failure), the dlPFC of the right hemisphere shows greater activation than under lower risk conditions (i.e., when the odds favor choosing correctly). Given that early adolescents and young adults do not differ in the magnitude of this activation (van Leijenhorst et al., 2006; Eshel et al., 2007), this region, however, may not notably contribute to developmental changes in risky decision-making.

More ventral portions of the PFC, such as the OFC, have

been more strongly and consistently linked to developmental changes in risk-taking behaviors. In a child-friendly version ("Hungry Donkey task") of traditional gambling tasks, children performed similarly to adults with brain damage sustained to a portion of the OFC (specifically, the vmPFC), with both groups making fewer advantageous choices than neurologically intact adults (Crone & van der Molen, 2004). Performance on the task improved during development, with 16- to 18-year-olds learning to make advantageous choices in the task more quickly than younger individuals. Activity in the OFC and other ventral regions such as the ventral ACC shows greater recruitment on high- than low-risk trials, again implicating these ventral regions in decisions involving risk. There is disagreement across studies, though, in terms of the ontogeny of these effects. In the van Leijenhorst study (2006), no age differences were seen in the magnitude of OFC recruitment during risky choices, although greater activation was seen in the ACC in young adolescents than adults, leading the authors to suggest that young adolescents may overrecruit in this brain region on risky trials because they have more difficulty than adults in responding under circumstances of uncertainty (van Leijenhorst et al., 2006). In contrast, under test conditions wherein not only probability of winning but also the magnitude of reward were varied, when making risky decisions adolescents have been reported to show less activation (or less focal activation) than adults in ventral regions of the frontal cortex thought to be involved in response inhibition and cognitive flexibility—regions varyingly identified as the vmPFC, ventrolateral PFC, OFC, and/or ventral ACC (Galvan et al., 2006; Bjork et al., 2007; see Eshel et al., 2007, for review and references).

Thus, although the limited fMRI data currently available consistently implicate ventral regions of the PFC in age-related changes in risky decision-making throughout adolescence, conclusions regarding the nature of those developmental changes and their regional specificity differ across studies. Among the critical differences across studies that could contribute to these varying findings are differences in the specific age range of the study participants as well as the nature of the task and the comparison/control conditions (e.g., whether probability of winning alone was varied across trials, or whether magnitude of reward/punishment was also varied). The specific neural regions and subregions targeted for analysis are also likely critical, and include not only portions of the PFC, but also subcortical regions involved in processing and responding to punishments and rewards.

Adolescent Risk-Taking and Development of the "Emotional Brain": The Amygdala, vmPFC, ACC, and Insula

Attenuated recruitment of the vmPFC may contribute to adolescent risk-taking in part because of its role in the processing of bodily (*somatic*) signs of emotions that are generated in response to rewards and losses (e.g., see Dalgleish, 2004). Patients with damage to the vmPFC are unable to interpret and utilize somatic signals of emotions (e.g., increases in heart rate, respiration, skin conductance) that are normally elicited in response to, or when anticipating, punishments and rewards. Along with the inability to use these somatic signals, these patients with vmPFC damage exhibit greater risky responding during gambling tasks (e.g., Bechara et al., 1999), a propensity for risk-taking reminiscent of that normally seen among adolescents. When making decisions involving risk, adolescents not only tend to show less recruitment in the vmPFC than adults, but also less activation in the insula and portions of the ACC relative to adults (Eshel et al., 2007). The ACC is activated by many types of emotional stimuli and is thought to be a key brain region for processing bodily information that provides cues about affective state and the nature of emotional experiences (see Dalgleish, 2004, for review). The insular region, hidden within the large fissure that separates the temporal and frontal lobes, likewise is thought to join the vmPFC in interpreting somatic signs of affect and emotions generated in response to rewards and losses (e.g., see Dalgleish, 2004).

It may be that adolescents show less recruitment during risky decision-making in brain regions processing somatic information in part because they are producing fewer somatic responses in risky situations. Indeed, although little explored to date, there is some evidence that adolescents are less capable of generating somatic signs in anticipation of rewards and punishments. In a gambling task modified for use with children as well as older individuals, it was not until 16–18 years that adult-typical anticipatory somatic responses were seen— that is, greater increases in skin conductance associated with decisions more likely to lead to punishment (Crone & van der Molen, 2007). This delayed emergence of a somatic state linked to risky decisions was not related to an inability to alter somatic state, per se, given that similar punishment-induced increases in skin conductance (and decreases in heart rate) were seen regardless of age (Crone & van der Molen, 2007). These findings are reminiscent of behavioral studies showing adolescents to be less sensitive to both positive and negative future consequences than adults (e.g., Crone & van der Molen, 2004).

The last component of the "emotional brain" to be introduced here is one of the most critical: the amygdala. This subcortical region is part of the limbic system and has long been linked to the processing of emotional stimuli, particularly those involving fear and social signals (Dalgleish, 2004). Patients with lesions disrupting the amygdala, like those with lesions of the vmPFC, failed to show somatic responses to rewards and punishments and likewise showed risky responding on gambling tasks (Bechara et al., 1999). Developmentally, adolescents were found to activate the amygdala less than adults when a hoped-for reward was not received (Ernst et al., 2005).

Networks involving frontal regions and the amygdala have been implicated in impulsivity in adults, with impulsivity during response inhibition, for instance, correlated with less activation of the ventral PFC and dorsal amygdala (Brown et al., 2006). We will return to discussion of the amygdala in the next chapter when reviewing neural systems activated when perceiving emotions in facial stimuli.

Risk-Taking as Sensation-Seeking: Adolescence, Reward Circuitry, and the Nucleus Accumbens

One other potentially important neural contributor to adolescent-typical increases in risk-taking and impulsivity is the remodeling in reward-related circuitry that occurs during adolescence. A prominent component of this neurocircuitry is the NAc, a brain region also frequently referred to as the ventral striatum. Activity in the NAc, along with closely interconnected regions such as the lateral OFC and ACC, is increased following receipt of rewards both in adolescents (Delgado et al., 2000) and adults (May et al., 2004). Based largely on studies conducted in laboratory animals, these brain regions have been shown to form a critical part of the neurocircuitry that attributes reward value and motivational salience to natural rewards such as food, social stimuli, and sex, along with novel, exciting, and thrilling stimuli (e.g., Bardo et al., 1996; Kelley et al., 2005). Alcohol, nicotine, and other drugs that are self-administered likewise appear to exert their rewarding effects via activation of this neurocircuitry (e.g., Nesse & Berridge, 1997; Volkow et al., 2002). Developmental changes in functional activity within this neurocircuitry could influence how reinforcing adolescents find new and exciting stimuli, and hence their propensity to seek out and take risks, including drug use.

Although the research to date has generally found rewarding stimuli to activate ("recruit") similar brain regions in adolescents as adults, the magnitude of that activation often differs across age. The findings vary, however, as to whether adolescence is associated with greater or lesser reward-related recruitment of activity in these regions. For instance, during anticipation of rewards, adolescents were found to exhibit less NAc activation than adults (Bjork et al., 2004), whereas in response to rewards, adolescents have varyingly been reported to show greater (Ernst et al., 2005), exaggerated (Galvan et al., 2006), or similar (Bjork et al., 2004) reward-related activation in NAc in relation to adults. Age-related differences in the NAc and other components of reward-related neurocircuitry are considered in more detail in Chapter 8 when we examine neural substrates of adolescent drug use (see also Eshel et al., 2007, for review).

The act of risk-taking itself may sometimes be sufficient to activate the NAc, with activity in this region greater on trials where risky choices were selected relative to trials on which safer choices were made (Matthews et al., 2004). Although the magnitude of the NAc activation in response to risky choices was not found to differ between adolescents and adults in a study by Eshel and colleagues (2007), individuals prone to take risks showed particularly pronounced risk-related recruitment in this region. Impulsivity and the propensity to take risks may also influence the extent to which rewarding stimuli activate the NAc. For instance, those individuals who were most impulsive in a delay discounting task showed greater activity in the NAc following both positive and negative feedback, relative to those individuals who responded less impulsively in this task (Hariri et al., 2006). Amount of activation in the NAc in response to reward was also found to be greater among individuals who reported that they were likely to engage in risk-taking relative to those viewing themselves as more risk-averse (Galvan et al., 2007). The NAc region was also activated more in individuals who anticipated positive consequences of engaging in risky behavior than in those individuals anticipating negative consequences (Galvan et al., 2007). Thus, although no notable age differences have been reported in the amount of NAc activation associated with risky decisions, significant individual differences are evident, with individuals prone to engage in risk-taking showing greater activation in response to risk behavior and rewards than those disinclined to take risks.

Neural Substrates of Impulsivity and Inhibitory Control during Adolescence

Regions of the PFC recruited during inhibitory tasks are connected via multiple networks with various other brain regions. These functional networks are complex, with adolescents and adults differing in the degree to which different networks are activated or suppressed during response inhibition tasks as well as in the connectivity relationships within specific networks (Stevens et al., 2007). Among the neurocircuitry implicated in inhibitory motor control is frontostriatal circuitry that interconnects the PFC and the motor control area of the dorsal striatum. More ventral regions of the PFC are thought to be particularly closely involved in inhibitory control and self-regulation, with delayed development in these regions thought to contribute to immaturities in inhibitory control of children and adolescents. There is less consensus, however, as to the specific PFC regions involved, and whether this delayed development reflects more diffuse or less focal PFC activation during inhibitory responding.

Several studies have found the PFC to be more diffusely activated in younger subjects when they attempt to inhibit a response than in older adolescents and adults (Casey et al., 1997b; Tamm et al., 2002). These data were interpreted to suggest that the strategies used by younger subjects may be less effective and require more widespread recruitment across PFC regions (see Tamm et al., 2002). The specific frontal regions undergoing age-related changes in activation during inhibitory responding (including whether the activation was evident in both cortical hemispheres or restricted to the left or right hemisphere) has varied somewhat across these studies (e.g., see Rubia et al., 2000), perhaps due to differences in age ranges assessed and inhibitory task used, with different portions of the PFC likely critical for different inhibitory processes (see Marsh et al., 2006). In general, though, the greater PFC activation reported in younger subjects involved more middle and dorsal regions, with older subjects displaying more focal activation in ventral PFC regions that are thought to play particularly critical roles in response inhibition (see Casey et al., 1997b; Tamm et al., 2002).

More diffuse PFC activation in children than adults during response inhibition tasks is not always observed, though, with some studies reporting developmental increases in activation in particular PFC regions (increased "frontalization" with age— see Rubia et al., 2000), with reports such as maturational increases in activation in lateral regions of the PFC during a task involving self-regulatory control (Marsh et al., 2006) and in middle and ventral frontal systems in a stop task (Rubia et al., 2000).

Effective inhibitory responding clearly involves much more than the PFC alone; hence developmental changes in inhibitory responding may involve changes in neurocircuitry connecting the PFC to other brain regions and relative amounts of task-related recruitment of activity in those regions as well. For instance, inhibitory responding has been associated with circuitry that includes motor control regions of the dorsal striatum, although findings of age-related increases in striatal activation during inhibitory responding (Marsh et al., 2006) contrast with other reports of greater inhibition-related striatal activation in adolescents than adults (Rubia et al., 2000). In other developmental fMRI studies, adults were found to engage posterior attention-related regions outside the PFC (i.e., in occipital and parietal regions) during inhibitory control tasks more so than children and adolescents. These findings were interpreted to suggest an age-related developmental transition from a reliance on "task-general" frontal systems to involvement of "more widely distributed circuitry that enables attentional and sensory regions, in addition to prefrontal executive regions, to assist with inhibitory control" (Velanova et al., 2008, p. 2519).

Thus, although developmental increases in focal activation of PFC regions, particularly in the OFC and other ventral regions of the PFC, are often seen during performance of inhibitory tasks through adolescence, some disparities are evident across studies as to the specific regions undergoing developmental change. Findings to date also differ as to whether the observed developmental patterns are best characterized as developmental increases in frontalization (Rubia et al., 2000), as a developmental switch from more diffuse to greater focal activation within the PFC (Casey et al., 1997b), or as increases in long-range functional connectivity that enable more posterior attention-related systems to join the PFC in processes of inhibitory control (Velanova et al., 2008).

SUMMARY AND CLOSING COMMENTS

Despite the potentially high cost of risky choices, adolescents often take risks. Their propensity for risk-taking is influenced by a number of interacting and multifaceted factors. Immaturity in ventral portions of the PFC and other brain regions critical for inhibitory control and decision making could increase the propensity of adolescents to engage impulsively in risk-taking. On the other hand, adolescents may be particularly keyed into potential benefits of risk-taking due to developmental alterations in the NAc and other reward-related neurocircuitry. Additionally or alternatively, adolescents may be less sensitive to the inhibitory effects of potential negative consequences of risky choices perhaps in part because of less robust recruitment of brain regions that process emotional somatic information, and maybe even because they are less likely to emit risk-relevant somatic signs, per se, when anticipating risk-related consequences.

Given the importance of the amygdala, vmPFC, ACC, and insula in the processing of emotions and social stimuli, age-related differences in recruitment of these components of the "emotional brain" could contribute to the propensity of adolescents to behave in risky and impulsive ways when with friends in the heat of the moment. Under these circumstances, the emotional context of the moment may favor reactive, "hot cognitions" rather than decisions based on rational, logic-based cognitive processing. It is to the topic of the neural processing of social stimuli and other emotionally laden stimuli to which we now turn in the next chapter.

CHAPTER SEVEN

Social Behavior and the Emotions of Adolescence

••

It may seem odd to consider social behavior—a prototypic, externally-focused behavior—along with the internal world of emotions and feelings. Yet, much of the emotional life of the adolescent is strongly colored by social interactions (or their absence). It has been argued that "emotion provides the principal currency in human relationships as well as the motivational force for what is best and worse in human behavior" (Dolan, 2002, p. 1191). As we shall see, certain components of the "emotional brain" that are critical for monitoring and modulating emotional reactions are also specialized for inferring emotional states in social contexts based on facial expressions of others. Indeed, brain regions critically involved in social behavior are largely the same as those activated by emotional stimuli. Of particular relevance here, these socially receptive and emotionally reactive brain areas are among those undergoing considerable change during adolescence.

THE SOCIAL WORLD OF THE ADOLESCENT

Adolescents spend much of their time with peers, and these social interactions are of particular importance to them. During an average school week, adolescents spend almost four times more time with peers than adults and report that they are most happy when interacting with peers (Csikszentmihalyi et al., 1977). Along with an increased emphasis on interacting socially with peers, adolescence is also frequently characterized by a greater emotional distance from, and conflict with, parents (Steinberg, 1987)—conflict that is especially pronounced early in adolescence (Laursen et al., 1998). This shift in social orientation from adults to peers during adolescence is highly conserved and is evident in adolescents of other mammalian species as well. For instance, even in a simple animal model of adolescence in the rat, adolescents spend more time interacting socially with peers and find these social interactions more reinforcing than do adults (e.g., Douglas et al., 2004). Likewise, elevations in conflicts with parents are not only seen in human adolescents, but are also evident during puberty among monogamous family groups in certain species of nonhuman primates as well (Caine, 1986; see also Steinberg, 1989).

During puberty, adolescents typically exhibit an increasing interest in the opposite sex. Although humans and other primates are "emancipated" from an absolute reliance on gonadal hormones to stimulate sexual interest and activity (Wallen, 2001), there is no doubt that the rising levels of gonadal hormones associated with puberty contribute to increases in sexual interest and motivation (e.g., Smith et al., 1985). Surveys conducted among adolescents in the United States have revealed that among young adolescents (grades 7 and 8), one in six reports that he or she has had sex, while one in two older adolescents (grades 9–12) reports that he or she is sexually active (Resnick et al., 1997). Among sexually active girls in high school, 20% report that they were currently, or had been, pregnant (Resnick et al., 1997). These rates undoubtedly would be much higher if puberty were not associated with a transient period of relative infertility immediately following sexual maturation (onset of menses) (Short, 1976).

In addition to showing alterations in adult- and peer-directed social interactions, adolescents exhibit an increasing focus on infants. This increasing interest in infants is sexually dimorphic and generally more prevalent in female adolescents than males (e.g., Weisfeld & Berger, 1983). Again this adolescent-typical switch in social focus is highly conserved and is apparent in human adolescents (e.g., Fullard & Reiling, 1976), nonhuman primates (e.g., Weisfeld & Berger, 1983), and even rodents (Mayer et al., 1979).

An increasing focus on social interactions with peers potentially serves a number of valuable functions for the adolescent. Interactions with individuals outside the family may be of adaptive significance for adolescents in helping to guide their behavioral choices, allowing them to practice more independent behavior patterns, and facilitating their development of social skills away from the home environment (e.g., Harris, 1995). Similar benefits may be seen among adolescents of other species as well; for instance, social interactions among adolescent rodents help to guide their food choices and allow for practice, in mock form, of certain behaviors (e.g., aggressive and sexual behaviors) that will later form part of the adult behavioral repertoire (Galef, 1977; Smith, 1982).

There are marked differences among adolescents in their susceptibility to peer influences. Interestingly, these differences were found to be associated with different patterns of neural activation in young adolescents when exposed to emotional (anger-related) stimuli. As discussed in more detail later, youth that showed high resistance to peer pressure exhibited greater coordinated activity in a network of brain regions associated with perception and decision-making when compared with their less peer-resistant counterparts (Grosbras et al., 2007).

THE EMOTIONAL LIFE OF THE ADOLESCENT

Before examining adolescent emotional expression, let's briefly consider what emotions are and why they are important. Emotions are mental states that attribute value to events and are often accompanied by physiological changes. Information provided by emotions can be used to encourage approach and maintenance of conditions associated with positive affect (positive emotions), while prompting withdrawal and avoidance of circumstances connected with negative affect/emotions. Stimuli capable of inducing emotional reactions vary across a wide range (e.g., consider the different affective reactions induced by a rabid dog vs. an appealing puppy). Social stimuli are particularly potent in generating emotions for a number of reasons. Humans (and most other mammalian species, for that manner) are social beings who typically require close social contact not only to survive during the infancy–juvenile period, but also to help ensure well-being throughout life. Few mammalian species have evolved with a solitary lifestyle.

By helping to direct behavior toward or away from positive versus negative circumstances, respectively, emotions play a prime role in decision-making, focusing attention on meaningful stimuli in the environment and facilitating learning about them. As a consequence, the stamp of affect can influence memory of, and behavior directed toward or away from, these beneficial or detrimental situations in the future. Intense emotions generated in one circumstance, however, may "bleed out" into other situations as well, coloring subsequent interactions and perceptions in ways that are not necessarily beneficial. Later in this chapter, we consider how intense emotions of the moment may bias or even suppress logical thinking—so-called "hot cognitions" (e.g., see Dahl, 2004), a form of emotion-related biasing of brain activity that is especially prevalent among adolescents, as noted in the previous chapter.

How Do Adolescents Differ Emotionally from Adults?

The adolescent period has often been characterized as a time of enhanced moodiness or emotionality. Several decades ago a number of studies reported that adolescents experience more intense emotions, albeit not necessarily more variable emotions, than children and adults (Larson & Lampman-Petraitis, 1989; Larson et al., 1990). For instance, when 9- to 15-year-old participants were queried periodically throughout the day as to their mood state, older individuals were more likely to report being in a mildly negative dysphoric state and less likely to report being in a highly positive state, leading the authors to conclude that "the adolescent's conscious experience includes many fewer occasions when the individual feels on top of the world and more occasions of feeling mildly negative" (Larson & Lampman-Petraitis, 1989, p. 1258). Indeed, as discussed in Chapter 6, adolescents have been reported to view positive situations as less pleasurable than both younger and older individuals (Larson & Richards, 1994).

In contrast, in an experience-sampling study of 7th and 10th graders, few overall age differences were seen in the dynamics of emotional experience, although the early adolescent group reported a greater incidence of anxiety than the older students (Silk et al., 2003). Others have reported that levels of anxiety and self-consciousness appear to peak in adolescence (see Buchanan et al., 1992). Notable individual differences in emotionality are apparent among adolescents, with those adolescents who show greater emotional intensity, more emotional volatility, and problems in regulating their emotions being more vulnerable to both internalizing and externalizing disorders (e.g., depression and aggression, respectively—see Chapter 9).

Clearly much more research is needed to explore the emotions and emotionality of adolescents. Under what circum-

159

stances do adolescents show greater negative affect? To what extent is this greater negative affect normative versus indicative of compromised cognitive/emotional functioning that signals greater vulnerability to psychological disorders? Do adolescents show increased vulnerability to stressors and greater stress reactivity, perhaps increasing their vulnerability for later psychopathology? We turn to these questions later.

THE PHYSIOLOGY AND HORMONES OF EMOTIONS AND SOCIALITY IN ADOLESCENCE

Although emotions are internal, psychological experiences, they are often expressed externally via behavior: verbal expressions, facial expressions, and other actions (e.g., crying, laughing, aggressing). Emotions are also expressed physiologically in terms of hormone release, alterations in heart rate (HR) and breathing patterns, facial flushing, and so on (see Dolan, 2002). These physiological concomitants of emotions provide a critical part of the emotional experience. Different emotions are associated with unique patterns of bodily (somatic) changes and, as we shall see, the sensing of these changes is thought to contribute to the emotional experience perceived (Collet et al., 1997). These physiological changes include the release of hormones, which also may help color emotional experiences and influence social interactions, a topic to which we now turn.

Hormones, Emotions, Social Behavior, and the Adolescent

The adolescent period is characterized by numerous hormonal changes that extend beyond the substantial increases in gonadal hormones and their releasing factors during puberty, which were discussed in Chapter 3. During adolescence, there are also changes in hormones regulating body metabolism, food intake, and growth, including such hormones as leptin, ghrelin, and growth hormone (e.g., Mann & Plant, 2002), along

160

with alterations in "prosocial" hormone systems, including oxytocin and vasopressin. In addition, there is some evidence of developmental increases in stress hormones during adolescence, which could be related to an increase in the average number of stressors to which adolescents are exposed, their greater reactivity to stressors, and/or to maturational changes in the systems contributing to the release of stress hormones. Of these hormonal alterations, those particularly likely to contribute to adolescent-typical socioemotional functioning include developmental alterations in stressors and stress-related hormones, as well as in prosocial hormones such as oxytocin. It is to these that we now turn. Later, the impact of puberty and pubertal-related hormonal changes will be revisited from the perspective of their potential role in triggering developmental alterations in reactivity to emotional stimuli in particular neural regions.

Stress, Stress Hormones, and Adolescents

Adolescence is often viewed as a stressful period of transition. It is challenging, however, to compare number and magnitude of stressors across age, with situations viewed as potentially stressful in adolescence (e.g., changing schools, rapid growth, undergoing puberty unusually early or late relative to peers, social pressures, demands for good grades) differing from those occurring in adulthood (e.g., job stress, debts and bill paying, infidelity), or childhood (e.g., not being chosen for the soccer team your friends are on). Even similar situations (social exclusion, parental divorce, death in the family) may be viewed differently across age. For instance, preadolescents and adolescents differ in the kinds of situations they view as stressful, with preadolescents more likely to focus on negative events associated with family matters and activities in the immediate surroundings, early adolescents more likely to experience negative outcomes associated with peer interactions, and older adolescents finding academic situations to be particularly stressful (e.g., Larson & Asmussen, 1991). There may be sex differences as well, with females being unusually vulnerable to stressors in early adolescence, perceiving events as more stressful than at other ages and than as perceived by males (e.g., Vik & Brown, 1998).

Despite these challenges in comparing number and significance of stressors across age, there is evidence that adolescents may be exposed to more overall stressful life events than at earlier or older ages (Ge et al., 1994; Gest et al., 1999). An additional contributor to the stressfulness of adolescence may be the phase delay in sleep onset normally seen during this time (Carskadon et al., 1993), often leading to some degree of sleep deprivation—especially during the school week, when early rising is typically mandated. Not only is sleep deprivation itself likely stressful (see Arnett, 1999), but depriving individuals of the restorative functions of sleep has been postulated to disrupt poststress recovery processes (Ackerman, 1999).

Adolescence may also be associated with increased levels of stress-related hormones. Exposure to a stressor activates a cascade of hormones: from the hypothalamus (corticotrophin releasing hormone [CRH]), pituitary (adrenocorticotropic hormone [ACTH]), and adrenal gland (corticosteroids [CORT] such as cortisol in humans and corticosterone in laboratory animals such as the rat). In laboratory animals, stress-induced activation of this hypothalamo–pituitary–adrenal (HPA) axis develops gradually with age to reach asymptotic levels during adolescence in males (e.g., Vázquez, 1998), with elevated levels in females relative to males beginning to emerge in late adolescence and becoming more pronounced in adulthood (e.g., Cirulli et al., 1996). Longer poststress hormonal recoveries have also been reported in adolescent rats when indexed in terms of time taken to restore low basal CORT levels following stress-induced rises in this hormone (Romeo & McEwen, 2006). It can be challenging to conduct similar CORT assessments in human adolescents due in part to (1) marked diurnal cycles in basal CORT levels, (2) the difficulty in obtaining true basal (non-stress-related) levels of CORT in a laboratory setting, and (3) difficulties in parsing HPA effects related to experimentally induced stressors from the consequences of other ongoing life experiences of the adolescent. Nevertheless, although the evidence is mixed (see Gunnar & Vazquez, 2006), adolescence in humans has sometimes been found to be associated with elevated basal CORT levels (Walker et al., 2001) and/or increased CORT release in stressful situations (see Walker et al., 1998; Gunnar & Quevedo, 2007, for review). Adolescent-associated increases in responsiveness to stressors may be evident not only in terms of HPA activation, but also via alterations in physiological reactivity (e.g., HR response) to stressors, a topic to which we turn later. To the extent that the incidence of, and response to, stressors increases at this time, these increases could contribute to the greater emotional reactivity that is sometimes evident during adolescence, as well as perhaps increasing susceptibility to the emergence of affective and other psychological disorders among more vulnerable adolescents. The issue of HPA dysregulation as a vulnerability factor for the emergence of psychopathology in adolescence is explored in Chapter 9.

Oxytocin and Adolescence

In addition to activation of the HPA axis, stressors (particularly social stressors) also induce the release of other hormones such as oxytocin. This hormone is produced primarily in the hypothalamus and is released both into the blood (via the pituitary gland) as well as in a variety of brain regions that contain oxytocin receptors. Oxytocin is often viewed as a prosocial hormone, with increases in levels of this hormone induced by social stressors (Taylor et al., 2006) thought to increase subsequent motivation for social contact (see DeAngelis, 2008). Sensitivity to positive social stimuli may be increased by oxytocin as well, with administration of oxytocin reported to facilitate recognition of positive words related to relationships or sexual activities, but not negative words in these categories or positively valenced words unrelated to social stimuli (Unkelbach et al., 2008). Oxytocin levels are low in individuals with clinical disorders involving deficits in the processing of social cues, such as autism (Green et al., 2001), and children neglected early in life (orphanage reared) show less of an increase in oxytocin when interacting with their adoptive mothers than do non-neglected children (Fries et al., 2005).

Oxytocin plays a number of other roles as well. For example, it facilitates the birth process, and is released during breastfeeding to stimulate milk ejection, induce relaxation, and perhaps enhance mother–infant bonding (e.g., see Young & Francis (2007). Indeed, the release of oxytocin in response to positive social contacts is thought to "orchestrate" a relaxation response (Uvnäs-Moberg, 1997). Basic research has shown that oxytocin plays a key role in facilitating social behavior and social affiliation. When injected into the brains of laboratory animals, oxytocin facilitates pair bonding, whereas administration of a drug that blocks oxytocin receptors can disrupt pair bonding (Young et al., 2001). Intriguingly, when examining two closely related species of voles that vary in whether they are monogamous (Prairie voles) or promiscuous (Montane voles), the monogamous voles were found to have significantly more oxytocin receptor sites in several mesolimbic brain regions than their promiscuous counterparts (Young & Francis, 2007). Thus, at a very simplistic neural level, promiscuity seems to be driven in part by attenuated sensitivity to oxytocin in critical brain regions.

Intriguingly, the limited developmental data available show considerable maturation of the oxytocin system during the pubertal/adolescent period. The number of receptors for oxytocin increases notably between midadolescence and adulthood in a number of brain regions, including portions of the hypothalamus and mesolimbic brain areas important in social motivation and the recognition of social cues (Tribollet et al., 1989). Likewise, amounts of the mRNA template necessary for producing oxytocin increase 4- to 10-fold across the adolescent period (Chibbar et al., 1990). These increases in oxytocin mRNA were found to be dependent in part on pubertal-related increases in gonadal hormones, in that this increase was partially, though not completely, blocked by removing the gonads of animals prior to puberty. Together these data suggest that during adolescence and especially around the time of puberty, there is a marked acceleration in development of the oxytocin system—both in terms of substantial increases in the mRNA necessary to produce this hormone, as well as in the prevalence of its receptors. With the increasing emphasis on peer-based social affiliations and development of romantic relationships during the adolescent/pubertal period, there appears to be a marked increase in activity of oxytocin—a hormone critical for social affiliation and social bonding. The timing could not be more perfect.

Emotions and the Body: The Autonomic Nervous System and Vagal Tone

The notion of the importance of physiological sensations to emotional perception was taken to an extreme by William James and Carl Lange back in the late 1800s, when each separately proposed that it is the experience of these physiological changes that results in emotion (see Dalgleish, 2004). According to this perspective, you're afraid because you run, rather than running because you are afraid. A more modern version of this perspective is the "somatic marker hypothesis" of Damasio that postulates that the collection of bodily responses (somatic state) to a particular rewarding or aversive stimulus serves to signal probable consequences of actions involving that stimulus, influencing decision-making and behavior (e.g., Verdejo-Garcia et al., 2006). While not necessarily endorsing this hypothesis, per se, most researchers concur that emotional expression does include important physiological signs. Where there is less agreement among researchers is the extent to which these physiological sensations influence perception of emotional intensity or merely reflect bodily manifestations of the emotional reaction (e.g., see Dunn et al., 2006). Nevertheless, as we shall see, examining physiological concomitants of emotional expression provides important clues regarding adolescent-characteristic emotional expression, control of emotions, and their neural substrates.

Emotions and stressors exert physiological changes in the body via activation of the autonomic nervous system (ANS). This portion of the nervous system forms a critical life support system, connecting the brain with the organs of the body to monitor and regulate such things as HR, blood pressure and blood flow, respiration, digestion and other aspects of gastrointestinal function, release of some hormones, sweating, salivating, blushing, erection of the penis, and so on. The ANS consists of two components that often act in opposition. The first component is the sympathetic nervous system (SNS): This system, when activated, facilitates "fight-or-flight" reactions, increasing HR, and shunting blood flow away from smooth muscles in the stomach/intestines that facilitate digestion to skeletal muscles that support action. In contrast, activation of the parasympathetic nervous system (PNS) subserves critical functions of rest, relaxation, growth and recovery, slowing HR, lowering blood pressure, facilitating digestion, suppressing activity, and conserving metabolic resources. Together these two components of the ANS rapidly (and often automatically) prepare the body for dealing with a wide variety of challenges, ranging from mild to life-threatening, and help the body recover thereafter.

PNS information is communicated from the brain to the periphery via the vagal system. The vagus normally exerts some level of inhibitory control, called "vagal tone," on peripheral organs such as the heart. Thus, stress-, arousal-, or excitement-induced increases in ANS activity can be mediated not only by increases in SNS activity, but also by decreasing activity of the vagal "brake" (vagal withdrawal). As a result, HR can be increased by vagal withdrawal, without having to resort to more metabolically costly increases in SNS activation (Porges, 2001). Baseline levels of vagal tone are important in that they have been associated with temperament differences, behavioral problems, and psychological disorders. For instance, low levels of vagal tone have been posited to increase stress vulnerability, in that individuals with a normally less active vagal system have a reduced capacity to alter their internal state, via vagal withdrawal, in response to stressors (Porges, 1995). Moderate vagal withdrawal during challenges has been suggested to be associated with optimal levels of involvement and responsiveness, whereas extreme vagal withdrawal is thought to be associated with negative emotional experiences such as panic attacks and anger (Beauchaine, 2001).

The Contribution of Physiological Responses to Emotions in Adolescence

Primary questions of interest for our purposes here are: When do ANS systems mature? What do they reveal about the development of emotional capacities during adolescence? Overall ANS functioning changes during development, with notable developmental declines seen in basal HR (Quas et al., 2000). HR variability is often used as an index of PNS efficiency (vagal tone) and has been shown to increase developmentally throughout childhood and into adolescence, suggesting a possible increase in vagal tone into adolescence (Lenard et al., 2004). Although straying a bit to the issue of psychopathology that is examined in a later chapter, it is interesting that the lower vagal tone characteristic of individuals with conduct disorder is not evident among preschoolers, but instead only emerges in middle childhood and into adolescence (Beauchaine et al., 2007).

Along with alterations in basal HR and vagal tone, developmental increases in activation of these systems by stressors or other challenges may occur. Indeed, it has been suggested that normative developmental alterations in ANS function and emotional reactivity might increase stressor reactivity during the pubertal/adolescent transition (Spear, 2000a, 2003, 2009; Walker et al., 2004; Gunnar et al., 2009). Few studies have provided data pertinent to the evaluation of these hypotheses, although relevant findings are beginning to emerge. For instance, in two recent studies, clear developmental increases in responsiveness to stressors were seen when examining activation of the ANS (Stroud et al., 2009) as well as the HPA stress axis (Gunnar et al., 2009; Stroud et al., 2009). Adolescent-associated increases in stressor sensitivity were evident in both studies in terms of increases in CORT levels and alterations in autonomic reactivity, although the specific autonomic measures affected varied across studies and stressors. Indeed, there may be intriguing differences in responsivity of different components of the ANS during development. For instance, in the study by Gunner et al. (2009) examining the cardiac response of 9- to 15-year-olds to social stressors, developmental changes emerged across this age span only in indices reflecting stress-induced alterations in SNS, but not vagal tone. In contrast, the vagal system was found to play a more prominent role in regulating physiological responses to stressors during adolescence than in adulthood in a study in laboratory animals where increases in HR induced by aversive stimuli were found to be associated with vagal withdrawal in adolescents, but with SNS activation in adults (Kurtz & Campbell, 1994). Thus, although there is increasing evidence that stress reactivity of the HPA and ANS increases during adolescence and may vary from the reactivity seen in adults, there are still many mysteries to solve regarding how different components of the ANS contribute to the dynamic changes in autonomic activity and reactivity to emotional stimuli seen during development.

But how do these changes in ANS functioning alter/reflect emotional functioning during development? As discussed earlier, there is evidence, albeit mixed, that emotion-specific patterns of autonomic and hormonal activation may serve as feedback cues to influence emotional perception (see Dunn et al., 2006). The few findings to date hint to the provocative possibility that these physiological responses to stressors and emotional challenges may not be as strongly linked to emotional expression during development as in adulthood. For instance, a study examining cardiovascular reactivity in response to emotional stimuli found "at best minimal associations between children's cardiovascular reactivity and emotional expressions" (Quas et al., 2000, p. 169), with children who showed greater cardiac reactivity (due to lower levels of vagal tone) displaying, if anything, a tendency to exhibit less behavioral evidence of negative affect/emotional distress to being punctured with a needle for blood collection. Likewise, the changes that Stroud et al. (2009) observed during the pubertal/adolescent transition in physiological responses to the stressors "were not mirrored by differences in *affective* responses to the stressors" (p. 62). Together these data raise the fascinating (albeit speculative) possibility that the ability to use physiological responses when attributing emotions may be very slow to develop, with children and adolescents displaying little evidence for a link between their physiological reactions and their perceived emotions. It is interesting that this seeming insensitivity to physiological cues may continue, to some extent, into adolescence, despite increases in the intensity of those cues resulting from pubertal- or age-related increases in autonomic (and HPA) reactivity.

Like the link between ANS activation and emotional attribution, the propensity to exhibit ANS responses in anticipation of emotional stimuli may also develop slowly. Indeed, as mentioned in Chapter 6, research using the galvanic skin response (GSR) as an index of ANS arousal in a gambling task found that children (8–10 years) and early adolescents (12–14 years) generated fewer somatic signs when anticipating punishment than older adolescents (16–18 years), whereas similar autonomic responses were seen to outcomes involving punishment at all ages (Crone & van der Molen, 2007). Thus, children and younger adolescents showed less anticipation of the future outcomes of their actions than did older adolescents, at least when that anticipation is indexed via changes in ANS activity.

Findings of alterations in the links between ANS and HPA reactivity and emotional anticipation and attribution during the adolescent transition perhaps should not be surprising, given evidence that brain regions critical for monitoring and regulating these physiological systems, like other brain regions sensitive to emotional and social stimuli, undergo considerable developmental change during adolescence. It is to these developmental changes that we now turn.

THE EMOTIONAL AND SOCIAL BRAIN OF THE ADOLESCENT

The adolescent brain differs from the more mature brain in its response to a variety of social and emotional stimuli. We start here with a discussion of a key region in the processing of emotional and social stimuli, including emotions in faces: the amygdala. Discussion then turns to fMRI studies relevant to a popular (although largely untested) hypothesis of a developmental dissociation during adolescence between an early maturing, possibly puberty-driven "affective" neural system and a later developing, inhibitory cognitive control system. Given the provocative—albeit speculative—suggestion that there may be weak links between physiological signs of emotional state and emotional attributions among children and young adolescents, developmental alterations in the brain systems interrelating ANS function and emotional perception will also be briefly discussed.

Face Perception, Emotions, and the Amygdala during Development

There has been a substantial focus on fMRI studies of brain regions activated when looking at faces and facial expressions. In one sense, this seems oddly specific—why faces? Why not fMRI studies of individuals looking at feet, or hands, or body shape, for that matter? A number of factors appear to contribute to the special emphasis on the neural processing of faces and facial expressions. Different brain regions are activated when perceiving faces than when looking at many other objects (e.g., Iidaka et al., 2001), at least in part because facial expressions provide an important external index of the emotional states of others. Indeed, facial expressions communicating specific emotions may convey not only affect information to others but, strangely enough, even to oneself. Asking individuals to physically move their facial musculature in ways commensurate with a specific emotional state (e.g., to purse the lips, furrow the forehead, draw eyebrows together) has been found to play a modest role in precipitating that emotional experience, as indexed by self-report as well as autonomic activation (e.g., Adelmann & Zajonc, 1989). Thus, facial expressions not only reflect, but also may sometimes contribute to, emotional state. Perhaps in part because of these dual roles, facial expressions serve as particularly sensitive indices of emotional reactivity and, indeed, are more strongly correlated with neuroendocrine and autonomic indices of emotional state than is self-report, per se (Lerner et al., 2007).

Given that the face often serves as an unusually sensitive window into inner emotional life, it is not surprising that even young infants are able to recognize facial expression, distinguishing among happy, sad, and surprised faces, for example, or between faces with different emotional intensities (Nelson & DeHaan, 1997). The adult-typical female superiority in recognition of facial expressions can be seen in infants as well as children and adolescents (McClure, 2000). Yet, despite the early ability to detect facial expressions, notable improvements in the capacity to recognize emotions from facial expressions occur throughout childhood and into adolescence when indexed both in terms of accuracy and speed of recognition (Herba & Phillips, 2004; Tonks et al., 2007). There are even reports that early adolescence may be characterized by a temporary developmental decline in face recognition abilities, with young adolescents performing more poorly than children and adults (Carey et al., 1980; McGivern et al., 2002, as mentioned previously in Chapter 5). The rather astoundingly slow emergence of the ability to recognize faces and detect emotional expression may be related in part to the subtlety of cues necessary to detect differences in emotional expression. The acquisition of these subtle cues may begin, though, relatively early in development and may be influenced by early experiences. For instance, abused and maltreated children were better able to distinguish facial expressions of anger than nonabused children, while generally processing other emotional expressions in ways similar to children who were not abused (Pollak & Kistler, 2002).

The slow maturation of expertise in the detection of facial expressions is also likely influenced by developmental alterations in the processing of facial expressions by the brain. For instance, consider the results of a study examining patterns of electrical activity recorded from electrodes on the skull in response to different facial versus nonfacial stimuli (Taylor et al., 1999). Although some adult-typical ERPs were seen to faces (but not other objects) in children and adolescents, expression of other face-related ERPs were not seen in youth younger than 12 years of age. Even when face-specific ERPs characteristic of adults were seen at younger ages, they differed considerably from mature ERPs in their strength and timing, with over a three-fold change in ERP magnitude, for instance, and about a 25% decrease in latency from adolescence (12- to 14-year-olds) to adulthood. Although it is difficult to know the precise neural alterations leading to these notable developmental differences, these findings provide electrophysiological evidence consistent with cognitive findings of delayed development of facial emotional recognition, and provide evidence that such developmental delays are likely related, in part, to developmental changes in the neural regions responsible for the processing of faces.

Turning to those neural regions, a number of face-sensitive regions have been identified, some of which are especially sensitive to particular types of emotional expressions, whereas others are sensitive to perception of faces, per se. For instance, the fusiform gyrus, a region located near the bottom of the temporal lobe, is selectively activated in adults by faces (regardless of emotional expression), but not other objects, unless an individual has developed an expertise for those objects (e.g., dogs for a dog show judge or breeder) (Gauthier et al., 1999). In contrast, other brain regions selectively respond to the emotional content of faces; for example, the adult amygdala responds particularly sensitively (although not exclusively) to facial expressions of fear, anger, and other negative-valenced emotions (e.g., Whalen et al., 2001).

Even when considering basic face perception, adult-typical patterns of brain activation emerge only gradually. Selective activation of the fusiform face area emerges only gradually, with 5- to 8-year-old children not showing face-selective activation but 11- to 14-year-olds showing this selectivity. Fine-tuning of face-selective activation of the fusiform gyrus and other face-sensitive areas of the cortex continues throughout adolescence, with increasingly selective and focal activation of face-sensitive regions occurring as individuals mature (Kadosh & Johnson, 2007). Given the slow maturation of processes involved in basic face perception, it is not surprising that the development of neural circuitry activated during detection of emotions in faces is at least as protracted.

Among the brain regions thought to play a critical role in the processing of emotional stimuli, including emotions conveyed via facial expressions, is a prominent group of subcortical nuclei that have been collectively termed the amygdala. This region is thought to be involved in the processing of, learning about, and remembering circumstances regarding emotional stimuli (especially stimuli inducing fear and other negative emotions) (Dalgleish, 2004; Zald, 2003), as well as in mounting defense responses (Deakin & Graeff, 1991) and processing social signals of emotion (Amaral et al., 2003). The amygdala contains receptors for various hormones that contribute to socioemotional expression—hormones such as estrogen and other sex hormones, CORT, and oxytocin (see LeDoux, 2007). The amygdala is sensitive not only to the emotional "juices" of the brain but is also responsive to emotional information, particularly aversive stimuli, conveyed via diverse sensory modalities (e.g., verbal tone, speech, touch, smell, vision). Particularly well studied in adults via fMRI investigations is amygdalar activation in response to emotions conveyed via facial expressions, again with aversive stimuli often reported as being particularly effective in activating the amygdala (see Zald, 2003).

A recent explosion of research has examined activation of the amygdala in response to emotional faces during adolescence. A number of these studies has reported greater amygdalar activation to fearful faces in adolescents than adults (Killgore et al., 2001; Monk et al., 2003; Guyer et al., 2008), or than both children and adults (Hare et al., 2008). Exaggerated amygdalar responses to emotional, relative to more neutral, facial stimuli are not always found among adolescents, however; some studies have reported equivalent levels of amygdalar activation to fearful faces among adolescents and adults (Pine et al., 2001; McClure et al., 2004; Deeley et al., 2008) or even greater amygdalar activation to fearful faces in adults than young adolescents (Thomas et al., 2001b). This diversity of findings across studies perhaps should not be surprising, given that amygdalar responses habituate rapidly, and studies have differed in test circumstances and in the emotional and nonemotional comparator stimuli used (remember that an fMRI examines changes in signal intensity in response to target stimuli relative to the response to control stimuli, so the nature of the control stimulus is essential). Moreover, basic research has shown that the amygdala consists of a variety of distinct subregions with different network connections and sometimes opposing functional effects (Swanson & Petrovich, 1998). These dissimilar subregions may be differentially tapped by variations in scanner strength and in the coordinates used to target the amygdala across studies (Zald, 2003).

Findings of greater emotion-precipitated amygdalar activation under some circumstances (e.g., when passively viewing faces with fearful emotional expressions) have been proposed to reflect an increased sensitivity of adolescents to the emotional properties of social stimuli (Monk et al., 2003; Nelson et al., 2005; Hare et al., 2008). This exaggerated emotional sensitivity may be related to reduced proficiency in speed of response to those stimuli. That is, amygdalar activity was correlated with slower reaction times to fearful faces in a go/no-go task (i.e., a task in which participants were asked to respond with a button push to faces displaying a particular facial expression but not to those with other expressions), with adolescents overall exhibiting slower response times than adults to fearful but not happy faces (Hare et al., 2008).

When considering the impact of emotion-related amygdalar activation in adolescence, it is important to consider how this region interacts with other brain areas in processing emotional stimuli. Indeed, as we shall see, a number of theories have emerged relating increases in emotional reactivity among adolescents to developmentally changing interrelationships between neural activation in cortical versus limbic (amygdalar) regions.

The Amygdala, Its Connectivity, and Adolescent Development

All areas of the amygdala receive some input from cortical regions, although more lateral regions (e.g., the basolateral nucleus of the amygdala [BLA]) provide the predominant entry point for sensory information (relayed from sensory areas of the cortex and thalamus) into the amygdala. Lateral regions also receive input from the hippocampus and receive and transmit information to the OFC and other ventral PFC regions. In contrast, central portions of the amygdala, such as the CeA, collect and process information from other amygdalar regions and serve as the major output for the amygdala, with prominent projections to a variety of subcortical regions, including hypothalamic and brainstem areas that control attention/arousal, emotion-related behaviors (e.g., immobility/freezing), hormone release, ANS activity, and so on (Armony

& LeDoux, 1997). As predicted by these anatomical connections, information from the PFC, including more dorsal and lateral regions of the PFC that do not directly project to the amygdala, may modulate the processing of emotional stimuli in the amygdala via influencing projections from the ventral PFC to the BLA. In contrast, emotion-related alterations in ANS activity seemingly are driven, in part, from amygdalar outputs generated via the CeA.

What is the state of amygdalar development and its connectivity with other brain regions during adolescence? The fMRI emotional perception data discussed earlier, showing adolescent-typical changes in amygdalar reactivity to emotional stimuli, are complemented by other data suggesting continued development of the amygdala throughout adolescence. As a matter of fact, developmental changes in the amygdala seem to play a critical role in the triggering of puberty during adolescence. It has long been known from animal studies that the amygdala is one of the rare forebrain regions where damage can markedly alter the timing of puberty, although both lesion-induced pubertal delays as well as precocious puberty have been reported (see Moltz, 1975), perhaps because of differential damage (across studies) to amygdalar subregions with opposing functional influences. Structural MRI studies have shown volume increases in the amygdala throughout adolescence in humans (Yurgelun-Todd et al., 2003), with basic research demonstrating puberty-associated increases in relative size of some specific amygdalar regions, and decreases in others (Romeo & Sisk, 2001). Amygdalar volumes were found to be correlated with amount of aggressive behavior among adolescents (Whittle et al., 2008a). These individual differences were interpreted as potentially reflecting predispositions for sustained negative affect, and vulnerability to affective and other psychological disorders whose incidence increases during adolescence, a topic to which we turn in Chapter 9. Develop-

177

mental changes in not only amygdalar volume but also in its connectivity are seen during adolescence, with anatomical studies showing that excitatory input from the BLA to the PFC, for instance, undergoes rapid elaboration during adolescence in a rodent model (Cunningham et al., 2002, 2008). Such continued development of connectivity throughout adolescence illustrates the importance of viewing amygdalar development within broader networks of interrelated brain regions.

Socioemotional Brain Systems in Adolescence

Many brain regions contribute to the processing, production, and utilization of emotional stimuli and their social ramifications, although, as is the case with all complex neurocognitive functions, much remains to be studied, argued, and resolved regarding the nuances of the involvement of particular regions and networks in these multifaceted processes. To guide this research, a number of models of how the brain processes emotional and social stimuli has been developed. Most such models include at least two contrasting systems thought to contribute to different aspects of socioemotional processing; although bearing basic similarities, the names assigned to these systems, their precise functions, and component brain constituents vary somewhat across models.

One system—varyingly termed ventral, affective, somatic marker, or bottom-up—is generally thought to involve identification and processing of emotional stimuli and social stimuli with emotional significance, along with the production of emotional affect. Structures typically attributed to this system include: (1) regions sensitive to somatic states such as the amygdala and insula; (2) the ventral striatum (i.e., NAc), a critical component of brain reward systems that receives substantial attention in Chapter 8; and (3) somewhat more controversially, ventral regions of the PFC and ACC (see Chapters 6 and 8) (e.g., Phillips et al., 2003; Killgore & Yurgelun-Todd,

2007; Wright et al., 2008). In contrast, processes involved in the integration of affective and cognitive information, and the inhibitory regulation of emotional responsiveness have been ascribed to a dorsal, cognitive, or top-down system consisting of the hippocampus and dorsal regions of the ACC and PFC. These two systems often are reciprocally activated, with the cognitive subdivision generally less active when the affective subdivision is activated, and vice versa (Bush et al., 2000). As suggested by the terms *bottom-up* and *top-down*, such inverse activation patterns have been interpreted to reflect a dynamic in which cognitive control processes associated with activation of sites in dorsal and lateral regions of the PFC exert top-down inhibitory influences on the stimulus-driven and often more automatic bottom-up emotional attribution processes that are located deeper in the frontal cortex (e.g., ventral PFC; OFC) and in subcortical regions such as the amygdala (Lewis & Stieben, 2004; Nelson et al., 2005).

One problem with the notion of a dorsal-PFC-based top-down regulation of the amygdala is anatomical evidence that there are few, if any, direct connections from dorsal regions of the PFC to the amygdala. There are, however, indirect connections through other brain regions, especially the ventral PFC; thus, portions of the ventral PFC may be critical for exerting top-down regulation over the amygdala and hence could be considered part of the top-down cognitive, rather than bottom-up affective, system. And, indeed, reciprocal patterns of activation have sometimes been reported between the ventral PFC and the amygdala (Quirk & Beer, 2006)—findings used to support a cognitive, top-down role of these ventral regions in the regulation of subcortical affective (Johnstone et al., 2007) and reward (e.g., Ernst et al., 2005; Casey et al., 2008) circuitry (see Chapters 6 & 8). Yet, under the test conditions used in other studies, ventral regions of the PFC were found to be activated under similar circumstances as the amygdala, data more consistent with the involvement of ventral PFC regions in the bottom-up affective system (e.g., Nelson et al., 2005). Clearly, more work is needed to dissect the role of ventral PFC regions in contributing to functioning within each of these systems under different test circumstances.

Adolescent Brain and Emotions: Bottom-Up before Top-Down Processing?

Intriguingly, these two socioemotional systems may mature at different rates and may play a major role in driving adolescent immaturities in emotional reactivity. Hypotheses of this nature have been generated by a number of research groups and can be summarized as follows: During adolescence, early emerging affective brain systems predominate, resulting in a bias for bottom-up emotional processing that gradually loses its competitive advantage with the emergence of more slowly developing dorsal, top-down cognitive regulatory systems (e.g., see Hare et al., 2008).

Although providing very general support for the notion of a developmental dissociation between bottom-up and top-down systems, fMRI studies of emotional development have yielded mixed findings, with some data consistent with this developmental model and others not. For example, in an emotional risk-taking task predicted to reveal conditioned development of regulatory cognitive control systems, adolescents were found to exhibit more activation than adults in one "affective" region (ventral ACC) but not another (e.g., amygdala), whereas they displayed less activation than adults in both dorsal ACC as well as certain ventral PFC regions (Eshel et al., 2007). In a study examining 8- to 50-year-old males, decreases in activation in the dorsomedial PFC and insula in response to negative emotions were seen with age, although, again, no age-related differences were seen in amygdalar activation in response to fearful faces (Deeley et al., 2008). Other examples of variations

180

in emotion-related reactivity of the adolescent amygdala across studies were discussed earlier. Thus, whereas the model of adolescent-typical prevalence of bottom-up processing would predict greater amygdalar activation in response to fearful faces in adolescents than adults, findings range across studies from reports of greater, less, to no differences in amygdalar activation in adolescents relative to adults.

Developmental differences in patterns of brain activation to emotional stimuli do appear to have functional relevance, with several studies showing associations between brain activation patterns and cognitive, emotional, or social performance measures. For instance, in an fMRI study of children, adolescents, and adults, greater amygdalar activity was found to be associated with slower reaction times to fearful stimuli, whereas activity in the ventral PFC was correlated with faster reaction times (Hare et al., 2008). Likewise, in an fMRI study using a fearful face perception task, activation in the amygdala, insula, and ventromedial PFC was found to be inversely correlated with indices of emotional and social capacities in a group of 8- to 15-year-olds (Killgore & Yurgelun-Todd, 2007). Keeping in mind that these activation differences are not necessarily causal, it is nevertheless interesting that elevated activity in a more affective bottom-up neural system often predicts poorer affect-relevant performance during development.

Although the hypothesis of a bottom-up affective system that predominates during adolescence prior to the emergence of a later maturing top-down cognitive regulatory system is logically appealing, the model has just begun to be tested, and as we have seen, the findings to date are often complex and mixed. This diversity is to be expected. Brain activation patterns to emotional stimuli among individuals of different ages are likely to be influenced by critical but sometimes subtle details of the test conditions and contexts, a number of which were discussed in Chapter 5. A strategy used by some researchers to complement assessments of stimulus-induced activation in particular target regions is to examine patterns of functional connectivity across regions—that is, which regions tend to be active together. As one example, consider a study by Grosbras and colleagues (2007) in which young adolescents were found to show increased fMRI activation to angry hand movements and facial movements in the premotor cortex and dorsolateral PFC, regardless of whether they showed high or low resistance to peer influences (Grosbras et al., 2007). Those adolescents who were resistant to peer influences, however, showed stronger correlations of activity among these and related brain regions than their peers who were susceptible to peer influences, suggesting that the greater self-control seen in influence-resistant youth is associated with more coordinated brain activity and enhanced neural interactions among brain regions involved in processing emotional stimuli and in planning and executing behavior.

A number of factors may complicate easy confirmation of the hypothesized developmental disparity in emotion-precipitated activation of bottom-up affective versus top-down regulatory systems. Indeed, important nuances included in the more detailed models developed by different researchers are lost in the simplified developmental model presented here. Neural responses to emotional stimuli are influenced not only by age but also by sex differences, nature of the task, emotional stimuli used, and laterality of the observed response. Dissecting these influences may be central to our understanding of the differences in age-related patterns of brain activation to emotional stimuli seen across studies. Consider first the issue of brain laterality. Laterality has long been thought to play a critical role in the brain processing of emotion, with the right cortical hemisphere traditionally thought to be more involved in holistic thinking, creativity, and the processing of emotions, in contrast to a left hemisphere more specialized for analytical judgments. As fMRI data have accumulated, however, it has become clear that emotional and stressful stimuli do not activate only the right hemisphere (Wager et al., 2003; Cerqueira et al., 2008); both left- and right-specific cortical and subcortical activation in response to emotional stimuli have been reported across different studies, laterality that is modulated by factors such as sex, age, and type of emotion. For instance, some studies have found regions of the right PFC (and right amygdala) to be more active during the processing of negative emotions, whereas the left PFC is particularly associated with positive emotions, with individual differences in the relative bias of left versus right PFC regions influencing overall affective style (Davidson, 2000).

Another significant consideration that might add diversity to observed age differences in brain activation patterns in response to social and emotional stimuli is the issue of task demands. For instance, emotional content, per se, was found to be critical for driving activation in affective bottom-up regions such as the amygdala and OFC in adolescents, whereas activation in these regions in adults was more influenced by task-related attentional demands within the emotion-laden test situation (Monk et al., 2003). Other potentially complicating factors are age-related differences in the overall amount of task-related brain activation. Similar to studies of the cognitive processing of nonemotional stimuli (see Chapter 5), the amount of the brain that is activated when processing emotional stimuli is often greater during adolescence than in the mature brain, even when behavioral performance is comparable across age (see Nelson et al., 2003). For instance, in a study examining ERPs recorded from the scalp of 5- to 16-year-olds performing an inhibitory go/no-go task under emotional test circumstances, cortical activity associated with inhibitory control became more limited and focally localized to PFC regions with age (Lewis et al., 2006). Thus, detection of age-related differences in which brain regions are recruited when confronted with socioemotional stimuli can be complicated by generally more widespread and less focal activation patterns in adolescents than in adults.

Puberty as a Trigger for Bottom-Up Affective Brain Systems: A Hypothesis

Puberty may be another important player. A relatively common theme among researchers in the field is the hypothesis that the early emergence of bottom-up emotional processing is driven by pubertal hormones (e.g., Dahl, 2001; Nelson et al., 2005; Casey et al., 2008). Indeed, some of the brain regions associated with the affective system, particularly portions of the amygdala, contain receptors for estrogen and testosterone (see Stevens, 2002), and hence activity in these regions seemingly would be modified, perhaps dramatically, by puberty-associated increases in gonadal hormones with receptor-mediated excitatory actions. Given the differences in the gonadal hormones that are released between males and females and the often notable sex differences in the timing of puberty, it would be expected that the timing and nature of some of the patterns of bottom-up emotional processing might differ between the sexes, and could contribute to the notable sex differences in incidence of affective disorders that emerge during adolescence, a topic explored in Chapter 9.

This suggestion of an increase in excitatory drive to the affective bottom-up emotional system triggered by puberty-related rises in sex hormones is reminiscent of the notion of "hormone-crazed" adolescents long evoked by the media and parents to explain adolescent behavioral peculiarities. This hypothesized pubertal bias toward bottom-up emotional processing contrasts with the second part of the hypothesis: that the later development of top-down regulatory systems is little influenced by pubertal hormones. Despite their appeal, experimental support of these hypotheses is relatively limited to date. There have been few attempts to systematically test either hypothesis, perhaps in part because of difficulties in convincingly dissociating age and pubertal effects in human studies (an issue raised in Chapter 3). And, even in basic science studies where gonadal hormonal action on affective brain regions has been shown to influence social behavior in adult animals, relatively few studies have explored the impact of pubertal hormonal manipulations on social and emotional behavior during adolescence (see Romeo et al., 2002; Schulz et al., 2009).

Adolescent Brain, Emotions, and the ANS

Many of the same brain regions identified as important components of socioemotional networks are sensitive to feedback cues associated with activation of the ANS and HPA and help regulate activation of these physiological and hormonal systems in response to social and emotional stimuli. There are receptors for the stress hormone CORT in the amygdala and PFC (Pryce, 2008), as well as for prosocial peptides such as oxytocin in the amygdala (Huber et al., 2005), and both regions have been shown to influence hypothalamic areas critical for regulating hormonal and autonomic responses to emotional stressors (Saper, 2004; Radley et al., 2006). Connections from these regions to the hypothalamus and other brain regions involved in autonomic and HPA control, however, are often indirect—that is, relayed through other brain regions (e.g., an area given the imposing name of the *bed nucleus of the stria terminalis*, which, along with the CeA and medial amygdala, forms part of a related group of structures termed the *extended amygdala*). Although the roles of these regions in the modulation of stress responses have yet to be detailed completely, in general, projections from the amygdala (CeA and medial amygdala) as well as ventral PFC regions facilitate HPA and autonomic stress reactions, whereas projections from more

185

dorsal regions of the PFC (dorsal ACC, dorsomedial PFC) are important for inhibiting stress responses (Herman et al., 2005; Radley et al., 2006). Thus, to the extent that emotional stimuli induce elevated activity in affective bottom-up regions of the amygdala and ventral PFC during adolescence, it would be expected that adolescents might be predisposed to exhibit greater autonomic and HPA responses to stressful stimuli than adults. And as previously discussed, evidence has begun to emerge to support this perspective.

In this earlier discussion, however, recent evidence was also presented that hints that the ability to use feedback from physiological responses when attributing emotions may develop slowly, with individuals often showing limited evidence of a link between their physiological reactions and their perceived emotions during adolescence (e.g., Quas et al., 2000; Stroud et al., 2009). Given that the amygdala is among the brain regions thought to be important for detecting body state information when responding to emotional stimuli (Killgore & Yurgelun-Todd, 2007), these findings of possibly delayed development of interrelationships between ANS/physiological reactivity and emotion perception/anticipation seem inconsistent with reports of exaggerated activation of the amygdala by emotional stimuli under certain circumstances during adolescence. It is not simply the case that amygdalar activation is dissociated from ANS activity in adolescence: Activity in the amygdala induced by emotional faces (happy, angry, and fearful) has been reported to be significantly correlated with HR and related indices of overall ANS activity in adolescents, as observed previously in adults (Yang et al., 2007).

It may be that brain regions other than the amygdala play a particularly critical role in linking somatic and hormonal indices of emotional state to perceived affect, and that development in these regions may be relatively delayed. Indeed, as detailed in Chapter 6, when making risky decisions, adolescents have been reported to show less activation in a number of cortical regions—the vmPFC, insula, and portions of the ACC (Eschel et al., 2007)—thought to be critical for detection and interpretation of somatic states (see Dalgleish, 2004). It is not always the case, though, that these regions are generally inactive in young individuals. For instance, in an fMRI study examining responses to emotional faces of individuals from 8 to 50 years of age, age-related decreases in activation of the insula in response to faces displaying disgust were seen (Deeley et al., 2008).

These initial hints of an adolescent immaturity in the neural systems serving to link physiological/hormonal indices of emotions with emotional perception and anticipation need further confirmation before strong conclusions can be drawn. Nevertheless, should these initial indications of an adolescent dissociation between bodily feelings and emotional affect/anticipation be confirmed, such a dissociation could provide an important clue as to why adolescents often respond differently in emotional contexts than do adults, and could help direct research efforts toward determining the neural basis for these ontogenetic differences in emotional responding.

Stress, Emotions, and the Adolescent Brain: "Hot Cognitions"

As discussed in Chapter 6, adolescents sometimes reach less-than-well-thought-out decisions in the "heat of the moment," and this poor decision-making likely contributes to their increased risk-taking. Although adolescents do not have a monopoly on "hot cognitions" (i.e., decisions reached under stressful, arousing, emotionally charged situations), such heat-of-the-moment decisions seem particularly prevalent at that time (see Dahl, 2001). Research has shown that stressful and emotionally arousing situations generally tend to increase activity in the amygdala and other subcortical regions necessary for rapid and instinctive behavioral responses (hot cognitions), while often attenuating activity in the PFC regions critical for logical thinking and executive control ("cold cognitions") (Arnsten, 1998). These findings obtained in the mature brain can be easily mapped onto the developmental model of a neural bias toward bottom-up, over top-down, emotional processing during adolescence, as detailed above. According to this model, when adolescents are confronted with emotional situations that are arousing or stressful, they are prone to show greater activation in amygdalar and ventral PFC regions than in emotion-regulatory cognitive regions located in more dorsal regions of the PFC. To the extent that developmental increases in reactivity in affective bottom-up brain regions are related to increases in pubertal hormones, as hypothesized (e.g., Dahl, 2001; Nelson et al., 2005; Casey et al., 2008), hot cognitions and risk-taking behaviors would be expected to rise at puberty and gradually decline with the later maturation of more dorsal top-down regulatory PFC regions (see Dahl, 2004). As developmental research in this area escalates, it will be interesting to see the extent to which these appealing hypotheses are supported, qualified, and refined.

SUMMARY AND CLOSING COMMENTS

This chapter began with a consideration of how the social life and emotions of adolescents differ from that of other-age individuals, and then turned to outlining major neural components of the socioemotional brain and how activity in those regions varies in adolescence from that seen in the mature brain. Focusing first on amygdalar activation to emotional stimuli, followed by a consideration of other interrelated structures, a popular model of emotional regulatory development was then reviewed, with increases in emotion-induced activation of a possibly puberty-facilitated affective bottom-up brain system (including the amygdala, NAc and ventral PFC regions) hypothesized to develop earlier than a more slowly maturing cognitive top-down system located in areas of the dorsal PFC thought to exert inhibitory descending control over these affective regions. While often emphasizing neural systems involved in emotional attribution and regulation in this discussion, these regions overlap considerably with those systems involved with identifying and responding to social stimuli (e.g., Truitt et al., 2007)—a close juxtaposition that should be anticipated, given that many social situations provide our most intense emotional stimulation as well.

The jury is still out as to the accuracy of the simple developmental model that adolescents show a bias toward emotion-based activation of affective (bottom-up) over cognitive (top down) brain regions. As research to test this model continues, new complexities are likely to emerge. Many of the brain regions implicated in socioemotional systems are the same as those whose activity is recruited by other demands and situations, and hence these areas also receive prominent play in the discussions of age-related changes in cognitive function, risk-taking, rewards and drug abuse, and so on. As a result of this neural multitasking, the interrelationships between attribution of emotions and how that attribution colors other aspects of cognitive and behavioral functioning are likely to be complex indeed—and with a story line that changes developmentally.

Even if the basics of this simple model are confirmed, many intriguing questions remain. Is the adolescent amygdala hyperreactive to emotional stimuli because its sensitivity to emotional stimuli matures early and is not countered by sufficient regulatory control by still-immature dorsal PFC regions? Or is the adolescent amygdala hyperexcitable because of an immaturity characterized by an increased excitatory drive, perhaps driven by excitatory actions of pubertal hormones on estrogen and testosterone receptors in the amygdala? How do developmental alterations in stress-induced somatic (ANS) responses and activation of the HPA and prosocial peptide systems (e.g., oxytocin) contribute to adolescent-typical emotional reactivity? And how does all this relate to preliminary findings that such somatic responses are poorly related to emotional attribution in adolescence? That is, are adolescents carried away by their emotions in part because they are less able to use bodily sensations as a deterrent to overly emotional responding? As answers to these questions unfold, they will undoubtedly raise new sets of questions, while contributing to our understanding of how the brain supports the social and emotional transitions of adolescence.

CHAPTER EIGHT

Alcohol and Drug Use and Abuse

••

It is during adolescence that individuals typically first initiate drug use, with a majority of adolescents in the United States having tried alcohol by around 14 years of age (e.g., Johnston et al., 2008), and having engaged in some exploratory use of illicit drugs by late adolescence. For instance, according to data from the 2007 National Institute of Drug Abuse Monitoring the Future Study, 19% of 8th graders, 36% of 10th graders, and 47% of 12th graders have used one or more illicit drugs (Johnston et al., 2008). By the time adolescents reach their senior year in high school, 42% have tried marijuana/hashish, 46% have smoked cigarettes, and 72% have used alcohol; analogous percentages for 8th graders are 14%, 22%, and 39%, respectively.

Alcohol use by adolescents often reaches "binge drinking" levels, with 26% of 12th graders, 22% of 10th graders, and 10% of 8th graders reporting that they had drunk five or more drinks in a row within the past 2 weeks (Johnston et al., 2008). Although adolescents drink fewer times per week than do adults, when they drink, they drink over twice as much per drinking episode as adults (Substance Abuse and Mental Health Services Administration [SAMHSA] combined 2005–2006 survey data, 2008). Although cultural factors undoubtedly influence levels of alcohol consumption, high levels of binge drinking are not merely a characteristic of adolescents in the United States. Indeed, adolescent binge-drinking rates are notably lower in the United States than in a variety of European countries where initial exposure to alcohol (especially wine) typically occurs during meals within a family setting (Ahlström & Österberg, 2004). For instance, the 9% rate of binge drinking within the past month among 15- to 16-year-olds in the United States reported by Ahlström and Österberg (2004) contrasts with rates of 27% among the same age range in England, 25% in Sweden, 24% in Norway, 28% in the Netherlands, 32% in Ireland, and 28% in Germany. Clearly, initial alcohol exposure within a family meal setting does not protect adolescents from engaging in binge drinking when they are away from home and out with their friends.

Initial experimentation with alcohol and other drugs leads to dependence and abuse for some adolescents. In marked contrast to the prototypic image of alcoholism conveyed by a middle-age, skid-row drunk, the highest incidence of alcoholism in the United States occurs during adolescence. More specifically, using criteria for abuse and dependence on alcohol described in the American Psychiatric Association's *Diagnostic and Statistical Manual of Mental Disorders* (4th ed.; DSM-IV), rates of alcohol abuse and alcohol dependence were found to be highest among individuals in the 18- to 23-year range, followed by 12- to 17-year-olds, with incidence rates declining in the 20s and thereafter, reaching the lowest levels among individuals in their 50s and older (Harford et al., 2005). Although numerous individuals successfully disengage from patterns of excessive alcohol use following their transition into adulthood, not all are successful in doing so. Indeed, as we shall see, evidence is mounting that early initiation of alcohol/drug use is associated with a greater incidence of a variety of problems, including substance abuse, in adulthood.

Multiple factors undoubtedly contribute to the increased propensity of adolescents to use alcohol and other rewarding drugs, sometimes excessively. There is a significant genetic component, as we shall see. In one sense, underage use of alcohol or cigarettes or use of illegal drugs (e.g., amphetamines, cocaine, heroin), like other illicit activities, are risk-taking activities akin to those discussed in Chapter 7, and with many similar contributing factors. Thus, to some extent, adolescent drug use may be impulsive, and may reflect immature capacities for self-control. Indeed, the reason most often given for substance abuse among college students is for "fun/thrills" (Pfefferbaum & Wood, 1994). As is the case with other types of risk-taking, the environment is likely to play an important role via such influences as cultural standards, peer-group attitudes, and drug/alcohol accessibility. Yet, use of drugs and alcohol is more than a cultural phenomenon. Even in a simple animal model, adolescent rats voluntarily self-administer alcohol and other drugs, with their alcohol intake, for instance, often two or three times greater relative to their body weights than intake levels of adults (e.g., see Doremus et al., 2005; Vetter et al., 2007). As we shall see, alcohol, nicotine, and illicit drugs of abuse interact with the same reward circuitry that evolved for responding to natural rewards. Hence, developmental changes during adolescence in these brain reward systems and related systems that support learning about, and directing motivation toward, rewards may increase the propensity to experiment with drugs and alcohol and sometimes use them excessively.

Stressors experienced by the adolescent may also play a contributory role, with stressful experiences sometimes altering drug effects or the propensity for their use. Such stress–drug interactions may be particularly relevant for adolescents, given that, as discussed previously, adolescence is associated with a variety of stressful transitions and experiences, with the physiological impact of stressors perhaps increasing as well. Intriguingly, adolescents may differ from adults in their sensitivity to alcohol and other drugs in ways that may also contribute to elevated use patterns. That is, adolescents may show elevated levels of drug/alcohol use in part because they are more sensitive to the rewarding properties of these drugs, as well as less sensitive to their aversive properties. Thus, adolescents may use relatively large amounts of drugs or alcohol in part because they can—due to their reduced sensitivity to aversive consequences that normally serve to moderate use.

Consideration of individual differences is woven throughout these discussions. Although some experimentation with alcohol becomes normative by midadolescence, not all adolescents experiment with drug use, and of those who do use alcohol and other drugs, many do not develop problems with abuse. Thus, normative neural and other biological changes of adolescence are not usually sufficient to precipitate substance abuse problems. Rather, substance abuse problems are more likely to arise when these age-related physiological changes interact with various predispositions and vulnerabilities associated with the adolescent's genetic background, epigenetic regulatory influences, and other consequences of early experiences and current environmental circumstances.

BRAIN REWARD SYSTEMS AND ADOLESCENT ALCOHOL AND DRUG USE

From an evolutionary perspective, organisms need to be able to consistently locate conditions and stimuli critical for survival and reproduction, including food, water, warmth, shelter, sexual and other social stimuli. Survival is dependent not only on locating rewarding stimuli such as these, but also on avoiding aversive stimuli that could damage or kill—stimuli such as toxic foods, temperature extremes, predators, and other sources of potential injury (e.g., unstable supports, heights), as well as loud noises and other intense stimuli that could signal danger. Because the survival necessities of seeking positive stimuli and avoiding potential sources of harm hold for all organisms, it perhaps should not be surprising that the basics of the neurocircuitry modulating responsiveness to rewarding and aversive stimuli in humans bear substantial commonalities with those seen in a wide variety of other species. For instance, one particularly important component in the circuitry of reward is the DA system, with projections from DA neurons in the brainstem to dorsal striatum and the NAc seen not only in the brains of all mammalian species, including humans, but in nonmammalian vertebrates as well (Nesse & Berridge, 1997). Indeed, the neurotransmitter DA plays an important role in feeding behavior even in slugs (see Nesse & Berridge, 1997). Alcohol and other drugs used for their rewarding effects activate different portions of these ancient brain motivational systems, potentially "hijacking" these systems with repeated drug use to precipitate continued drug use, dependence, and cravings when the drug is no longer available.

Neural Substrates of Reward: Major "Players" and Potential Roles

Major components of the brain reward systems are shown in Figure 8.1. This interconnected network includes a number of brain regions that should be quite familiar from discussions in earlier chapters, given their involvement in other adolescent-typical behaviors and evidence of their remodeling during adolescence. A central component of the reward system has long been attributed to the NAc and its DA input from the VTA. The NAc also receives substantial excitatory (glutamate) input from ventral portions of the PFC (e.g., the OFC and ACC) and from limbic brain regions such as the amygdala and hippocampus.

195

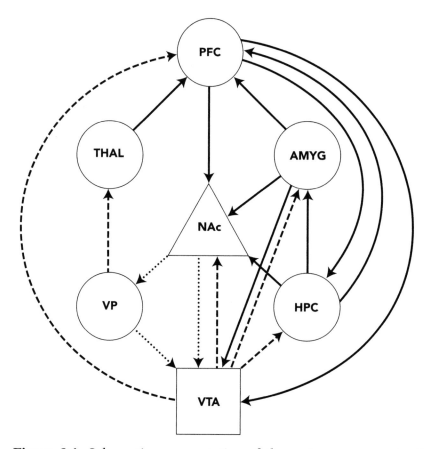

Figure 8.1. Schematic representation of the major components of the brain reward system. Pathways using the excitatory neurotransmitter glutamate are represented by solid lines. Pathways using the inhibitory neurotransmitter GABA are represented by dotted lines. DA pathways are represented by dashed lines.

PFC = prefrontal cortex; AMYG = amygdala; HPC = hippocampus; NAc = nucleus accumbens; VTA = ventral tegmental area; VP = ventral pallidum; THAL = thalamus.

Like the NAc, each of these reward-related regions also receives substantial DA input projecting from DA cell bodies located in the VTA in the midbrain; collectively, these DA projections to limbic and frontal cortical regions are sometimes referred to as the *mesocorticolimbic DA system*. In turn, the NAc projects back to DA cell body regions and to the ventral pallidum and other brain regions involved in directing emotional, hormonal, and behavioral responses to reward-relevant stimuli.

Although all rewarding stimuli ultimately interface with components of this neurocircuitry, they do not necessarily do so in the same manner. For instance, although blocking DA activity in the NAc decreases self-administration of most drugs, the reinforcing effects of opiates and alcohol are not always dependent on intact DA activity in that region (see Caine et al., 2007, for references). Moreover, when electrical activity in neurons in the NAc was recorded in response to food, water, or intravenous cocaine, the majority of neurons examined showed similar activation patterns in response to food and water, while showing very different patterns of activation to cocaine (Carelli, 2002). Thus, although all stimuli viewed as rewarding ultimately do so via interactions with portions of this reward circuitry, different rewards tap into this circuitry in unique ways, many details of which remain to be resolved.

Much of the challenge relates to the issue of how to relate specific aspects of reward-related processing to functioning within particular reward regions. That is, different regions of the brain may respond to a given reward stimulus when it is expected than when it appears unexpectedly, or when it is initially paired with a particular cue, or when it doesn't appear when it should have. Studies examining the effects of damage to particular regions or stimulation of those regions in laboratory animals have proved valuable in helping to unravel the ways in which different reward-related processes are modulated by the brain (e.g., see Baxter & Murray, 2002; Cardinal et al., 2002, for review). There is still considerable controversy, however, as to the role(s) of specific brain regions in attributing reward value to a stimulus, determining its motivational relevance, and guiding behavior to obtain the desired reward. To illustrate these controversies, let's consider DA projection systems—a central component long thought to play a critical role in reward. Much of the evidence for the involvement of

DA in reward-related processes has been based on animal studies, given challenges with imaging small DA cell body regions and detecting DA levels in human imaging studies. Although the rapid pace of technological improvements is rapidly removing these limitations (e.g., Kareken et al., 2004; D'Ardenne et al., 2008), studies using more invasive approaches with animal models will undoubtedly still be essential for disentangling the considerable intricacies between DA activity and the processing of rewards.

One important theory views DA projections to reward-related regions in the forebrain as being critical for mediating the positive affective value of rewards. According to this view, repeated drug use leading to addiction impairs the degree to which these DA systems are activated by natural and drug rewards, precipitating high levels of drug use in an attempt to compensate for this DA deficiency (e.g., Bowirrat & Oscar-Breman, 2005; Volkow et al., 2007). Other researchers have postulated essentially the opposite: that forebrain DA projection systems are not critical for mediating affective reactions to rewards ("liking"), but rather are critical for attributing motivational drive (*incentive salience*) to these stimuli. According to this theory, repeated drug use increases activation of these DA projections in the NAc, leading to increased "wanting" behavior—that is, drug craving—thereby elevating drug use (Robinson & Berridge, 2003). "Liking" responses, in turn, are postulated to be facilitated by opiate, cannabinoid, and other neurochemical systems in small "hot spots" within the NAc and other reward-relevant areas (Smith & Berridge, 2005). Yet other theories have focused on the importance of mesolimbic DA projections in learning about reward, citing work suggesting that DA release may be critical for "stamping in" reward learning and for notifying reward-related regions throughout the forebrain when expected rewards are not received, thereby serving as "teaching signals" for new learning in these regions (see Hollerman et al., 2000; Berridge, 2007). Thus, while disagreeing on many of the specifics, these theories all attribute crucial roles to DA projections to the forebrain in reward-related processes.

Generally speaking, forebrain components of reward-related networks integrate this DA input with other reward-relevant information, the contingencies under which the reward was obtained, or the internal state of the organism, and pass along these findings to the NAc and other regions within the reward network. For instance, the PFC is thought to process information about the reward significance of stimuli and alert the NAc, the amygdala, and other subcortical regions accordingly (Kelley et al., 2005), whereas the OFC appears to play a particularly critical role in modulating the motivational significance of rewards based on need state and status of conflicting rewards (see Hollerman et al., 2000; Berridge & Kringelbach, 2008, for review). Many of the specifics relating these neural regions and their interconnected networks to particular reward-related functions are still a matter of active debate and ongoing research, reminiscent of the continuing efforts to parse the varying roles of DA projection systems in reward function discussed above.

Adolescent Brain Transformations in the Neural Substrates of Motivation and Reward

There is substantial evidence from basic research studies that reward-related brain regions and their neurocircuitry are among the brain regions undergoing the most marked developmental change during adolescence. Consistent with the relatively delayed development of the PFC and other frontal regions (e.g., see Spear, 2007a), emergence of neurocircuitry interrelating the PFC and subcortical reward-related regions continues throughout adolescence. Excitatory (glutamate) projections from the BLA to GABA interneurons in the PFC are largely elaborated in adolescence (Cunningham et al., 2008), despite the overall decline in excitatory synaptic input to PFC at this time (see Spear, 2007a, for review and references). The number of DA projections to the PFC likewise increases into adolescence (Benes et al., 2000), as does the inhibitory control exerted by these DA inputs on the PFC (Tseng & O'Donnell, 2006). Downstream connections from the PFC to subcortical regions also continue to emerge during adolescence, with the number of PFC neurons (i.e., pyramidal cells) that project to the NAc, for instance, increasing significantly during adolescence (Brenhouse et al., 2008). The percentage of these PFC projection neurons that contain the D1 form of DA receptors (DRD1) peaks late in adolescence at levels considerably higher (40%) than at younger or older ages (4–5%). This finding is of particular interest given evidence that these PFC projections to the NAc are important for drug-seeking behaviors (e.g., Kalivas et al., 2005) and that DRD1 receptors in the PFC play a role in attributing reward value to drugs (see Brenhouse et al., 2008).

DA Systems in Adolescence

Evidence obtained from research in laboratory animals showing a transient rise in DRD1-containing pyramidal cells in the PFC during late adolescence and decline thereafter is reminiscent of recent findings from human autopsy material (Weickert et al., 2007). In that study, levels of mRNA for DRD1 receptors were observed to peak during adolescence and early adulthood (age range from 14–24 years) at levels significantly higher than in infants, children, and adults over 30. This peak in DA receptor gene expression in human PFC was specific to the DRD1 form of the receptor, and was not evident when examining expression patterns of DRD2 or DRD4. Post-peak declines in DA receptors in PFC during early-to-mid adulthood have also been reported in receptor binding studies in laboratory animals as well (Andersen et al., 2000).

Such relatively delayed pruning of DA receptors in PFC contrasts with earlier DA receptor elimination in subcortical regions. In the dorsal striatum, developmental increases during adolescence in levels of DRD1 and the D2 form of DA receptors (DRD2) are followed by a loss of one-third to one-half or more of these DA receptors during the transition from adolescence into young adulthood, with these declines evident both in human autopsy material and in studies using animal models (e.g., Seeman et al., 1987; Tarazi & Baldessarini, 2000; Teicher et al., 2003). A similar developmental rise and subsequent pruning of DA receptors has been reported in the NAc, although the pruning there is more modest, with a significant loss of about 20–35% of DRD1 and DRD2 receptors sometimes (Tarazi & Baldessarini, 2000; Andersen, 2002), but not always (e.g., Andersen et al., 2000), reported between early adolescence and young adulthood. Such inverted U-shaped patterns—characterized by receptor peaks in adolescence followed by later declines—have been particularly well-studied with DA receptors, but are evident with certain other receptor systems as well. For instance, levels of cannabinoid receptors—that is, the receptors through which delta-9-tetrahydrocannabinol (THC) and other cannabinoids in marijuana exert their actions on the brain—increase developmentally to peak throughout adolescence in striatum and limbic regions, declining thereafter to reach adult-typical levels (Rodriguez de Fonseca et al., 1993).

As impressive as the transient adolescent peaks in the density of DA receptors are, they have not proved easy to link to reward-related functioning of the adolescent. Part of the challenge is within the highly regulated DA system itself—that is, if one component of the DA system is altered, other portions of that system may partially compensate or even overcompensate in an attempt to restore balance. Thus, when exploring the significance of the adolescent-peculiar peaks in DA receptors, other components of the DA system also need to be considered. One approach that has been used to estimate overall levels of DA activity ("impulse flow") in particular DA terminal regions in laboratory animals is to lower probes into the brain to collect and analyze levels of DA outside neurons in a target brain region via a technique called *microdialysis*. Using this technique, basal levels of extracellular DA in the NAc (but not the striatum) were found to be lower early in adolescence than in adulthood, data interpreted to suggest that impulse activity in the DA projections to the NAc is immature early in adolescence (Cao et al., 2007). Likewise, using neurochemical measures to examine how much DA is made and how rapidly it is used (i.e., its "turnover"), DA synthesis and turnover in the NAc and dorsal striatum were found to be low early in adolescence and to rise during adolescence, whereas an opposite developmental pattern was evident in the PFC (e.g., Teicher et al., 1993; Andersen et al., 1997). When turning the focus to neurons receiving DA input in the NAc and striatum, neurochemical measures used to estimate baseline levels of DA impact on these neurons (i.e., DA "tone") were found to be two to seven times higher late in adolescence than in adulthood, with the PFC again showing an opposite developmental pattern (that is, higher basal DA tone in adults than in adolescents—Andersen, 2002). Elevations in basal DA tone, however, were associated with a lower functional response to activation of these receptors, which was evident neurochemically and behaviorally (Bolanos et al., 1998; Andersen, 2002).

What can be concluded from this mishmash of findings? First, age-related patterns of DA receptor density (e.g., peaking in early adolescence in the dorsal striatum and NAc) often contrast with neurochemical estimates of DA activity reflected in measures of impulse flow, turnover, and tone in these regions (where levels are generally higher later than early in adolescence). Secondly, when DA projections to the dorsal striatum and NAc are compared with DA projections to the PFC, opposite developmental shifts in indices of DA activity and tone are often seen. These opposite developmental patterns of DA activity in the PFC versus the NAc and dorsal striatum are reminiscent of the often reciprocal relationship seen between DA activity in these regions in adults (e.g., Wilkinson, 1997). Together these findings have led to the suggestion of a developmental shift in balance between these regions during adolescence (Spear, 2000a; Andersen, 2003), with functional levels of DA activity in the NAc and dorsal striatum low early in adolescence and increasing later in adolescence, at which time DA activity in the PFC is relatively low (see Spear, 2000a, for review).

As for how developmental alterations in DA projections to reward-relevant regions might influence drug use and other reward-related behaviors during adolescence, there are a number of possibilities, depending on which DA theory of reward you prefer. For instance, to the extent that late adolescence is characterized by DA hyperactivity in the NAc/dorsal striatum, this hyperactivity could be varyingly associated with increased incentive wanting (Berridge, 2007), or a greater sensitivity to natural/drug rewards (e.g., Volkow et al., 2007; Andersen & Teicher, 2008), or perhaps even unusual proclivities to associate environmental cues with drug use (e.g., Hollerman et al., 2000). Thus, although clearly DA projections to reward-related forebrain regions undergo meaningful and substantial alterations during adolescence that include a culling of up to 50% of the DA receptors in some regions, along with marked (two- to seven-fold) changes in regional DA tone, the question of how these marked changes influence the propensity of adolescents to initiate, use, and abuse drugs still remains.

Reward-Related Regions and Adolescence: fMRI Data

One rapidly escalating area of fMRI study has focused on whether human adolescents and adults differ in their regional brain activation patterns in response to anticipating and receiving rewards (or not receiving expected rewards) under varying levels of risk. Of the studies including adolescent samples that have been published to date, most have focused on signal changes in the NAc and in various regions of PFC. Although few in number, these fMRI studies of neural recruitment during reward have led to several theories of the neurobiology of adolescent reward processing that emphasize early developing and/or heightened subcortical (NAc) responses to rewards during adolescence, along with immature and more slowly developing behavioral control (supervisory) regions located in the PFC (Chambers & Potenza, 2003; Ernst et al., 2005b; Casey et al., 2008). A weak "harm-avoidant" system (amygdala) was added as a third component system by Ernst and colleagues (2005) as well.

Turning first to the PFC and frontal control, when making risky decisions, as discussed in Chapter 6, adolescents often have been shown to exhibit less recruitment in ventral regions of the PFC than adults (see Eshel et al., 2007, for review). Age differences in frontal recruitment may vary with the magnitude of the risk, with adolescents found to show less activation in a ventral portion of the ACC than adults when making moderately risky decisions, but similar levels of activation when threats of penalties were severe (Bjork et al., 2007). Such findings are reminiscent of other neuroanatomical and imaging data suggesting relatively delayed development of PFC control regions (see Casey et al., 2008, for review).

Adolescents, in contrast, sometimes shown greater NAc recruitment when receiving rewards than adults, although the findings to data are not unanimous on this point. For instance, reports that adolescents show greater (Ernst et al., 2005a) or exaggerated (Galvan et al., 2006) activation of the NAc when receiving rewards relative to adults contrast with other work showing no difference between adolescents and adults in NAc recruitment during receipt of rewards (Bjork et al., 2004). Possible differences in perceived reward value across studies potentially could contribute to these differences, given intriguing data from Galvan et al. (2006) suggesting that the relationship between NAc activation and reward magnitude normally seen in adults is exaggerated during adolescence, with adolescents showing more dramatic increases in signal change with larger rewards than adults, but tending to show weaker recruitment in response to small rewards. Age differences in NAc recruitment may also differ more during reward anticipation than upon receipt of the reward (reminiscent of the *wanting* versus *liking* distinction advocated by others—e.g., Berridge, 2007). For instance, Bjork and colleagues (2004) found that adolescents showed less recruitment of the NAc than adults when anticipating a reward, whereas both ages responded similarly to the receipt of the reward, per se, showing increased activation in both the NAc and the medial part of the PFC. These data were interpreted to suggest that "adolescents selectively show reduced recruitment of motivational but not consummatory components of reward-directed behavior" (Bjork et al., 2004, p. 1793).

There is some evidence, although correlational in nature, suggesting that the magnitude of NAc recruitment predicts excitement (Bjork et al., 2004, 2008) and positive affect (Ernst et al., 2005a) in response to receiving rewards, as well as levels of sensation-seeking (Bjork et al., 2008) and risk-taking (Galvan et al., 2007). These data support the notion that individual differences in hedonic responses to rewards and risky behaviors may be related to magnitude of reward-related recruitment of NAc, effects that are largely independent of age. Ernst and colleagues (2005a), however, reported that level of NAc recruitment correlated with positive emotion in response to a reward receipt only among adolescents, with adults showing a correlation between negative emotion and decreased amygdalar activation on trials involving reward omission. These data are reminiscent of work by van Duijvenvoorde et al. (2008), wherein brain regions were found to be recruited by positive feedback earlier than negative feedback; for instance, the dlPFC was activated more strongly by positive feedback in 8- to 9-year-olds, equally by positive or negative feedback at 11–13 years of age, but only by negative feedback in 18- to 25-year-olds. Likewise, Crone and colleagues (2008) observed that adult-typical increases in activation of the OFC, ACC, dlPFC, and parietal cortex in response to negative feedback developed only gradually, becoming adult-typical by 8–11 years of age in the OFC and by 14–15 years in the parietal cortex, whereas adult-like activation patterns to negative feedback were not still not evident in the ACC or dlPFC even at 14–15 years of age.

Taken together, these initial fMRI findings of reward sensitivity in adolescents suggest that adolescents may show (1) less NAc activation in anticipation of (when *wanting*?) positive rewards, (2) more recruitment in response to receipt of particularly compelling rewards (more *liking*?) under some circumstances than adults, and (3) greater sensitivity to positive, but less sensitivity to negative, feedback and rewards than adults. Although of course substantial more research is needed to confirm or reject such speculations, it is nevertheless interesting that studies examining reward sensitivity in simple animal models of adolescence in the rat have yielded some intriguing parallels to these speculations, a topic to which we now turn.

SENSITIVITY TO REWARDS DURING ADOLESCENCE

It would be astonishing, indeed, if developmental changes in reward-related regions of the brain and their neurocircuitry during adolescence were not associated with alterations in reward-related behaviors of the adolescent. Given challenges in disentangling the multitude of factors influencing behavior toward rewarding stimuli among adolescents, a variety of research groups have turned to studies in laboratory animals to systematically compare adolescents and adults in the motivational value they attribute to rewarding stimuli such as drugs, novelty, social peers, and so on. One approach often used in these types of studies is to examine associations formed between the rewarding stimulus of interest and a distinctive place—a form of conditioning termed *conditioned place preference* (CPP). During conditioning trials, exposure to the stimulus is paired with placement in a distinctive location (paired location); animals also receive equal exposure to a different location, but in the absence of the stimulus object. At the time of testing, animals are allowed to choose between the two locations, with no stimulus present. To the extent that the stimulus is rewarding, animals should spend more time on the side previously paired with that stimulus than spent by control animals who received the same amount of exposure during conditioning to both locations, but in the absence of the rewarding stimulus.

Such tests have often revealed stronger CPP for natural rewards during adolescence than in adulthood. Consider first social CPP: Adolescent rats were found to develop significant CPP for a location previously paired with a same-sex, same-age peer, even when the adolescents being conditioned were housed with other animals and hence not socially deprived (Douglas et al., 2004). In contrast, social CPP only emerged in adults that were housed alone—that is, deprived of social interactions except during conditioning episodes. Similar findings were found in adolescent and adult male rats in a study examining novelty CPP; conditioning in this situation involved exposing experimental animals to a new novel stimulus in the paired location on each training trial (Douglas et al., 2003).

CPP for drugs of abuse has been studied more extensively than natural rewards, with adolescents again often showing more robust conditioning than adults. For instance, adolescents have been reported to exhibit greater CPP to nicotine than adults (e.g., Vastola et al., 2002; Shram et al., 2006; Torres et al., 2008), and have often (e.g., Brenhouse & Andersen, 2008; Brenhouse et al., 2008; Zakharova et al., 2009a, 2009b), but not always (e.g., Campbell et al., 2000; Adriani & Laviola, 2003; Mathews & McCormick, 2007), been found to exhibit more robust CPP to psychomotor stimulants such as cocaine and methamphetamine as well. Although methodological difficulties make it challenging to use CPP to probe the motivational effects of ethanol during development in a rat model, other approaches are beginning to be used, with these studies providing initial evidence that adolescent rats may likewise find ethanol more motivationally rewarding than do adults (e.g., Pautassi et al., 2008; Ristuccia & Spear, 2008).

From these basic science studies, evidence is accumulating that adolescents seemingly attribute greater motivational value than do adults to a variety of different natural and drug rewards. To the extent that these data reflect developmental changes in evolutionarily ancient neural reward systems that have been conserved across species, an enhanced impetus to seek out rewarding stimuli could contribute to the avidity with which human adolescents seek out and use alcohol, nicotine, and other drugs, as well as seek out social peers and novel, potentially risky, situations. Yet, findings are beginning to mount that reveal another side to this story—that adolescents may exhibit an attenuated response to the aversive consequences of drugs—a topic to which we now turn.

ADOLESCENCE AND THE AVERSIVE CONSEQUENCES OF DRUGS AND ALCOHOL

Positive and negative rewarding stimuli may not represent opposite ends of the same continuum, but rather may be processed along separable dimensions. Whereas both positive and negative outcomes involve DA signaling to some extent (e.g., Klein et al., 2007), certain brain systems are differentially activated, with negative outcomes activating regions of the PFC and insula associated with negative emotional states (e.g., Bechara et al., 2002; Liu et al., 2007; see Chapters 6 and 7). Indeed, many stimuli have multiple consequences, some that are characteristically viewed as positive, and others, negative. As one example, very spicy foods may activate pain receptors but may also be viewed as pleasurable for their overall taste. Of particular relevance here, alcohol and other drugs are well-known for presenting a mixed profile of both positive and negative consequences—with the pleasurable tasting, positive rewarding, relaxing, anxiety-reducing, socially facilitating effects of alcohol, for example, contrasting with slurred speech, unsteadiness and other signs of motor impairment, sedation, nausea, and general dysphoria, not to mention hangover-related headaches, nausea, extensive thirst, and so on. Age-related changes in sensitivity to such aversive effects also could contribute to developmental differences in the propensity to use drugs and the amount of that use.

Differences across age in the aversive properties of drugs have been explored in studies in laboratory animal in a number of different ways. Place conditioning can be used to examine not only the positively rewarding effects of drugs, but their negative consequences as well. That is, at relatively high-exposure levels, drugs often induce conditioned place aversions rather than the CPP often evident at lower doses. Aversive internal consequences of drugs that are associated with consumption of particular foods or tastes often inhibit later ingestion of those substances, due to the undoubtedly adaptive propensity to develop taste aversions to substances inducing nausea and internal malaise. Using these approaches, adolescent rats have been revealed, even within the same experimental series, to demonstrate both greater CPP to low doses of nicotine but weaker place aversions at higher nicotine doses than adults (Torres et al., 2008), and to show stronger CPP but weaker conditioned taste aversions (CTA) for nicotine as well (Shram et al., 2006). An attenuated sensitivity of adolescents to the aversive effects of nicotine may extend to nicotine withdrawal as well, with adolescent rats showing less marked signs of nicotine withdrawal than adults (e.g., O'Dell et al., 2006; Wilmouth & Spear, 2006; Kota et al., 2007). Enhanced positive and attenuated negative effects may be seen to other drugs during adolescence as well. That is, in contrast to evidence of enhanced rewarding properties of alcohol and psychomotor stimulants such as cocaine and amphetamine during adolescence (Brenhouse & Andersen, 2008; Brenhouse et al., 2008; Pautassi et al., 2008; Ristuccia & Spear, 2008; Zakharova et al., 2009a, 2009b), adolescent rats have been found to be less sensitive than adults to both the aversive properties of alcohol (Anderson et al., 2008) and stimulants (Infurna & Spear, 1979; Schramm-Sapyta et al., 2006) when indexed via CTA. Adolescent rats have been reported to be less sensitive to aversive effects of THC than adults as well (Schramm-Sapyta et al., 2007).

Enhanced positive but attenuated negative effects experienced during adolescence may also be seen under some circumstances with natural rewards. For instance, using facial responses shown to reflect positive and negative affect reactions to sweet and bitter tastes, respectively, in species ranging from rats and nonhuman primates to human infants, adolescent rats were consistently found to exhibit enhanced positive taste responses to sucrose, but fewer aversive responses to the bitter taste of quinine, than adults (Wilmouth & Spear, 2009). Adolescents are even less likely than adults to form a CTA to a nonaddictive but aversive substance, lithium chloride (Schramm-Sapyta et al., 2006). Not all data are consistent with a simple shift in aversive–positive reward balance to natural rewards during adolescence, however (e.g., see Willey et al., 2009), which should perhaps not be surprising given that work in this area is just beginning.

Differential sensitivities to positive versus aversive effects of alcohol and other drugs could influence use/abuse propensity in at least two ways. First, in response to first use: that is, individuals experiencing largely negative drug effects when first trying a drug presumably would be less likely to want to use that drug again than if they experienced predominantly rewarding and pleasurable effects of the drug (see Kendler & Prescott, 2006). Also, alterations in the propensity to use large amounts of alcohol or other drugs may be influenced not only by how rewarding the substance is, but also by sensitivity to aversive consequences that likely serve as feedback cues to terminate intake. Indeed, Bechara and colleagues (2002) have suggested that whereas some drug abusers exhibited exaggerated processing of drug-related rewards, others are characterized by an attenuated sensitivity to aversive consequences; still others may exhibit impulsivity problems.

ADOLESCENT-TYPICAL SHIFTS IN ALCOHOL/DRUG SENSITIVITY AS RISK FACTORS FOR PROBLEMATIC USE

Adolescents may differ from adults not only in their sensitivity to the general rewarding and aversive properties of alcohol and other drugs, but also in their sensitivity to other drug effects that may also influence their risk for abuse and dependence. These effects have been particularly well studied in the case of alcohol, again with a focus on animal models of adolescence, given ethical constraints against administering alcohol to underage youth.

Such studies have revealed that adolescents are notably more sensitive than adults to a few restricted effects of alcohol. These unusual sensitivities include not only the positive rewarding properties of alcohol mentioned earlier (Fernández-Vidal et al., 2003; Philpot et al., 2003; Pautassi et al., 2008; Ristuccia & Spear, 2008), but also the socially facilitative effects of alcohol. That is, adolescent rats exposed to relatively low doses of alcohol markedly increase their social interactions—a social facilitation effect of alcohol that is not normally seen in adults (e.g, Varlinskaya et al., 2001; Varlinskaya & Spear, 2002; see Spear & Varlinskaya, 2005, for review). Ethanol-induced social facilitation has long been viewed as a critical component of drinking for human adolescents as well; for instance, a study of high school survey data concluded that "the most important factor across all of the measures of alcohol abuse was drinking for social facilitation" (Beck et al., 1993, p. 166).

Adolescent rats have also been shown to be more vulnerable than adults to alcohol-induced disruptions of a form of brain plasticity called *long-term potentiation* as well as to alcohol-related memory impairments (see White & Swartzwelder, 2005, for review). A similar enhanced sensitivity to the memory-impairing effects of alcohol has also been reported during (late) adolescence in humans; 21- to 24-year-olds who were trained and tested under the influence of a moderate (0.6 g/kg) dose of ethanol showed impaired performance on both verbal and nonverbal learning tasks relative to 21- to 24-year-olds who were given a comparably smelling and tasting placebo solution that did not contain alcohol. In contrast, 25- to 29-year-olds showed little sign of impairment in either task at this same alcohol dose (Acheson et al., 1998). Thus, even when comparing relatively late human adolescents with individuals several years their senior, enhanced sensitivity to the memory-impairing effects of alcohol was seen in late adolescence as has been observed and well characterized in basic animal studies.

Aside from these few restricted effects of alcohol, adolescents are notably less sensitive than adults to most alcohol effects. As discussed earlier, like other drugs, this insensitivity extends to the general aversive properties of alcohol as indexed via CTA (Anderson et al., 2008), as well as to hangover-related anxiogenic effects (Doremus et al., 2003). Adolescents are also less sensitive than adults to a variety of alcohol effects that may normally serve as cues to limit intake, including alcohol-induced motor impairment, activity suppression, social impairment, and sedation (see Spear & Varlinskaya, 2005, for review). This relative insensitivity can be pronounced. For instance, whereas adult animals are highly sedated from a high dose of alcohol and remain "passed out" for 8 or so hours, adolescent animals given the same dose recover in less than half the time—in about 3 hours (Silveri & Spear, 1998).

Studies to determine whether human adolescents might exhibit a similar insensitivity to these aversive and intoxicating effects of ethanol are extremely rare due to ethical issues associated with administration of alcohol to underage youth. There is, however, one older study by Behar and colleagues (1983) that did examine 8- to 15-year-old boys following an intoxicating dose of alcohol. After examining a variety of behavioral and subjective consequences of alcohol in these boys who were presumably undergoing their first experience with alcohol, the investigators noted that they "were impressed by how little gross behavioral change occurred in the children . . . after a dose of alcohol which had been intoxicating in an adult population" (p. 407).

The insensitivity of adolescents to many alcohol effects is not simply related to alterations in how quickly they are able to break down (metabolize) and eliminate alcohol from their brains and bodies. Overall metabolic rate, as well as rate of metabolism of alcohol and other drugs, tends to be elevated somewhat in adolescence (which may contribute in part to the seeming ability of many adolescent boys to eat prodigious amounts of junk food without gaining an ounce of fat). Yet, the slight elevation in the rate of alcohol metabolism sometimes seen in adolescents is insufficient to account for their attenuated sensitivity to so many alcohol effects. Rather, basic science studies have revealed that this relative resistance appears to result in part from very rapid adaptations within the brain, termed acute tolerance, which develops within a single alcohol exposure period. These brain adaptations to alcohol begin rapidly upon entry of alcohol into the brain and are much more pronounced in adolescents than adults (e.g., see Silveri & Spear, 1998; Varlinskaya & Spear, 2003).

If human adolescents are indeed relatively insensitive to many intoxicating effects of ethanol, why would it matter? On one hand, it could be argued that this attenuated sensitivity, although not sufficient to protect completely against overdose deaths, could partially protect adolescents from adverse consequences associated with moderately overimbibing alcohol. Yet, to the extent that adolescents are insensitive to alcohol cues that normally serve to moderate drinking, this may permit them to drink more, contributing to the comparatively high incidence of binge drinking seen during adolescence, and consistent with evidence discussed earlier that human and nonhuman adolescents drink twice as much alcohol per occasion, on average, than do adults. Higher levels of alcohol intake by adolescents during drinking episodes would lead to increased brain exposure to alcohol, possibly placing vulnerable adolescents on a trajectory for later problems.

Indeed, decreased sensitivity to the intoxicating effects of alcohol has been shown to be a risk factor for problematic alcohol involvement, with "a lower sensitivity to moderate doses of alcohol [being] associated with a significant increase in the risk of future alcoholism, perhaps through increasing the chances that a person will drink more heavily" (Schuckit, 1994, p. 184). A lowered sensitivity to alcohol intoxication is a major risk factor associated with a family history of alcoholism, with sons of alcoholics typically showing attenuated responses to the intoxicating and aversive effects of alcohol (perhaps along with an increased sensitivity to the euphoric/reward effects of ethanol) (e.g., Newlin & Thomson, 1990; Begleiter & Porjesz, 1999; Schuckit, 1994). A similar insensitivity to the aversive and sedating effects of alcohol are seen in rodent lines selectively bred for high levels of alcohol consumption (McBride & Li, 1998; Green & Grahame, 2008). A history of exposure to stressors also may attenuate the inhibitory effects of higher doses of alcohol, while enhancing alcohol-induced social facilitation and social motivation (Doremus-Fitzwater et al., 2007). Repeated use of alcohol likewise often induces chronic tolerance, which develops at least as rapidly (if not more rapidly) among adolescents than adults; such tolerance would further attenuate ethanol sensitivity (e.g., Varlinskaya & Spear, 2007).

Thus, developmental insensitivities to the aversive and intoxicating effects of alcohol normally seen during adolescence, when combined with genetic-based attenuations in alcohol intoxication along with insensitivities induced by stressful circumstances and/or tolerance associated with early and persistent alcohol use, could potentially act as triple or quadruple "whammies" to precipitate high levels of alcohol intake when genetically at-risk youth living in stressful life circumstances begin to drink—a pattern of elevated use and brain exposure to alcohol that could place them on a trajectory for later problems. The greater sensitivity of adolescents to alcohol-induced social facilitation may likewise encourage further drinking, given that most adolescent drinking occurs in, and is likely encouraged by, a social context (see Beck & Treiman, 1996). Together, these patterns of decreased and increased sensitivities to alcohol may serve as permissive factors to precipitate relatively high levels of drinking among vulnerable adolescents. Yet, at the same time, adolescents display unusual sensitivity relative to adults to the memory-impairing effects of alcohol and to alcohol-induced disruptions in brain plasticity—a disconcerting combination indeed.

Similar developmental patterns of altered drug sensitivities can be seen with other drugs as well. Particularly compelling is work showing that, although less sensitive to the aversive effects of cannabinoids such as THC (Schramm-Sapyta et al., 2007), adolescents are more sensitive to cannabinoid-induced impairments in cognitive performance (Cha et al., 2006) and display marked cannabinoid-induced social stimulation (see Trezza et al., 2008, for review)—patterns of developmental sensitivities strikingly similar to those seen with alcohol. More generally speaking, the developmental insensitivities to aversive, but enhanced sensitivities to rewarding, drug effects that are evident with a variety of drugs during adolescence likely contribute to enhanced drug/alcohol use at this time.

STRESS AS A PREDISPOSING FACTOR FOR ADOLESCENT ALCOHOL/DRUG ABUSE

Returning to what is now probably a familiar refrain, the adolescent period in humans is often associated with an increased overall exposure to stressors, particularly those stressors related to individual behavior and life choices (e.g., Gest et al., 1999), along with an increase in biological reactivity to stressors (see Walker et al., 2004, for an excellent review of this literature). Time to recover from stressors may also be greater during adolescence than in maturity, at least when indexed by time taken to restore baseline levels of CORT following stress-induced elevations in this hormone (Romeo & McEwen, 2006). Relative to the levels of dysphoria reported in children and adults, (Arnett, 1999) adolescence has been reported to be characterized by greater overall levels of negative affect (see Silberg et al., 1999; Rice et al., 2003). There is likely to be substantial individual differences among adolescents in amount of stressor exposure as well as in their vulnerability to stressors, due to genetic factors and the presence or absence of early adverse experiences (see Walker et al., 2004).

Stress is thought to play a significant role in the initiation and progression of drug abuse, and in relapse to drug-seeking behavior following withdrawal in dependent adults (see Koob & Kreek, 2007; Wand, 2008, for review). This relationship is also evident during adolescence, with perceived level of stress joining a number of other factors that predict use and abuse of alcohol and other drugs in human adolescents (e.g., DeWit et al., 1999). Indeed, in an older review of the human literature, stress was found to be more strongly associated with alcohol consumption among adolescents than adults, with the data substantially more mixed in adults (Pohorecky, 1991). Wagner (1993) concluded that the two most powerful predictors of adolescent alcohol/drug use were peer drug use and levels of perceived stress. The relationship between drug use and stress under many circumstances is likely bidirectional, with stress not only leading to increased drug use, but with drug use itself perhaps increasing stressful circumstances (e.g., Johnstone et al., 1997). A history of early life stressors may further increase vulnerability to stress-related drug problems during adolescence via long-lasting sensitization of stress response systems (Andersen & Teicher, 2008). Intriguingly, though, both increases and decreases in HPA reactivity serve as potential risk factors for developing substance abuse disorders. That is, HPA hyperactivity, as often occurs in adolescents with internalizing disorders, may mark overreaction to stressors, whereas the HPA hypoactivity sometimes seen in youth with externalizing disorders may represent underreaction to stressors, with both forms of HPA dysfunction associated with increased risk for substance abuse problems among adolescents (see Schepis et al., 2008). These intriguing differences in HPA axis function among adolescents with internalizing versus externalizing disorders are discussed in more detail in Chapter 9.

There are many intersections between the HPA stress axis and the reward-related brain regions that undergo developmental remodeling during adolescence. Novelty, drugs of abuse, and stressors induce HPA activation in both systems, increasing CORT levels, elevating DA activity (e.g., Piazza et al., 1991), and triggering similar synaptic adaptations in DA neurons (Saal et al., 2003). Receptors for CORT are found in reward-related regions, including DA neurons themselves, as well as the amygdala, PFC, and NAc (Piazza et al., 1991; Romeo & McEwen, 2006). Presumably via interaction with these receptors, stress-induced increases in CORT stimulate DA transmission in regions such as the NAc and PFC (Imperato et al., 1989; Piazza et al., 1996). Reward-relevant regions conversely influence stress reactivity as well, with activity, size, and functional connectivity in the amygdala, for instance, influencing responsivity to stressors (Gianaros et al., 2008).

Little is known about interrelationships between stressors and these reward-related systems during adolescence. CORT receptors are abundant in regions such as the amygdala and PFC during adolescence, suggesting that these regions are stress-sensitive (Romeo & McEwen, 2006). There is some evidence, however, of changes in the relative stressor sensitivity of different reward-related areas across developmental periods that include adolescence. A study examining brain regions activated by a chemical stressor in developing rats found that the stressor predominantly induced PFC activation in postpubertal rats, while more equivalently inducing activation of the PFC, NAc, and dorsal striatum in preadolescent animals (Lyss et al., 1999). In another study by the same group, adolescent rats were found to exhibit little stress-induced activation in a number of brain regions (e.g., the amygdala and ACC) that were quite sensitive to stressor activation in adults (Kellogg et al., 1998). Thus, although many of the details still await clarification, there is reasonable support for the speculation that developmental changes in stress-sensitive, reward-related brain regions during adolescence likely contribute to stress-exacerbated propensities for use and abuse of drugs by adolescents.

GENETICS AND ADOLESCENT DRUG USE

The results of twin studies have consistently shown relatively large genetic contributions to the vulnerability for developing substance abuse disorders. For instance, heritability estimates for development of alcohol dependence or abuse or nicotine dependence are generally in the range of 50–60%, with estimates of the genetic contribution to overall risk for abuse/dependence of any illicit drug in the range of 60–80% (Kendler & Prescott, 2006). Of course, what is inherited is a vulnerability for developing problematic use—a vulnerability that may never be challenged if individuals with genetic predispositions never try drugs. Indeed, it is possible that different genetic risk factors might contribute to the probability of initially deciding to try the drug versus the propensity to develop abuse once use has been initiated. The story here seems to vary for alcohol versus illicit drugs. For instance, when genetic contribution to the initiation of illicit drug use and progression to abuse/dependence was examined in the twin studies reported by Kendler and Prescott (2006), these researchers concluded that "although there clearly are genes whose only action is to alter the risk for progressing to abuse or dependence after first trying a drug, the bulk of the genetic risk factors act at both stages" (Kendler & Prescott, 2006, p. 233). Indeed, about three-fourths of the genetic contributions in their study were found to affect both the probability that individuals will initially try an illicit drug as well as their propensity to develop abuse/dependence with continued use.

In contrast, initiation of alcohol use appears to be less influenced by genetic factors, with heritability rates varying across studies from essentially zero (e.g., Rose, 1998) to about 25% (Fowler et al., 2007); onset of alcohol use seems to be particularly influenced by environmental effects such as sibling and peer influences, amount of urbanization, and other regional differences (see Rose, 1998). However, once drinking is initiated, heritability rates of about 55–65% have been estimated for drinking frequency and the amount drunk per drinking episode (Rose, 1998; Fowler et al., 2007) as well as the risk for alcohol abuse/dependence (Kendler & Prescott, 2006). Thus, in the case of alcohol, initiation of use and progression to later use seem to be regulated differently, whereas genetic similarities contributing to both initial use and dependence are stronger for illicit drugs (Kendler & Prescott, 2006; Fowler et al., 2007) as well as nicotine (Fowler et al., 2007). Nevertheless, twin studies have revealed considerable overlap in the genetic liability for developing dependence on alcohol versus other drugs. These common genetic influences across drugs appear to be largely shared "through a general predisposition toward externalizing disorders, which may manifest in different ways" (Dick & Agrawal, 2008, p. 112), with some individuals abusing drugs or alcohol and others displaying conduct disorder or other sorts of antisocial behaviors (see Chapter 9).

Although twin studies of heritability provide valuable information regarding the relative genetic contribution to initiation of drug/alcohol use and propensity for abuse, such studies provide no insight as to the specific genes involved. The task of identifying such genes is somewhat daunting because of the multitude of genes likely involved. In an integration of data from all studies from 1976 to 2007 that examined links between addiction and specific genes or particular chromosome regions, Li and colleagues (2008) identified 1,500 genes related to human addiction (i.e., dependence on cocaine, alcohol, heroin and other opiates, nicotine). Expression of these genes was particularly enriched in five types of molecular pathways, involving neurotransmitter–receptor interactions and their signaling pathways, hormone signaling pathways, control of junctions between cells, and neural plasticity (long-term potentiation).

Perhaps the best example of work to identify specific genes linked to dependence is in the field of alcohol. It has long been known that polymorphisms in the genes that code for the alcohol metabolizing enzymes differ not only between alcoholics and non-alcoholics but also cross-culturally, contributing to across-cultural differences in alcohol drinking and dependence (e.g., lower metabolic rates of alcohol and lower incidence of dependence among Asians) (Thomasson et al., 1991; Whitfield, 2005). Given the importance of DA in reward systems, early focus for candidate genes was also placed on genes related to DA receptors. These studies revealed a particular variant (called the A1+ allele) of the DRD2 gene that is associated with reduced numbers of DA D2 receptors (e.g., Pohjalainen et al., 1998), as well as an increased propensity for development of alcohol dependence and other substance use disorders (e.g., see Noble, 2003). Among a vulnerable group of adolescents (children of alcoholics), those having the A1+ form of the DRD2 receptor allele were characterized by an earlier onset age of marijuana use, greater frequency of alcohol intoxication, greater probability of being a smoker, and the use of more illicit drugs than those without this allele (Conner et al., 2005).

Genes for other neurotransmitter receptors affected by alcohol have also emerged as important, including particular subtypes of GABA (Whitfield, 2005; Enoch, 2008), glutamate (Schumann et al., 2008), and opiate (Barr et al., 2007) receptors. In the case of opiate receptors, for instance, expression of a particular variant of the gene coding the mu opiate receptor

221

(OPRM1) was found to be associated with increases in alcohol preference, alcohol consumption, and drinking to intoxication in rhesus monkeys (Barr et al., 2007). This variant was likewise found to be associated with the propensity to develop alcohol dependence in some (but not all) human studies (see van der Zwaluw et al., 2007) and, among alcoholics, with the probability of benefiting from treatment with the opiate receptor blocking drug, naltrexone (Anton et al., 2006). Although little explored, normal developmental changes in expression of these opiate, GABA, and glutamate receptor systems during adolescence (see Spear & Varlinskaya, 2005; Schepis et al., 2008, for review and references) could reveal genetic variants in receptor expression, perhaps contributing to the rise in incidence of alcohol dependence late in adolescence and into young adulthood.

DOES ADOLESCENT ALCOHOL/DRUG USE PRODUCE LASTING CONSEQUENCES?

Thus far in this chapter, we have focused on why adolescents differ from adults in their propensity to use alcohol and other drugs, and why notable numbers of them use these drugs excessively. We now turn to the critical question of whether there are lasting consequences of adolescent drug exposure. On the one hand, it could be hypothesized that neural alterations occurring during adolescence might be unusually sensitive to disruption by specific drugs; on the other hand, this remodeling could reflect a window of opportunity for unusual plasticity and recovery.

Is Early Substance Use Particularly Problematic?

Relative to individuals initiating drug use in adulthood, those whose drug use began in adolescence exhibit "accelerated dependency courses, with shorter times from first exposure to dependence for alcohol and cannabis and shorter times between their first and second dependencies" (Clark et al., 1998, p. 120). Even within adolescence, the younger individuals are when they begin to drink alcohol or use other drugs, the more likely they are to exhibit dependence or abuse of alcohol or other drugs in adulthood (e.g., see Spear, 2000b, for review and references). For instance, in a study using twin data, males who began drinking before 15 years of age were found to be twice as likely to develop alcohol dependence than those whose began drinking when they were 15 or older, with early drinking females being four times more likely than later-onset females to become dependent (Kendler & Prescott, 2006). But, in what may be a familiar refrain, correlations like these do not necessarily reflect causal relationships—that is, it may not be the early exposure, per se, that increases later probability of dependence. Instead, it is possible that some third factor, such as conduct disorder or elevated novelty-seeking behaviors, may not only increase the risk for both early alcohol use but also perhaps induce a pattern of persistent alcohol/drug involvement that leads to lasting problems with dependence. Indeed, high novelty-seeking in preteens was found to predict alcohol abuse at 27 years (Cloninger et al., 1988), and is one of a number of traits that is associated with early initiation of alcohol and other drug use (Baumrind, 1987). Moreover, in the Kendler and Prescott (2006) twin study, virtually all of the relationship between age at first drink and later alcohol dependence was found to be mediated by common genetic factors, with no significant environmental contribution associated with the impact of early onset-drinking, per se. Such findings are consistent with the conclusion that early use merely serves as a risk marker, but is not causal, in leading to later problems.

A powerful approach for disentangling whether early substance use is causal for later problems with abuse/dependence is to examine youth repeatedly, beginning well prior to the time of initiation of use and continuing through adolescence and into adulthood. A few such prospective, longitudinal studies have been recently published and provide initial evidence that there may indeed be some lasting consequences associated with early use (e.g., Dooley et al., 2005; Brook et al., 2008; Odgers et al., 2008). In one such longitudinal study, a group of over a thousand children from a birth cohort in New Zealand were examined every 2–6 years from the age of 3 to 32. Among the data that were collected was the presence or absence of conduct problems (at 7, 9, 11, and 13 years), early use (i.e., by 15 years of age) of alcohol, cannabis, inhalants, or other drugs, and a variety of outcome measures assessed at 32 years (Odgers et al., 2008). Individuals who had initiated substance use prior to 15 years as well as those who had not were followed prospectively into adulthood to determine whether there was an impact of early substance exposure on adult outcome. Importantly, estimate of effects between the two groups was adjusted for incidence of conduct disorder as well as a variety of other factors (e.g., socioeconomic status, incidence of early maltreatment, family history of alcohol/drug disorders, ADHD, maternal intelligence quotient [IQ] scores, and so on) to balance the groups on key factors that could otherwise have influenced outcome differences between the groups.

The results clearly demonstrated that early substance use, both by individuals with and without a history of conduct disorders, affected a variety of adult outcomes at 32 years of age. Specifically, early use was associated with an increased probability of substance dependence at age 32, early pregnancy (in females prior to age 21), and an increased number of criminal convictions between 17 and 32 years. Conduct disorder in childhood was associated with a two-fold increased probability that the affected adolescents would engage in early substance use. Yet, even the approximately 50% of early users who did not have conduct problems were at increased risk for these negative adult outcomes, with the risk further elevated among early substance users with a history of conduct disorders. When the type of substance used was examined, early alcohol exposure alone was found to significantly increase risk for negative adult outcomes, although early use of multiple drugs was associated with greater risks. Thus, in contrast to conclusions reached using twin data (Kendler & Prescott, 2006), this longitudinal study provides some evidence that early use of alcohol or illicit drugs may play a causal role in contributing to a number of later problems, including drug abuse (Odgers et al., 2008). Distinguishing between these possibilities continues to be a focus of ongoing work and is a quest important for guiding prevention efforts—that is, for informing policy decisions as to whether significant substance abuse prevention funds should be allocated to efforts aimed at reducing early substance use.

Are There Lasting Consequences of Adolescent Substance Use on Brain and Behavioral Function?

Lasting behavioral consequences of early alcohol/drug exposures may extend beyond an influence on later substance use and abuse. For example, marijuana (cannabis) users who began use prior to midadolescence were found to have lower verbal IQ scores, reduced focused attention, and poorer performance on a variety of neuropsychological and cognitive tests than later-onset users and nonusers (e.g., Ehrenreich et al., 1999; Pope et al., 2003). Imaging studies have revealed that the brains of individuals with a history of adolescent alcohol and substance abuse differ in a number of respects from the brains of those without a history of abuse. Included among these differences seen in individuals with a history of adolescent alcohol abuse are smaller volumes of hippocampus and prefrontal cortex (De Bellis et al., 2000, 2008), abnormalities in white matter, reduced brain activation during memory tasks, and disrupted memory performance (see Tapert & Schweinsburg, 2005, for review).

But, yet again, the issue of causality arises: Are these changes a result of excessive alcohol use during adolescence, or did they exist prior to such use, perhaps contributing to the tendency to use alcohol excessively? One approach that has been used to address this issue examines the correlation between volume of the target brain area and age of onset of the alcohol use disorder and its duration. The thinking is that if toxic effects of alcohol disrupt maturation in the brain region of interest, then the earlier the onset age (and hence the longer the duration of excessive alcohol use), the greater the influence should be on the target region. In contrast, the absence of a correlation between the volume of the brain region of interest and age of onset or duration of the alcohol use disorder would be more consistent with an interpretation that the regional volume difference reflects an inherent vulnerability (risk factor) for development of a pattern of excessive alcohol use during adolescence. Using this approach, De Bellis and colleagues (2000, 2005) concluded that the decrease in hippocampal volume associated with adolescent-onset alcohol use disorders is likely to be associated with toxic effects of the early alcohol exposure per se, whereas the decrease in PFC volume is more consistent with a pattern of delayed PFC maturation reflecting an increased risk for emergence of an alcohol use disorder in adolescence.

As discussed earlier, another strategy for addressing causality is to use longitudinal prospective studies to examine the brains of youth from families with strong histories of alcoholism (high risk) and those without this family history (low risk) over time. Using this approach, high-risk youth with minimal alcohol use were found to have reduced right amygdalar volumes relative to low-risk youth, suggesting that this volume difference represents an antecedent rather than a consequence of alcohol/substance abuse (Hill et al., 2001). Additional brain scans of the high-risk youth in this longitudinal population have revealed altered right–left laterality in volume of OFC and larger cerebellar volumes than low-risk youth; although by the time of these imaging sessions, many of the youth were already using alcohol and other drugs, a variety of approaches was used to suggest that these volume differences were likely not a consequence of alcohol/drug use, per se, but instead may reflect genetic risk factors (Hill et al., 2001, 2007, 2009).

Clear evidence for causality can be obtained through basic research studies in laboratory animals where drug exposures and other experiences can be highly controlled. Although often methodologically challenging (Spear, 2007b), work in this area is progressing rapidly, and a few consistent themes are beginning to emerge. Substance exposure during adolescence clearly can disrupt ongoing brain development. For instance, exposure to a large amount of alcohol potently inhibits the normally high levels of neurogenesis seen in the adolescent brain, resulting in lower numbers of neurons that are still evident in adulthood; in contrast, even higher levels of brain exposure to alcohol had relatively little impact on neurogenesis in adults (Crews et al., 2006). More marked consequences of chronic alcohol exposure during adolescence than in adulthood on measures of GABA receptor function have also been reported (Grobin et al., 2001). Adolescent exposure to alcohol has also been found to produce more pronounced brain damage in some regions, particularly frontal areas, than seen in adults (Crews et al., 2000). Turning to nicotine as a second example, adolescent nicotine exposure has been reported to increase dendritic length of neurons in the NAc, whereas this structural plasticity was not evident following nicotine exposure in adulthood (McDonald et al., 2007). Exposure to nicotine during adolescence was also found to induce long-term alterations in synaptic activity and in expression of nicotine receptors (Slotkin, 2002) and certain subtypes of glutamate receptors (Adriani et al., 2004)—adaptations that differ notably from those seen in response to similar nicotine exposure in adulthood. Such findings led Slotkin (2002) to conclude that nicotine induces "misprogramming" of neural and synaptic functioning during adolescence.

From such studies, it is clear that alcohol/drug exposure during adolescence can alter ongoing brain development and exert long-term influences on the brain (see Smith, 2003, for review). What still remains to be determined is whether the amount of exposure necessary to induce these effects is relevant to the levels of alcohol exposure seen in human adolescents. For example, alcohol exposures used to produce brain damage and disrupt neurogenesis were generally high enough that the animals were essentially sedated and remained "passed out" for hours. Yet, drinking until one passes out is not unheard of among high schooler or college kids. The issue is that high-enough levels of just about *anything* can cause problems.

Laboratory animal studies focusing on behavioral consequences in adulthood following adolescent drug exposure typically use relatively low-drug exposure levels, including those produced by allowing animals to voluntarily self-administer the drug, thereby regulating their own exposure levels. Such studies have often reported long-lasting behavioral consequences of adolescent exposures to drugs such as alcohol, nicotine, cocaine, and cannabinoids, although the number of studies available to date is limited and findings are diverse. Reported effects include sometimes subtle cognitive alterations, as well as lasting alterations in behavioral sensitivity to that drug and often other drugs in adulthood (see Smith, 2003; Schneider, 2008; Trezza et al., 2008, for review). For one example, chronic exposure to alcohol during adolescence, but not in adulthood, was found to decrease the later aversive consequences of alcohol when indexed via CTA in adulthood (Graham & Diaz-Granados, 2006; Diaz-Granados & Graham, 2007).

To the extent that adolescent alcohol use results in the retention of an adolescent-like insensitivity to the aversive effects of alcohol into adulthood (as suggested by the work of Gram & Diaz-Granados, 2006; Diaz-Granados & Graham, 2007), it might be expected that these animals would likewise retain an increased capacity to drink alcohol as adults. Indeed, under some circumstances, they do. When animals from a line of rats selectively bred to prefer alcohol ("P rats") were allowed to self-administer alcohol during adolescence, they showed greater alcohol self-administration in adulthood than their counterparts who were not given alcohol access during adolescence; in contrast, when the initial alcohol access period was delayed into adulthood, there was no effect on later self-administration of alcohol (Rodd-Henricks et al., 2002a, 2002b). This effect is less consistently seen among standard laboratory animals that were not genetically selected for high alcohol intake (e.g., compare Vetter et al., 2007, and Tambour et al., 2008, with Siciliano & Smith, 2001). Thus, at least among animals with a genetic predisposition for high levels of alcohol use, access to alcohol during adolescence may result in the retention of adolescent-typical elevations in alcohol intake into adulthood.

A few hints have begun to emerge, at least in the stimulant literature, suggesting that adolescent drug exposure may sometimes have less pronounced long-term consequences than comparable drug exposure in adulthood. One published example is the work of Kerstetter and Kantak (2007), wherein rats during adolescence or in adulthood were either allowed to self-administer cocaine daily or given equivalent amounts of cocaine or a control substance (saline) daily without having to work for access. Later, when all animals were adults, they were trained and tested in a learning task. Animals self-administering or passively given cocaine in adulthood showed marked learning impairments, whereas cocaine-exposed adolescents did not. Thus, it may not always be the case that adolescent drug exposure produces more pronounced effects than comparable exposures in adulthood.

Taken together, the available data provide strong evidence for long-lasting alterations in brain and behavior following adolescent drug exposure. Yet, the data to date are limited and need to be interpreted cautiously (see Spear, 2007b, for discussion). Drug effects are likely to be dose and timing specific. Indeed, in a number of studies, particularly those focusing on lasting neuroanatomical consequences, the doses used may not always have been pharmacologically relevant to typical exposure levels among human adolescents. Moreover, at this early stage in research in this area, some of the studies have not included another age comparison group, without which it cannot be determined whether adolescence represents a sensitive period for inducing lasting drug effects, or whether effects induced by adolescent exposures are similar to, or even less than, might be seen following equivalent exposures in adulthood or some other time of life. Thus, although the very limited amount of basic research to date has documented a number of long-lasting functional consequences of adolescent exposure to alcohol and other drugs at relevant levels, more research is needed to characterize the magnitude, dose- and drug-dependency, and significance of these effects.

SUMMARY AND CLOSING COMMENTS

Drugs of abuse clearly interact with forebrain reward systems that undergo considerable remodeling during adolescence. Developmental changes in reward systems likely contribute to the increased propensity of adolescents to use and abuse alcohol and other drugs, perhaps in part through elevating their sensitivity to the positive rewarding properties of these substances.

Yet, basic research suggests that elevated substance use during adolescence may also be driven by an adolescent-associated resistance to undesired and aversive effects of these substances that normally serve to limit their intake.

Individuals rarely use and abuse drugs in isolation, with use of multiple drugs the norm among adolescents as well as adults (Deas et al., 2000). Use of drugs in combination may present even greater risks, escalating problems relative to those associated with each drug in isolation. For instance, one popular combination among older adolescents is the mixing of alcohol with highly caffeinated energy drinks, a combination used by about one-fourth of current college drinkers. Consumption of alcohol with energy drinks is associated with increased heavy drinking, double the rate of drunkenness, and an increased incidence of a host of alcohol-related negative consequences, as compared to the consumption of similar amounts of alcohol alone (O'Brien et al., 2008). Despite the popularity of such drug combinations and the elevated risks for negative outcome they may provide, there has been little exploration of the potential mechanisms underlying such apparently synergistic effects.

Excessive and problematic use of alcohol/drugs during adolescence clearly reflects multiple factors that include the usual triad of developmental changes in brain, genetics, and environmental influences (including stressors). Drug abuse rarely occurs in isolation; individuals who abuse drugs often exhibit a constellation of other problems as well, including externalizing and internalizing disorders (which are the focus of the next chapter). One drug–disorder association that is receiving substantial current attention is the surprising link between adolescent use of cannabis (marijuana/hashish) and the later emergence of schizophrenia; this intriguing story is considered in Chapter 9 as well.

CHAPTER NINE

Adolescence and the Emergence of Psychological Disorders

• •

"Mental disorders . . . have their strongest foothold in youth, with substantially lower risk among people who have matured out of the high-risk age range."

—Kessler et al. (2005, p. 601)

Unlike the risks of developing chronic physical disorders, which continue to increase throughout life, the greatest risk for the emergence of psychological disorders generally occurs during development, especially during the adolescent years. For instance, the median age of onset of anxiety disorders is 11 years (social phobias, in particular: 13 years); externalizing disorders such as oppositional defiant disorder (ODD) and conduct disorder (CD) is 13 years; and substance abuse disorders is 20 years (Kessler et al., 2005). And even though major depression has a median age of onset in the early 30s (Kessler et al., 2005), the incidence of depression begins to increase notably during adolescence, particularly among young females, leading to a greater prevalence rate of depression in females than males that persists into adulthood (e.g., Kessler et al., 1998). Psychotic symptoms leading to a diagnosis of schizophrenia also typically emerge during late adolescence to early adulthood (e.g., see Walker & Walder, 2003), although in some cases the onset of overt symptoms of the disease may begin in childhood (child-onset schizophrenia), a type of schizophrenia that perhaps reflects an unusually severe form of the disease. As will be discussed, regardless of time of onset of the disorder, schizophrenia is thought to have developmental underpinnings that are established much earlier, even during fetal life.

This chapter focuses on three types of psychological disorders that increase in incidence during adolescence: schizophrenia; externalizing disorders such as CD; and internalizing disorders, with an emphasis on depression and anxiety. Although not a focus here, adolescence is also associated with an increase in the incidence of other psychological disorders, including not only the alcohol and drug abuse problems discussed in the preceding chapter, but also bulimia, anorexia, and other eating disorders, "cutting," gambling problems, and so on. Still other disorders, such as ADHD and Tourette's syndrome (a disorder characterized by repetitive motor and vocal tics), tend to show the largest developmental increase in prevalence prior to adolescence. It has been suggested that psychological disorders with a typical preadolescent onset may involve disruptions in the relatively early maturing basal ganglia (which include striatal and related regions involved in motor control), whereas disorders having a more typical onset in adolescence may be characterized by disruptions in development of temporal lobe regions (e.g., amygdala) (see Durston et al., 2001, for review). Frontal regions as well, especially the PFC, have also been implicated in adolescent-onset disorders, as we shall see.

Although less common than developmental increases in disorder incidence, for some disorders prevalence rates decline during adolescence. For instance, incidence of Tourette's syndrome declines from childhood into adolescence, and only about 10% of youth with seizures during childhood continue to exhibit signs of epilepsy in adolescence and at maturity (Kurlan, 1992; Saugstad, 1994). Thus, although adolescence is associated with an increase in prevalence of a variety of psychological disorders, there are notable exceptions as well.

WHY IS ADOLESCENCE ASSOCIATED WITH AN ELEVATED INCIDENCE OF PSYCHOLOGICAL DISORDERS?

Most youth traverse the bumps of adolescence with only occasional adjustment problems that do not evolve into psychological disorders. Yet, for other individuals, problems become more pronounced during adolescence and eventually emerge as a diagnosable psychological disorder. Contributors to the rise in these disorders during adolescence are to some extent disorder-specific. Nevertheless, psychological disorders are not mutually exclusive, multiple diagnoses (*comorbidity*) are frequent, and vulnerabilities to these disorders share a number of commonalities. These vulnerabilities are considered briefly before moving to a discussion of specific disorders.

Stressors and Other Environmental Challenges

As discussed in Chapters 7 and 8, adolescence can be a relatively stressful developmental transition. The HPA stress axis and its neural modulators undergo maturational changes during this time (see Spear, 2000a; Walker et al., 2004, for review) that are akin to, although much less dramatic than, the reawakening of the HPG axis at puberty. Yet, whereas the incidence of stressful situations and the physiological response to those stressors may increase to some extent during adolescence, large individual differences are seen in the mental health consequences of those stressful situations. The *stress–diasthesis model* focuses on this notion of stressors as affecting different individuals differently. This model postulates that, among individuals who are unusually sensitive to stress because of

genetic vulnerabilities or early adversities, the stressors of adolescence may precipitate the emergence of psychological disorders, whereas less vulnerable youth may take similar stressful
situations in stride (Walker & Walder, 2003; Walker et al.,
2004).

Among the developmental alterations in the HPA axis reported during adolescence are increases in basal levels of the
stress-related hormone CORT, along with enhanced CORT responses to stressors under some occasions, although these
findings are by no means ubiquitous (Walker et al., 2001; see
Gunnar & Vazquez, 2006, for extensive review). Mixed findings as to whether CORT levels increase in adolescence are
seemingly driven in part by challenges associated with assessing basal and stress-related CORT levels in humans (see Mc-
Burnett et al., 2003, for discussion). For one thing, levels of
CORT are highest shortly after awakening and decline notably
during the day, a daily cycle that can obscure baseline differences across age or groups if time of day is not tightly controlled. Shifts in cyclicity (e.g., age differences in onset and
offset of sleep) could masquerade as baseline differences in
CORT. Baseline levels obtained from individuals shortly after
they enter the laboratory may not reflect true baselines, but
rather a reaction to the novelty of the laboratory experience,
hassles associated with getting to the laboratory, or the stress
of sample collection (particularly when CORT is assessed from
blood rather than saliva). Even if basal CORT levels are determined from saliva samples collected at home, these samples
may not reflect true baseline values if the adolescent has
recently received an upsetting text message, or fought with a
sibling, or is worried about an upcoming test. And any such
elevations in "baseline" CORT levels could compromise the
ability to detect CORT increases to the experimental challenges, per se.

Elevations in CORT levels around the onset of awakening

and in response to stressors serve to mobilize energy stores and shunt energy from digestive/growth processes to muscle, heart, respiratory, and other systems necessary to get going during the day and to orchestrate effective responding to stressful situations, respectively. Yet, continued elevations in CORT levels deplete reserves and can be maladaptive, altering brain function, leading to the emergence of various stress-related diseases (see Korte et al., 2005), and perhaps triggering the onset of psychological disorders among vulnerable individuals (Gunnar & Vazquez, 2006). Not surprisingly, given the considerable cost of long-term elevations in CORT levels, HPA-related CORT release is normally under close negative feedback regulation, with receptors for CORT in brain regions such as the hippocampus and other mesolimbic brain regions monitoring CORT levels and inhibiting activation of the HPA when CORT levels are elevated. Thus, CORT levels are normally under close surveillance and carefully regulated within a moderate range to support CORT-facilitated adaptive functioning while avoiding CORT toxicity.

Due to genetic- or early-adversity-induced alterations in the functioning of neural and hormonal stress-sensitive systems, certain youth appear to enter adolescence with an increased vulnerability to even normal developmental risks associated with exposure to stressors or other environmental challenges. Childhood adversity alone may not typically be sufficient to precipitate the emergence of a psychological disorder in adolescence. Rather, it is the combination of poor coping resources induced by early adversity along with additional stressors or other threats to coping capacity that appear most likely to lead to the expression of psychological problems (Masten et al., 2006). Among the physiological vulnerabilities associated with poor coping are alterations in HPA regulation. Such HPA alterations can take a variety of forms: from elevated basal levels of CORT and perhaps a hyperreactive HPA axis that responds strongly to even mild stressors (Pajer, 2007) to a hypofunctioning HPA axis along with lower CORT levels (see Gunnar & Vazquez, 2006, for review). Intriguingly, both higher-than-normal as well as atypically low CORT levels are associated with particular psychological disorders. As we shall see later, the latter is prevalent in youth with externalizing disorders, whereas elevated CORT levels and HPA activity are often associated with schizophrenia, anxiety, and (to some extent) depression.

It is interesting that both increases and decreases in CORT levels can prove problematic. Some of the bias toward high versus low HPA activity appears to be genetic, with personality types typified by boldness, aggressiveness, and high risk-taking (called *hawks*) characterized by unusually low HPA activity, and the more cautious, nonaggressive, low risk-taking types (called *doves*) exhibiting higher HPA activity (Korte et al., 2005). Early adversity-induced alterations in the functioning of neural and hormonal stress-sensitive systems also appear to play a role, although the directionality of those effects (towards hyper- or hyporesponsiveness of the HPA axis) is complexly influenced by variables such as the type and developmental timing of the stressors and their interaction with genetic vulnerabilities (see Gunnar & Vazquez, 2006, for review). For instance, the timing of early sexual abuse has been shown to differentially affect stress-sensitive brain regions critical for feedback regulation of HPA function, with sexual abuse at ages 3–5 years or 11–13 years associated with smaller volumes of the hippocampus, whereas frontal cortex volumes were found to be smaller in individuals who had been sexually abused at 14–16 years of age (Andersen et al., 2008). Even in adults, basic research has demonstrated that repeated exposure to stressors sometimes results in tolerance and other times precipitates sensitization to further stressors (e.g., Post et al., 2003; see Herman et al., 2005, for review). Thus, although much remains to be learned as to why HPA dysregulations in youth take dramatically opposite forms, likely critical contributors include the nature of early adversities and the type, timing, and chronicity of the stressors to which the adolescent is exposed—all interacting with the dynamics of development of the HPA axis and its neural modulations (see Gunnar & Vazquez, 2006). Genetic background, to which we now turn, is also likely to play a critical role.

Genetics

Gene expression in the adolescent brain is developmentally unique. Indeed, as discussed in Chapter 2, a number of human genetic studies have found genetic factors to exert a *greater* impact on psychological functioning during adolescence than early in life. For instance, Silberg and colleagues (1999) examined variation in the influence of genetic and environmental factors on the incidence of depression in a large cohort of MZ and DZ twins between the ages of 8 and 16 years. They found that proportion of variance accounted for by genetic factors increased developmentally, with stronger genetic influences on depression seen in postpubertal than prepubertal females. Genetic-based vulnerabilities that alter production or efficacy of particular gene product(s) have effects only when those genes are normally expressed during development, raising the possibility that adverse consequences of some "susceptibility" genes may begin to be detectable only when their expression levels increase during adolescence.

When thinking about genetic contributors to psychological disorders, it is important to remind ourselves that genetic factors do not exist in isolation, and that gene expression occurs within, and can be strongly modified by, the environmental context. Genetic background may even influence the nature of the environmental contexts that are experienced. For instance, part of the genetic heritability of depression has been reported to be related to genetically induced predispositions to experience stressful life events (Silberg et al., 1999).

Developmental Remodeling of the Brain

The substrate through which stressors and genetic vulnerabilities exert their influences on the incidence of psychological disorders is ultimately, of course, the brain. Indeed, developmental transformations occurring in the adolescent brain may alter propensity for developing psychological disorders. Synaptic pruning and shifts in functional balance across brain regions during adolescence may uncover hidden dysfunctions induced early in life by abnormalities in gene expression and/ or exposure to stressors or other environmental insults. This possibility has been modeled in basic research largely by examining how the brain responds to, and recovers from, damage across age. This model is not meant to imply that psychological disorders are generally a result of actual brain injury (and indeed there is substantial evidence that this is *not* the case). Rather, these lesion studies can be viewed as providing "proof of principle" that developmental changes occurring in the brain throughout adolescence can unmask previously hidden dysfunctions under some circumstances, while, under other circumstances, eliminating signs of disorders.

It has long been known that greater recovery is seen following some types of early brain damage than when that injury is sustained in adulthood; such enhanced recovery after early brain injury is termed the *Kennard principle* (see Kolb & Gibb, 2007, for historical review). For instance, after early lesions of the OFC in rhesus monkeys, lesion-induced deficits resolved considerably as animals matured though adolescence (Goldman, 1971). Likewise, when the medial PFC is lesioned in infant rat pups, no signs of behavioral recovery nor indication of dendritic adaptations were seen when animals were examined during the preadolescent period, whereas substantial behavioral recovery along with increases in dendritic spine density had emerged by late adolescence/early adulthood (Kolb & Gibb, 1993).

Conversely, in a number of instances, laboratory animals have been shown to "grow into their deficits" during adolescence following certain types of early brain damage—findings reminiscent of the delayed emergence of signs of schizophrenia and other psychological disorders seen in adolescent humans. For instance, there are few signs of functional disruption in infant rhesus monkeys following early lesions of the dlPFC, with consequences of the damage becoming progressively more apparent as the animals reach maturity (Goldman, 1971). Similarly, lesions of the ventral hippocampus in neonatal rats have few consequences initially, but result in the emergence, by adolescence or early adulthood, of neuropathological and behavioral features that mimic schizophrenia in certain respects, including stress hyperresponsiveness and abnormalities in DA-related behaviors (Lipska & Weinberger, 2002); these effects were not apparent following comparable lesions in adult rats (Lipska et al., 1993). In this study similar schizophrenic-like functional effects also emerged following only transient disruption of the ventral hippocampus early in development. Delayed consequences have also been reported in response to some early insults other than brain lesions. For instance, characteristic disruptions in stress responsiveness, arousal, and attention in rats exposed prenatally to diazepam often do not become apparent until late adolescence (Kellogg, 1991).

Delayed emergence of symptomology has also been reported following damage to some brain regions in humans. Consider, for example, damage to the cerebellum. Effects of cerebellar damage in adults are now known to extend far beyond motor deficits, per se, to impairments in executive function and affective regulation (Schmahmann & Sherman, 1998) that are presumably associated with disruptions of neural circuits linking the cerebellum to the PFC and thalamus (Middleton & Strick, 2001). Although the available study population of young individuals who have sustained cerebellar damage is limited, deficits characteristic of this "cerebellar cognitive affective syndrome" were found to be more pronounced in older than younger individuals among a group of 3- to 16-year-olds with cerebellar damage, suggesting that expression of this syndrome may intensify during adolescence (Levisohn et al., 2000).

Together, these types of studies demonstrate that developmental changes in the brain during adolescence can alter propensity to express signs of symptomology following brain injury or other insults sustained early in life. Yet, the details of which developmental alterations precipitate the exacerbation or alleviation of which particular dysfunctions still remain largely unknown, although certain suspects are beginning to emerge—candidates that are presented in the discussions of particular psychological disorders.

Rises in Gonadal Hormone Levels

Increases in the release of testosterone, estrogen, and other sex hormones from the gonads at puberty could potentially contribute to the rise in psychological disorders during adolescence by altering the adolescent's sensitivity to environmental stressors/challenges and via triggering certain brain changes. Physiological and behavioral changes induced by pubertal increases in gonadal hormones also alter how the adolescent is perceived by others, contributing to the potential stressfulness of his or her environment. For instance, across many species, increases in size and apparent virility of postpubertal males may elicit aggression toward them by mature males—aggression that adult males would not exhibit against prepubertal individuals (e.g., de Waal, 1993). In humans, early attempts of young adolescents to become more independent from parental influences are often accompanied by transient increases in family tension and fighting with parents (Laursen et al., 1998).

Gonadal hormones can also directly influence gene expression. There are two types of receptors for gonadal hormones: membrane-bound receptors similar to most neurotransmitter receptors, as well as receptive areas within the cell that can control DNA synthesis (e.g., see McEwen & Alves, 1999). Thus, via action on the genome through the latter type of receptors, rising levels of gonadal hormones at puberty can directly influence gene expression, perhaps contributing to the selective rise in expression of certain genes (and declines in other genes) seen during adolescence. To the extent that the actions of the products of these gene variants influence susceptibility for particular psychological disorders, pubertally triggered increases in activity of these genes could reveal abnormalities in their expression that contribute to symptom emergence during adolescence—a possibility yet to be systematically examined. It is also possible that puberty-associated activation of gonadal hormone receptors may alter neural activity in brain regions such as the amygdala that undergo developmental change during adolescence, contributing to the unveiling of psychopathological signs.

Gonadal hormone influences are particularly suspect in psychological disorders where notable sex differences in incidence emerge postpubertally. The prototypic example of these sex-linked differences is a female predominance in the prevalence of depression that first emerges in adolescence and continues into adulthood, a topic to which we return later.

SCHIZOPHRENIA

Schizophrenia is a brain disorder characterized by considerable impairments in thinking, emotions, and behavior. Symptoms of this psychosis typically include both positive symptoms of delusions, hallucinations, and agitation as well as negative symptoms that include a lack of normal social behaviors, little motivation for, or ability to enjoy, positive rewarding situations, and a "poverty" of speech. Such identifiable symptoms of schizophrenia typically emerge in late adolescence or early adulthood. Yet, as we shall see, there is a great deal of evidence that points to schizophrenia as a disorder initiated very early in development.

Schizophrenia as a Developmental Disorder

Although symptomology consistent with a diagnosis of schizophrenia typically does not become fully expressed and recognizable until at least adolescence (except in relatively rare child-onset cases), multiple lines of evidence suggest that the roots of the disorder begin very early in life (e.g., see Walker & Walder, 2003). Autopsy studies have found that in individuals with schizophrenia, some cortical neurons are abnormally located in the wrong cortical layers; given that developing neurons migrate to reach their target location in the cortex during the second trimester, these findings suggest a fetal origin of schizophrenia (Akbarian et al., 1993). Similar alterations in neuronal location are seen in other regions such as the hippocampus (Scheibel & Conrad, 1993), further supporting the suggestion that the foundation for the later emergence of schizophrenia—or at least a vulnerability to its later development—may be laid prior to birth. Additional evidence cited to support this "fetal origins" perspective are reports of modest increases in the risk of developing schizophrenia among offspring of women exposed to nutritional deprivation (Susser et al., 1996), illnesses such as rubella (Brown et al., 2000), or a variety of other obstetric complications during pregnancy (see Lewis & Levitt, 2002; Rapoport et al., 2005, for review).

Consistent with the notion of schizophrenia as a disorder with roots in early life is evidence that children who eventually develop schizophrenia differ in a number of respects from others. These children often show developmental delays (Jones et al., 1994) and exhibit minor physical anomalies (e.g., low-set

243

or unusually shaped ears, curved fingers) that are typically associated with disturbances in fetal development and hence may serve as an index of early risk (Lewis & Levitt, 2002; Walker & Walder, 2003). They also show neuromotor abnormalities that are distinguishable in early home movies from the motor behavior of their siblings who do not develop the disorder later (Walker et al., 1994). Socially and cognitively they are different as well, tending to be anxious and socially withdrawn (Done et al., 1994) and exhibiting lower cognitive abilities (Ott et al., 1998) than children who do not develop schizophrenia. Importantly, though, these neurodevelopmental abnormalities are often relatively subtle and also evident in some individuals who develop other types of psychopathological disorder or who are not later diagnosed with a psychological disorders at all. Hence, these neurodevelopmental characteristics do not lie sufficiently outside the normal range to be diagnostically useful in identifying preschizophrenic youth. These early signs of nonoptimal development add credence, however, to the notion of schizophrenia as a neurodevelopmental disorder. Because early identification of youth on a likely trajectory toward later expression of schizophrenia could provide critical opportunities for prevention and early intervention, attempts continue to determine ways to identify a *prodrome* (early predictive signs) among preschizophrenic youth, including consideration of some combination of behavior and biological indices that collectively may be more predictive of the later development of schizophrenia than any single measure alone (e.g., Walker & Walder, 2003).

Emergence of Diagnosable Schizophrenia: Why Late Adolescence or Later?

If schizophrenia is a disorder of early development, why does it take so long for diagnosable symptoms of the disease to emerge? Many of the possibilities that have been suggested share the common theme of the disorder as representing the accumulation of progressive developmental perturbations that culminate in the expression of diagnosable symptoms of schizophrenia, per se. Theories tend to differ in their emphasis on what type of developmental events during the late-adolescent to adult transition might be particularly critical for precipitating disease expression, with the emphasis generally falling into three types of categories: (1) neural (disruptions in cortical pruning or other adolescent-typical brain alterations), (2) genetic (disruptions in normal developmental patterns of gene expression during adolescence or expression during adolescence of gene variants increasing susceptibility), or (3) environmental (e.g., stress-induced triggering of the overt expression of the disease). These factors are inextricably interrelated, and all likely contribute to the developmental course of the emergence of this disease. For instance, early neural dysfunctions precipitated genetically and perhaps exacerbated by adverse pregnancy or birth events may increase subsequent vulnerability to stressors that, when the individual is exposed to an accumulation of stressors during adolescence, may culminate in a stress-related disruption of normal genetically instigated neurodevelopmental changes of adolescence, resulting in the emergence of the disease (e.g., Walker & Diforio, 1997).

Developmental Neurobiology of Schizophrenia

Determining the neurobiological basis for the late-adolescent emergence of overt schizophrenia has proved challenging in part because the actual neuropathology is still unknown. Traditional approaches to characterize the schizophrenic brain focused on comparing autopsy samples of the brains of people with schizophrenia and controls, whereas the emphasis more recently has focused on imaging studies. Neuropathological findings include not only the abnormally located neurons in the cortex and hippocampus mentioned earlier, but also slight decreases in overall brain volume; reductions in gray matter and abnormalities in white matter in some regions; and lower numbers of specific types of neurons, dendrites, synapses, and glia that form myelin (see Harrison & Weinberger, 2005, for review). Such alterations are not always seen reliably across studies and seemingly could reflect either causes or consequences of the disease process.

One strategy to explore early neural changes associated with the emergence of the schizophrenic disease state is to use structural MRI to scan the brains of children and adolescents with child-onset schizophrenia (COS), although it remains to be determined whether the etiology of this early-onset disease reflects a more severe form of schizophrenia than that which emerges later, or whether it reflects a distinct disease entity with a different etiology than the schizophrenia diagnoses that are made in late adolescence/early adulthood (see Luna & Sweeney, 2001). The brains of youth with COS have been shown to exhibit a progressive series of changes, including decreases in size of the hippocampus and total brain volume, along with increases in size of the ventricles (Giedd et al., 1999b). Imaging studies focusing on the neocortex have revealed developmental declines in gray matter that are accelerated and more dramatic than those seen in low-risk individuals. Developmental declines in gray matter in frontal brain regions were found to peak at a rate of about 1% per year in nonpsychotic adolescents, but at rates of > 5% year in adolescents with COS; these gray matter declines were regionally specific, being more marked in the medial frontal cortex than in the adjacent ACC (Vidal et al., 2006). Areas of accelerated gray matter declines were reported to spread progressively across cortical regions in COS, starting in parietal regions and gradually extending to temporal and frontal regions (Thompson et al., 2001). Although dramatic, these gray matter declines may not be associated with the onset of the disease, but instead may represent a vulnerability factor (Bartzokis, 2002). Consistent with this suggestion, cortical gray matter reductions are also seen in normal relatives of individuals diagnosed with schizophrenia (Baare et al., 2001).

In contrast, a recent surge of studies has reported the emergence of white matter alterations at the onset of the disease state, per se. These white matter alterations include tract-specific declines in white matter volume (Whitford et al., 2007) and white matter integrity (indexed via DTI) (Price et al., 2007) in individuals undergoing their first episode of psychosis, as well as in youth with COS or adolescent-onset schizophrenia (Douaud et al., 2007; White et al., 2007). Although these findings suggest that impaired connectivity among brain regions associated with disruptions in myelin production and efficacy may be central to the initial expression of the disease, myelin disruptions also continue to occur after disease onset and may even be influenced by the type of antipsychotic drug used to treat the illness (Bartzokis et al., 2007).

In the search for triggers of schizophrenia, other research has focused on molecular changes at the synaptic level. Indeed, one of the earliest theories of the neural substrates underlying schizophrenia is that it results from dysregulation of forebrain DA systems. The details of the developmental derailment of DA in schizophrenia are complex and have been hypothesized to involve both regionally specific disruptions in both baseline (tonic) and stimulus-associated (phasic) DA release driven by abnormal cortical regulatory control (Moore et al., 1999). Generally speaking, though, these alterations can be summarized as reflecting attenuated DA activity in frontal regions, presumably contributing to negative symptoms, but with elevated DA activation in subcortical limbic regions leading to positive symptoms (see Cohen et al., 2008). Interestingly, as discussed in Chapter 8, there are signs that late adolescence is associated with a shift toward greater subcortical and less cortical DA activity (see Spear, 2000a). This late readjustment of DA balance across these regions not only has a timing coincident with the typical emergence of schizophrenic symptomology, but also shifts DA balance in the same direction, although presumably in a manner less marked, than that generally seen in schizophrenia. To descend into conjecture, perhaps this late adolescent shift in DA balance might be exaggerated or otherwise dysfunctional in individuals at risk for schizophrenia, contributing to the emergence of psychosis or negative signs of schizophrenia. Although highly speculative, this hypothesis nevertheless illustrates how normal developmental changes could potentially trigger symptoms of schizophrenia in vulnerable individuals.

Recent advances in molecular biology and neurogenetics have been co-opted to the quest of uncovering the developmental neuropathology of schizophrenia. These approaches have proved fruitful, with increasing evidence that schizophrenia represents a "developmental and dynamic shift in the normal regulation of synaptic connectivity and activity" (Harrison & Weinberger, 2005, p. 57). Synaptic signaling is disrupted in schizophrenia, particularly in forebrain regions such as the dorsal PFC. As just discussed, DA projections to mesolimbic and PFC regions have long been suspected to play a major role in schizophrenia, buoyed up, no doubt, by the fact that the primary action of antipsychotic drugs used in the treatment of schizophrenia is to chemically block certain types of DA receptors (e.g., Seeman, 1987). There is also evidence of the involvement of other neurotransmitter systems as well, including cannabinoid, glutamate, and GABA systems (see Cohen et al., 2008). The cannabinoid (CB) system and its primary receptors in brain, CB1 receptors, is currently a favorite neural target for investigation by schizophrenia researchers, largely because (1) CB1 receptors have been found to be largely localized to presynaptic endings, where they serve as important regulators of neuronal input to DA target regions, ultimately influencing DA systems thought to be dysfunctional in schizophrenia (see Cohen et al., 2008, for review); (2) levels of CB1 receptors as well as the endogenous cannabinoid, anandamide, are elevated in frontal regions of people with schizophrenia, relative to non-schizophrenic individuals (Dean et al., 2001; Leweke et al., 2007); and (3) cannabis (marijuana) use has been shown to increase risk of schizophrenia, an intriguing association to which we return later.

Developmental Genetics of Schizophrenia

Examining genetic contributors to the development of schizophrenia has reinforced the notion that disrupted signaling in DA, CB, and other neurotransmitter systems may represent core dysfunctions in schizophrenia. This disease is predominantly a genetic disorder, with heritability estimates of about 80% (Sullivan et al., 2003). With recent advances in molecular genetics, research to identify susceptibility genes in schizophrenia has escalated rapidly. To determine which genes are important, the genetic profiles of people with schizophrenia and genetically vulnerable individuals (i.e., close family members) have been compared, using a variety of genetic approaches, with those of nonschizophrenic individuals without a family history. Each such study typically generates many dozens of gene variants that vary between individuals with schizophrenia (and those at risk) and nonschizophrenic controls. When the multitudes of gene polymorphisms revealed in these sorts of studies are compared for commonalities across studies, a smaller subset of candidate "susceptibility genes" emerges. Although the functions of most of these gene variants have yet to be systematically detailed, those with known functions often involve neural development, synaptic plasticity, and neurotransmission in DA, GABA, glutamate, cannabinoid, and other neurotransmitter systems (see Harrison & Weinberger, 2005; Rapoport et al., 2005, for review). Only a few examples are given here.

One susceptibility gene produces catechol-O-methyl-transferase (COMT), an enzyme that regulates synaptic DA levels and plays a particularly critical role in the PFC (see Harrison & Weinberger, 2005), where other means for regulating synaptic DA levels are limited once maturity is reached (Teicher et al., 1991). Another example is the dysbindin gene whose expression is lower in the dorsal PFC and hippocampus of people with schizophrenia than of controls, with particularly notable effects on glutaminergic excitatory systems in those regions. Another susceptibility gene, neuroregulin (NRG1), is a huge gene that can give rise to at least 15 different peptides, depending on which portions of the gene are transcribed and how the resulting mRNA is spliced. These diverse peptides have separable functions that exert different influences during development, ranging from early influences on the migration of brain cells and formation of synapses to later functions in modulating neurotransmission and synaptic plasticity throughout life (see Harrison & Weinberger, 2005). This highly diverse gene illustrates how a given gene can be expressed at multiple times during the lifespan and serve different functions at different points in development and at maturity.

Environmental Contributors to the Emergence of Schizophrenia

Considerable attention has focused on potential environmental triggers for the development of schizophrenia, two examples of which are given here. First, increases in stress hormones associated with maturational changes in the HPA axis and its increasing activation by stressors during the adolescent transition have been suggested to serve as a trigger for expression of psychosis in vulnerable individuals. Using the stress–diasthesis model discussed earlier, the emergence of symptomology of schizophrenia in late adolescence is viewed as an "unfolding of aberrant biodevelopmental processes" that reflects stress-related triggering of underlying genetic vulnerabilities that increase susceptibility to stressors (Walker & Walder, 2003). Evidence supporting this theory includes, for example, data showing that preschizophrenic youth with high CORT levels exhibit more severe schizophrenia-like symptoms upon follow up several years later than similar youth with more moderate CORT levels at the initial assessment (Walker et al., 2001).

Another potential environmental trigger that has emerged relatively recently is the use of marijuana and other cannabinoids (e.g., hashish). Studies drawn across a variety of different countries have reported that regular use of cannabis is associated with an increased risk of schizophrenia (see Degenhardt & Hall, 2006). The relationship between marijuana use and psychopathology may not be entirely specific for psychosis, with some evidence that cannabis use may also be associated with risk of other psychological disorders, particularly internalizing (mood) disorders (e.g., Leweke & Koethe, 2008), although schizophrenia has been, by far, the best studied and documented effect. This effect is not subtle, with cannabis use increasing the relative risk of schizophrenia about two- or three-fold, and with earlier onset and more frequent use more strongly related to later psychosis (reviewed in Degenhardt & Hall, 2006). It is not the case, however, that regular cannabis use or abuse predisposes otherwise nonvulnerable individuals to develop schizophrenia; indeed the vast majority of cannabis abusers never develop symptoms of schizophrenia. Rather, cannabis use increases the probability that individuals already at high risk for schizophrenia will convert to a full-blown version of the disease (see Hall et al., 2004). For instance, when a sample of adolescents and young adults at high risk for developing schizophrenia (because of either family history and/or expression of minor "subsyndromal" signs of psychotic symptoms at the initial examination) was reexamined 1 year later, 12.5% had become psychotic during the year. Of those developing psychosis, 83% were cannabis abusers, whereas only 26% of those who had not developed psychosis engaged in cannabis abuse (Kristensen & Cadenhead, 2007). Although cannabis exposure has sometimes been reported to improve some aspects of cognitive function in people with schizophrenia (Coulston et al., 2007), there is little evidence overall that individuals use cannabis to "self-medicate"—that is, in an attempt to improve functioning or otherwise reduce unpleasant signs of impending psychosis or schizophrenia (see Hall et al., 2004).

In much of this literature relating cannabis use with relative risk of developing schizophrenia, cannabis use and abuse were initiated in adolescence, although the importance of this timing typically has not been investigated systematically. Caspi and colleagues (2005), however, used a longitudinal study approach to compare adolescent-onset cannabis users (beginning at < 15 years or at least monthly before 18 years) and adult-onset users (monthly use at 21 or 26 years, but not < 18 years) and to examine functional polymorphism in the COMT gene thought to be a susceptibility factor for schizophrenia (as discussed above). Adolescent-onset cannabis use was associated with an increased risk of developing psychosis within the next decade, but *only* among individuals with the high-risk-associated variant of the COMT gene. In contrast, adult-onset cannabis users were not at increased risk of psychosis regardless of which form of the COMT gene they carried. These data are particularly important in demonstrating that a specific environmental risk factor may be unmasked only in individuals with a particular genetic vulnerability, and vice versa.

Multifactorial Determinants for the Emergence of Schizophrenia in Late Adolescence

Although individual studies examining the developmental psychopathology of schizophrenia have often focused on one type of risk factor, it is clear that there are multiple determinants that contribute to the generally delayed developmental appearance of psychosis and other symptoms of schizophrenia. That is, the emergence of schizophrenia may represent the end result of a series of vulnerabilities and their underlying pathophysiological consequences that accumulate over time (Marenco & Weinberger, 2000), and may be modified in their trajectory by ongoing experiences. For instance, early neural dysfunctions that are precipitated genetically and/or by adverse pregnancy or birth events may increase subsequent vulnerability to stressors, which in turn may increase negative outcomes associated with childhood adverse experiences, culminating in the emergence of the disease when this high-risk individual is exposed to multiple stressors or begins to abuse cannabis in adolescence (e.g., Walker & Diforio, 1997).

EXTERNALIZING DISORDERS

Certain psychological disorders are characterized by what individuals do—that is, they are defined by external manifestations viewed as inappropriate, undesirable, or antisocial. Externalizing disorders/antisocial behaviors have been broken up into separate groups based largely on the age of the individual and the nature of the problem behaviors: ODD is often used to refer to younger children with externalizing problems or those with less severe forms of the disorder, whereas CD is a diagnosis typically given to older children and adolescents, with antisocial personality disorder (also called sociopathy or psychopathy) used to refer to individuals whose problems in this area continue to escalate into adulthood. Individuals with externalizing disorders typically are hostile, defiant, uncooperative, and rebellious. Children with ODD are often temperamental, deliberately annoying, spiteful, argumentative, and refuse to follow rules; although many kids exhibit such behaviors occasionally, these behaviors are habitual for children with OCC, and exhibited with a frequency that often frustrates parents and teachers. In CD, aggressive and antisocial acts can escalate into truancy, running away from home, lying, property damage, fighting, cruelty to animals, and robbery, with these latter types of behavior problems leading to increasing involvement with the law for adults with psychopathy. Many of these disruptive behaviors are thought to be related to problems with the inhibitory control of behavior and emotions. Indeed, children with externalizing disorders may also be diagnosed with other disorders that involve impaired inhibitory control, including ADHD and substance abuse disorders. Because of the substantial comorbidity of ODD/CD and ADHD, it is sometimes difficult to disentangle the substrates underlying these two types of psychological disorders. Hence, although the focus here is on ODD/CD, studies to determine genetic, neural, and hormonal contributors to ODD/CD in clinical populations may be complicated by the dual diagnoses of many of these youth, as well as by the medications used to treat one or both disorders.

Environmental–Hormonal Interactions in ODD/CD

Children and adolescents with ODD/CD often appear physiologically underaroused in baseline circumstances. This underarousal is evident in terms of lower baseline HR (Ortiz & Raine, 2004) as well as lower basal levels of the stress hormone CORT (for review, see McBurnett et al., 2003). Lower baseline CORT levels presumably reflect attenuated activation of the HPA system (van Goozen et al., 2007), whereas lower basal

HRs are seemingly driven by lower baseline levels of SNS activity, along with deficiencies in PNS (vagal) tone emerging in early adolescence (see Beauchaine et al., 2007). Underarousal is not characteristic of other types of psychological disorders and hence may be helpful in distinguishing youth with ODD/CD from those with other disorders. Indeed, several studies have found low resting levels of CORT during childhood and adolescence to be predictive of later delinquency and externalizing behaviors (Shoal et al., 2003; van de Wiel et al., 2004), although this relationship is not always evident, especially among adolescents (see Alink et al., 2008). Associations between low basal CORT and externalizing problems also may be less apparent or even in the opposite direction during the toddler and preschool years (Gunnar & Vazquez, 2006; Alink et al., 2008).

Significant numbers of youth with ODD/CD not only show lower resting arousal levels but also an attenuated reactivity to stressors and other types of challenges, including rewarding stimuli. For instance, youth with ODD/CD often show less of an increase in the stress hormone CORT when challenged with a stressor than other children (van Goozen et al., 2007, but see also van Bokhoven et al., 2005), with those children showing the most blunted CORT response having more serious forms of the disorder and being particularly unlikely to show improvement with treatment (van de Wiel et al., 2004). Indeed, those children who failed to show stress-induced increases in CORT were the most aggressive, findings that suggest a decoupling between physiology and subjective emotional reactions (Snoek et al., 2004)—that is, "a mismatch between subjective and physiological arousal" (van Goozen et al., 2007, p. 157). This association between lower CORT levels and increased aggression is seen even in animal studies, with research showing that rats chronically depleted of CORT are more aggressive and show deficits in normal social behaviors (Haller et al.,

255

2004). An attenuated reactivity to challenge has also been seen in antisocial youth in terms of SNS reactivity. For instance, children and adolescents with ODD/CD sometimes show less SNS activation in response to rewarding or arousing stimuli than their agemates without an externalizing disorder (Beauchaine et al., 2007).

Insensitivity to arousing, rewarding, or threatening stimuli has been hypothesized to contribute to chronic underarousal, dissatisfaction, and irritability in individuals with ODD/CD, leading them to avidly seek new sensations, larger rewards, and greater thrills to increase arousal and obtain reinforcing effects, thereby promoting sensation-seeking and externalizing behaviors (see Beauchaine et al., 2007; Gunnar & Vazquez, 2006, for review). In older children and adolescents with ODD/CD, these SNS and HPA insensitivities to reward, arousal, and threat appear to be joined by an ineffective vagal system for emotional regulation (Beauchaine et al., 2007). In the absence of effective vagal buffering of emotional reactions, youth with ODD/CD are thought to overreact to negative situations, leading to hostility, aggression, and rebellion. According to this theory, then, the adolescent with ODD/CD is in double jeopardy: engaging in chancy, rule-breaking activities in an attempt to relieve the dissatisfaction precipitated by underarousal and an underactive reward system, while overreacting to negative consequences ensuing from those activities. And these negative consequences often have stressful ramifications of their own (e.g., punishment, arrest, social rejection, school failure) (van Goozen et al., 2007).

In the extreme, insensitivity to rewarding, arousing, and threatening stimuli becomes particularly pronounced in adults who continue to exhibit antisocial personality disorder, with incarcerated adult psychopaths typically exhibiting a lack of fear to aversive effects, along with a general insensitivity to both rewarding and aversive stimuli (Herpertz et al., 2001).

Thus, the blunted hormonal and physiological reactions seen in some youth with ODD/CD become even more pronounced in individuals whose conduct problems develop into psychopathy in adulthood, an emotional hyporesponsiveness that is not seen with other types of personality disorders.

This pattern of underresponsive physiological and hormonal reactivity is not characteristic, however, of all youth with ODD/CD. Rather, it is seen only in individuals with a nonanxious, underresponsive type of ODD/CD who are also typically characterized by notable aggression, "undersocialization" (e.g., delinquency that is typically not instigated by peers), and a relatively early (childhood) onset of CD (McBurnett et al., 2003). In contrast, youth whose ODD/CD is accompanied by anxiety often exhibit greater hormonal and physiological reactivity to threatening and stressful stimuli than youth without ODD/CD (e.g., see Gunnar & Vazquez, 2006). The ODD/CD in these individuals generally has a later onset (in adolescence) and is not accompanied by significant aggression (McBurnett et al., 2003). Thus, for individuals with ODD/CD that is comorbid with an anxiety disorder, their CORT reactivity to stressful and other emotional stimuli appears to be characterized by hyperemotionality and enhanced HPA reactivity reminiscent of that seen with anxiety disorders (see later discussion). Research that does not distinguish between youth whose ODD/CD symptoms are characterized by underreactive HPA activity (i.e., nonanxious, aggressive forms of the disorder) and those whose symptomology involves HPA overreactivity (the anxious, nonaggressive subtype of ODD/CD) would end up averaging across these two extremes, perhaps resulting in overall levels of HPA activity similar (though more variable across individuals) to those seen in normal youth. This is a good example of the importance of distinguishing among potential subtypes of psychological disorders when trying to determine their underlying physiological and neural substrates.

Genetics of ODD/CD

Twin studies have generally revealed evidence of modest genetic and shared environmental contributions to CD, with estimates of 26% genetic, 25% shared environment, and 49% nonshared, individual environmental influences on probability of CD when collapsing across both sexes in an adolescent sample (Kendler & Prescott, 2006). Although the low lifetime prevalence of CD in females (4.4%) relative to males (19.1%) provided insufficient power to conclusively demonstrate sex differences in heritability, the propensity for CD in adolescent females appeared to be more strongly driven by genetic influences (accounting for 60% of the total variance) than in their male counterparts (16%). Intriguingly, when males were examined across age, there was little evidence for genetic influences on antisocial behavior in early adolescence (with estimates of genetic variance of only 6%), whereas by late adolescence, the genetic influence increased considerably (to 42% of the variance). In contrast, the shared environmental influence declined from 28 to 6% of the variance over the adolescent period, with individual-specific factors contributing to the largest share of the variance at both ages (64% and 52%, respectively). Thus, the relative importance of shared environmental factors in the production of CD declines with age, whereas genetic factors increase in significance (see Kendler & Prescott, 2006).

But which genes matter? While many of the players have still to be identified, a couple of important gene polymorphisms have emerged in the research to date. One polymorphism involves a variant of the gene coding monoamine oxidase A (MAO-A), an enzyme critical for breaking down the neurotransmitters DA, norepinephrine, and serotonin (5-HT). Individuals with a low-activity variant of this gene are slower to metabolize these neurotransmitters, thereby elevating their levels in the brain. Among males with the low-activity variant of the MAO-A gene who were severely maltreated during childhood or early adolescence, 85% developed some form of CD (Caspi et al., 2002). No elevation in CD prevalence was seen, though, among individuals with the same low-activity variant if they were not maltreated. Nor was risk for CD increased by childhood maltreatment among those having high MAO-A activity. Thus, the risk for CD is increased by severe maltreatment only among individuals who are already vulnerable due to a gene polymorphism producing low MAO-A activity.

Another potential candidate gene implicated in CD is the gene coding the DRD4 subtype of DA receptor. The longer form of this gene apparently codes for a less active DRD4 receptor and has been sometimes (but not always) linked to increases in novelty-seeking, attention, aggression, and externalizing behaviors (see Schmidt et al., 2007, for review). The mixed nature of these findings may reflect critical interactions of the DRD4 gene with other genes. For instance, children with both the long variant of the DRD4 gene and a short (less active) functional polymorphism in a gene coding for the 5-HT transporter (that modulates synaptic levels of 5-HT) show increases in externalizing and internalizing behaviors than are not seen in youth with neither variant or either of these variants alone (Schmidt et al., 2007). Thus, although evidence is mounting for the involvement of certain specific genes in the development of CD, the search is likely to be complicated by modulatory interactions of these genes with other genes and environmental risk factors.

Neural Contributors to ODD/CD

Adolescents with CD exhibit regionally selective reductions in gray matter when their brains are compared with those from age-, sex-, and IQ-matched controls. Although the precise brain regions affected vary somewhat across studies, reductions in gray matter volume in the amygdala have been reported consistently, along with study-specific findings of gray matter reductions in the hippocampus, orbitofrontal cortex, and insular cortex (Sterzer et al., 2007; Huebner et al., 2008). Intriguingly, in the Sterzer et al. (2007) study, greater declines in insular volume were found to be correlated with lower empathy scores, findings which they interpreted as supporting the hypothesis that a lack of empathy serves to bias individuals toward aggression (Sterzer et al., 2007).

Studies are just beginning to be conducted using fMRI to explore how the brains of youth with ODD/CD differ in their responsiveness to emotional stimuli and in their brain activation patterns during cognitive tasks requiring inhibitory responding. Some fMRI findings suggest that CD may be associated with a reduced neural responsiveness to affective information, a conclusion reminiscent of the underresponsive physiological and hormonal reactivity often seen in youth with the nonanxious, aggressive form of ODD/CD that was discussed earlier. For instance, when examining alterations in fMRI responses to aversive stimuli relative to neural stimuli, youth with CD exhibited less amygdalar (or L-amygdala) activation to fearful facial stimuli (Marsh et al., 2008) and to negative affective pictures (Sterzer et al., 2005) than age-matched controls without CD. When responding to negative affective pictures, youth diagnosed with CD also showed reduced ACC activation (Stadler et al., 2007) or actual suppression of ACC activity below baseline levels under circumstances where controls showed no change (Sterzer et al., 2005). Yet, at least one recent fMRI study reports data inconsistent with the conclusion that youth with CD exhibit reductions in neural processing of affective stimulation. In this study, male adolescents with CD (and often comorbid ADHD) were found to exhibit greater activation of the left amygdala in response to aversive pictures than same-age ADHD youth as well as normal controls, while not showing the decline in activation of the PFC and insular regions typically seen in normal controls when viewing aversive stimuli (Herpertz et al., 2008).

Youth with ODD/CD often exhibit cognitive impairments in decision-making tasks involving reversal learning and active response inhibition, and fMRI studies are beginning to determine brain regions that are activated differently by these tasks in youth with CD and their control age-mates. For instance, when making punished errors on a reversal task, adolescents with severe ODD/CD exhibited increased activation in the caudate and vmPFC regions, rather than the typical decreases in activation in these regions seen when normal children commit the same errors (Finger et al., 2008). These findings were interpreted to suggest that reversal learning deficits in youth with CD are associated with dysfunctions in the neural processing of reward information. In a study examining fMRI during a task requiring active inhibition, on trials for which individuals failed to inhibit responding, youth with CD exhibited less activation than normal youth in the ACC and in temporal/parietal regions thought to form part of a system that monitors task performance (Rubia et al., 2008). Attenuated activation in these regions were interpreted as reflecting that youth with CD are "undermotivated and respond less to negative feedback than comparison subjects" (Rubia et al., 2008, p. 894).

Clearly, research to determine neural substrates underlying ODD/CD is just beginning, and much work remains. Gene polymorphisms suggesting important candidate genes are not well integrated yet with findings from neuroimaging studies, although both very generally support the importance of differences in forebrain neurocircuitry involving frontal cortical and limbic (amygdala, insular cortex) regions. Studies using fMRI have not fully exploited analyses of functional connectivity among brain regions—connectivity differences that may provide particularly critical information as to how brain neurocircuitry is altered in youth with ODD/CD (e.g., see Marsh et al., 2008). Single fMRI studies are often more suggestive than conclusive, arguing for the importance of replication to build consensus. Research exploring how youth with externalizing disorders vary from normal children in how their brains respond to aversive stimuli or reversal/inhibition failures will likely be aided by continued attention to comorbidities and subtypes of ODD/CD (e.g., under- vs. overreactive HPA subtypes), and even perhaps individual differences in temperament traits (e.g., Whittle et al., 2008b).

INTERNALIZING DISORDERS

There are two major types of internalizing (mood) disorders, depression and anxiety, each consisting of a heterogeneous grouping of conditions. About 3–5% of children and adolescents suffer from an anxiety disorder at any point in time. The most commonly observed anxiety disorders among youth include generalized anxiety disorder, social phobias, and other specific phobias. Panic disorder, posttraumatic stress disorder, and obsessive–compulsive disorders appear less frequently in youth (Evans et al., 2005). Depression is characterized by extended dysphoria (despondency, sad feelings), anhedonia (not deriving pleasure from normally pleasurable activities), and irritability; other common symptoms include disruptions in sleep, eating, thought, and motor behavior, along with low self-esteem (see Miller, 2007, for review). Incidence of major depression is low in childhood (with about 2% of children exhibiting depression at any point in time) and increases during adolescence to reach lifetime prevalence rates of 14% by mid- to late adolescence (Evans et al., 2005). The rise in rates of depression during adolescence is more marked in females than males, with rates of depression among young women more than twice the rates in young men by late adolescence; these increases appear to be related more to pubertal status than to age, per se (Angold et al., 1998). Although originally thought to be rare in youth, there is increasing evidence that some depressed children and adolescents may exhibit manic episodes—a combination of symptoms that defines bipolar disorder (Birmaher et al., 2006). Diagnosis of bipolar disorder in youth has proved somewhat challenging and controversial. Manic episodes in adolescents are rarely expressed as a euphoric mood such as that often seen in adults with bipolar disorder, but instead may appear as irritability, agitation, and "affective storms" characterized by outbursts of temper or aggression (Biederman et al., 2004). These symptoms have been suggested to cycle more rapidly and be greater in severity than the manic symptoms of bipolar disorder characteristic of adults (Birmaher et al., 2006).

There is considerable comorbidity among these disorders and with other psychological disorders in children and adolescents, with estimates that up to 90% of depressed youth have one or more other psychological disorders. About 25% of youth with depression are also diagnosed with ODD/CD and/or ADHD, and in about 25–50%, their depression is comorbid with anxiety (see Miller, 2007). Anxiety disorders generally precede depression in their appearance during development, and hence anxiety has been suggested to reflect a risk factor for developing depression (see Axelson & Birmaher, 2001). Because of the increase in incidence of depression during adolescence, it is the primary focus here. Nevertheless, given the high comorbidity between anxiety disorders and major depression during adolescence, along with notable similarities in postulated genetic and neural substrates of these two types of internalizing disorders, data on anxiety are also presented, highlighting similarities and differences in these two disorders, when possible.

Environmental–Hormonal Interactions in Internalizing Disorders

Anxious youth sometimes have been found to have higher base-line CORT levels or greater CORT responses to stressors (e.g., Greaves-Lord et al., 2007; Kallen et al., 2008). Not all studies have found these differences, though—perhaps in part because of differences in the types of challenges to HPA axis activity used across studies. That is, given that activation of the HPA axis is important when dealing with challenges, even well-adapted individuals should demonstrate elevations in CORT when anticipating or dealing with a challenge. Thus, when faced with novel challenges or stressors, anxious youth may not differ in their initial CORT response from their nonanxious agemates. However, anxious individuals may display slower habituation as the novel situation becomes more familiar, as well as delayed HPA axis recovery postchallenge. Consequently, anxious youth may exhibit greater CORT levels than well-adapted youth under familiar circumstances (see Gunnar & Vazquez, 2006, for references and an excellent discussion of these points).

Given the considerable comorbidity between anxiety and depression in youth, it might be expected that depressed youth, like their anxious counterparts, would exhibit dysfunctions in the HPA axis. Yet, the studies to date suggest minimal dysregulation in this stress hormone system among depressed youth—despite robust evidence for HPA axis dysregulation among depressed adults (e.g., see Ryan, 1998; Miller, 2007, for review). For instance, tests of the ability of a synthetic CORT derivative (dexamethasone) to activate negative feedback systems, inhibiting further HPA activity, typically reveal little evidence for dexamethasone suppression among adults with clinical depression, whereas this negative feedback deficit is rarely seen among depressed youth (see Ryan, 1998, for review). Given the delayed appearance of this HPA axis dysregulation relative to depression onset, it likely represents a consequence rather than a cause of the depressive disorder (Miller, 2007).

Nevertheless, there does appear to be a special relationship between stress and depression in adolescence. Immediate life stressors (e.g., breakup of a relationship, peer rejection) are more likely to initiate first depressive episodes in adolescence than later episodes (see Davey et al., 2008, for review). Moreover, overall level of lifetime exposure to adversity was found to be associated with an increased risk of developing depressive and/or anxiety disorders among a group of college-age individuals (Turner & Lloyd, 2004). Thus, whereas there may not be notable dysfunction of the HPA stress axis at the onset of depression, life events viewed as particularly stressful may initiate a depressive episode in anxious youth or other adolescents who are already at risk for the development of internalizing disorders.

Genetics of Internalizing Disorders

Twin studies examining the genetics of different internalizing disorders have generally revealed modest genetic heritability, accounting for 30–40% of the variance in the incidence of depression and 28–32% of the variability for generalized anxiety disorder and panic disorder (Kendler & Prescott, 2006). Much of the genetic liability for the development of clinical depression and anxiety disorders is similar across these disorders (e.g., Todd & Heath, 1996), with some theoretical models proposing that perhaps the timing of stressful life circumstances induces a differential trajectory toward one or the other disorder, with genetically vulnerable individuals developing anxiety following early life stress, but depression following significant stress in adolescence (see Axelson & Birmaher, 2001). In twin studies, shared environmental factors did not contribute significantly to the risk for either depression or anxiety, with individual-specific effects thus exerting the greatest influence on liability to develop internalizing disorders. Individual-specific stressful life events may precipitate a depressive episode if the impact of an acute stressful life episode surpasses the capacity of the genetically vulnerable individual to cope with that stressor. Fortunately, longitudinal data from these studies suggest that the increased risk associated with any particular stressful life event is relatively short-lived, elevating depression liability for only a few months (see Kendler & Prescott, 2006).

Polymorphisms in a number of candidate genes have been postulated to play a role in internalizing disorders, although each polymorphism generally has been found to account for only 3–4% of the variance. Thus, as with other psychological disorders, it is likely that multiple genetic influences interact to influence the susceptibility of youth to developing depression and anxiety.

The nature of the genetic contributions to internalizing disorders remains to be characterized, to a large extent. A number of researchers has focused on temperament variables as likely influenced by genetic loading. One aspect of temperament that has been speculated to reflect genetic vulnerability is "negative affectivity"—that is, the bias toward experiencing negative emotions and/or an impaired ability to regulate negative emotions. Indeed, youth with high negative affectivity appear to be at greater risk for the development of both depression and anxiety, although the extent to which this affective bias is genetically driven and the specific genes involved are unknown (see Axelson & Birmaher, 2001).

A few likely candidate genes contributing to vulnerability for internalizing disorders have been identified. As mentioned during discussion of CD and other externalizing disorders, combined polymorphisms at both the 5-HT transporter and DRD4 have been reported to influence the incidence of both externalizing and internalizing behaviors (Schmidt et al., 2007). Intriguingly, both fMRI and genetic studies have found the 5-HT transporter polymorphism to be associated with the amygdalar response to fearful stimuli, with individuals having the short (less active) variant of the 5-HT transporter gene showing amygdalar hyperactivation to angry and fearful faces (Hariri et al., 2002); as discussed below, amygdalar hyperactivation to negative affective faces is commonly seen in adolescents and adults with internalizing disorders, and even in adolescents at risk for these disorders. Thus, genetic vulnerabilities may be expressed in part by altered neural sensitivity to activation by emotionally arousing affective stimuli. Vulnerabilities induced by the short variant of the 5-HT transporter gene also may depend on environmental experience. In a study of young (21- to 26-year-old) adults, the less active short form of the 5-HT transporter gene was associated with more symptoms of depression only when individuals with this form of the gene were also exposed to multiple stressful life events during the adolescent-to-adult transition (Caspi et al., 2003). A similar gene × environmental interaction also emerged in a study of 12- to 20-year-olds, although in this case the elevated risk of depression reached significance only among female adolescents (Eley et al., 2004). In this study, several other genes related to 5-HT functioning also predicted incidence of depression, independent of environmental stressors or sex.

Neurobiology of Internalizing Disorders

An additional sign of the importance of 5-HT in depressive disorders emerges when considering effective pharmacotherapies for its treatment. Although it is not always the case that drugs effective in treating a particular disorder necessarily relate to the root cause of the disorder, it is nevertheless interesting that SSRIs such as fluoxetine have been shown to be effective in the treatment of depression (as well as in the treatment of anxiety disorders) in children, adolescents, and adults. In contrast, however, although tricyclic antidepressants (TCAs) have long been known to be effective in treating depression in adults, drugs of this class have little, if any, therapeutic benefit in children and adolescents (for review, see Evans et al., 2005; Miller, 2007). What underlies the age difference in effectiveness of these two types of drugs is unknown. Both types of drugs ultimately boost levels of 5-HT, whereas TCAs also affect the norepinephrine (NE) system, again suggesting a potentially important role for 5-HT mechanisms in depression reminiscent of the genetic discussion above. Among the other consequences of TCAs and SSRIs is to block certain adverse effects of stress on the brain, including stress-induced suppression of neurogenesis (i.e., formation of new neurons) and stress-related inhibition in the production of a brain-derived neurotrophic factor, BDNF, that is critical for the survival and functioning of mature neurons (see Duman, 2002). These findings have led to a number of popular theories focusing on stress, neurogenesis, and neurotrophic factors in depression (e.g., Jacobs et al., 2000; Duman et al., 2002) that are discussed later. Whether there are age differences in these stress-suppressing effects of antidepressants is unknown.

Age differences in the effectiveness of TCAs bring to mind other developmental discontinuities characteristic of depression, such as the less marked hyperresponsiveness of the HPA axis seen in depressed youth than in adults with depression discussed earlier. Such findings have led some to question how similar the biology of depression is in children and adolescents relative to adults (e.g., Kaufman & Charney, 2003). Nevertheless, alterations in many of the same neural systems—especially 5-HT systems, the amygdala, the PFC, and HPA axis regulatory systems—emerge both in studies of adolescents with depression and/or anxiety as well as in studies of adults with these internalizing disorders.

Depressed adolescents differ from nondepressed adolescents in the size of particular brain regions (e.g., MacMillan et al., 2003), as do their adult counterparts (e.g., Frodl et al., 2003). There is little consensus yet, however, as to the specific nature of these alterations in adolescence; for instance, volumes of gray and white matter in the frontal cortex and in limbic regions such as the amygdala varyingly have been reported to be smaller or larger in adolescents with depression than in nondepressed adolescents (see Miller, 2007, for review). Such across-study variance is likely due in part to small sample sizes, the limited number of studies available, and characteristics of the adolescents studied, including whether the depressed adolescents had comorbid anxiety or other disorders. Overall these reports of differences in size of frontal and limbic areas in adolescent depression have been postulated to reflect "developmental abnormalities in medial frontal and related areas that modulate autonomic and neuroendocrine stress responses and reward sensitivity" (Miller, 2007, p. 56). It should not be assumed, though, that such brain-size alterations necessarily reflect permanent neural dysfunctions. For instance, the increased volume of the amygdala characteristic of the first depressive episode in adults is no longer evident in adults who have had recurrent episodes of depression (along with long-term exposure to antidepressants) (Frodl et al., 2003).

Depressed adolescents differ from nondepressed individuals not only in relative size of particular brain regions, but also in their brain activation patterns to emotional stimuli (usually, faces with different expressions), with these activation patterns generally similar to those found in fMRI studies of depressed adults. For instance, adults with depression have been reported to show greater activation in the amygdala and NAc in response to faces showing negative affect (i.e., fearful or sad faces) than do nondepressed adults, while showing less activation in the amygdala in response to happy faces (Surguladze et al., 2005). These functional alterations are sensitive to treatment: The greater activation in the amygdala and other limbic regions in response to sad faces seen during episodes of depression is reduced by antidepressants (Fu et al., 2004). Findings reminiscent of those seen in adults with depression are seen in adolescents with clinical depression as well, with reports of enhanced activation in the amygdala under some test circumstances when depressed adolescents look at faces displaying various emotions, but less activation in response to positive rewards in the striatal and other reward-related brain regions (Roberson-Nay et al., 2006; Forbes et al., 2006; although see also Thomas et al., 2001a).

When children and adolescents at high risk for depression (because their parents had the disorder) were asked to view faces with various emotional expressions, they showed greater activation of the amygdala and NAc in response to fearful facial expressions, but less activation in response to happy faces, than controls without a family history of internalizing or psychotic disorders (Monk et al., 2008). Differences in these regions were not seen when the adolescents' attention was captured by the addition of a task requiring them to focus on specific, nonemotional aspects of the faces. Performance on this task, in contrast, was associated with activation of medial portions of the PFC, with this activation greater in at-risk than control adolescents. This elevated activation was speculated to be necessary to "normalize" excessive emotion-related limbic activation among at-risk adolescents (see Monk et al., 2008). Adolescents at risk for anxiety disorders due to a behaviorally inhibited temperament likewise have been reported to show amygdalar hyperactivation when exposed to emotional and/or threatening faces under some test circumstances (Pérez-Edgar et al., 2007). Given that these differences in amygdalar and PFC activation are evident in at-risk youth before the emergence of clinical signs of internalizing disorders, these activation differences seemingly represent neural markers of vulnerability rather than concomitants of expressing a mood disorder, per se.

The amygdala and PFC have emerged as regions whose activity is altered in adolescents and adults with anxiety disorders as well. The higher vigilance of clinically anxious adults for threat-related stimuli (e.g., threatening faces) has consistently been shown to be related to greater amygdalar activation, with the magnitude of activation correlated with the severity of anxiety (e.g., Phan et al., 2006). Under similar test conditions, an enhanced amygdalar response to threatening faces is sometimes (e.g., Thomas et al., 2001a) but not always (Monk et al., 2006) seen in adolescents with anxiety disorders, perhaps because, once the threat is detected, anxious adolescents direct their attention away from it in an attempt to reduce anxiety levels (Monk et al., 2006). Indeed, where the threatening stimuli are presented so briefly that processing is autonomic and not conscious, adolescents with anxiety disorders consistently exhibit greater (right) amygdalar activation than their nonanxious counterparts (Monk et al., 2008). Thus, adolescents and adults with clinical anxiety are often characterized by amygdalar hyperactivation during the initial processing of threatening stimuli—findings akin to the greater amygdalar response to negative affective stimuli seen in depressed adolescents and adults.

In fMRI studies comparing clinically anxious with nonanxious adolescents, activation differences were seen not only in the amygdala but also in the ventrolateral part of the PFC during the processing of threatening stimuli. In these studies greater ventrolateral PFC activation to threatening stimuli was generally associated with less activation in the amygdala, consistent with the interpretation that this portion of the PFC serves to moderate the amygdala's response to threat. This PFC inhibitory influence appears to be weaker in more anxious individuals, with less PFC modulatory activity seen in anxious than nonanxious adolescents (Monk et al., 2008) and in clinically anxious adolescents with greater anxiety than those expressing lower anxiety levels (Monk et al., 2006).

One exciting new set of hypotheses regarding the neurobiology of depression is based largely on basic research findings showing that antidepressants increase neurogenesis and expression of BDNF and reverse stress-induced impairments in these functions. For instance, one recent hypothesis regarding the neurobiology of depression is that stress-related increases in the stress hormone CORT (along with other stress effects, such as declines in 5-HT activity) suppress neurogenesis in the hippocampus, thereby precipitating depressive episodes, an effect particularly marked in individuals with hyperreactive HPA systems (Jacobs et al., 2000; Nestler et al., 2002). The hippocampus is thought to be a particular target because it has especially high levels of CORT receptors and is also one of the few brain regions where new neurons are formed throughout life. According to this theory, the hippocampus is critical for the formation of new memories, and when neurogenesis is disrupted there by stressful events that induce depressive thoughts, it becomes more difficult to replace these memories by new memories that could help the individual "escape" depressive ruminations (Jacobs et al., 2000). Thus, "waxing and waning of neurogenesis in the hippocampal formation [are thought to be] causal factors . . . in the precipitation of, and recovery from, episodes of clinical depression" (Jacobs et al., 2000, p. 264).

A related hypothesis is that stress-induced decreases in BDNF in the hippocampus, amygdala, and frontal cortex (but not other brain regions—e.g., hypothalamus) disrupt functioning and promote cell death of neurons and glia in these regions. These neurotoxic effects are reversed, to some extent, by antidepressant-induced increases in BDNF (see Nestler et al., 2002, for discussion and references). The largely hippocampal emphasis in these hypotheses follows from basic research examining animal models of depression and antidepressant actions, and contrasts with human imaging studies where there has been little focus to date on this brain region, other than a few reports of volume reductions among long-term depressed individuals (e.g., Shah et al., 1998; Sheline et al., 1996). Nevertheless, this new generation of hypotheses, focusing on neuronal plasticity as a critical process disrupted during depressive episodes and restored by antidepressants, opens new and exciting opportunities for the development of therapeutic agents (see Duman et al., 2000; Duman, 2002).

Yet, if depression is associated with disruptions in neural plasticity, why would the incidence of depression increase during adolescence, particularly in females? Generally, these hypotheses have not included a developmental dimension—at least, not yet. Any adolescent-associated increase in the amount of stressor exposure or in stressor reactivity, however, could seemingly contribute to disruptions in neurogenesis and declines in BDNF, precipitating depression among vulnerable adolescents. It also does not seem to be too much of a stretch to suggest that normal developmental declines in neurogenesis, and to a certain extent, levels of BNDF and other neurotrophic factors normally seen during adolescence, could contribute to a rise in the incidence of depression. Rates of neurogenesis, for example, decline developmentally throughout adolescence and into adulthood (e.g., Lemaire et al., 2000; He & Crews, 20007), a finding considered in some detail in the next chapter. In studies using animal models of adolescence, developmental declines in BDNF have also been reported in certain brain regions (Maisonpierre et al., 1990), including the neocortex (Katoh-Semba et al., 1998) and a brainstem region that contains cell bodies of DA neurons (Numan et al., 2005).

273

What Is It About Females That Increases Their Sensitivity to Developing Depression During the Pubertal and Adolescent Transitions?

Sex differences in the brain have not received much attention in prior chapters, principally because the relationship between the often modest sex differences emerging during brain development and the often marked sex differences in behavior, emotional expression, cognition, and sexual attitudes are still largely unknown. When searching for evidence as to why the incidence of depression increases during adolescence, however, consideration of sex differences may provide important clues, given that the increase in prevalence rate of depression is more pronounced in adolescent females than males. That is, from a slightly greater incidence of depression in males than females seen during late childhood, the 2:1 female:male ratio in the incidence of depression typically seen in adults emerges between 10 and 15 years of age (Angold et al., 1998). This rise in the prevalence of depressive disorders in females has been reported to be more strongly linked to pubertal status than to chronological age, per se, with a notable increase in risk for depression evident from midpuberty on in females but not their male counterparts (Angold et al., 1998).

It is not known what sex-typical change(s) might contribute to the rising vulnerability to depression among adolescent females, although evidence is beginning to build using several different approaches. One approach has focused on sex differences and the impact of gonadal hormones on stressor responsiveness and functioning of the HPA axis. At a physiological level, males and females differ in how different levels of the HPA axis function and are regulated (e.g., Young, 1998; Kirschbaum et al., 1999). For instance, females have been reported to sometimes show greater responsiveness to, and delayed post-stress recovery from, stress-related increases in CORT due to an attenuation in HPA feedback regulation, effects that appear partly related to elevations in gonadal hormones such as estrogen (Young, 1998). Sex differences were also apparent in 17- to 23-year-olds in the types of situations eliciting HPA activation, with females showing greater CORT release following a social rejection stressor, but males showing greater release of CORT when faced with a stressor related to an achievement challenge (Stroud et al., 2002). Given that the majority (about 75%) of depressive episodes are precipitated by stressful life events and that social stressors are particularly prevalent during adolescence, sex differences in vulnerability to social stressors, perhaps along with greater physiological reactivity to such stressors, may contribute to the increased vulnerability to depression seen in female adolescents.

Sex differences in brain function, perhaps engendered in part by puberty-associated increases in estrogen and other gonadal hormones, may also contribute to the greater rise in the incidence of depression in female than male adolescents. Estrogen acts directly on the brain via interaction with estrogen receptors that are localized in high concentrations in the hypothalamus and amygdala, and at more moderate levels in areas of the mesolimbic DA system, the hippocampus, neocortex, and regions containing cell bodies of 5-HT neurons (the dorsal raphe). There are a number of different types of estrogen receptors in these regions, and when activated by estrogen, they serve to influence transcription of genetic information, alter excitability of neurons, and even exert neuroprotective effects (see McEwen & Alves, 1999, for review). Via these means, rising levels of estrogen and other sex hormones at puberty may act at various places in the brain to impact neural functioning in sex-specific ways, potentially contributing to the greater prevalence of depression seen in female adolescents (see Chapter 3 for more discussion of the potential role of pubertal hormones in adolescent neurobehavioral function).

Although this general outline makes sense, it is entirely

speculative: What sex hormones are specifically doing to the brain during puberty and where they are doing it is still largely a mystery. One can envision a variety of possible culprits. For instance, given the complex (and incompletely understood) role of estrogen in regulating 5-HT activity (see McEwen & Alves, 1999), developmental rises in estrogen during adolescence could exert regionally specific alterations in 5-HT function (Okazawa et al., 2000) that serve to increase vulnerability to depression in females. As another example, studies in laboratory animals have revealed notable sex differences in regional brain concentrations of BDNF and other neurotrophic factors in adults (Angelucci et al., 2000); these differences could induce sex-dependent protective influences critical for imparting resistance to depression, which may begin to emerge during the normal developmental decline in levels of these protective factors during adolescence as discussed above.

SUMMARY AND CLOSING COMMENTS

Research exploring the developmental neuroscience of psychological disorders has multiplied over the past decade, due in large part to concerns regarding the substantial number of youth that are affected with these disorders, as well as advances made in characterizing the human genome and in developing powerful scanners for the noninvasive imaging of the developing brain. The hope is that findings obtained using these emergent techniques, when interfaced with results from basic research in areas such as gene–neuron interactions during development and long-term consequences of early and recent experiences on gene expression and neural function, may ultimately lead to more effective strategies for strengthening adolescent resiliency to the development of psychological disorders.

In such studies there is an increasing recognition that even genetic vulnerabilities for developmental psychopathology can be moderated considerably by experiences early in life, as well as by experiences faced by vulnerable youth as they enter adolescence. Even genetically "identical" twins may differ in whether or not they express any of these psychological disorders during adolescence, arguing for the critical importance of environmental contexts and experiences in determining whether vulnerability ultimately morphs into psychopathology. Indeed, many of the hypotheses discussed above regarding mechanisms underlying specific psychological disorders and their rise during adolescence are not mutually exclusive. Rather, they likely reflect different components of the multifactorial contributors that interact to produce any given disorder. For instance, the impact of genetic vulnerabilities may be moderated or exacerbated by life experiences (e.g., Gotlib et al., 2008) and associated with different patterns of regional brain activation in response to particular target stimuli (e.g., Hariri et al., 2005; Munafò et al., 2008).

As illustrated in this chapter, although expression of, or even increased vulnerability to, a particular disorder may be associated with regional differences in brain activation patterns in response to certain types of stimuli, such activation differences may no longer be evident following pharmacotherapeutic treatments (e.g., Fu et al., 2004). Even differences in the size of particular brain regions between those affected or not affected with a particular disorder are not necessarily permanent, and may wax and wane with life experiences and therapy over time (e.g., Frodl et al., 2003). This is good news. As more is learned about precipitators of, and protections against, the emergence of specific psychological disorders, clinicians, psychologists, and others working with susceptible youth may be able to design more supportive environmental contexts and novel drug- and other therapeutic approaches for prevention and treatment of these disorders early in their developmental course.

A Few Words on Resiliency

In the discussion thus far, I have largely emphasized vulnerabilities and risk factors—that is, those elements that make certain youth susceptible to the development of psychological disorders during adolescence. An important alternative approach focuses instead on protective factors and resiliency, and often extends indices of healthy functioning beyond the absence of diagnosable psychological disorders to include attainment of age-appropriate goals through the adolescent-to-adult transition in areas such as education, work, and social functioning (marriage, parenting skills, friendship base). Using a resiliency model, the question becomes why certain youth, despite exposure to high levels of adversity beginning in childhood, either do not develop psychological disorders or problematic behaviors or manage to get "back on track" after a transient period of less-than-optimal socioemotional functioning. These positive outcomes contrast with the more typical pattern of persisting problems that carries into adulthood among youth with similar histories of recurring life adversities (e.g., see Masten et al., 2006). Resilient youth not only escape psychopathology but often thrive in many aspects of their life, showing educational and job-related accomplishments that equal or even exceed those of low-risk youth who were not exposed to significant adversities (e.g., see Werner, 2005, for brief review).

Quite a bit is known about what makes a young person resilient. Such resiliency is likely partly genetic. As one example, although earlier in this chapter I emphasized the association between the short variant of the 5-HT transporter gene and enhanced vulnerability to stress-induced precipitation of depressive episodes, these data can be conversely viewed as supporting the suggestion that the long variant of the 5-HT transporter gene serves a protective role, with very low rates of stress-induced depression occurring in individuals having only the long variant of this gene (Caspi et al., 2003). Other critical resilient-promoting factors have been divided into external assets and internal assets, with youth displaying many of these assets being dramatically less likely to exhibit drug/alcohol use, antisocial behaviors, depression, and other problem behaviors than those youth having few such assets (see Benson et al., 1998).

External assets include environmental components that foster healthy emotional growth by supporting and empowering youth, establishing boundaries, setting expectations, providing constructive activities, and so on (see Benson et al., 1998). Sources providing such "scaffolding" for young adolescents include families, schools, and religious and neighborhood organizations. For older youth in the throes of the adolescent-to-adult transition, additional sources of potential scaffolding include military service, higher education, work apprenticeships, and perhaps marriage (under the best of circumstances) (see Werner, 2005).

Internal assets include skills, competencies, positive values, and self-image that youth develop over time, with resilient youth typically being goal-directed, future oriented, motivated for change, planful, autonomous, and, importantly, possessing good self-regulatory skills (e.g., see Masten et al., 2006; Masten, 2007). The development of the adaptive functioning characteristic of resilient youth is promoted by continued maturation of executive functions during adolescence, as well as via support provided by various external assets, with particularly critical predictors of positive outcomes associated with adult support outside the family (Masten et al., 2006) as well as after-school activities (Benson et al., 1998). Interestingly, youth who develop resiliency often actively seek out external supports to strengthen their capacities even further, for instance, frequently "recruiting" their own sources of adult mentorship and support (Werner, 2005).

This focus on resiliency emphasizes the importance of positive environmental experiences and the development of internal adaptive capacities during adolescence to promote positive psychological health. This notion is developed further as we now turn to the topic of whether the normal remodeling of the adolescent brain provides a time of special vulnerability as well as opportunity for experiences to "customize" the maturing brain.

CHAPTER TEN

Adolescent Vulnerabilities and Opportunities

••

As discussed in Chapter 4, much of the remodeling of the adolescent brain contributes to an increase in brain efficiency, seemingly associated with a shift from a more inefficient but "plastic" juvenile brain to the more efficient but less plastic adult brain. That is not to say, however, that the mature brain is insensitive to experience. The brain retains substantial plasticity in some respects throughout life, with estimates of a 7% synaptic turnover, *per week*, in the adult neocortex (Stettler et al., 2006). After all, the brain is specialized for learning and modifying behavior based on past experiences, and this type of learning mandates some degree of plasticity.

Although the brain is most malleable to experience-induced modification early in life, there is growing evidence that significant neuroplasticity is retained in some regions well into adolescence. Such plasticity could potentially provide continued opportunities for the adolescent brain to be sculpted and "customized" to match the proclivities, activities, and experiences of the adolescent. This matching of the brain function to environmental circumstances during adolescence may represent a relatively delayed example of "developmental programming" of the brain—programming that is particularly pronounced and well characterized during the prenatal and early postnatal periods.

DEVELOPMENTAL PROGRAMMING

Very early in development, the brain is developmentally pro- grammed along a number of dimensions, influencing brain function, behavior, and health throughout life. Developmental periods of enhanced plasticity, when particular brain systems appear to be programmed or "tuned" to match characteristics of the environment, are called "critical periods" or "sensitive periods." There are many such periods, each sensitive to par- ticular environmental stimuli. For instance, shortly after vision begins, research conducted in kittens has shown that there is a critical period for *orientation selectivity* when neurons in the visual cortex become "tuned" to the types of visual input they receive; for example, more neurons become responsive to horizontal than vertical lines when the visual environment contains many horizontal, but few vertical, lines. Likewise, children and adolescents born with bilateral cataracts on both eyes (and hence deprived of pattern vision) exhibit permanent deficits in their acuity for visual patterns, even when their cat- aractous lenses were removed and replaced with contact lenses within the first 9 months of life (Lewis & Mauer, 2005). Some- what later in development, visual input from both eyes is re- quired to maintain normal binocular vision, with a disruption of vision in one eye during this critical period for *ocular domi- nance* permanently impairing vision in that eye. There are oth- er sensitive periods in the visual system as well, each with its own developmental timing and stimulus characteristics (see Lewis & Maurer, 2005, for review).

While critical periods have been associated most often with the fine-tuning of sensory systems (Hensch, 2004), during its development the brain can also be modulated ("programmed") more globally by other types of environmental experiences. As mentioned in Chapter 4, one such type of developmental programming is the establishment of body weight regulatory systems based on nutritional availability during the prenatal and early postnatal period. For instance, individuals who are heavy at birth are more likely to become obese later in life than those with average birthweights (Armitage et al., 2005). Through such developmental programming, the brain and physiology of the growing organism are tuned to the environment—an environment that serves as the best-guess predictor of future life circumstances. Such early programming can occasionally backfire when there is a mismatch between early experience and the later environment. For instance, both individuals who are heavy at birth as well as those born with *low* birthweights are more likely to be obese later in life than those with average birth weights (e.g., Taylor & Poston, 2007). This seemingly paradoxical relationship between low birth weights and later obesity has been hypothesized to result from developmental programming of metabolic setpoint systems. That is, low birthweight associated with less than optimal exposure to nutrients prenatally is thought to lead to the development of a "thrifty phenotype," whereby the offspring's metabolism is set to maximize available nutrient sources. While this adaptation would help support adequate weight gain under circumstances of continued nutritional insufficiencies throughout life, under conditions where food is plentiful, this early metabolic adaptation can lead to weight gain and obesity. This adaptation has been suggested as one factor contributing to the high rate of obesity among the offspring of immigrants to the United States from developing countries (see Gluckman & Hanson, 2004).

Another prominent example of developmental programming is the influence of early maternal care on later stress-related functioning. Basic research has shown that when infant animals receive extensive tactile stimulation from their mothers (i.e., offspring of high-LG mothers discussed in Chapter 2), their brains develop in a way to maximize function in low-stress environments, whereas the opposite is true for animals exposed to little maternal care. For instance, adult offspring who received high levels of maternal tactile stimulation and care learn better under low-stress conditions than those receiving less maternal care, although they may perform worse under high-stress conditions (Champagne et al., 2008). Tactile stimulation has also been shown to be critical for offspring development in humans. For instance, preemies in neonatal intensive care units grow faster when given tactile "massages" than when not stimulated in this manner (see Field et al., 2007). In general, early environmental adversities (e.g., pronounced maternal separation in laboratory animals; childhood physical abuse or neglect in humans) appear to developmentally program the brain to be more responsive to environmental stressors throughout life (Gutman & Nemeroff, 2003). While this adaptation facilitates short-term capacity to deal with stressors, under continued stressful circumstances, this greater reactivity would result in repeated extranormal activation of stress systems, increasing vulnerability to chronic stress-related diseases (e.g., Seckl & Meaney, 2004).

Developmental programming may exert lifelong influences on the emergence of diverse medical and psychological disorders via these influences on stress reactivity and the propensity for the emergence of obesity. Even the course of aging may be influenced: Recent evidence suggests that the incidence of aging-related diseases such as Alzheimer's disease may be influenced by early developmental experiences (Ross et al., 2007).

The developmental programming and neuroplasticity characteristic of early life decline gradually thereafter. There are numerous examples of greater plasticity of the brain of the child than that of more mature individuals. For instance: (1) feral children develop notably better language skills if introduced to language before 10 years of age than thereafter; (2) damage to the language-dominant hemisphere prior to 10 years of age results in greater recovery of language function than if the damage occurs thereafter; and (3) there is lasting damage to vision in individuals with a "lazy eye" if they are not forced, prior to about 10 years of age, to use the lazy eye by temporarily blocking input to the dominant eye (see Chugani, 1998). In these examples, plasticity of the developing brain appears to be maintained at some level throughout childhood, but declines around the transition into adolescence. In other cases, however, developmental neuroplasticity may extend into the adolescent brain.

DEVELOPMENTAL NEUROPLASTICITY IN ADOLESCENCE

Although there has been little consideration of developmental programming in adolescence, there are a number of hints that some degree of developmental neuroplasticity extends into adolescence—perhaps providing one last opportunity for the brain to be customized before full maturity is reached. Although much of the evidence for greater plasticity in the adolescent than mature brain has been obtained from basic research, signs of similar plasticity are also beginning to emerge in studies with human adolescents as well.

Formation of New Neurons

New neurons are formed at very high rates prenatally, with the vast majority of neurons seen in the adult brain being formed prior to birth. Nevertheless, modest amounts of new neurons are formed throughout life. These later-forming neurons are derived from small populations of stem cells (i.e., cells that are still capable of dividing) and are destined for a few targeted brain regions such as the hippocampus. Rates of this neurogenesis are four- to five-fold higher among adolescents than adults (Lemaire et al., 2000; He & Crews, 2007). The functional impact of this marked neurogenesis for the adolescent remains to be identified. At least among adult animals, neurogenesis has been shown to be critical for some types of learning and may also facilitate brain repair, under some circumstances, following damage (e.g., Kozorovitskiy & Gould, 2003). Rates of production and survival of neurons generated in adulthood are enhanced by physical activity and enriched environmental experiences, and are disrupted by exposure to stressors (see Kozorovitskiy & Gould, 2003). Thus, it seems possible, if not likely, that the higher neurogenesis rates of the adolescent brain could contribute to elevated neuroplasticity, perhaps reflecting one of the ways by which environmental experiences could help customize the adolescent brain.

Synaptic Dynamics

Adolescence is characterized not only by more synaptic pruning than seen in the mature brain, but also by considerable remodeling of synapses as well. Axons and their presynaptic endings show considerable fluidity during adolescence, with axonal endings often extending or retracting on the order of minutes—a dynamic process that is much less evident and notably slower in mature neurons (Gan et al., 2003). Likewise, there appears to be substantially more fluidity in the postsynaptic component of synapses during adolescence than in adulthood. One way in which this fluidity has been studied is to investigate changes over time in the number and appearance of synaptic spines: those spiny extensions of dendrites that provide the postsynaptic targets for most of the excitatory input to the cortex. In addition to a sizable reduction in number of synaptic spines in the cortex during adolescence, the turnover rate (i.e., rate of breakdown and replacement) of those spines is also much faster in the adolescent than the mature brain. For instance, 13–20% of the spine population in sensory, motor, and frontal cortices was eliminated over a 2-week period in adolescent mice, with 5–8% of these spines replaced by new spines, whereas only 3–5% of spines were eliminated and a comparable number formed over the same 2-week period in these regions in adulthood (Zuo et al., 2005b). While there is general agreement that adolescence is characterized by substantial turnover in spines along with a considerable decline in overall number of spines, the jury is still out as to the extent to which the relatively constant number of spines in the adult reflect relatively static spines (Zuo et al., 2005b; Grutzendler et al., 2002) or spines that are being dynamically eliminated and replaced in a balanced manner (Trachtenberg et al., 2002; Stettler et al., 2006).

Greater plasticity has also been reported in adolescence than in adulthood in terms of the rate and extent to which synapses recover from brain damage. When axons are damaged, the portion of each axon separated from the cell body dies, along with its presynaptic endings. Under some circumstances, unaffected axons in nearby regions may sprout into the damaged area and generate new synaptic endings, replacing some synapses that were lost and potentially enhancing recovery. Studies in laboratory animals have shown that these processes—postdamage loss and replacement of synapses—are faster during adolescence than in adulthood. For instance, following damage at different ages to a group of axons projecting to the hippocampus, number of synapses initially declined markedly and then began to increase; number of synapses had recovered to almost normal levels 8 days postdamage in adolescence, whereas comparable amounts of recovery took months in adulthood (McWilliams & Lynch, 1983).

POSSIBLE EXPERIENCE-INFLUENCED BRAIN PLASTICITY IN ADOLESCENCE

Evidence is gradually emerging that the marked transformations occurring in the brain during adolescence may be, in part, environmentally dependent. Two particularly notable alterations in the adolescent brain that may be influenced by ongoing experiences are the processes of axonal myelination and synaptic pruning.

Myelination

As discussed in Chapter 4, myelination of axons has been shown to be driven partly by the amount of activity (i.e., amount of impulse flow) in those axons (Stevens et al., 2002). Given that amount of axonal activity in many fiber tracts reflects input from the environment, such activity-driven myelination provides one means by which the environment could help sculpt the brain of the adolescent. Indeed, substantial research has shown that animals raised throughout adolescence in enriched environments, when compared with those reared in restricted environments, have brains that are more heavily myelinated and have a larger corpus callosum—that is, the huge bundle of myelinated and unmyelinated axons that crosses the midline to connect the left and right sides of the neocortex (Markham & Greenough, 2004).

Studies using diffusion tensor imaging (DTI; see Chapter 4) to examine the development of white matter integrity in juvenile and adolescent humans have revealed substantial individual differences in myelin production—individual differences that could be driven partly by environmental experiences. For instance, more developed white matter pathways were correlated with higher IQs in a group of children and young adolescents, data interpreted to suggest that "efficient organization of white matter association fibers is essential for optimal cognitive performance" (Schmithorst et al., 2005, p. 5). The extent to which these white matter changes contribute to cognitive functioning per se, however, is unclear, as is the degree to which individual differences in white matter reflect the accumulation of prior experiences.

This issue was more directly explored in a study briefly mentioned in Chapter 4 that examined the structural integrity of white matter in different axonal tracts of professional pianists. White matter integrity was found to be correlated with the amount of time these musicians practiced the piano as children (< 11 years of age), as adolescents (12–16 years), and as late adolescent/adults (> 17 years). Intriguingly, the amount of practice during the two younger age intervals was correlated with development in more tracts than at the older age, even though the pianists spent less time practicing at earlier ages than when they reached late adolescence/young adulthood and began performing professionally (Bengtsson et al., 2005). Tracts that were most susceptible to experience varied with age, with late-maturing pathways connecting frontal regions with other brain regions most sensitive to amount of practice later in adolescence and in young adulthood.

From such correlational data alone it is not possible to determine causality—that is, whether it was the amount of practice, per se, that led to the alterations in white matter. Nevertheless, the results of the study by Bengtsson and colleagues (2005) are consistent with the suggestion that the intensity of myelin development (and hence speed of information flow in those tracts) can be increased by experience, with the strongest experience effects seen through midadolescence. The converse may also be the case, with individuals subjected to neglect as children differing from non-neglected individuals in having a smaller-size corpus callosum (Teicher et al., 2004). Likewise, the amount of exposure to parental verbal abuse during childhood and adolescence was recently reported to be associated with reduced white matter integrity in a variety of axonal pathways implicated in cognitive and psychological functioning (Choi et al., 2009). Taken together, these findings are consistent with the suggestion that extent and structural integrity of myelination—and hence speed of information flow across specific brain regions—can be bidirectionally influenced by different types of experiences during childhood and adolescence, perhaps contributing to individual differences in vulnerabilities or resiliencies to future life challenges and adversities.

Synaptic Pruning and Gray Matter Density

Another major developmental transformation of the adolescent brain that may be experience-dependent, to some extent, is the process of synaptic pruning. Although there is substantial evidence that the number of synapses declines significantly during adolescence in cortical and some subcortical regions, the contributing factors to this synaptic decline are less than clear. The cause does not seem to be the same as with the synaptic pruning that occurs early in life, where the loss seems to follow a "survival of the fittest" principle, with weaker, more immature synapses selectively culled (Le Be & Markram, 2006). That is, in contrast to this early elimination of immature synapses, the synapses lost during adolescence have characteristics of functionally mature connections and appear indistinguishable from those that are retained (Gonzalez-Burgos et al., 2008). In this case, rather than merely reflecting a loss of weaker synapses, fate decisions about survival or loss of synapses in adolescence may be partly based on type and location of synapse, with excitatory synapses on dendritic spines, for example, lost more commonly than inhibitory synapses (De Felipe et al., 1997; Gonzalez-Burgos et al., 2008), and connections within a given cortical region (intrinsic circuitry) losing more synaptic connections than so-called "association" projections that connect different brain regions (Woo et al., 1997; Zuo et al., 2005a).

Of particular relevance for our interest here, the synaptic culling of adolescence may be partly experience-dependent. Zuo and colleagues (2005a) explored the effects of experience on synapse elimination, as indexed by declines in the number of dendritic spines. Surprisingly, they found that normal adolescent declines in spine numbers in the sensory cortex required stimulation from the environment and did not occur when the cortical region was deprived of its input during adolescence. Thus, in this instance the adolescent-typical *decline* in number of synaptic contacts between neurons was dependent on normal experience, with sensory-deprived adolescents retaining more spines (i.e., more synapses) than adolescents who were not deprived of sensory experience. At first blush, these data are difficult to reconcile with other evidence that increased environmental stimulation (such that provided by rearing in an enriched environment) is associated with increased numbers of spines and synapses in a number of brain regions (Markham & Greenough, 2004). Yet, the finding that adolescent-typical synaptic declines sometimes require stimulation from the environment is reminiscent of other findings in the developmental literature (see Lichtman & Colman, 2000). For instance, early imprinting in chicks is associated with synapse elimination, with this reduction in spine synapses thought to serve as a means of retaining information learned early in life (Bock & Braun, 1999). Activity-dependent increases in both the production of spines as well as in spine pruning are seen in the mature brain (Segal, 2005), along with changes in spine structure that may alter the strength of synapses associated with those spines (Carpenter-Hyland & Chandler, 2007). Thus, spine genesis and demise may not be related in any simple fashion to expression of brain plasticity, either during development or in adulthood, with both spine loss as well as spine formation sometimes linked to environmentally induced plasticity, depending on factors such as the neural region involved, the nature of the environmental deprivation or stimulation, and its timing (see Carpenter-Hyland & Chandler, 2007; Zuo et al., 2005a).

Number of synapses and spines cannot be examined in intact humans but rather requires autopsy material; thus, it is not surprising that studies of experience effects on the culling of synapses during adolescence have not been extended to human adolescents. Effects of childhood and adolescent experiences on brain structure and function have been explored, however, through examining experience effects on gray matter density using brain imaging. As discussed in Chapter 4, gray matter density is influenced by a number of factors in addition to synaptic density, including amount of dendritic branching as well as numbers of neurons and glia in that region. These studies have revealed evidence of experience effects during time periods that include adolescence, although the relative sensitivity to experience effects across age has been little detailed. For instance, in a study that examined bilingual individuals who began their second language acquisition at ages ranging from infancy to the mid-30s, the earlier the second language exposure began, the greater the amount of gray matter in the left inferior parietal cortex, a brain region critical for verbal fluency and whose size (amount of gray matter) was greater in bilinguals than monolinguals and correlated with proficiency in the second language (Mechelli et al., 2004). These findings support the conclusion that early experiences continuing throughout adolescence and into adulthood can impact density of gray matter in performance-relevant brain regions. Training young adults (with an average age in the early 20s) to juggle likewise was found to increase gray matter volume of brain regions involved in visual perception of moving objects; these effects were transient and gradually declined posttraining when juggling was no longer practiced (Draganski et al., 2004).

Experience-related effects have been reported in middle-aged adults as well. Adults (mean age of 44 years) licensed as taxi drivers in London—who hence have extensive knowledge of the spatial location of streets and locales—were found to differ from an age-matched control group in terms of distribution of gray matter in their hippocampus, with the taxi drivers having relatively more gray matter in the posterior hippocampus, a brain region important for spatial representations of the environment, than the anterior hippocampus, and the magnitude of this redistribution correlating with amount of time as a taxi driver (Maguire et al., 2002). Thus, the brain can change structurally with experience well into adulthood, although the extent (and perhaps longevity) of these effects seems to be less marked under some circumstances in adulthood than after comparable experience as juveniles or adolescents (see results of Bengtsson et al., 2005; Mechelli et al., 2004).

WHY DOES NEUROPLASTICITY DECLINE DEVELOPMENTALLY?

A central thesis of this chapter is that neuroplasticity is most pronounced early in life and shows system-specific declines thereafter, with significant residual plasticity still evident in some systems into and throughout adolescence. Why does plasticity decline—or, in other words, what is it about the maturing brain that normally constrains the degree to which neuroplasticity can be exhibited? The answer to this question is likely complex, given that there are many different sensitive periods, each with its own timing of onset and offset—a timing likely driven by specific molecular mechanisms and environmental influences. Although many emerging constraints on plasticity have yet to be identified, research has begun to reveal a few of the limiting factors.

Changing Molecular Characteristics, Inhibitory/Excitatory Balance

Differing critical periods likely have unique molecular mechanisms and environmental influences. For instance, the timing of two different forms of plasticity in the visual system mentioned earlier in this chapter—orientation selectivity and ocular dominance—is controlled via very different molecular mechanisms. In the case of orientation selectivity, sensory experience (light) triggers alterations in N-methyl-D-aspartate (NMDA) receptors for the excitatory neurotransmitter glutamate, with receptor alterations in turn permitting development of orientation selectivity of neurons in the visual cortex (Fagiolini et al., 2003). In contrast, exposure to visual stimuli induces increases in activity of the inhibitory neurotransmitter GABA, with this increase in turn setting the stage for both the onset and offset of the critical period for ocular dominance (Berardi et al., 2003). Interestingly, the absence of appropriate visual experience delays expression of this critical period, whereas drugs that stimulate GABA receptors (e.g., diazepam and other antianxiety agents) speed up the timing of both its onset and termination (Fagiolini et al., 2004).

Alterations in glutaminergic excitatory neurotransmission play a key role not only in controlling the timing of the critical period for orientation selectivity, but also in the control of sensitive periods for other forms of plasticity (e.g., see Lamprecht & LeDoux, 2004). Likewise, a shift in the balance of excitatory and inhibitory inputs toward greater inhibition is thought to play an essential role in the timing of the critical period not only for ocular dominance but also in regulating the timing and duration of critical periods for responsivity to other, non-visual sensory stimuli (see Hensch & Fagiolini, 2004). These examples of critical periods in the visual system also support the suggestion that experience-triggered neural changes may precipitate not only a transient period of induced plasticity, but also the decline in plasticity that follows on its heels, thereby stabilizing the plasticity-induced neural changes for use by the mature brain.

Maturation of Neurocircuitry

Pyramidal cells in the cortex have two different types of excitatory projections: (1) extrinsic "association" projections that extend from that cortical region to different cortical regions or subcortical areas; and (2) intrinsic projections that connect with other pyramidal cells and smaller, inhibitory "local circuit" neurons within the same cortical region. Much of the synaptic pruning seen in the cortex during adolescence occurs in the intrinsic projections—particularly in synapses between pyramidal cells in the same horizontal layer of the cortex (Woo et al., 1997). The net effect is a refinement of the horizontal circuitry of pyramidal cell interconnections, resulting in a clustering of these neurons into discrete functional networks that allow for more focused neural activation. Similar refinements in intrinsic cortical circuitry are also seen within the visual cortex at the close of critical periods and hence at the time that various aspects of visual perception are specified (e.g., orientation selectivity) (Burkhalter et al., 1993; Durack & Katz, 1996). Whereas synaptic pruning-related refinement in neurocircuitry seems to be straightforwardly related to specification and loss of environmentally sensitive plasticity in the visual system, the function of pruning in regions of the association cortex such as the PFC are less clear. Does the refinement in neurocircuitry with synaptic culling in the adolescent PFC signal the maturation and closing of a sensitivity period, during which environmental experiences influence circuit specification? If so, what kinds of experiences are influential, and how would they alter PFC neurocircuitry? Clearly, this is a ripe area for further investigation.

Myelination as a Plasticity Terminator

Another potential brake on plasticity is the process of myelination, per se. In a recent study of adolescents diagnosed with alcohol use disorders, these adolescents unexpectedly showed evidence of *earlier* myelination than was seen in a matched group of adolescents without an alcohol/drug disorder (De Bellis et al., 2008). The researchers conducting this study speculated that such early myelination might reflect a premature shutting down of brain plasticity that signals a less than optimal timing of development. Indeed, there is some indication from basic research that myelination may serve to "consolidate neural circuitry by suppressing plasticity" (McGee et al., 2005, p. 2225). In a general sense, the process of myelination limits the plasticity of the myelinated axons by constraining their capacity to grow in different directions, sprout new extensions, and so on. In at least some brain areas, myelin also releases chemicals that serve to block plasticity of surrounding neurons. For instance, in the visual cortex, myelin releases a protein called *nogo* that activates specific nogo receptors (abbreviated *NgR*) on cortical neurons; this receptor activation in turn inhibits outgrowth of neuronal processes necessary for the formation of new synapses (McGee et al., 2005). Animals with a genetic mutation of NgR, rendering them insensitive to this myelin-released protein continued to show experience-dependent visual plasticity into adulthood. Although this nogo–NgR pathway is not required for termination of plasticity in all brain regions, these data illustrate how chemical signals released from myelin during the process of axonal myelination can serve to terminate developmental neuroplasticity in a regionally specific manner. Other myelin signals serving to constrain neural plasticity continue to be identified and studied for their role in normal and atypical development (Fields, 2008).

ADOLESCENT NEUROPLASTICITY: CUSTOMIZING THE BRAIN OF THE ADOLESCENT?

The adolescent brain is characterized by a number of dynamic changes that includes marked and highly specific synaptic pruning, along with myelination of a number of axonal tracts. As discussed above, there are hints that both synaptic pruning and myelination may be environmentally influenced, with the extent of axon myelination in part influenced by the level of activity in those axons, and with adolescent-typical declines in synaptic spines requiring environmental experience in at least some instances (best characterized in the visual system). Moreover, evidence is gradually emerging that during this sculpting, the adolescent brain demonstrates greater neuroplasticity than the brain at maturity, at least when indexed via rates of neurogenesis and synaptic dynamism. Taken together, these data are consistent with the hypothesis that adolescence represents a sensitive period in which environmental interactions influence these sculpting processes. But what might be the functional consequences of this brain neuroplasticity for the adolescent? Does adolescence represent one last-ditch developmental programming effort to match the maturing brain to environmental circumstances? Or is this period of rapid neural changes a time of particular vulnerability for the growing brain? Or are both scenarios possible, depending on the target brain system as well as the individual's genetic heritage, past experiences, and current environment? Although it would be at best speculative to assert any firm answers to these questions, some considerations and data of possible relevance to these issues are discussed below.

Adolescent Brain Sculpting as a Time of Opportunity

If developmental programming continues into adolescence, it could provide a final opportunity to match the maturing brain to environmental circumstances. The networks most likely to be affected seemingly would be those involving brain regions that change notably during adolescence—"higher" cortical regions such as the PFC and other frontal cortical regions, along with the cerebellum, amygdala, and other interconnected limbic regions. This combination of a speeding-up of information flow within networks interconnecting these cortical regions with more distant areas, in combination with a decline in number of synaptic contacts within these regions, could potentially provide a time of particular sensitivity to education and the social environment. For instance, consider the changes in social interactions that occur during adolescence—starting from an emphasis on same-sex playmates and substantial parental control and evolving to perhaps serious relationships with the opposite sex (for heterosexual individuals) and less parental involvement. Given the dramatic nature of these changes, alterations in brain regions critical for various social behaviors might be expected to be particularly sensitive to social experience during adolescence. Indeed, basic research has shown that adolescent social experience can dramatically alter postlesion recovery of sociosexual behavior, with lesions in a region of the hypothalamus (medial preoptic area) that markedly disrupts male sexual behavior in animals lesioned either prepubertally or in adulthood being almost completely ameliorated when prepubertally lesioned animals are reared in mixed social groups through adolescence (Twiggs et al., 1978). Moreover, social stress during adolescence (created by housing animals in a new social situation daily) has been found to induce alterations in brain regions such as the CeA, an area of the amygdala critical for socioemotional control and adaptation to social and other types of stressors (McCormick et al., 2007). The extent to which particular social experiences during adolescence can "program" the social brain in humans is as yet unknown, however.

Maturational changes in the PFC and related brain regions during adolescence have been suggested to be associated with development of certain executive functions (see Chapter 5), although it is not known whether particular educational or environmental experiences during adolescence could trigger enhanced functioning in these regions. The possibilities are exciting, although very speculative at this point. Consider *mul-*

titasking—that is, engagement in more than one activity at a time. What with the proliferation of text messaging, iPods, YouTube, online chat rooms, and so on, multitasking seems considerably more common among today's youth than in past generations. Brain regions critical for attention, divided attention, and prioritizing among stimuli include forebrain areas such as PFC that undergo developmental sculpting during adolescence. Is it possible that such extensive experience multitasking might developmentally program the maturing brain to provide greater capacity for dividing attention and processing multiple stimuli? On the other hand, with such sources of constant stimulation, along with "free time" that is often highly scheduled with extracurricular activities, practices, clubs, and games, not to mention homework, kids and adolescents today seem to have less time for nonstructured thinking than prior generations. Could this context constrain development of cortical regions in the right hemisphere critical for creative, empathic, holistic thinking (see Taylor, 2008)?

Exercise and nutrition may exert additional influences on the sculpting of the brain during adolescence. It has long been known that what we eat influences levels of brain neurotransmitters, brain function, and behavior (e.g., Wurtman et al., 2003). Indeed, in a study of the impact of nutritional supplementation on antisocial behavior among late-adolescent/young-adult prisoners, intake of a supplement containing vitamins, minerals, and essential fatty acids markedly reduced the number of disciplinary incidences and episodes of violence (Gesch et al., 2002). These data are particularly compelling given that the study design used was double-blind and placebo-controlled—the "gold standard" for human studies, whereby neither those receiving the supplements nor those providing them knew which prisoners received nutritional supplements or the similarly appearing placebo. Yet, despite general recognition that sound nutrition is critical to help the brain reach

its full potential during developmental spurts that include adolescence (House, 2007), much of the focus in developmental
nutrition has emphasized ensuring nutritional adequacy during gestational/neonatal periods. Although it is well-known
that the physiological changes of adolescence are accompanied by increases in food intake and a considerable growth
spurt (Post & Kemper, 1993), the impact of quality, quantity,
and type of food for facilitating the structural and molecular
changes associated with the remodeling of the adolescent brain
nevertheless has received little attention. Likewise, basic research studies have shown that exercise increases cell proliferation and numbers of neurons in the hippocampus of
adolescents (Uysal et al., 2005) as well as adults (e.g., Kim et
al., 2002), although it remains to be determined whether the
adolescent brain is more, less, or similarly sensitive to exercise
effects when compared to the mature brain. Could there be
consequences for adolescent brain sculpting of the considerable reduction in physical activity currently seen as youth enter adolescence, with recent reports that almost all 9-year-olds
meet recommended amounts of physical activity, whereas only
about 25% of 15-year-olds do so (Nader et al., 2008)?

Another intriguing possibility is that developmental experiences through adolescence could alter *brain reserve*—a term
used for the capacity to respond adaptively later in life when
confronted with new challenges, including the disruption in
brain function associated with brain injury (e.g., a stroke) or
diseases such as Alzheimer's disease. Brain reserve is thought
to consist of a number of neural properties such as number of
neurons and their interconnections, and is thought to be reflected cognitively by the variety and sophistication of cognitive problem-solving strategies (Mortimer, 1997). For an
example of data interpreted within a brain reserve framework,
consider findings from the so-called nun study, a longitudinal
study examining cognitive–linguistic abilities of an order of

nuns from the time they joined their order through the aging process and until their brains were examined at death (see Mortimer et al., 2007). Larger brain sizes and higher levels of education were found to serve as protective factors that delayed the onset of signs of dementia, although not altering the physical brain changes associated with the process of Alzheimer's disease, per se (Mortimer et al., 2007). That is, although level of education during adolescence (high school and college) did not affect the timing of the onset of neuropathology associated with Alzheimer's disease, those individuals with higher levels of education (or larger brain sizes) were less likely to exhibit dementia and other clinical signs of the disease. These data support the suggestion that the amount of educational experience during adolescence is associated with greater brain reserve later in life. Yet, to wave the causality flag once again, from these data alone it is not possible to determine whether the amount of education during adolescence was causal in inducing the later protection from Alzheimer's dementia. For instance, one possible alternative explanation of these data is that individuals with higher IQs may be not only more likely to seek out and obtain more education, but also may have brains that retain more neurological function in the presence of Alzheimer's related neuropathology. Nevertheless, these data are intriguing in demonstrating a correlation between level of educational achievement during adolescence and clinical manifestation of a brain disease many decades later.

Brain reserve could also be functionally expressed a number of other ways. Adolescence is often accompanied by many environmental changes, as teens must learn to function in new social contexts, changing educational situations, new types of stressful circumstances, and so on. Some of these situations may be more reflective of the environment to be expected at maturity than situations experienced early in life. To the extent that exposure to these new contexts influences the brain during its adolescent remodeling, it could be wildly speculated that this neuroplasticity might provide additional adaptive programs that could be tapped beyond those programs established early in life. Brain research broadly supporting such a speculation is seen in studies examining the development of sensory maps of the environment in owls, which need to form matching visual and auditory maps of their environment to locate prey under low light conditions. When owls were raised through adolescence first with normal vision and then wearing prisms that distorted the visual field, they developed two sets of auditory–visual map pairings, with the inappropriate set actively inhibited by the inhibitory neurotransmitter GABA until such time as it might be needed (Zheng & Knudsen, 1999). These basic science data provide "proof of concept" that the brain may hold more than one "program" for adaptive responding, each of which could be potentially activated under the appropriate environmental demands. Yet, whether this conditional adaptive programming occurs outside of the sensory system and is evident in humans is unknown—and may present insurmountable challenges for investigation in studies with human adolescents.

Basic research provides some support for the idea that adaptive programs induced by environmental stimulation during the neuroplasticity of adolescence might not only protect against the later emergence of maladaptive neurobehavioral function, but also might help ameliorate unfavorable consequences of early developmental adversity. As discussed above, broad-based social experience during adolescence was sufficient to allow for expression of male sexual behavior following prepubertal hypothalamic lesions that normally block sexual activity (Twiggs et al., 1978). Likewise, raising animals in enriched environments through adolescence results in fewer long-lasting adverse consequences of prenatal or postnatal stressors than when animals are raised under nonenriched conditions (Francis et al., 2002; Laviola et al., 2004), and reverses a number of neurochemical consequences resulting from low levels of maternal care (seen in offspring of LG rat moms—see Chapter 2) (Bredy et al., 2004). Animals reared through adolescence in enriched environments also choose to self-administer less amphetamine than nonenriched animals (Cain et al., 2006).

Another potential way that the brain could be customized during adolescence is through variations in the timing of puberty-activated hormones. Adolescents who enter puberty early fare differently on a number of dimensions from those undergoing puberty later in life, with late-maturing girls and early-maturing boys generally benefiting from their pubertal timing (see Chapter 3 for discussion and references). Factors that contribute to these differences are undoubtedly many, including not only puberty-related appearance changes that alter how these adolescents are perceived by others, but also perhaps pubertal hormone influences on regionally specific brain remodeling that occurs at different points during adolescence (see Zehr et al., 2006; Neufang et al., 2009).

Thus, there is emerging evidence that normal developmental alterations in the adolescent brain may represent a period of neuroplasticity during which the brain undergoes some final "customizing" prior to the gradual emergence of the mature brain. As exciting as these possibilities are, however, it should be remembered that much of the pertinent data have been derived from basic research, and the degree to which similar neuroplasticity would be seen among human adolescents is often unknown, in part because many areas of interest are difficult to study in human populations.

Adolescent Brain Sculpting as a Time of Vulnerability

The remodeling of the adolescent brain and its neuroplasticity may be a time not only of opportunity and possibility, but also of potential vulnerability. This vulnerability potentially arises from two different sources. First, neuroplasticity that continues into adolescence may help not only to adapt the maturing brain to positive aspects of the environment experienced during adolescence (e.g., education, athletic or musical practice, other enriching experiences), but also to aversive components of the environment to which the adolescent is exposed either passively (e.g., stressful living circumstances) or actively (e.g., use of licit or illicit drugs, anabolic steroids). As discussed in previous chapters, repeated exposure to stimuli such as stressors or drugs of abuse during adolescence can sometimes exert long-term effects on later psychosocial functioning, which may not be seen after comparable experiences in adulthood. Thus, under some circumstances, the neuroplastic adolescent brain may adapt to the presence of the aversive stimulus and begin to consider and seek out that state as "normal," perhaps resulting in the emergence of drug dependence and setting the stage for long-term drug abuse. Likewise, exposure to anabolic steroids during the time when rising levels of sex hormones exert organizational influences on the brain (see Chapter 3) has the potential to influence this second period of sexual differentiation of the brain, resulting in lasting neurobehavioral alterations, including possible disruptions in sexual behaviors and increases in aggression (Sato et al., 2008).

It is also possible that the adolescent brain may exhibit particular vulnerability at times when the ongoing processes of brain remodeling normally result in periods of transient instability. Some of the normal developmental transitions of the adolescent brain seemingly must disrupt, at least temporarily, delicate excitatory–inhibitory balances of brain activity and disturb the precision of input timing—possibly inducing periods of particular vulnerability for the maturing adolescent brain. Consider first the importance of excitatory–inhibitory balance for effective cortical functioning. If left unchecked, experience-related increases in the strength of excitatory activity produce instability: As excited synapses become stronger, they become more excitable, making them more excited and even stronger, and ultimately resulting in "runaway" excitability. While experience-related changes in synaptic strength are critical for learning and memory, even modest instabilities produced by alterations in the excitatory–inhibitory balance must be countered by compensatory processes to reestablish homeostasis (Turrigiano & Nelson, 2004). During adolescence, there is a marked decline (up to 50% in some areas) in excitatory input to the cortex, with little to no loss of inhibitory synapses (e.g., Woo et al., 1997). Much remains to be understood regarding how the delicate balance of excitation to inhibition is restored in the face of massive declines in excitatory input to the cortex during adolescence; readjustments in synaptic strength of residual synapses (i.e., strengthening remaining excitatory synapses, while weakening inhibitory ones) may play a critical role (Turrigiano & Nelson, 2004). Such a marked downward shift in excitatory–inhibitory balance, while perhaps helping to drive or terminate critical periods (Hensch, 2005), would seemingly present a considerable threat to homeostasis, with the time required to reestablish this delicate balance perhaps introducing a period of particular vulnerability, as noted, to perturbations that serve to further alter this balance. Indeed, many manipulations, such as alterations in sensory input, alcohol and other drugs of abuse, as well as exposure to stressors, can influence the balance of excitation to inhibition during adolescence (e.g., see Turrigiano & Nelson, 2004; Romeo & McEwen, 2006; Carpenter-Hyland & Chandler, 2007).

Another potential threat to brain stability during adolescence is the process of myelination, with its resulting marked alterations in input timing. As previously discussed, the process of myelination considerably speeds up information flow of an axon, with an unmyelinated axon taking perhaps 50–100 milliseconds to transmit information from one side of the cortex to the other, but taking only 1–2 milliseconds when myelinated (see Markham & Greenough, 2004). Thus as axons become myelinated, there is a considerable acceleration in transmission of that information throughout its associated neural circuitry. Yet, temporal summation of multiple inputs converging on the same neuron is critical for determining the impact of each input, and the relative timing of each impulse often plays a decisive role. Differences of 20 milliseconds or less in the timing with which different inputs impinge on the same neuron can influence the synaptic strength of each of these inputs in opposite ways (Dan & Poo, 2004). Thus, as axons connecting more distant cortical regions (or cortical and subcortical regions) become myelinated, the influence exerted by these generally excitatory connections is likely to increase markedly, perhaps serving to offset, to some extent, the decline in excitatory connectivity associated with the often extensive pruning of excitatory synapses among pyramidal cells within the same cortical regions, and changing the source of primary excitatory drive from within cortical areas to more distant regions. Given the critical importance of timing for brain function and plasticity, any alterations in the timing of myelination seemingly could perturb the dynamics of input timing (see Fields, 2008), markedly shifting (and perhaps transiently destabilizing) relative activity across brain regions within the affected networks.

One common substance that may influence timing or extent of myelination is caffeine. As mentioned in Chapter 4, basic research has shown that the myelination of axons by glia is driven in part by the level of activity in those axons, with glia containing receptors sensitive to chemical(s), such as adenosine, that are released by axons when they are actively transmitting impulses (Stevens et al., 2002). Blocking these receptors with an adenosine receptor antagonist could potentially hinder the ability of glia to monitor axonal activity, possibly disturbing activity-dependent myelination during adolescence. Prominent among the drugs that block these adenosine receptors is caffeine—a chemical found not only in coffee but in many soft drinks as well, and particularly highly concentrated in energy drinks. Although there is a recent report from research in laboratory animals showing that chronic exposure to caffeine late in adolescence leads to long-lasting changes in emotional reactivity in adulthood (Anderson & Hughes, 2008), it is unknown whether amount of caffeine exposure could be related to the timing, characteristics, or integrity of myelination among human adolescents. Although work in this area is just beginning, given the possible influence of caffeine on adenosine systems, it is somewhat disconcerting to realize that extensive use of caffeinated drinks, including energy drinks and the latest craze—alcohol-containing energy drinks (e.g, O'Brien et al., 2008)—is becoming increasingly common among children and adolescents (see Bramstedt, 2007).

SUMMARY AND CLOSING COMMENTS

There are numerous hints in the research literature that some developmental neuroplasticity is retained into adolescence. This residual plasticity, along with the remodeling of the adolescent brain that normally occurs during this developmental period, may permit adolescent experiences to channel the sculpting of the adolescent brain in ways that are not evident following similar experiences in adulthood. Thus, experiences occurring during adolescence may serve to customize the maturing brain in a way commensurate with those experiences. Depending on the nature of such experiences, their timing, and hence their consequences, this customizing of the brain can be viewed as a time of opportunity, as well as vulnerability. Under some circumstances, adolescent brain neuroplasticity may provide an enhanced opportunity for the nervous system to recover from drug exposure, brain damage, or other challenges, with the result of fewer lasting consequences and greater recovery than after comparable experiences at older ages. Under other conditions, experiences of the adolescent may channel sculpting of the adolescent brain to produce a different brain, resulting in long-lasting alterations in neural functioning not seen after comparable experiences in adulthood.

Much of the evidence for these conclusions is derived from basic research in laboratory animals—often necessarily so, with many questions of interest difficult, if not impossible, to examine through experimentation with human adolescents. Hence, the conclusions reached are often more speculative than definitive, and we are far from being able to identify means of directing adolescent experiences to channel brain sculpting in a beneficial way, or to parse which types of environmental experiences might be advantageous, necessary, or damaging to the maturing brain of particular adolescents. These tasks are even more challenging when considering that the efficacy of particular experiences and their timing are likely to be influenced markedly by individual differences, with adolescents being active agents in helping to create their own life experiences. By the time of adolescence, individual differences among adolescents are a complex mosaic of genetic predispositions of temperament, intellect, activity level, neural function, and so on, as critically modulated by, and influencing, the experiences of life and how others view and treat them.

Developmental neuroplasticity reaches its "swan song" during adolescence and, along with the normal remodeling of the adolescent brain, provides a time of opportunity—and vulnerability—for experiences to customize the maturing brain. Certainly, much remains to be determined regarding the relationship between specific environmental experiences and the maturing brain. What is clear is that environmental circumstances of the adolescent matter, and the maturing brain during adolescence is not immutable to those experiences.

References

Acheson, S. K., Stein, R. M., & Swartzwelder, H. S. (1998). Impairment of semantic and figural memory by acute ethanol: Age-dependent effects. *Alcoholism: Clinical and Experimental Research, 22*(7), 1437–1442.

Ackerman, S. J. (1999). *Uncovering the importance of sleep: NCRR reporter.* Bethesda, MD: National Institutes of Health, National Center for Research Resources.

Adair, L. S. (2001). Size at birth predicts age at menarche. *Pediatrics, 107*(4), U95–U101.

Adelmann, P. K., & Zajonc, R. B. (1989). Facial efference and the experience of emotion. *Annual Review of Psychology, 40*, 249–280.

Adleman, N. E., Menon, V., Blasey, C. M., White, C. D., Warsofsky, I. S., Glover, G. H., et al. (2002). A developmental fMRI study of the Stroop color-word task. *NeuroImage, 16*, 61–75.

Adriani, W., Chiarotti, F., & Laviola, G. (1998). Elevated novelty seeking and peculiar *d*-amphetamine sensitization in periadolescent mice compared with adult mice. *Behavioral Neuroscience, 112*(5), 1152–1166.

Adriani, W., Granstrem, O., Macri, S., Izykenova, G., Dambinova, S., & Laviola, G. (2004). Behavioral and neurochemical vulnerability during adolescence in mice: Studies with nicotine. *Neuropsychopharmacology, 29*(5), 869–878.

Adriani, W., & Laviola, G. (2003). Elevated levels of impulsivity and reduced place conditioning with *d*-amphetamine: Two behavioral features of adolescence in mice. *Behavioral Neuroscience, 117*(4), 695–703.

Ahlström, S. K., & Österberg, E. L. (2004). International perspectives on adolescent and young adult drinking. *Alcohol Research and Health, 28*(4), 258–268.

Akbarian, S., Bunney, W. E., Jr., Potkin, S. G., Wigal, S. B., Hagman, J. O., Sandman, C. A., et al. (1993). Altered distribution of nicotinamide-adenine dinucleotide phosphate-diaphorase cells in frontal lobe of schizophrenics implies disturbances of cortical development. *Archives of General Psychiatry, 50,* 169–177.

Alessi, S. M., & Petry, N. M. (2003). Pathological gambling severity is associated with impulsivity in a delay discounting procedure. *Behavioral Processes, 64*(3), 345–354.

Alföldi, P., Tobler, I., & Borbély, A. A. (1990). Sleep regulation in rats during early development. *American Journal of Physiology, 258,* R634–R644.

Alink, L. R. A., van IJzendoorn, M. H., Bakermans-Kranenburg, M. J., Mesman, J., Juffer, F., & Koot, H. M. (2008). Cortisol and externalizing behavior in children and adolescents: Mixed meta-analytic evidence for the inverse relation of basal cortisol and cortisol reactivity with externalizing behavior. *Developmental Psychobiology, 50,* 427–450.

Alvarez, J. A., & Emory, E. (2006). Executive function and the frontal lobes: A meta-analytic review. *Neuropsychology Review, 16*(1), 17–42.

Amaral, D. G., Capitanio, J. P., Jourdain, M., Mason, W. A., Mendoza, S. P., & Prather, M. (2003). The amygdala: Is it an essential component of the neural network for social cognition? *Neuropsychologia, 41*(2), 235–240.

American Psychiatric Association. (1994). *The diagnostic and statistical manual of mental disorders* (4th ed.). Washington, DC: Author.

Amsterdam, A., Nissen, R. M., Sun, Z., Swindell, E. C., Farrington, S., & Hopkins, N. (2004). Identification of 315 genes essential for early zebrafish development. *Proceedings of the National Academy of Sciences, 101*(35), 12792–12797.

Andersen, S. L., Dumont, N. L., & Teicher, M. H. (1997). Developmental differences in dopamine synthesis inhibition by (+/-)-7-OH-DPAT. *Naunyn-Schmiedeberg's Archives of Pharmacology, 352*(2), 173–181.

Andersen, S. L. (2002). Changes in the second messenger cyclic amp during development may underlie motoric symptoms in attention deficit/hyperactivity disorder (ADHD). *Behavioural Brain Research, 130,* 197–201.

Andersen, S. L. (2003). Trajectories of brain development: Point of vulnerability or window of opportunity? *Neuroscience and Biobehavioral Reviews, 27*(1–2), 3–18.

Andersen, S. L., & Teicher, M. H. (2008). Stress, sensitive periods and maturational events in adolescent depression. *Trends in Neuroscience, 31*(4), 183–191.

Andersen, S. L., Thompson, A. T., Rutstein, M., Hostetter, J. C., & Teicher, M. H. (2000). Dopamine receptor pruning in prefrontal cortex during the periadolescent period in rats. *Synapse, 37*(2), 167–169.

Andersen, S. L., Tomada, A., Vincow, E. S., Valente, E., Polcari, A., & Teicher, M. H. (2008). Preliminary evidence for sensitive periods in the effect of childhood sexual abuse on regional brain development. *Journal of Neuropsychiatry and Clinical Neuroscience, 20*(3), 292–301.

Anderson, N. L., & Hughes, R. N. (2008). Increased emotional reactivity in rats following exposure to caffeine during adolescence. *Neurotoxicology and Teratology, 30*, 195–201.

Anderson, R. I., Varlinskaya, E. I., & Spear, L. P. (2008). Restraint stress, sucrose intake and ethanol-induced conditioned taste aversion in adolescent and adult male rats. *Alcoholism: Clinical and Experimental Research, 32*(1), 31A.

Anderson, V. A., Anderson, P., Northam, E., Jacobs, R., & Catroppa, C. (2001). Development of executive functions through late childhood and adolescence in an Australian sample. *Developmental Neuropsychology, 20*(1), 385–406.

Andersson, N., Amlie, C., & Ytteroy, E. A. (2002). Outcomes for children with lesbian or gay parents. A review of studies from 1978 to 2000. *Scandinavian Journal of Psychology, 43*(4), 335–351.

Angelucci, F., Aloe, L., Vasquez, P., & Mathé, A. A. (2000). Mapping the differences in the brain concentration of brain-derived neurotrophic factor (BDNF) and nerve growth factor (NGF) in animal model of depression. *Neuroreport, 11*(6), 1369–1373.

Angold, A. (2003). Adolescent depression, cortisol, and DHEA: editorial. *Psychological Medicine, 33*(4), 573–581.

Angold, A., Costello, E. J., & Worthman, C. M. (1998). Puberty and depression: The roles of age, pubertal status, and pubertal timing. *Psychological Medicine, 28*, 51–61.

Anton, R. F., O'Malley, S. S., Ciraulo, D. A., Cisler, R. A., Couper, D., Donavan, D. M., Gastfriend, D. R., Hosking, J. D., Johnson, B. A., LoCastro, J. S., Longabaugh, R., Mason, B. J., Mattson, M. E., Miller, W. R., Pettinati, H. M., Randall, C. L., Swift, R., Weiss, R. D., Williams, L. D., & Zweben, A. (2006). Combined pharmacotherapies and behavioral interventions for alcohol dependence. *JAMA–Journal of the American Medical Association, 295*(17), 2003–2017.

Armitage, J. A., Taylor, P. D., & Poston, L. (2005). Experimental models of developmental programming: Consequences of exposure to an energy rich diet during development. *Journal of Physiology, 565*(1), 3–8.

Armony, J. L., & LeDoux, J. E. (1997). How the brain processes emotional information. *Annals of the New York Academy of Sciences, 821*, 259–270.

Arnett, J. (1992a). Reckless behavior in adolescence: A developmental perspective. *Developmental Review, 12*, 339–373.

Arnett, J. (1992b). The soundtrack of recklessness: Musical preferences and reckless behavior among adolescents. *Journal of Adolescent Research, 7*(3), 313–331.

Arnett, J. J. (1999). Adolescent storm and stress, reconsidered. *American Psychologist, 54*(5), 317–326.

Arnett, J. J. (2004). *Emerging Adulthood: The Winding Road From the Late Teens Through the Twenties.* New York: Oxford University Press.

Arnsten, A. F. T. (1998). The biology of being frazzled. *Science, 280*, 1711–1712.

Ashburner, J., & Friston, K. J. (2000). Voxel-based morphometry: The methods. *NeuroImage, 11*, 805–821.

Ashtari, M., Cervellione, K. J., Hasan, K. M., Wu, J. Y., McIlree, C., Kester, H., et al. (2007). White matter development during late adolescence in healthy males: A cross-sectional diffusion tensor imaging study. *NeuroImage, 35*(2), 501–510.

Attwell, D., & Iadecola, C. (2002). The neural basis of functional brain imaging signals. *Trends in Neuroscience, 25*(12), 621–625.

Austin, M. P., Leader, L. R., & Reilly, N. (2005). Prenatal stress, the hypothalamic–pituitary–adrenal axis, and fetal and infant neurobehavior. *Early Human Development, 81*(11), 917–926.

Axelson, D. A., & Birmaher, B. (2001). Relation between anxiety and depressive disorders in childhood and adolescence. *Depression and Anxiety, 14*, 67–78.

Baare, W. F. C., van Oel, C. J., Hulshoff Pol, H. E., Schnack, H. G., Durston, S., Sitskoorn, M. M., et al. (2001). Volumes of brain structures in twins discordant for schizophrenia. *Archives of General Psychiatry, 58*, 33–40.

Bailey, J. M., & Bell, A. P. (1993). Familiality of female and male homosexuality. *Behavior Genetics, 23*(4), 313–322.

Bailey, J. M., & Pillard, R. C. (1991). A genetic study of male sexual orientation. *Archives of General Psychiatry, 48*(12), 1089–1096.

Bailey, K. R., Rustay, N. R., & Crawley, J. N. (2006). Behavioral phenotyping of transgenic and knockout mice: Practical concerns and potential pitfalls. *Institute of Laboratory Animal Resources, 47*(2), 124–131.

Banaschewski, T. (2007). Annotation: What electrical brain activity tells us about brain function that other techniques cannot tell us—a child psychiatric perspective. *Journal of Child Psychology and Psychiatry, 48*(5), 415–435.

Bardo, M. T., Donohew, R. L., & Harrington, N. G. (1996). Psychobiology of novelty seeking and drug seeking behavior. *Behavioural Brain Research, 77*, 23–43.

Barnea-Goraly, N., Menon, V., Eckert, M., Tamm, L., Bammer, R., Karchemskiy, A., et al. (2005). White matter development during childhood and adolescence: A cross-sectional diffusion tensor imaging study. *Cerebral Cortex, 15*(12), 1848–1854.

Barr, C. S., Schwandt, M., Lindell, S. G., Chen, S. A., Goldman, D., Suomi, S. J., et al. (2007). Association of a functional polymorphism in the mu-opioid receptor gene with alcohol response and consumption in male rhesus macaques. *Archives of General Psychiatry, 64*(3), 369–376.

Barreto, M. C., Hernandez, M., Doremus, T. L., & Spear, L. P. (2005, June). *Adolescence, impulsivity, and voluntary alcohol consumption: Studies in an animal model.* Paper presented at the Research Society on Alcoholism, Santa Barbara, CA.

Bartzokis, G. (2002). Schizophrenia: Breakdown in the well-regulated lifelong process of brain development and maturation. *Neuropsychopharmacology, 27*(4), 672–683.

Bartzokis, G., Lu, P. H., Nuechterlein, K. H., Gitlin, M., Doi, C., Edwards, N., et al. (2007). Differential effects of typical and atypical antipsychotics on brain myelination in schizophrenia. *Schizophrenia Research, 93*(1–3), 13–22.

Batch, J. A., Williams, D. M., Davies, H. R., Brown, H. R., Evans, B. A., Hughes, I. A., et al. (1992). Role of the androgen receptor in male sexual differentiation. *Hormone Research, 35*(5–6), 226–229.

Baumrind, D. (1987). A developmental perspective on adolescent risk taking in contemporary America. In C. Irwin, Jr. (Ed.), *Adolescent social behavior and health* (pp. 93–125). San Francisco: Jossey-Bass.

Baxter, M. G., & Murray, E. A. (2002). The amygdala and reward. *Nature Reviews Neuroscience, 3*(7), 563–573.

Bean, J. W. (1983). *Cross-cultural variation in maturation rates in relation to marriage system.* Unpublished master's thesis, University of Chicago, Chicago.

Beauchaine, T. (2001). Vagal tone, development, and Gray's motivational theory: Toward an integrated model of autonomic nervous system functioning in psychopathology. *Development and Psychopathology, 13*, 183–214.

Beauchaine, T. P., Gatzke-Kopp, L., & Mead, H. K. (2007). Polyvagal theory and developmental psychopathology: Emotion dysregulation and conduct problems from preschool to adolescence. *Biological Psychology, 74,* 174–184.

Bechara, A., Damasio, H., Damasio, A. R., & Lee, G. P. (1999). Different contributions of the human amygdala and ventromedial prefrontal cortex to decision-making. *Journal of Neuroscience, 19*(13), 5473–5481.

Bechara, A., Dolan, S., & Hindes, A. (2002). Decision-making and addiction (Part ii): Myopia for the future or hypersensitivity to reward? *Neuropsychologia, 40,* 1690–1705.

Beck, K. H., Thombs, D. L., & Summons, T. G. (1993). The social context of drinking scales: Construct validation and relationship to indicants of abuse in an adolescent population. *Addictive Behaviors, 18*(2), 159–169.

Beck, K. H., & Treiman, K. A. (1996). The relationship of social context of drinking, perceived social norms, and parental influence to various drinking patterns of adolescents. *Addictive Behaviors, 21*(5), 633–644.

Begleiter, H., & Porjesz, B. (1999). What is inherited in the predisposition toward alcoholism?: A proposed model. *Alcoholism: Clinical and Experimental Research, 23,* 1125–1135.

Behar, D., Berg, C. J., Rapoport, J. L., Nelson, W., Linnoila, M., Cohen, M., et al. (1983). Behavioral and physiological effects of ethanol in high-risk and control children: A pilot study. *Alcoholism: Clinical and Experimental Research, 7*(4), 404–410.

Belsky, J., Houts, R. M., DeHart, G., Roisman, G. I., Steinberg, L. D., Friedman, S. L., et al. (2007). Family rearing antecedents of pubertal timing. *Child Development, 78*(4), 1302–1321.

Benes, F. M., Taylor, J. B., & Cunningham, M. C. (2000). Convergence and plasticity of monaminergic systems in the medial prefrontal cortex during the postnatal period: Implications for the development of psychopathology. *Cerebral Cortex, 10*(10), 1014–1027.

Benes, F. M., Turtle, M., Khan, Y., & Farol, P. (1994). Myelination of a key relay zone in the hippocampal formation occurs in the human brain during childhood, adolescence, and adulthood. *Archives of General Psychiatry, 51*(6), 477–484.

Bengtsson, S., Nagy, Z., Skare, S., Forsman, L., Forssberg, H., & Ullen, F. (2005). Extensive piano practicing has regionally specific effects on white matter development. *Nature Neuroscience, 8*(9), 1148–1150.

Benson, P. L., Leffert, N., Scales, P. C., & Blyth, D. A. (1998). Beyond the "village" rhetoric: Creating healthy communities for children and adolescents. *Applied Developmental Science, 2*(3), 138–159.

Benthin, A., Slovic, P., & Severson, H. (1993). A psychometric study of adolescent risk perception. *Journal of Adolescence, 16,* 153–168.

Berardi, N., Pizzorusso, T., Ratto, G. M., & Maffei, L. (2003). Molecular basis of plasticity in the visual cortex. *Trends in Neuroscience, 26*(7), 369–378.

Berenbaum, S., & Hines, M. (1992). Early androgens are related to childhood sex-typed toy preferences. *Psychological Science, 3*(3), 203–206.

Bergen, S. E., Gardner, C. O., & Kendler, K. S. (2007). Age- related changes in heritability of behavioral phenotypes over adolescence and young adulthood: A meta-analysis. *Twin Research and Human Genetics, 10*(3), 423–433.

Berridge, K. C. (2007). The debate over dopamine's role in reward: The case for insentive salience. *Psychopharmacology, 191*(3), 391–431.

Berridge, K. C., & Kringelbach, M. L. (2008). Affective neuroscience of pleasure: Reward in humans and animals. *Psychopharmacology, 199*, 457–480.

Berridge, K. C., & Robinson, T. E. (1998). What is the role of dopamine in reward?: Hedonic impact, reward learning, or incentive salience? *Brain Research Reviews, 28*, 309–369.

Beyer, C., Pilgrim, C., & Reisert, I. (1991). Dopamine content and metabolism in mesencephalic and diencephalic cell cultures: Sex differences and effects of sex steroids. *Journal of Neuroscience, 11*(5), 1325–1333.

Bickel, W. K., Odum, A. L., & Madden, G. J. (1999). Impulsivity and cigarette smoking: Delay discounting in current, never, and ex-smokers. *Psychopharmacology, 146*(4), 447–454.

Biederman, J., Faraone, S., Wozniak, J., Mick, E., Kwon, A., & Aleardi, M. (2004). Further evidence of unique developmental phenotypic correlates of pediatric bipolar disorder: Findings from a large sample of clinically referred preadolescent children assessed over the last 7 years. *Journal of Affective Disorders, 82S*, S45–S58.

Birmaher, B., Axelson, D., Strober, M., Gill, M. K., Valeri, S., Chiappetta, L., et al. (2006). Clinical course of children and adolescents with bipolar spectrum disorders. *Archives of General Psychiatry, 63*, 175–183.

Biro, P. A., Abrahams, M. V., Post, J. R., & Parkinson, E. A. (2004). Predators select against high growth rates and risk-taking behaviour in domestic trout populations. *Proceedings of the Royal Society of London Series B, 271*(1554), 2233–2237.

Biro, P. A., Post, J. R., & Abrahams, M. V. (2005). Ontogeny of energy allocation reveals selective pressure promoting risk-taking behaviour in young fish cohorts. *Proceedings of the Royal Society of London Series B, 272*(1571), 1443–1448.

Bixler, R. H. (1992). Why littermates don't: The avoidance of inbreeding depression. *Annual Review of Sex Research, 3*, 291–328.

317

Bjork, J. M., Knutson, B., Fong, G. W., Caggiano, D. M., Bennett, S. M., & Hommer, D. W. (2004). Incentive-elicited brain activation in adolescents: Similarities and differences from young adults. *Journal of Neuroscience, 24*(8), 1793–1802.

Bjork, J. M., Knutson, B., & Hommer, D. W. (2008). Incentive-elicited striatal activation in adolescent children of alcoholics. *Addiction, 103,* 1308–1319.

Bjork, J. M., Smith, A. R., Danube, C. L., & Hommer, D. W. (2007). Developmental differences in posterior mesofrontal cortex recruitment by risky rewards. *Journal of Neuroscience, 27*(18), 4839–4849.

Blackwelder, T. L., & Golub, M. S. (1996). Pubertal weight gain in female rhesus macaques. *American Journal of Physical Anthropology, 99,* 449–454.

Blakemore, C. (1974). Developmental factors in the formation of feature extracting neurons. In F. O. Schmitt & F. G. Worden (Eds.), *The neurosciences: Third study program* (pp. 105–112). Cambridge, MA: MIT Press.

Blakemore, S.-J., & Choudhury, S. (2006). Development of the adolescent brain: Implications for executive function and social cognition. *Journal of Child Psychology and Psychiatry, 47*(3–4), 296–312.

Blanchard, R. (2004). Quantitative and theoretical analyses of the relation between older brothers and homosexuality in men. *Journal of Theoretical Biology, 230,* 173–187.

Blanchard, R., & Bogaert, A. F. (1996). Homosexuality in men and number of older brothers. *American Journal of Psychiatry, 153*(1), 27–31.

Blanchard, R., Zucker, K., Cavacas, A., Allin, S., Bradley, S., & Schachter, D. (2002). Fraternal birth order and birth weight in probably prehomosexual feminine boys. *Hormones and Behavior, 41,* 321–327.

Bock, J., & Braun, K. (1999). Blockade of n-methyl-*d*-aspartate receptor activation suppresses learning-induced synaptic elimination. *Proceedings of the National Academy of Sciences, 96,* 2485–2490.

Bogaert, A. F. (1997). Birth order and sexual orientation in women. *Behavioral Neuroscience, 111*(6), 1395–1397.

Bolanos, C. A., Glatt, S. J., & Jackson, D. (1998). Subsensitivity to dopaminergic drugs in periadolescent rats: A behavioral and neurochemical analysis. *Developmental Brain Research, 111,* 25–33.

Booth, A., Johnson, D. R., Granger, D. A., Crouter, A. C., & McHale, S. (2003a). Testosterone and child and adolescent adjustment: The moderating role of parent–child relationships. *Developmental Psychology, 39*(1), 85–98.

Booth, J. R., Burman, D. D., Meyer, J. R., Lei, Z., Trommer, B. L., Davenport,

N. D., et al. (2003b). Neural development of selective attention and response inhibition. *Neuroimage, 20,* 737–751.

Bowirrat, A., & Oscar-Berman, M. (2005). Relationship between dopaminergic neurotransmission, alcoholism, and reward deficiency syndrome. *American Journal of Medical Genetics, 123B,* 29–37.

Brake, S. C., Burdette, D. R., Chen, J. S., & Amsel, A. (1980). Retention of response persistence in weanling and adolescent rats. *Journal of Comparative and Physiological Psychology, 94,* 1060–1068.

Bramstedt, K. A. (2007). Caffeine use by children: The quest for enhancement. *Substance Use and Misuse, 42,* 1237–1251.

Bratbert, G. H., Nilsen, T. I. L., Holmen, T. L., & Vatten, L. J. (2007). Early sexual maturation, central adiposity and subsequent overweight in late adolescence: A four-year follow-up of 1,605 adolescent Norwegian boys and girls: The Young–Hunt Study. *BMC Public Health, 7*(54), 1–7.

Bredy, T. W., Zhang, T. Y., Grant, R. J., Diorio, J., & Meaney, M. J. (2004). Peripubertal environmental enrichment reverses the effects of maternal care on hippocampal development and glutamate receptor subunit expression. *European Journal of Neuroscience, 20*(5), 1355–1362.

Bremner, J. D. (2005). *Brain imaging handbook.* New York: Norton.

Brenhouse, H. C., & Andersen, S. L. (2008). Delayed extinction and stronger reinstatement of cocaine conditioned place preference in adolescent rats, compared to adults. *Behavioral Neuroscience, 122*(2), 460–465.

Brenhouse, H. C., Sonntag, K. C., & Andersen, S. L. (2008). Transient d_1 dopamine receptor expression on prefrontal cortex projection neurons: Relationship to enhanced motivational salience of drug cues in adolescence. *Journal of Neuroscience, 28*(10), 2375–2382.

Brook, D. W., Brook, J. S., Zhang, C., Cohen, P., & Whiteman, M. (2008). Drug use and the risk of major depressive disorder, alcohol dependence, and substance use disorders. *Archives of General Psychiatry, 59,* 1039–1044.

Brooks-Gunn, J., Graber, J. A., & Paikoff, R. L. (1994). Studying links between hormones and negative affect: Models and measures. *Journal of Research on Adolescence, 4,* 469–486.

Brown, A. S., Cohen, P., Greenwald, S., & Susser, E. (2000). Nonaffective psychosis after prenatal exposure to rubella. *American Journal of Psychiatry, 157,* 438–434.

Brown, S. M., Manuck, S. B., & Flory, J. D. (2006). Neural basis of individual differences in impulsivity: Contributions of corticolimbic circuits for behavioral arousal and control. *Emotion, 6*(2), 239–245.

Brown, T. T., Lugar, H. M., Coalson, R. S., Miezin, F. M., Petersen, S. E., & Schlaggar, B. L. (2005). Developmental changes in human cerebral functional organization for word generation. *Cerebral Cortex, 15*, 275–290.

Brunell, S. C., & Spear, L. P. (2005). Effect of stress on the voluntary intake of a sweetened ethanol solution in paired-house adolescent and adult rats. *Alcoholism: Clinical and Experimental Research, 29*(9), 1641–1653.

Buchanan, C. M., Eccles, J. S., & Becker, J. B. (1992). Are adolescents the victims of raging hormones?: Evidence for activational effects of hormones on moods and behavior at adolescence. *Psychological Bulletin, 111*(1), 62–107.

Bunge, S. A., & Wright, S. B. (2007). Neurodevelopmental changes in working memory and cognitive control. *Current Opinion in Neurobiology, 17*, 243–250.

Burkhalter, A., Bernardo, K. L., & Charles, V. (1993). Development of local circuits in human visual cortex. *Journal of Neuroscience, 13*(5), 1916–1931.

Bush, G., Luu, P., & Posner, M. I. (2000). Cognitive and emotional influences in anterior cingulate cortex. *Trends in Cognitive Science, 4*(6), 215–222.

Bussey, K., & Bandura, A. (1999). Social cognitive theory of gender development and differentiation. *Psychological Review, 106*(4), 676–713.

Cabeza, R., & Nyberg, L. (2000). Imaging cognition: II. An empirical review of 275 PET and fMRI studies. *Journal of Cognitive Neuroscience, 12*(1), 1–47.

Cain, M. E., Green, T. A., & Bardo, M. T. (2006). Environmental enrichment decreases responding for visual novelty. *Behavioral Processes, 73*(3), 360–366.

Caine, N. G. (1986). Behavior during puberty and adolescence. In G. Mitchell & J. Erwin (Eds.), *Comparative primate biology: Vol. 2a. Behavior, conservation, and ecology* (pp. 327–361). New York: Liss.

Caine, S. B., Thomsen, M., Gabriel, K. I., Berkowitz, J. S., Gold, L. H., Koob, G. F., et al. (2007). Lack of self-administration of cocaine in dopamine d₁ receptor knock-out mice. *Journal of Neuroscience, 27*(48), 13140–13150.

Campbell, J. O., Wood, R. D., & Spear, L. P. (2000). Cocaine and morphine-induced place conditioning in adolescent and adult rats. *Physiology and Behavior, 68*(4), 487–493.

Cantor, J., Blanchard, R., Patterson, A., & Bogaert, A. F. (2002). How many gay men owe their sexual orientation to fraternal birth order? *Archives of Sexual Behavior, 31*(1), 63–71.

Cao, J., Lotfipour, S., Loughlin, S. E., & Leslie, F. M. (2007). Adolescent maturation of cocaine-sensitive neural mechanisms. *Neuropsychopharmacology, 32*(11), 2279–2289.

Cardinal, R. N., Parkinson, J. A., Hall, J., & Everitt, B. J. (2002). Emotion and motivation: The role of the amygdala, ventral striatum, and prefrontal cortex. *Neuroscience and Biobehavioral Reviews, 26*(3), 321–352.

Carelli, R. M. (2002). Nucleus accumbens cell firing during goal-directed behaviors for cocaine vs. "natural" reinforcement. *Physiology and Behavior, 76,* 379–387.

Carey, S., Diamond, R., & Woods, B. (1980). Development of face recognition: A maturational component? *Developmental Psychology, 16,* 257–269.

Carpenter-Hyland, E., & Chandler, L. (2007). Adaptive plasticity of NMDA receptors and dendritic spines: Implications for enhanced vulnerability of the adolescent brain to alcohol addiction. *Pharmacology, Biochemistry, and Behavior, 86,* 200–208.

Carskadon, M. A., Vieira, C., & Acebo, C. (1993). Association between puberty and delayed phase preference. *Sleep, 16*(3), 258–262.

Casey, B. J., Galvan, A., & Hare, T. A. (2005). Changes in cerebral functional organization during cognitive development. *Current Opinion in Neurobiology, 15*(2), 239–244.

Casey, B. J., Getz, S., & Galvan, A. (2008). The adolescent brain. *Developmental Review, 28*(1), 62–77.

Casey, B. J., Giedd, J. N., & Thomas, K. M. (2000). Structural and functional brain development and its relation to cognitive development. *Biological Psychology, 54*(1–3), 241–257.

Casey, B. J., Thomas, K. M., Davidson, M. C., Kunz, K., & Franzen, P. L. (2002). Dissociating striatal and hippocampal function developmentally with a stimulus–response compatibility task. *Journal of Neuroscience, 22*(19), 8647–8652.

Casey, B. J., Tottenham, N., Liston, C., & Durston, S. (2005b). Imaging the developing brain: What have we learned about cognitive development? *Trends in Cognitive Sciences, 9*(3), 104–110.

Casey, B. J., Trainor, R., Giedd, J., Vauss, Y., Vaituzis, C. K., Hamburger, S., et al. (1997a). The role of the anterior cingulate in automatic and controlled processes: A developmental neuroanatomical study. *Developmental Psychobiology, 30,* 61–69.

Casey, B. J., Trainor, R. J., Orendi, J. L., Schubert, A. B., Nystrom, L. E., Giedd, J. N., et al. (1997b). A developmental functional MRI study of prefrontal activation during performance of a go-no-go task. *Journal of Cognitive Neuroscience, 9*(6), 835–847.

Caspi, A., McClay, J., Moffitt, T. E., Mill, J., Martin, J., Craig, I. W., et al. (2002). Role of genotype in the cycle of violence in maltreated children. *Science, 297,* 851–854.

Caspi, A., Moffitt, T. E., Cannon, M., McClay, J., Murray, R., Harrington, H., et al. (2005). Moderation of the effect of adolescent-onset cannabis use on adult psychosis by a functional polymorphism in the catechol-O-methyltransferase gene: Longitudinal evidence of a gene × environment interaction. *Biological Psychiatry, 57,* 1117–1127.

Caspi, A., Sugden, K., Moffitt, T. E., Taylor, A., Craig, I. W., Harrington, H., et al. (2003). Influence of life stress on depression: Moderation by a polymorphism in the 5-HTT gene. *Science, 301,* 386–389.

Cauffman, E., & Steinberg, L. (2000). (Im)maturity of judgment in adolescence: Why adolescents may be less culpable than adults. *Behavioral Sciences and the Law, 18*(6), 741–760.

Cerqueira, J. J., Almeida, O. F. X., & Sousa, N. (2008). The stressed prefrontal cortex. Left? Right! *Brain, Behavior, and Immunity, 22,* 630–638.

Cha, Y. M., White, A. M., Kuhn, C. M., Wilson, W. A., & Swartzwelder, H. S. (2006). Differential effects of delta⁹-THC on learning in adolescent and adult rats. *Pharmacology, Biochemistry, and Behavior, 83*(3), 448–455.

Chambers, R. A., & Potenza, M. N. (2003). Neurodevelopment, impulsivity, and adolescent gambling. *Journal of Gambling Studies, 19*(1), 53–84.

Champagne, D. L., Bagot, R. C., van Hasselt, F., Ramakers, G., Meaney, M. J., De Kloet, E. R., et al. (2008). Maternal care and hippocampal plasticity: Evidence for experience- dependent structural plasticity, altered synaptic functioning, and differential responsiveness to glucocorticoids and stress. *Journal of Neuroscience, 28*(23), 6037–6045.

Chibbar, R., Toma, J. G., Mitchell, B. F., & Miller, F. D. (1990). Regulation of neural oxytocin gene expression by gonadal steroids in pubertal rats. *Molecular Endocrinology, 4*(12), 2030–2038.

Choi, J., Jeong, B., Rohan, M. L., Polcari, A. M., & Teicher, M. H. (2009). Preliminary evidence for white matter tract abnormalities in young adults exposed to parental verbal abuse. *Biological Psychiatry, 65*(3), 227–234.

Chugani, H. T. (1994). Development of regional brain glucose metabolism in relation to behavior and plasticity. In G. Dawson & K. Fischer (Eds.), *Human behavior and the developing brain* (pp. 153–175). New York: Guilford Press.

Chugani, H. T. (1996). Neuroimaging of developmental nonlinearity and developmental pathologies. In R. W. Thatcher, G. R. Lyon, J. Rumsey, & N. Krasnegor (Eds.), *Developmental neuroimaging: Mapping the development of brain and behavior* (pp. 187–195). San Diego: Academic Press.

Chugani, H. T. (1998). Biological basis of emotions: Brain systems and brain development. *Pediatrics, 102*(5), 1225–1229.

Chugani, H. T. (1998). A critical period of brain development: Studies of cerebral glucose utilization with PET. *Preventive Medicine, 27*, 184–188.

Cirulli, F., Terranova, M. L., & Laviola, G. (1996). Affiliation in periadolescent rats: Behavioral and corticosterone response to social reunion with familiar or unfamiliar partners. *Pharmacology, Biochemistry, and Behavior, 54*, 99–105.

Clark, D. B., Kirisci, L., & Tarter, R. E. (1998). Adolescent versus adult onset and the development of substance use disorders in males. *Drug and Alcohol Dependence, 49*, 115–121.

Cloninger, C. R., Sigvardsson, S., & Bohman, M. (1988). Childhood personality predicts alcohol abuse in young adults. *Alcoholism: Clinical and Experimental Research, 12*, 494–505.

Cohen, M., Solowij, N., & Carr, V. (2008). Cannabis, cannabinoids, and schizophrenia: Integration of the evidence. *Australian and New Zealand Journal of Psychiatry, 42*(5), 357–368.

Collet, C., Vernet-Maury, E., Delhomme, G., & Dittmar, A. (1997). Autonomic nervous system response patterns specificity to basic emotions. *Journal of the Autonomic Nervous System, 62*(1), 45–57.

Conklin, H. M., Luciana, M., Hooper, C. J., & Yarger, R. S. (2007). Working memory performance in typically developing children and adolescents: Behavioral evidence of protracted frontal lobe development. *Developmental Neuropsychology, 50*(12), 975–990.

Conner, B. T., Noble, E. P., Berman, S. M., Okaragoz, T., Ritchie, T., Antolin, T., et al. (2005). DRD2 genotypes and substance use in adolescent children of alcoholics. *Drug and Alcohol Dependence, 79*, 379–387.

Coulston, C. M., Perdices, M., & Tennant, C. C. (2007). The neuropsychological correlates of cannabis use in schizophrenia: Lifetime abuse/dependence, frequency of use, and recency of use. *Schizophrenia Research, 96*, 169–184.

Crews, F. T., Braun, C. J., Hoplight, B., Switzer, R. C., III, & Knapp, D. J. (2000). Binge ethanol consumption causes differential brain damage in young adolescent rats compared with adult rats. *Alcoholism: Clinical and Experimental Research, 24*(11), 1712–1723.

Crews, F. T., Mdzinarishvili, A., Kim, D., He, J., & Nixon, K. (2006). Neurogenesis in adolescent brain is potently inhibited by ethanol. *Neuroscience, 137*(2), 437–445.

Crockett, C. M., & Pope, T. R. (1993). Consequences of sex differences in dispersal for juvenile red howler monkeys. In M. E. Pereira & L. A. Fairbanks (Eds.), *Juvenile primates* (pp. 104–118, 367–415). New York: Oxford University Press.

Crone, E. A., & van der Molen, M. W. (2004). Developmental changes in real life decision making: Performance on a gambling task previously shown to depend on the ventromedial prefrontal cortex. *Developmental Neuropsychology, 25*(3), 251–279.

Crone, E. A., & van der Molen, M. W. (2007). Development of decision making in school-aged children and adolescents: Evidence from heart rate and skin conductance analysis. *Child Development, 78*(4), 1288–1301.

Crone, E. A., Wendelken, C., Donohue, S., van Leijenhorst, L., & Bunge, S. A. (2006). Neurocognitive development of the ability to manipulate information in working memory. *Proceedings of the National Academy of Sciences, 103*(24), 9315–9320.

Crone, E. A., Zanolie, K., Van Leijenhorst, L., Westenberg, P. M., & Rombouts, S. A. R. B. (2008). Neural mechanisms supporting flexible performance adjustment during development. *Cognitive, Affective, and Behavioral Neuroscience, 8*(2), 165–177.

Csikszentmihalyi, M., & Larson, R. (1978). Intrinsic rewards in school crime. *Crime and Delinquency, 24*, 322–335.

Csikszentmihalyi, M., Larson, R., & Prescott, S. (1977). The ecology of adolescent activity and experience. *Journal of Youth and Adolescence, 6*, 281–294.

Cunningham, M. G., Bhattacharyya, S., & Benes, F. M. (2002). Amygdalocortical sprouting continues into early adulthood: Implications for the development of normal and abnormal function during adolescence. *Journal of Comparative Neurology, 453*(2), 116–130.

Cunningham, M. G., Bhattacharyya, S., & Benes, F. M. (2008). Increasing interaction of amygdalar afferents with GABAergic interneurons between birth and adulthood. *Cerebral Cortex, 18*, 1529–1535.

Dahl, R. E. (2001). Affect regulation, brain development, and behavioral/emotional health in adolescence. *CNS Spectrums, 6*(1), 60–72.

Dahl, R. E. (2004). Adolescent brain development: A period of vulnerabilities and opportunities. *Annals of the New York Academy of Sciences, 1021*, 1–23.

Dahl, R. E., & Lewis, D. S. (2002). Pathways to adolescent health sleep regulation and behavior. *Journal of Adolescent Health, 31*(6 Suppl.), 175–184.

Dalgleish, T. (2004). The emotional brain. *Nature Reviews Neuroscience, 5*(7), 582–589.

Dan, Y., & Poo, M.-M. (2004). Spike timing-dependent plasticity of neural circuits. *Neuron, 44*, 23–30.

D'Ardenne, K., McClure, S. M., Nystrom, L. E., & Cohen, J. D. (2008). BOLD responses reflecting dopaminergic signals in the human ventral tegmental area. *Science, 319*(5867), 1264–1267.

Davey, C. G., Yücel, M., & Allen, N. B. (2008). The emergence of depression in adolescence: Development of the prefrontal cortex and the representation of reward. *Neuroscience and Biobehavioral Reviews, 32*, 1–19.

Davidson, M. C., Amso, D., Anderson, L. C., & Diamond, A. (2006). Development of cognitive control and executive functions from 4 to 13 years: Evidence from manipulations of memory, inhibition, and task switching. *Neuropsychologia, 44*, 2037–2078.

Davidson, R. J. (2000). Affective style, psychopathology, and resilience: Brain mechanisms and plasticity. *American Psychologist, 55*(11), 1196–1214.

Davies, P. L., Segalowitz, S. J., & Gavin, W. J. (2004). Development of error-monitoring event-related potentials in adolescents. *Annals of the New York Academy of Sciences, 1021*, 324–328.

De Bellis, M. D., Clark, D. B., Beers, S. R., Soloff, P. H., Boring, A. M., Hall, J., et al. (2000). Hippocampal volume in adolescent-onset alcohol use disorders. *American Journal of Psychiatry, 157*(5), 737–744.

De Bellis, M. D., Narasimhan, A., Thatcher, D. L., Keshavan, M. S., Soloff, P., & Clark, D. B. (2005). Prefrontal cortex, thalamus, and cerebellar volumes in adolescents and young adults with adolescent-onset alcohol use disorders and comorbid mental disorders. *Alcoholism: Clinical and Experimental Research, 29*(9), 1590–1600.

De Bellis, M. D., Van Voorhees, E., Hooper, S. R., Gibler, N., Nelson, L., Hege, S. G., et al. (2008). Diffusion tensor measures of the corpus callosum in adolescents with adolescent onset alcohol use disorders. *Alcoholism: Clinical and Experimental Research, 32*(3), 395–404.

De Felipe, J., Marco, P., Fairén, A., & Jones, E. G. (1997). Inhibitory synaptogenesis in mouse somatosensory cortex. *Cerebral Cortex, 7*, 619–634.

de Muinck Keizer-Schrama, S. M. P. F., & Mul, D. (2001). Trends in pubertal development in Europe. *Human Reproduction Update, 7*(3), 287–291.

de Waal, F. B. M. (1993). Codevelopment of dominance relations and affiliative bonds in rhesus monkeys. In M. E. Pereira & L. A. Fairbanks (Eds.), *Juvenile primates* (pp. 259–270, 367–415). New York: Oxford University Press.

Deakin, J. F. W., & Graeff, F. G. (1991). Critique: 5-HT and mechanisms of defense. *Journal of Psychopharmacology, 5*(4), 305–315.

Dean, B., Sundram, S., Bradbury, R., Scarr, E., & Copolov, D. (2001). Studies on [3h]cp-55490 binding in the human central nervous system: Regional specific changes in density of cannabinoid-1 receptors associated with schizophrenia and cannabis use. *Neuroscience, 103*, 9–15.

DeAngelis, T. (2008). The two faces of oxytocin. *APA Monitor, 39*(2), 30–32.

Deardorff, J., Gonzales, N. A., Christopher, F. S., Roosa, M. W., & Millsap, R. E. (2005). Early puberty and adolescent pregnancy: The influence of alcohol use. *Pediatrics, 116*(6), 1451–1456.

Deas, D., Riggs, P., Langerbucher, J., Goldman, M., & Brown, S. (2000). Adolescents are not adults: Developmental considerations in alcohol users. *Alcoholism: Clinical and Experimental Research, 24*(2), 232–237.

Deeley, Q., Daly, E. M., Azuma, R., Surguladze, S., Giampietro, V., Brammer, M. J., et al. (2008). Changes in male brain responses to emotional faces from adolescence to middle age. *Neuroimage, 40*(1), 389–397.

Degenhardt, L., & Hall, W. (2006). Is cannabis use a contributory cause of psychosis? *Canadian Journal of Psychiatry, 51*(9), 556–565.

Delemarre-van de Waal, H. A., van Coeverden, S. C. C. M., & Engelbregt, M. J. T. (2002). Factors affecting onset of puberty. *Hormone Research, 57*(Suppl. 2), 15–18.

Delgado, M. R., Nystrom, L. E., Fissell, C., Noll, D. C., & Fiez, J. A. (2000). Tracking the hemodynamic responses to reward and punishment in the striatum. *Journal of Neurophysiology, 84*(6), 3072–3077.

Demerens, C., Stankoff, B., Logak, M., Anglade, P., Allinquant, B., Couraud, C., et al. (1996). Induction of myelination in the central nervous system by electrical activity. *Proceedings of the National Academy of Science of the United States of America, 93*, 9887–9892.

Demetriou, A., Christou, C., Spanoudis, G., & Platsidou, M. (2002). The development of mental processing: Efficiency, working memory, and thinking. *Monographs of the Society for Research in Child Development, 67*(1), i–viii, 1–155.

Dempster, F. N. (1992). The rise and fall of the inhibitory mechanism: Toward a unified theory of cognitive development and aging. *Developmental Review, 12*, 45–75.

Devous, M. S., Altuna, D., Furl, N., Cooper, N., Gabbert, G., Ngai, W., et al.

(2006). Maturation of speech and language functional neuroanatomy in pediatric normal controls. *Journal of Speech, Language, and Hearing Research, 49*(4), 856–866.

Dewing, P., Shi, T., Horvath, S., & Vilain, E. (2003). Sexually dimorphic gene expression in mouse brain precedes gonadal differentiation. *Molecular Brain Research, 118*, 82–90.

DeWit, D. J., MacDonald, K., & Offord, D. R. (1999). Childhood stress and symptoms of drug dependence in adolescence and early adulthood: Social phobia as a mediator. *American Journal of Orthopsychiatry, 69*(1), 61–72.

Diaz-Granados, J. L., & Graham, D. (2007). The effects of continuous and intermittent ethanol exposure in adolescence on the aversive properties of ethanol during adulthood. *Alcoholism: Clinical and Experimental Research, 31*(12), 2020–2027.

Diamond, A., & Goldman-Rakic, P. S. (1989). Comparison of human infants and rhesus monkeys on Piaget's AB task: Evidence for dependence on dorsolateral prefrontal cortex. *Experimental Brain Research, 74*(1), 24–40.

Diamond, R., Carey, S., & Back, K. J. (1983). Genetic influences on the development of spatial skills during early adolescence. *Cognition, 13*, 167–185.

Dick, D. M., & Agrawal, A. (2008). The genetics of alcohol and other drug dependence. *Alcohol Research and Health, 31*(2), 111–118.

Dick, D. M., Bierut, L., Hinrichs, A., Fox, L., Bucholz, K. K., Kramer, J., et al. (2006). The role of GABRA2 in risk for conduct disorder and alcohol and drug dependence across developmental stages. *Behavior Genetics, 36*(4), 577–590.

Dittmann, R. W., Kappes, M. E., & Kappes, M. H. (1992). Sexual behavior in adolescent and adult females with congenital adrenal hyperplasia. *Psychoneuroendocrinology, 17*(2–3), 153–170.

Dolan, R. J. (2002). Emotion, cognition, and behavior. *Science, 298*, 1191–1194.

Done, D. J., Crow, T. J., Johnstone, E. C., & Sacker, A. (1994). Childhood antecedents of schizophrenia and affective illness: Social adjustment at ages 7 and 11. *British Medical Journal, 309*, 699–703.

Dooley, D., Prause, J., Ham-Rowbottom, K. A., & Emptage, N. (2005). Age of alcohol drinking onset: Precursors and the mediation of alcohol disorder. *Journal of Child and Adolescent Substance Abuse, 15*(2), 19–37.

Doremus, T. L., Brunell, S. C., Rajendran, P., & Spear, L. P. (2005). Factors influencing elevated ethanol consumption in adolescent relative to adult rats. *Alcoholism: Clinical and Experimental Research, 29*(10), 1796–1808.

Doremus, T. L., Brunell, S. C., Varlinskaya, E. I., & Spear, L. P. (2003). Anxiogenic effects during withdrawal from acute ethanol in adolescent and adult rats. *Pharmacology, Biochemistry, and Behavior, 75*, 411–418.

Doremus, T. L., & Spear, L. P. (2005). Influence of stress on operant self-administration of ethanol in adolescent and adult rats. *Alcoholism: Clinical and Experimental Research, 29*(S1), 20A.

Doremus-Fitzwater, T. L., Varlinskaya, E. I., & Spear, L. P. (2007, October/November). *Impact of repeated stress responsivity to ethanol-induced changes in social behavior in adolescent and adult rats.* Society for Neuroscience. Chicago, IL.

Douaud, G., Smith, S., Jenkinson, M., Behrens, T., Johansen-Berg, H., Vickers, J., et al. (2007). Anatomically related grey and white matter abnormalities in adolescent-onset schizophrenia. *Brain, 130*, 2375–2386.

Douglas, L. A., Varlinskaya, E. I., & Spear, L. P. (2003). Novel object place conditioning in adolescent and adult male and female rats: Effects of social isolation. *Physiology and Behavior, 80*, 317–325.

Douglas, L. A., Varlinskaya, E. I., & Spear, L. P. (2004). Rewarding properties of social interactions in adolescent and adult male and female rats: Impact of social vs. isolate housing of subjects and partners. *Developmental Psychobiology, 45*, 153–162.

Draganski, B., Gaser, C., Volker, B., Schuierer, G., Bogdahn, U., & May, A. (2004). Changes in grey matter induced by training. *Nature, 427*, 311–312.

Dubas, J. S. (1991). Cognitive abilities and physical maturation. In R. M. Lerner, A. C. Petersen, & J. Brooks-Gunn (Eds.), *Encyclopedia of adolescence* (Vol. 1, pp. 133–138). New York: Garland.

Duman, R. S. (2002). Pathophysiology of depression: The concept of synaptic plasticity. *European Psychiatry, 17*(3), 306–310.

Duman, R. S., Malberg, J., Nakagawa, S., & D'Sa, C. (2000). Neuronal plasticity and survival in mood disorders. *Biological Psychiatry, 48*(8), 732–739.

Dunn, B. D., Dalgleish, T., & Lawrence, A. D. (2006). The somatic marker hypothesis: A critical evaluation. *Neuroscience and Biobehavioral Reviews, 30*, 239–271.

Durack, J. C., & Katz, L. C. (1996). Development of horizontal projections in layer 2/3 ferret visual cortex. *Cerebral Cortex, 6*, 178–183.

Durston, S., Davidson, M. C., Tottenham, N., Galvan, A., Spicer, J., Fossella, J. A., et al. (2006). A shift from diffuse to focal cortical activity with development. *Developmental Science, 9*(1), 1–20.

Durston, S., Hulshoff Pol, H. E., Casey, B. J., Giedd, J. N., Buitelaar, J. K., & van Engeland, H. (2001). Anatomical MRI of the developing human brain: What have we learned? *Journal of the American Academy of Child and Adolescent Psychiatry, 40*(9), 1012–1020.

Eaves, L. J., Long, J., & Heath, A. C. (1986). A theory of developmental change in quantitative phenotypes applied to cognitive development. *Behavior Genetics, 16*(1), 143–162.

Ehrenreich, H., Rinn, T., Kunert, H.-J., Moeller, M. R., Poser, W., Schilling, W., et al. (1999). Specific attentional dysfunction in adults following early start of cannabis use. *Psychopharmacology, 142*, 295–326.

Eley, T. C., Sugden, K., Corsico, A., Gregory, A. M., Sham, P., McGuffin, P., et al. (2004). Gene–environment interaction analysis of serotonin system markers with adolescent depression. *Molecular Psychiatry, 9*, 908–915.

Ellis, L., Ames, M. A., Peckham, W., & Burke, D. (1988). Sexual orientation of human offspring may be altered by severe maternal stress during pregnancy. *Journal of Sex Research, 25*(1), 152–157.

Ellis, L., & Cole-Harding, S. (2001). The effects of prenatal stress, and of prenatal alcohol and nicotine exposure, on human sexual orientation. *Physiology and Behavior, 74*(1–2), 213–226.

Enoch, M.-A. (2008). The role of GABA A receptors in the development of alcoholism. *Pharmacology, Biochemistry, and Behavior, 90*, 95–104.

Enright, R. D., Levy, V. M., Jr., Harris, D., & Lapsley, D. K. (1987). Do economic conditions influence how theorists view adolescents? *Journal of Youth and Adolescence, 16*, 541–559.

Eriksson, P. S., Perfilieva, E., Bjork-Eriksson, T., Alborn, A.-M., Nordborg, C., Perterson, D. A., et al. (1998). Neurogenesis in the adult human hippocampus. *Nature Medicine, 4*(11), 1313–1317.

Ernst, M., Nelson, E. E., Jazbec, S., McClure, E. B., Monk, C. S., Leibenluft, E., et al. (2005a). Amygdala and nucleus accumbens in responses to receipt and omission of gains in adults and adolescents. *NeuroImage, 25*(4), 1279–1291.

Ernst, M., Pine, D. S., & Hardin, M. (2005b). Triadic model of the neurobiology of motivated behavior in adolescence. *Psychological Medicine, 36*(3), 299–312.

Eshel, N., Nelson, E. E., Blair, R. J., Pine, D. S., & Ernst, M. (2007). Neural substrates of choice selection in adults and adolescents: Development of the ventrolateral prefrontal and anterior cingulate cortices. *Neuropsychologia, 45*, 1270–1279.

Evans, D. L., Foa, E. B., Gur, R. E., Hendin, H., O'Brien, C. P., Seligman, M. E. P., et al. (Eds.). (2005). *Treating and preventing adolescent mental health disorders*. New York: Oxford University Press.

Fagiolini, M., Fritschy, J. M., Löw, K., Möhler, H., Rudolph, U., & Hensch, T. K. (2004). Specific GABAa circuits for visual cortical plasticity. *Science, 303*, 1681–1683.

Fagiolini, M., Katagiri, H., Miyamoto, H., Mori, H., Grant, S. G. N., & Mishina, M. (2003). Separable features of visual cortical plasticity revealed by n-methyl-d-aspartate receptor 2a signaling. *Proceedings of the National Academy of Sciences, 100*(5), 2854–2859.

Fair, D. A., Cohen, A. L., Dosenbach, N. U. F., Church, J. A., Miezin, F. M., Barch, D. M., et al. (2008). The maturing architecture of the brain's default network. *Proceedings of the National Academy of Sciences, 105*(10), 4028–4032.

Fair, D. A., Cohen, A. L., Power, J. D., Dosenbach, N. U. F., Church, J. A., Niezin, F. M., et al. (2009). Functional brain networks develop from a "local to distributed" organization. *PLoS Computational Biology, 5*(5), 1–14.

Fair, D. A., Dosenback, N. U. F., Church, J. A., Cohen, A. L., Brahmbhatt, S., Miezin, F. M., et al. (2007). Development of distinct control networks through segregation and integration. *Proceedings of the National Academy of Sciences, 104*(33), 13507–13512.

Fecteau, S., Knoch, D., Fregni, F., Sultani, N., Boggio, P. S., & Pascual-Leone, A. (2007a). Diminishing risk-taking behavior by modulating activity in the prefrontal cortex: A direct current stimulation study. *Journal of Neuroscience, 27*(46), 12500–12505.

Fecteau, S., Pascual-Leone, A., Zald, D. H., Liguori, P., Théoret, H., Boggio, P. S., et al. (2007b). Activation of prefrontal cortex by transcranial direct current stimulation reduces appetite for risk during ambiguous decision making. *Journal of Neuroscience, 27*(23), 6212–6218.

Fedigan, L. M., & Zohar, S. (1997). Sex differences in mortality of Japanese macaques: Twenty-one years of data from Arashiyama West population. *American Journal of Physical Anthropology, 102*, 161–175.

Feinberg, I., Higgins, L. M., Khaw, W. Y., & Campbell, I. G. (2006). The adolescent decline of nREM delta, an indicator of brain maturation, is linked to age and sex but not to pubertal stage. *American Journal of*

Physiology: Regulatory, Integrative, and Comparative Physiology, 291, R1724–R1729.

Fernández-Vidal, J. M., Spear, N. E., & Molina, J. C. (2003). Adolescent rats discriminate a mild state of ethanol intoxication likely to act as an appetitive unconditioned stimulus. *Alcohol, 30*(1), 45–60.

Field, T. M. (1998). Massage therapy effects. *American Psychologist, 53*(12), 1270–1281.

Field, T. M., Diego, M., & Hernandez-Reif, M. (2007). Massage therapy research. *Developmental Review, 27,* 75–89.

Fields, R. D. (2008). White matter in learning, cognition and psychiatric disorders. *Trends in Neurosciences, 31*(7), 361–370.

Finger, E. C., Marsh, A. A., Mitchell, D. G., Reid, M.E., Sims, C., Budhani, S., et al. (2008). Abnormal ventromedial prefrontal cortex function in children with psychopathic traits during reversal learning. *Archives of General Psychiatry, 65*(5), 586–594.

Fishbein, D. H., Eldreth, D. L., Hyde, C., Matochik, J. A., London, E. D., Contoreggi, C., et al. (2005). Risky decision making and the anterior cingulate cortex in abstinent drug abusers and nonusers. *Cognitive Brain Research, 23,* 119–136.

Flannery, D. J., Rowe, D. C., & Gulley, B. L. (1993). Impact of pubertal status, timing, and age on adolescent sexual experience and delinquency. *Journal of Adolescent Research, 8*(1), 21–40.

Forbes, E. E., May, J. C., Siegle, G. J., Ladouceur, C. D., Ryan, N. D., Carter, C. S., et al. (2006). Reward-related decision-making in pediatric major depressive disorder: An fMRI study. *Journal of Child Psychology and Psychiatry, 47*(10), 1031–1040.

Fowler, T., Lifford, K., Shelton, K., Rice, F., Thapar, A., Neale, M. C., et al. (2007). Exploring the relationship between genetic and environmental influences on initiation and progression of substance use. *Addiction, 101,* 413–422.

Francis, D. D., Diorio, J., Liu, D., & Meaney, M. J. (1999). Nongenomic transmission across generations of maternal behavior and stress responses in the rat. *Science, 286,* 1155–1158.

Francis, D. D., Diorio, J., Plotsky, P. M., & Meaney, M. J. (2002). Environmental enrichment reverses the effects of maternal separation on stress reactivity. *Journal of Neuroscience, 22*(18), 7840–7843.

Frantz, K. J., O'Dell, L. E., & Parsons, L. H. (2007). Behavioral and neurochemical responses to cocaine in periadolescent and adult rats. *Neuropsychopharmacology, 32,* 625–637.

Fries, A. B., Ziegler, T. E., Kurlan, J. R., Jacoris, S., & Pollak, S. D. (2005). Early experience in humans is associated with changes in neuropeptides critical for regulating social behavior. *Proceedings of the National Academy of Sciences, 102*(47), 17237–17240.

Frisch, R. E. (1984). Body fat, puberty, and fertility. *Biological Reviews of the Cambridge Philosophical Society, 59*(2), 161–188.

Frisch, R. E. (1991). Puberty and body fat. In R. M. Lerner, A. C. Petersen, & J. Brooks-Gunn (Eds.), *Encyclopedia of adolescence* (pp. 884–892). New York: Garland.

Frodl, T., Meisenzahl, E. M., Zetzsche, T., Born, C., Jäger, M., Groll, C., et al. (2003). Larger amygdala volumes in first depressive episode as compared to recurrent major depression and healthy control subjects. *Biological Psychiatry, 53*, 338–244.

Fryer, S. L., Tapert, S. F., Mattson, S. N., Paulus, M. P., Spadoni, A. D., & Riley, E. P. (2007). Prenatal alcohol exposure affects frontal-striatal bold response during inhibitory control. *Alcoholism: Clinical and Experimental Research, 31*(8), 1–10.

Fu, C. H. Y., Williams, S. C. R., Cleare, A. J., Brammer, M. J., Walsh, N. D., Kim, J., et al. (2004). Attenuation of the neural response to sad faces in major depression by antidepressant treatment. *Archives of General Psychiatry, 61*, 877–889.

Fullard, W., & Reiling, A. M. (1976). An investigation of Lorenz's babyness. *Child Development, 47*, 1191–1193.

Galef, B. G. Jr. (1977). Mechanisms for the social transmission of food preferences from adult to weanling rats. In L. M. Barker, M. Best, & M. Domjan (Eds.), *Learning mechanisms in food selection* (pp. 123–148). Waco, TX: Baylor University Press.

Galef, B. G., Jr. (1981). The ecology of weaning: Parasitism and the achievement of independence by altricial mammals. In D. J. Gubernick & P. Klopfer (Eds.), *Parental care in mammals* (pp. 211–241). New York: Plenum Press.

Galvan, A., Hare, T. A., Parra, C. E., Penn, J., Voss, H., Glover, G., et al. (2006). Earlier development of the accumbens relative to oribitofrontal cortex might underlie risk-taking behavior in adolescents. *Journal of Neuroscience, 26*(25), 6885–6892.

Galvan, A., Hare, T., Voss, H., Glover, G., & Casey, B. J. (2007). Risk-taking and the adolescent brain: Who is at risk? *Developmental Science, 10*(2), F8–F14.

Gan, W.-B., Kwon, E., Feng, G., Sanes, J. R., & Lichtman, J. W. (2003). Synaptic dynamism measured over minutes to months: Age-dependent decline in an autonomic ganglion. *Nature Neuroscience, 6*(9), 956–960.

Gardner, M., & Steinberg, L. (2005). Peer influence on risk taking, risk preference, and risky decision making in adolescence and adulthood: An experimental study. *Developmental Psychology, 41*(4), 625–635.

Gaspar de Moura, E., & Passos, M. C. F. (2005). Neonatal programming of body weight regulation and energetic metabolism. *Bioscience Reports, 25*(3–4), 251–269.

Gathercole, S. E., Pickering, S. J., Ambridge, B., & Wearing, H. (2004). The structure of working memory from 4 to 15 years of age. *Developmental Psychology, 40*(1), 177–190.

Gauthier, I., Tarr, J. M., Anderson, A. W., Skudlarski, P., & Gore, J. C. (1999). Activation of the middle fusiform "face area" increases with expertise in recognizing novel objects. *Nature Neuroscience, 2*(6), 568–573.

Ge, X., Conger, R. D., & Elder, J., G. H. (1996). Coming of age too early: Pubertal influences on girls' vulnerability to psychological distress. *Child Development, 67*(6), 3386–3400.

Ge, X., Lorenz, F. O., Conger, R. D., Elder, G. H., Jr., & Simons, R. L. (1994). Trajectories of stressful life events and depressive symptoms during adolescence. *Developmental Psychology, 30*(4), 467–483.

Gesch, C. B., Hammond, S. M., Hampson, S. E., Eves, A., & Crowder, M. J. (2002). Influence of supplementary vitamins, minerals and essential fatty acids on the antisocial behaviour of young adult prisoners. *British Journal of Psychiatry, 181*, 22–28.

Gest, S. D., Reed, M.-G. J., & Masten, A. S. (1999). Measuring developmental changes in exposure to adversity: A life chart and rating scale approach. *Development and Psychopathology, 11*(1), 171–192.

Gianaros, P. J., Sheu, L. K., Matthews, K. A., Jennings, J. R., Manuck, S. B., & Hariri, A. R. (2008). Individual differences in stressor-evoked blood pressure reactivity vary with activation, volume, and functional connectivity of the amygdala. *Journal of Neuroscience, 28*(4), 990–999.

Giedd, J. N., Blumenthal, J., Jeffries, N. O., Castellanos, F. X., Liu, H., Zijdenbos, A., et al. (1999a). Brain development during childhood and adolescence: A longitudinal MRI study. *Nature Neuroscience, 2*(10), 861–863.

Giedd, J. N., Jeffries, N. O., Blumenthal, J., Castellanos, F. X., Vaituzis, A. C., Fernandez, T., et al. (1999b). Childhood- onset schizophrenia: Progressive brain changes during adolescence. *Biological Psychiatry, 46*(7), 869–870.

Glantz, M. D., & Chambers, J. C. (2006). Prenatal drug exposure effects on subsequent vulnerability to drug abuse. *Development and Psychopathology, 18*(3), 893–922.

Gluckman, P. D., & Hanson, M. A. (2004). The developmental origins of the metabolic syndrome. *Trends in Endocrinology and Metabolism, 15*(4), 183–187.

Godfrey, K. M., & Barker, D. J. P. (2000). Fetal nutrition and adult disease. *American Journal of Clinical Nutrition, 71*, 1344–1352.

Gogtay, N., Giedd, J. N., Lusk, L., Hayashi, K. M., Greenstein, D., Vaituzis, A. C., et al. (2004). Dynamic mapping of human cortical development during childhood through early adulthood. *Proceedings of the National Academy of Sciences of the United States of America, 101*(21), 8174–8179.

Goldman, P. S. (1971). Functional development of the prefrontal cortex in early life and the problem of neuronal plasticity. *Experimental Neurology, 32*, 366–387.

Goldman-Rakic, P. S., Isseroff, A., Schwartz, M. L., & Bugbee, N. M. (1983). The neurobiology of cognitive development. In P. H. Mussen (Ed.), *Infancy and developmental psychobiology* (Vol. II, pp. 281–344). New York: Wiley.

Gonzalez-Burgos, G., Kroener, S., Zaitsev, A., Povysheva, N., & Krimer, L. (2008). Functional maturation of excitatory synapses in layer 3 pyramidal neurons during postnatal development of the primate prefrontal cortex. *Cerebral Cortex, 18*(3), 626–637.

Goodyer, I. M., Herbert, J., & Tamplin, A. (2003). Psychoendocrine antecedents of persistent first-episode major depression in adolescents: A community-based longitudinal enquiry. *Psychological Medicine, 33*(4), 601–610.

Gorski, R. (2002). Hypothalamic imprinting by gonadal steroid hormones. *Advances in Experimental Medicine and Biology, 511*, 601–610.

Gotlib, I. H., Joormann, J., Minor, K. L., & Hallmayer, J. (2008). HPA axis reactivity: A mechanism underlying the associations among 5-HTTLPR, stress, and depression. *Biological Psychiatry, 63*(9), 847–851.

Graham, D. L., & Diaz-Granados, J. L. (2006). Periadolescent exposure to ethanol and diazepam alters the aversive properties of ethanol in adult mice. *Pharmacology, Biochemistry, and Behavior, 84*(3), 406–414.

Greaves-Lord, K., Ferdinand, R. F., Oldehinkel, A. J., Sondeijker, F. E., Ormel, J., & Verhuist, F. C. (2007). Higher cortisol awakening response in young adolescents with persistent anxiety problems. *Acta Psychiatrica Scandinavica, 116*(2), 137–144.

Green, A. S., & Grahame, N. J. (2008). Ethanol drinking in rodents: Is free-choice drinking related to the reinforcing effects of ethanol? *Alcohol, 42*(1), 1–11.

Green, L., Fein, D., Modahl, C., Feinstein, C., Waterhouse, L., & Morris, M. (2001). Oxytocin and autistic disorder: Alterations in peptide forms. *Biological Psychiatry, 50*(8), 609–613.

Green, L., Fry, A. F., & Myerson, J. (1994). Discounting of delayed rewards: A life-span comparison. *Psychological Science, 5*(1), 33–36.

Greene, K., Krcmar, M., Walters, L. H., Rubin, D. L., Hale, J., & Hale, L. (2000). Targeting adolescent risk-taking behaviors: The contributions of egocentrism and sensation-seeking. *Journal of Adolescence, 23*, 439–461.

Grobin, A. C., Matthews, D. B., Montoya, D., Wilson, W. A., Morrow, A. L., & Swartzwelder, H. S. (2001). Age-related differences in neurosteroid potentiation of muscimol-stimulated (36)Cl(-) flux following chronic ethanol treatment. *Neuroscience, 105*(3), 547–552.

Grosbras, M., Jansen, M., Leonard, G., McIntosh, A., Osswald, K., Poulsen, C., et al. (2007). Neural mechanisms of resistance to peer influence in early adolescence. *Journal of Neuroscience, 27*(30), 8040–8045.

Grumbach, M. M. (2002). The neuroendocrinology of human puberty revisited. *Hormone Research, 57*(Suppl. 2), 2–14.

Grutzendler, J., Kasthuri, N., & Gan, W.-B. (2002). Long-term dendritic spine stability in adult cortex. *Nature, 420*, 812–816.

Gunnar, M. R., & Quevedo, K. (2007). The neurobiology of stress and development. *Annual Review of Psychology, 58*, 145–173.

Gunnar, M. R., & Vazquez, D. (2006). Stress neurobiology and developmental psychopathology. In D. Chicchette & D. J. Cohen (Eds.), *Developmental psychopathology: Developmental neuroscience* (pp. 533–577). New York: Wiley.

Gunnar, M. R., Wewerka, S., Frenn, K., Long, J. D., & Griggs, C. (2009). Developmental changes in hypothalamo–pituitary–adrenal activity over the transition to adolescence: Normative changes and associations with pubertal stage. *Development and Psychopathology, 21*(1), 69–85.

Gutman, D. A., & Nemeroff, C. B. (2003). Persistent central nervous system effects of an adverse early environment: Clinical and preclinical studies. *Physiology and Behavior, 79*, 471–478.

Guyer, A. E., Monk, C. S., McClure-Tone, E. B., Nelson, E. E., Roberson-Nay, R., Adler, A. D., et al. (2008). A developmental examination of amygdala response to facial expressions. *Journal of Cognitive Neuroscience, 20*(9), 1565–1582.

Hall, W., Degenhardt, L., & Teesson, M. (2004). Cannabis use and psychotic disorders: An update. *Drug and Alcohol Review, 23*, 433–443.

Haller, J., Halász, J., Mikics, E., & Kruk, M. R. (2004). Chronic glucocorticoid deficiency-induced abnormal aggression, autonomic hypoarousal, and social deficit in rats. *Journal of Neuroendocrinology, 16*, 550–557.

Hare, T. A., Tottenham, N., Galvan, A., Voss, H. U., Glover, G. H., & Casey, B. J. (2008). Biological substrates of emotional reactivity and regulation in adolescence during an emotional go-no-go task. *Biological Psychiatry, 63*(10), 927–934.

Harford, T. C., Grant, B. F., Yi, H., & Chen, C. M. (2005). Patterns of DSM-IV alcohol abuse and dependence criteria among adolescents and adults: Results from the 2001 National Household Survey on Drug Abuse. *Alcoholism: Clinical and Experimental Research, 29*(5), 810–828.

Hariri, A. R., Brown, S. M., Williamson, D. E., Flory, J. D., de Wit, H., & Manuck, S. B. (2006). Preference for immediate over delayed rewards is associated with magnitude of ventral striatal activity. *Journal of Neuroscience, 26*(51), 13213–13217.

Hariri, A. R., Drabant, E. M., Munoz, K. E., Kolachana, B. S., Mattay, V. S., Egan, M. F., et al. (2005). A susceptibility gene for affective disorders and the response of the human amygdala. *Archives of General Psychiatry, 62*(2), 146–152.

Hariri, A. R., Mattay, V. S., Tessitore, A., Kolachana, B., Fera, F., Goldman, D., et al. (2002). Serotonin transporter genetic variation and the response of the human amygdala. *Science, 297*, 400–403.

Harrell, J. S., Bangdiwala, S. I., Deng, S., Webb, J. P., & Bradley, C. (1998). Smoking initiation in youth. *Journal of Adolescent Health, 23*, 271–279.

Harris, J. R. (1995). Where is the child's environment? A group socialization theory of development. *Psychological Review, 102*(3), 458–489.

Harrison, P. J., & Weinberger, D. R. (2005). Schizophrenia genes, gene expresson, and neuropathology: On the matter of their convergence. *Molecular Psychiatry, 10*, 40–68.

He, J., & Crews, F. T. (2007). Neurogenesis decreases during brain maturation from adolescence to adulthood. *Pharmacology, Biochemistry, and Behavior, 86*, 327–333.

Hensch, T. K. (2004). Critical period regulation. *Annual Review of Neuroscience, 27*, 549–579.

Hensch, T. K. (2005). Critical period plasticity in local cortical circuits. *Nature Reviews Neuroscience, 6*, 877–888.

Hensch, T. K., & Fagiolini, M. (2004). *Excitatory–inhibitory balance: Synapses, circuits, systems.* New York: Plenum Press.

Herba, C., & Phillips, M. (2004). Annotation: Development of facial expression recognition from childhood to adolescence: Behavioral and neurological perspectives. *Journal of Child Psychology and Psychiatry, 45*(7), 1185–1198.

Herman, J. P., Ostrander, M. M., Mueller, N. K., & Figueiredo, H. (2005). Limbic system mechanisms of stress regulation: Hypothalamo–pituitary–adrenocortical axis. *Progress in Neuro-Psychopharmacology and Biological Psychiatry, 29,* 1201–1213.

Heron, M. P., & Smith, B. L. (2007). Deaths: Leading causes for 2003. *National Vital Statistics Reports, 55*(10), 16–52.

Herpertz, S. C., Huebner, T., Marx, I., Vloet, T. D., Fink, G. R., Stoecker, T., et al. (2008). Emotional processing in male adolescents with childhood-onset conduct disorder. *Journal of Child Psychology and Psychiatry, 49*(7), 781–791.

Herpertz, S. C., Werth, U., Luckas, G., Qunaibi, M., Schuerkens, A., Kunert, H.-J., et al. (2001). Emotion in criminal offenders with psychopathy and borderline personality disorder. *Archives of General Psychiatry, 58,* 737–745.

Higley, J. D., Mehlman, P. T., Higley, S. B., Fernald, B., Vickers, J., Lindell, S. G., et al. (1996a). Excessive mortality in young free-ranging male nonhuman primates with low cerebrospinal fluid 5-hydroxyindoleacetic acid concentrations. *Archives of General Psychiatry, 53,* 537–543.

Higley, J. D., Suomi, S. J., & Linnoila, M. (1996b). A nonhuman primate model of type II excessive alcohol consumption? Part 1. Low cerebrospinal fluid 5-hydroxyindoleacetic acid concentrations and diminished social competence correlate with excessive alcohol consumption. *Alcoholism: Clinical and Experimental Research, 20*(4), 629–642.

Hill, S. Y., De Bellis, M. D., Keshavan, M. S., Lowers, L., Shen, S., Hall, J., et al. (2001). Right amygdala volume in adolescent and young adult offspring from families at high risk for developing alcoholism. *Biological Psychiatry, 49*(11), 894–905.

Hill, S. Y., Muddasani, S., Prasad, K., Nutche, J., Steinhauer, S. R., Scanlon, J., McDermott, M., & Keshavon, M. (2007). Cerebellar volume in offspring from multiplex alcohol dependence families. *Biological Psychiatry, 61,* 41–47.

Hill, S. Y., Wang, S., Kostelnik, B., Carter, H., Holmes, B., McDermott, M., et al. (2009). Disruption of orbitofrontal cortex laterality in offspring from multiplex alcohol dependence families. *Biological Psychiatry, 65*, 129–136.

Hollerman, J. R., Tremblay, L., & Schultz, W. (2000). Involvement of basal ganglia and orbitofrontal cortex in goal-directed behavior. *Progress in Brain Research, 126*, 193–215.

House, S. H. (2007). Nurturing the brain nutritionally and emotionally from before conception to late adolescence. *Nutrition and Health, 19*, 143–161.

Huber, D., Veinante, P., & Stoop, R. (2005). Vasopressin and oxytocin excite distinct neuronal populations in the central amygdala. *Science, 308*, 245–248.

Huebner, T., Vloet, T. D., Marx, I., Konrad, K., Fink, G. R., Herpertz, S. C., et al. (2008). Morphometric brain abnormalities in boys with conduct disorder. *Journal of the American Academy of Child and Adolescent Psychiatry, 47*(5), 540–547.

Huttenlocher, P. R., & Dabholkar, A. S. (1997). Regional differences in synaptogenesis in human cerebral cortex. *Journal of Comparative Neurology, 387*, 167–178.

Iidaka, T., Omori, M., Murata, T., Kosaka, H., Yonekura, Y., Okada, T., et al. (2001). Neural interaction of the amygdala with the prefrontal and temporal cortices in the processing of facial expressions as revealed by fMRI. *Journal of Cognitive Neuroscience, 13*(8), 1035–1047.

Imperato, A., Puglisi-Allegra, S., Casolini, P., Zocchi, A., & Angelucci, L. (1989). Stress-induced enhancement of dopamine and acetylcholine release in limbic structures: Role of corticosterone. *European Journal of Pharmacology, 165*, 337–338.

Inder, T. E., & Huppi, P. S. (2000). In vivo studies of brain development by magnetic resonance techniques. *Mental Retardation and Developmental Disabilities Research Reviews, 6*, 59–67.

Infurna, R. N., & Spear, L. P. (1979). Developmental changes in amphetamine-induced taste aversions. *Pharmacology, Biochemistry, and Behavior, 11*(1), 31–35.

Irwin, C. E., Jr. (1989). Risk-taking behaviors in the adolescent patient: Are they impulsive? *Pediatric Annals, 18*, 122–133.

Irwin, C. E., Jr. (1993). Adolescence and risk taking: How are they related? In N. J. Bell & R. W. Bell (Eds.), *Adolescent risk taking* (pp. 7–28). Newbury Park, CA: Sage.

Irwin, C. E., Jr., Burg, S. J., & Uhler Cart, C. (2002). America's adolescents: Where have we been, where are we going? *Journal of Adolescent Health, 31*(Suppl. 6), 91-121.

REFERENCES

REFERENCES

Irwin, C. E., Jr., & Millstein, S. G. (1992). Correlates and predictors of risk-taking behavior during adolescence. In L. P. Lipsitt & L. L. Mitnick (Eds.), *Self-regulatory behavior and risk taking: Causes and consequences* (pp. 3–21). Norwood, NJ: Ablex.

Jacobs, B. L., van Praag, H., & Gage, F. H. (2000). Adult brain neurogenesis and psychiatry: A novel theory of depression. *Molecular Psychiatry, 5,* 262–269.

Jacobson, S. (1963). Sequence of myelinization in the brain of the albino rat: A. Cerebral cortex, thalamus, and related structures. *Journal of Comparative Neurology, 121,* 5–29.

James, W. (2006). Two hypotheses on the causes of male homosexuality and paedophilia. *Journal of Biosocial Science, 38*(6), 745–761.

Jessor, R., Donovan, J. E., & Costa, F. (1996). Personality, perceived life chances, and adolescent behavior. In K. Hurrelmann & S. F. Hamilton (Eds.), *Social problems and social contexts in adolescence* (pp. 219–233). New York: Aldine de Gruyter.

Johansson, T., & Ritzén, E. M. (2005). Very long-term follow-up of girls with early and late menarche. *Endocrine Development, 8,* 126–136.

Johnson, M. H. (2001). Functional brain development in humans. *Neuroscience, 2*(7), 475–483.

Johnston, L. D., O'Malley, P. M., & Bachman, J. G. (2003). *Monitoring the future national results on adolescent drug use* (Publication No. 03-5374). Bethesda, MD: National Institute on Drug Abuse.

Johnston, L. D., O'Malley, P. M., Bachman, J. G., & Schulenberg, J. E. (2008). *Monitoring the future: National Survey Results on Adolescent Drug Use: Overview of key findings, 2007* (Publication No. 08-6418). Bethesda, MD: National Institutes of Health.

Johnstone, B. M., Garrity, T. F., & Straus, R. (1997). The relationship between alcohol and life stress. In T. W. Miller (Ed.), *Clinical disorders and stressful life events* (pp. 247–279). Madison, CT: International Universities Press.

Johnstone, T., van Reekum, C. M., Urry, H. L., Kalin, N. H., & Davidson, R. J. (2007). Failure to regulate: Counterproductive recruitment of top-down prefrontal–subcortical circuitry in major depression. *Journal of Neuroscience, 27*(33), 8884–8887.

Jones, P., Rodgers, B., Murray, R., & Marmot, M. (1994). Child developmental risk factors for adult schizophrenia in the British 1946 birth cohort. *Lancet, 344,* 1398–1402.

Jung, R. E., & Haier, R. J. (2007). The parieto-frontal integration theory

(P-FIT) of intelligence: Converging neuroimaging evidence. *Behavioral and Brain Sciences, 30*, 135–187.

Jurado, M. B., & Rosselli, M. (2007). The elusive nature of executive functions: A review of our current understanding. *Neuropsychology Review, 17*, 213–233.

Kadosh, K. C., & Johnson, M. H. (2007). Developing a cortex specialized for face perception. *Trends in Cognitive Science, 11*(9), 367–369.

Kail, R. (1991). Developmental change in speed of processing during childhood and adolescence. *Psychological Bulletin, 109*(3), 490–501.

Kaiser, U. B., & Kuohung, W. (2005). Kiss-1 and GPR54 as new players in gonadotropin regulation and puberty. *Endocrine, 26*(3), 277–284.

Kalivas, P. W., Churchill, L., & Klitenick, M. A. (1993). The circuitry mediating the translation of motivational stimuli into adaptive motor responses. In P. W. Kalivas & C. D. Barnes (Eds.), *Limbic motor circuits and neuropsychiatry* (pp. 237–287). Boca Raton, FL: CRC.

Kalivas, P. W., Volkow, N., & Seamans, J. (2005). Unmanageable motivation in addiction: A pathology in prefrontal–accumbens glutamate transmission. *Neuron, 45*(5), 647–650.

Kallen, V. L., Tulen, J. H., Utens, E. M., Treffers, P. D., De Jong, F. H., & Ferdinand, R. F. (2008). Associations between HPA axis functioning and level of anxiety in children and adolescents with an anxiety disorder. *Depression and Anxiety, 25*(2), 131–141.

Kaplan, H. B., Johnson, R. J., & Bailey, C. A. (1987). Deviant peers and deviant behavior: Further elaboration of a model. *Social Psychology Quarterly, 50*, 277–284.

Kareken, D. A., Claus, E. D., Sabri, M., Dzemidzic, M., Kosobud, A. E., Radnovich, A. J., Hector, D., Ramchandani, V. A., O'Connor, S. J., Lowe, M., & Li, T. K. (2004). *Alcoholism: Clinical and Experimental Research, 28*(4), 550–557.

Karlberg, J. (2002). Secular trends in pubertal development. *Hormone Research, 57*(Suppl. 2), 19–30.

Katoh-Semba, R., Semba, R., Takeuchi, I. K., & Kato, K. (1998). Age-related changes in levels of brain-derived neurotrophic factor in selected brain regions of rats, normal mice, and senescence-accelerated mice: A comparison to those of nerve growth factor and neurotrophin-3. *Neuroscience Research, 31*, 227–234.

Kaufman, J., & Charney, D. (2003). The neurobiology of child and adolescent depression. In D. Cicchetti & E. Walker (Eds.), *Neurodevelopmental mechanisms in psychopathology* (pp. 461–490). Cambridge, UK: Cambridge University Press.

Keane, B. (1990). Dispersal and inbreeding avoidance in the white-footed mouse, *Peromyscus leucopus*. *Animal Behaviour, 40*, 143–152.

Keating, D. (2004). Cognitive and brain development. In Steinberg, L. D. (Ed.), *Handbook of adolescent psychology* (2nd ed.). New York: Wiley.

Kelley, A. E., & Berridge, K. (2002). The neuroscience of natural rewards: Relevance to addictive drugs. *Journal of Neuroscience, 22*(9), 3306–3311.

Kelley, A. E., Schiltz, C. A., & Landry, C. F. (2005). Neural systems recruited by drug- and food-related cues: Studies of gene activation in corticolimbic regions. *Physiology and Behavior, 86*(1–2), 11–14.

Kellogg, C. K. (1991). Postnatal effects of prenatal exposure to psychoactive drugs. *Pre- and Post-Natal Psychology, 5*(3), 233–251.

Kellogg, C. K., Awatramani, G. B., & Piekut, D. T. (1998). Adolescent development alters stressor-induced Fos immunoreactivity in rat brain. *Neuroscience, 83*(3), 681–689.

Kendler, K., & Prescott, C. (2006). *Genes, environment, and psychopathology*. New York: Guilford Press.

Kendler, K., Thorton, L., Gilman, S., & Kessler, R. (2000). Sexual orientation in a U.S. national sample of twin and non-twin sibling pairs. *American Journal of Psychiatry, 157*(11), 1843–1846.

Kerstetter, K. A., & Kantak, K. M. (2007). Differential effects of self-administered cocaine in adolescent and adult rats on stimulus–reward learning. *Psychopharmacology, 194*, 403–411.

Kessler, R. C., Berglund, P., Demler, O., Jin, R., Merikangas, K. R., & Walters, E. E. (2005). Lifetime prevalence and age-of-onset distributions of DSM-IV disorders in the National Comorbidity Survey replication. *Archives of General Psychiatry, 62*, 593–602.

Kessler, R. C., & Walters, E. E. (1998). Epidemiology of DSM-III-R major depression and minor depression among adolescents and young adults in the National Comorbidity Survey. *Depression and Anxiety, 7*, 3–14.

Killgore, W. D. S., Oki, M., & Yurgelun-Todd, D. A. (2001). Sex-specific developmental changes in amygdala responses to affective faces. *NeuroReport, 12*(2), 427–433.

Killgore, W. D. S., & Yurgelun-Todd, D. A. (2007). Neural correlates of emotional intelligence in adolescent children. *Cognitive, Affective, and Behavioral Neuroscience, 7*(2), 140–151.

Kim, K., & Smith, P. K. (1998). Childhood stress, behavioural symptoms and mother–daughter pubertal development. *Journal of Adolescence, 21,* 231–240.

Kim, S.-H., Kim, H.-B., Jang, M.-H., Lim, B.-V., Kim, Y.-J., Kim, Y.-P., et al. (2002). Treadmill exercise increases cell proliferation without altering of apoptosis in dentate gyrus of Sprague–Dawley rats. *Life Sciences, 71,* 1331–1340.

Kimmel, M. (2008). *Guyland: The perilous world where boys become men.* New York: Harper Collins.

Kirschbaum, C., Kudielka, B. M., Gaab, J., Schommer, N. C., & Hellhammer, D. H. (1999). Impact of gender, menstrual cycle phase, and oral contraceptives on the activity of the hypothalamus–pituitary–adrenal axis. *Psychosomatic Medicine, 61,* 154–162.

Klein, T. A., Neumann, J., Reuter, M., Hennig, J., von Cramon, D. Y., & Ullsperger, M. (2007). Genetically determined differences in learning from errors. *Science, 318,* 1642–1645.

Klingberg, T., Forssberg, H., & Westerberg, H. (2002). Increased brain activity in frontal and parietal cortex underlies the development of visuospatial working memory capacity during childhood. *Journal of Cognitive Neuroscience, 14*(1), 1–10.

Klump, K. L., McGue, M., & Iacono, W. G. (2003). Differential heritability of eating attitudes and behaviors in prepubertal versus pubertal twins. *International Journal of Eating Disorders, 33*(3), 287–292.

Knoch, D., Gianotti, L. R. R., Pascual-Leone, A., Treyer, V., Regard, M., Hohmann, M., et al. (2006). Disruption of right prefrontal cortex by low-frequency repetitive transcranial magnetic stimulation induces risk-taking behavior. *Journal of Neuroscience, 26*(24), 6469–6472.

Kodituwakku, P. W., Kalberg, W., & May, P. A. (2001). The effects of prenatal alcohol exposure on executive functioning. *Alcohol Research and Health, 25*(3), 192–198.

Kolb, B., & Gibb, R. (1993). Possible anatomical basis of recovery of function after neonatal frontal lesions in rats. *Behavioral Neuroscience, 107*(5), 799–811.

Kolb, B., & Gibb, R. (2007). Brain plasticity and recovery from early cortical injury. *Developmental Psychobiology, 49,* 107–118.

Koob, G. F., & Kreek, M. J. (2007). Stress, dysregulation of drug reward pathways, and the transition to drug dependence. *American Journal of Psychiatry, 164*(8), 1149–1159.

Koob, G. F., & Le Moal, M. (2006). *Neurobiology of addiction.* San Diego, CA: Elsevier.

Korte, S. M., Koolhaas, J. M., Wingfield, J. C., & McEwen, B. S. (2005). The Darwinian concept of stress benefits of allostasis and costs of allostatic load and the trade-offs in health and disease. *Neuroscience and Biobehavioral Reviews, 29,* 3–38.

Kota, D., Martiin, B. R., Robinson, S. E., & Damaj, M. I. (2007). Nicotine dependence and reward differ between adolescent and adut male mice. *Journal of Pharmacology and Experimental Therapeutics, 322*(1), 399–407.

Kozorovitskiy, Y., & Gould, E. (2003). Adult neurogenesis: A mechanism for brain repair? *Journal of Clinical and Experimental Neuropsychology, 25*(5), 721–732.

Kristensen, K., & Cadenhead, K. S. (2007). Cannabis abuse and risk for psychosis in a prodromal sample. *Psychiatry Research, 151,* 151–154.

Kuhl, B. A., Dudukovic, N. M., Kahn, I., & Wagner, A. D. (2007). Decreased demands on cognitive control reveal the neural processing benefits of forgetting. *Nature Neuroscience, 10*(7), 908–914.

Kurlan, R. (1992). The pathogenesis of Tourette's syndrome: A possible role for hormonal and excitatory neurotransmitter influences in brain development. *Archives of Neurology, 49,* 874–876.

Kurtz, M. M., & Campbell, B. A. (1994). Paradoxical autonomic responses to aversive stimuli in the developing rat. *Behavioral Neuroscience, 108*(5), 962–971.

Kwon, H., Reiss, A. L., & Menon, V. (2002). Neural basis of protracted developmental changes in visuo-spatial working memory. *Proceedings of the National Academy of Sciences, 99*(20), 13336–13341.

Ladd, C. O., Huot, R. L., Thrivikraman, T., Nemeroff, C. B., Meaney, M. J., & Plotsky, P. M. (2000). Long-term behavioral and neuroendocrine adaptations to adverse early experience. *Progress in Brain Research, 122,* 79–101.

Lamm, C., Zelazo, P. D., & Lewis, M. D. (2006). Neural correlates of cognitive control in childhood and adolescence: Disentangling the contributions of age and executive function. *Neuropsychologia, 44,* 2139–2148.

Lamprecht, R., & LeDoux, J. (2004). Structural plasticity and memory. *Nature Reviews Neuroscience, 5,* 45–54.

Landau, S. M., & D'Esposito, M. (2006). Sequence learning in pianists and nonpianists: An fMRI study. *Cognitive, Affective, and Behavioral Neuroscience, 6*(3), 246–259.

Langley-Evans, S. C. (2007). Developmental programming of health and disease. *Proceedings of the Nutrition Society, 65*(1), 97–105.

343

Larson, R., & Asmussen, L. (1991). Anger, worry, and hurt in early adolescence: An enlarging world of negative emotions. In M. E. Colten & S. Gore (Eds.), *Adolescent stress: Causes and consequences* (pp. 21–41). New York: Aldine de Gruyter.

Larson, R., & Lampman-Petraitis, C. (1989). Daily emotional states as reported by children and adolescents. *Child Development, 60,* 1250–1260.

Larson, R., & Richards, M. H. (1994). *Divergent realities: The emotional lives of mothers, fathers, and adolescents.* New York: Basic Books.

Larson, R. W., Richards, M. H., Raffaelli, M., Ham, M., & Jewell, L. (1990). Ecology of depression in late childhood and early adolescence: A profile of daily states and activities. *Journal of Abnormal Psychology, 99*(1), 92–102.

Laursen, B., Coy, K. C., & Collins, W. A. (1998). Reconsidering changes in parent–child conflict across adolescence: A meta-analysis. *Child Development, 69*(3), 817–832.

Laviola, G., Rea, M., Morley-Fletcher, S., Di Carlo, S., Bacosi, A., De Simone, R., et al. (2004). Beneficial effects of enriched environment on adolescent rats from stressed pregnancies. *European Journal of Neuroscience, 20*(6), 1655–1664.

Le Be, J. V., & Markram, H. (2006). Spontaneous and evoked synaptic rewiring in the neonatal neocortex. *Proceedings of the National Academy of Sciences, 103,* 13214–13219.

LeDoux, J. (2007). The amygdala. *Current Biology, 17*(20), R868–R874.

Lemaire, V., Koehl, M., Le Moal, M., & Abrous, D. N. (2000). Prenatal stress produces learning deficits associated with an inhibition of neurogenesis in the hippocampus. *Proceedings of the National Academy of Sciences of the United States of America, 97*(20), 11032–11037.

Lenard, Z., Studinger, P., Mersich, B., Kocsis, L., & Kollai, M. (2004). Maturation of cardiovagal autonomic function from childhood to young adult age. *Circulation, 110,* 2307–2312.

Lenroot, R. K., & Giedd, J. N. (2006). Brain development in children and adolescents: Insights from anatomical magnetic resonance imaging. *Neuroscience and Biobehavioral Reviews, 30*(6), 718–729.

Lenroot, R. K., & Giedd, J. N. (2008). The changing impact of genes and environment on brain development during childhood and adolescence: Initial findings from a neuroimaging study of pediatric twins. *Development and Psychopathology, 20*(4), 1161–1175.

Lenroot, R. K., Gogtay, N., Greenstein, D. K., Wells, G. L., Clasen, L. S., Blumenthal, J. D., et al. (2007). Sexual dimorphism of brain developmental

344

trajectories during childhood and adolescence. *Neuroimage, 36*(4), 1065–1073.

Leon-Carrion, J., García-Orza, J., & Pérez-Santamaría, F. J. (2004). Development of the inhibitory component of the executive functions in children and adolescents. *International Journal of Neuroscience, 114*(10), 1291–1311.

Lerner, J. S., Dahl, R. E., Hariri, A. R., & Taylor, S. E. (2007). Facial expressions of emotion reveal neuroendocrine and cardiovascular stress responses. *Biological Psychiatry, 61*, 253–260.

Lerner, R. M., & Galambos, N. L. (1998). Adolescent development: Challenges and opportunities for research, programs, and policies. *Annual Review of Psychology, 49*, 413–446.

LeVay, S. (1991). A difference in hypothalamic structure between heterosexual and homosexual men. *Science, 277*, 1659–1662.

Levenson, R. W. (2003). Blood, sweat, and fears: The autonomic architecture of emotion. *Annals of the New York Academy of Sciences, 1000*, 348–366.

Levisohn, L., Cronin-Golomb, A., & Schmahmann, J. D. (2000). Neuropsychological consequences of cerebellar tumour resection in children: Cerebellar cognitive affective syndrome in a paediatric population. *Brain, 123*, 1041–1050.

Leweke, F. M., Giuffrida, A., Koethe, D., Schreiber, D., Nolden, B. M., Kranaster, L., et al. (2007). Anandamide levels in cerebrospinal fluid of first-episode schizophrenic patients: Impact of cannabis use. *Schizophrenia Research, 94*, 29–36.

Leweke, F. M., & Koethe, D. (2008). Cannabis and psychiatric disorders: It is not only addiction. *Addiction Biology, 13*, 264–275.

Lewis, D. A. (1997). Development of the prefrontal cortex during adolescence: Insights into vulnerable neural circuits in schizophrenia. *Neuropsychopharmacology, 16*(6), 385–398.

Lewis, D. A., & Levitt, P. (2002). Schizophrenia as a disorder of neurodevelopment. *Annual Review Neuroscience, 25*, 409–432.

Lewis, M. D., Lamm, C., Segalowitz, S. J., Stieben, J., & Zelazo, P. D. (2006). Neurophysiological correlates of emotion regulation in children and adolescents. *Journal of Cognitive Neuroscience, 18*(3), 430–443.

Lewis, M. D., & Stieben, J. (2004). Emotion regulation in the brain: Conceptual issues and directions for developmental research. *Child Development, 75*(2), 371–376.

Lewis, T. L., & Maurer, D. (2005). Multiple sensitive periods in human visual development: Evidence from visually deprived children. *Developmental Psychobiology, 46*, 163–183.

Li, C.-Y., Mao, X., & Wei, L. (2008). Genes and (common) pathways underlying drug addiction. *PLoS Computational Biology, 4*(1), 0028–0034.

Lichtman, J. W., & Colman, H. (2000). Synapse elimination and indelible memory. *Neuron, 25*, 269–278.

Lipska, B. K., Jaskiw, G. E., & Weinberger, D. R. (1993). Postpubertal emergence of hyperresponsiveness to stress and to amphetamine after neonatal excitotoxic hippocampal damage: A potential animal model of schizophrenia. *Neuropsychopharmacology, 9*, 67–75.

Lipska, B. K., & Weinberger, D. R. (2002). A neurodevelopmental model of schizophrenia: Neonatal disconnection of the hippocampus. *Neurotoxicity Research, 4*(5–6), 469–475.

Liu, J., Morrow, A. L., Devaud, L., Grayson, D. R., & Lauder, J. M. (1997). GABA(a) receptors mediate trophic effects of GABA on embryonic brainstem monoamine neurons in vitro. *Journal of Neuroscience, 17*(7), 2420–2428.

Liu, X., Powell, D. K., Wang, H., Gold, B. T., Corbly, C. R., & Joseph, J. E. (2007). Functional dissociation in frontal and striatal areas for processing of positive and negative reward information. *Journal of Neuroscience, 27*(17), 4587–4597.

Luciana, M., & Nelson, C. A. (2002). Assessment of neuropsychological function through use of the Cambridge neuropsychological testing automated battery: Performance in 4- to 12-year-old children. *Developmental Neuropsychology, 22*(3), 595–624.

Luna, B., Garver, K. E., Urban, T. A., Lazar, N. A., & Sweeney, J. A. (2004). Maturation of cognitive processes from late childhood to adulthood. *Child Development, 75*(5), 1357–1372.

Luna, B., & Sweeney, J. A. (2001). Studies of brain and cognitive maturation through childhood and adolescence: A strategy for testing neurodevelopmental hypotheses. *Schizophrenia Bulletin, 27*(3), 443–455.

Luna, B., & Sweeney, J. A. (2004). The emergence of collaborative brain function. *Annals of the New York Academy of Sciences, 1021*, 296–309.

Luna, B., Thulborn, K. R., Munoz, D. P., Merriam, E. P., Garver, K. E., Minshew, N. J., et al. (2001). Maturation of widely distributed brain function subserves cognitive development. *NeuroImage, 13*(5), 786–793.

Lyss, P. J., Andersen, S. L., LeBlanc, C. J., & Teicher, M. H. (1999). Degree of neuronal activation following FG-7142 changes across regions during development. *Brain Research: Developmental Brain Research, 116*(2), 201–203.

MacMillan, S., Szeszko, P. R., Moore, G. J., Madden, R., Lorch, E., Ivey, J., et al. (2003). Increased amygala–hippocampal volume ratios associated with severity of anxiety in pediatric major depression. *Journal of Child and Adolescent Psychopharmacology, 13*, 65–73.

Maggs, J. L., Almeida, D. M., & Galambos, N. L. (1995). Risky business: The paradoxical meaning of problem behavior for young adolescents. *Journal of Early Adolescence, 15*, 344–362.

Maguire, E. A., Gadian, D. G., Johnsrude, I. S., Good, C. D., Ashburner, J., Frackowiak, R. S., et al. (2002). Navigation-related structural change in the hippocampi of taxi drivers. *Proceedings of the National Academy of Sciences, 97*(8), 4398–4403.

Mainero, C., Caramia, F., Pozzilli, C., Pisani, A., Pestalozza, I., Borriello, G., et al. (2004). fMRI evidence of brain reorganization during attention and memory tasks in multiple sclerosis. *NeuroImage, 21*, 858–867.

Maisonpierre, P. C., Belluscio, L., Friedman, B., Alderson, R. F., Wiegand, S. J., Furth, M. E., et al. (1990). NT-3, BDNF, and NGF in the developing rat nervous system: Parallel as well as reciprocal patterns of expression. *Neuron, 5*, 501–509.

Mann, D. R., & Plant, T. M. (2002). Leptin and pubertal development. *Seminars in Reproductive Medicine, 20*(2), 93–102.

Marenco, S., & Weinberger, D. R. (2000). The neurodevelopmental hypothesis of schizophrenia: Following a trail of evidence from cradle to grave. *Development and Psychopathology, 12*(3), 501–527.

Markham, J. A., & Greenough, W. T. (2004). Experience-driven brain plasticity: Beyond the synapse. *Neuron Glia Biology, 1*, 351–363.

Marsh, A. A., Finger, E. C., Mitchell, D. G. V., Reid, M. E., Sims, C., Kosson, D. S., et al. (2008). Reduced amygdala response to fearful expressions in children and adolescents with callous-unemotional traits and disruptive behavior disorders. *American Journal of Psychiatry, 165*, 712–720.

Marsh, R., Zhu, H., Schultz, R. T., Quackenbush, G., Royal, J., Skudlarski, P., et al. (2006). A developmental fMRI study of self-regulatory control. *Human Brain Mapping, 27*, 848–863.

Marsh, R., Zhu, H., Wang, Z., Skudlarski, P., & Peterson, B. S. (2007). A developmental fMRI study of self-regulatory control in Tourette's syndrome. *American Journal of Psychiatry, 164*(6), 955–066.

Martin, R. P., Wisenbaker, J., Baker, J., & Huttunen, M. O. (1997). Gender differences in temperament at six months and five years. *Infant Behavior and Development, 20*(3), 339– 347.

Masten, A. S. (2007). Resilience in developing systems: Progress and promise as the fourth wave rises. *Development and Psychopathology, 19,* 921– 930.

Masten, A. S., Obradovic, J., & Burt, K. (2006). Resilience in emerging adulthood: Developmental perspectives on continuity and transformation. In J. J. Arnett & J. L. Tanner (Eds.), *Emerging adults in America: Coming of age in the 21st century* (pp. 173–190). Washington, DC: American Psychological Association.

Mathews, I. Z., & McCormick, C. M. (2007). Female and male rats in late adolescence differ from adults in amphetamine-induced locomotor activity, but not in conditioned place preference for amphetamine. *Behavioural Pharmacology, 18,* 641–650.

Matthews, S. C., Simmons, A. N., Lane, S. D., & Paulus, M. P. (2004). Selective activation of the nucleus accumbens during risk-taking decision making. *Neuroreport, 15*(13), 2123–2127.

May, J. C., Delgado, M. R., Dahl, R. E., Stenger, V. A., Ryan, N. D., Fiez, J. A., & Carter, C. S. (2004). Event-related functional magnetic resonance imaging of reward-related brain circuitry in children and adolescents. *Biological Psychiatry, 55,* 359–366.

Mayer, A. D., Freeman, N. C. G., & Rosenblatt, J. S. (1979). Ontogeny of maternal behavior in the laboratory rat: Factors underlying changes in responsiveness from 30 to 90 days. *Developmental Psychobiology, 12,* 425– 439.

McArdle, P. (2008). Use and misuse of drugs and alcohol in adolescence. *British Medical Journal, 337,* 46–50.

McBride, W. J., & Li, T.-K. (1998). Animal models of alcoholism: Neurobiology of high alcohol-drinking behavior in rodents. *Critical Reviews in Neurobiology, 12*(4), 339–369.

McBurnett, K., King, J., & Scarpa, A. (2003). The hypothalamic–pituitary–adrenal system (HPA) and the development of aggressive, antisocial, and substance abuse disorders. In D. Cicchetti & E. Walker (Eds.), *Neurodevelopmental mechanisms in psychopathology* (pp. 324–344). Cambridge, UK: Cambridge University Press.

McClure, E. B. (2000). A meta-analytic review of sex differences in facial expression processing and their development in infants, children, and adolescents. *Psychological Bulletin, 126*(3), 424–453.

McClure, E. B., Monk, C. S., Nelson, E. E., Zarahn, E., Leibenluft, E., Bilder,

R. M., et al. (2004). A developmental examination of gender differences in brain engagement during evaluation of threat. *Biological Psychiatry, 55*(11), 1047–1055.

McCord, J. (1990). Problem behaviors. In S. S. Feldman & G. R. Elliott (Eds.), *At the threshold: The developing adolescent* (pp. 414–430). Cambridge, MA: Harvard University Press.

McCormick, C. M., Merrick, A., Secen, J., & Helmreich, D. L. (2007). Social instability in adolescence alters the central and peripheral hypothalamic–pituitary–adrenal responses to a repeated homotypic stressor in male and female rats. *Journal of Neuroendocrinology, 19*(2), 116–126.

McCracken, J., Smalley, S. L., McGough, J. J., Crawford, L., Del'Homme, M., Cantor, R. M., et al. (2000). Evidence for linkage of a tandem duplication polymorphism upstream of the dopamine D4 receptor gene (DRD4) with attention deficit hyperactivity disorder (ADHD). *Molecular Psychiatry, 5*(5), 531–536.

McDonald, C. G., Eppolito, A. K., Brielmaier, J. M., Smith, L. N., Bergstrom, H. C., Lawhead, M. R., et al. (2007). Evidence for elevated nicotine-induced structural plasticity in nucleus accumbens of adolescent rats. *Brain Research, 1151*, 211–218.

McEwen, B. S., & Alves, S. E. (1999). Estrogen actions in the central nervous system. *Endocrine Reviews, 20*(3), 279–307.

McGee, A. W., Yang, Y., Fischer, Q. S., Daw, N. W., & Strittmatter, S. M. (2005). Experience-driven plasticity of visual cortex limited by myelin and nogo receptor. *Science, 309*, 2222–2226.

McGivern, R. F., Andersen, J., Byrd, D., Mutter, K. L., & Reilly, J. (2002). Cognitive efficiency on a match to sample task decreases at the onset of puberty in children. *Brain and Cognition, 50*(1), 73–89.

McIntosh, A. R. (2000). Towards a network theory of cognition. *Neural Networks, 13*, 861-870.

McLaughlin, N. C. R., Paul, R. H., Grieve, S. M., Williams, L. M., Laidlaw, D., DiCarlo, M., et al. (2007). Diffusion tensor imaging of the corpos callosum: A cross-sectional study across the lifespan. *International Journal of Developmental Neuroscience, 25*, 215–221.

McWilliams, J. R., & Lynch, G. (1983). Rate of synaptic replacement in denervated rat hippocampus declines precipitously from the juvenile period to adulthood. *Science, 221*(4610), 572–574.

Meaney, M. J. (2001). Maternal care, gene expression, and the transmission of individual differences in stress reactivity across generations. *Annual Review of Neuroscience, 24*, 1161–1192.

Meaney, M. J., Szyf, M., & Secki, J. R. (2007). Epigenetic mechanisms of perinatal programming of hypothalamic–pituitary–adrenal function and health. *Trends in Molecular Medicine, 13*(7), 269–277.

Mechelli, A., Crinion, J. T., Noppeney, U., O'Doherty, J., Ashburner, J., Frackowiak, R. S., et al. (2004). Structural plasticity in the bilingual brain. *Nature, 431*, 757.

Meyer-Bahlburg, H. F. L., Ehrhardt, A. A., Rosen, L. R., Gruen, R. S., Veridiano, N. P., Vann, F. H., et al. (1995). Prenatal estrogens and the development of homosexual orientation. *Developmental Psychobiology, 31*(1), 12–21.

Middleton, F. A., & Strick, P. L. (2001). Cerebellar projections to the prefrontal cortex of the primate. *Journal of Neuroscience, 21*(2), 700–712.

Miller, A. (2007). Social neuroscience of child and adolescent depression. *Brain and Cognition, 65*(1), 47–68.

Miller, D. C., & Byrnes, J. P. (1997). The role of contextual and personal factors in children's risk taking. *Developmental Psychology, 33*(5), 814–823.

Millstein, S. G. (1993). Perceptual, attributional, and affective processes in perceptions of vulnerability through the life span. In N. J. Bell & R. W. Bell (Eds.), *Adolescent risk taking* (pp. 55–65). Newbury Park, CA: Sage.

Mishra, G., & Kuh, D. (2006). Perceived change in quality of life during the menopause. *Social Science and Medicine, 62*(1), 93–102.

Mody, M., Cao, Y., Cui, Z., Tay, K.-Y., Shyong, A., Shimizu, E., et al. (2001). Genome-wide gene expression profiles of the developing mouse hippocampus. *Proceedings of the National Academy of Sciences of the United States of America, 98*(15), 8862–8867.

Moffitt, T. E. (1993). Adolescence-limited and life-course-persistent antisocial behavior: A developmental taxonomy. *Psychological Review, 100*, 674–701.

Moltz, H. (1975). The search for the determinants of puberty in the rat. In B. E. Eleftheriou & R. L. Sprott (Eds.), *Hormonal correlates of behavior: A lifespan view* (Vol. 1, pp. 35–154). New York: Plenum Press.

Monk, C. S., McClure, E. B., Nelson, E. E., Zarahn, E., Bilder, R. M., Leibenluft, E., et al. (2003). Adolescent immaturity in attention-related brain engagement to emotional facial expressions. *NeuroImage, 20*, 420–428.

Monk, C. S., Nelson, E. E., McClure, E. B., Mogg, K., Bradley, B. P., Leibenluft, E., et al. (2006). Ventrolateral prefontal cortex activation and attentional bias in response to angry faces in adolescents with generalized anxiety disorder. *American Journal of Psychiatry, 163*(6), 1091–1097.

Monk, C. S., Teizer, E. H., Mogg, K., Bradley, B. P., Mai, X., Louro, H. M., et al. (2008). Amygdala and ventrolateral prefrontal cortex activation to masked angry faces in children and adolescents with generalized anxiety disorder. *Archives of General Psychiatry, 65*(5), 568–576.

Moore, H., West, A. R., & Grace, A. A. (1999). The regulation of forebrain dopamine transmission: Relevance to the pathophysiology and psychopathology of schizophrenia. *Biological Psychiatry, 46*(1), 40–55.

Moore, J. M. (1992). Dispersal, nepotism, and primate social behavior. *International Journal of Primatology, 13*, 361–378.

Mortimer, J. A. (1997). Brain reserve and the clinical expression of Alzheimer's disease. *Geriatrics, 52*, S50–S53.

Mortimer, J. A., Snowdon, D. A., & Markesbery, W. R. (2007). Brain reserve and risk of dementia: Findings from the nun study. In Stern, Y. (Ed.), *Cognitive reserve: Theory and applications* (pp. 237–249). New York: Taylor & Francis.

Mukamel, R., Gelbard, H., Arieli, A., Hasson, U., Fried, I., & Malach, R. (2005). Coupling between neuronal firing, field potentials, and fMRI in human auditory cortex. *Science, 309*, 951–954.

Munafò, M. R., Brown, S. M., & Hariri, A. R. (2008). Serotonin transporter (5-HTTLPR) genotype and amygdala activation: A meta-analysis. *Biological Psychiatry, 63*(9), 852–857.

Muuss, R. E., & Porton, H. D. (1998). *Increasing risk behavior among adolescents.* Boston: McGraw Hill College.

Nader, P. R., Bradley, R. H., Houts, R. M., McRitchie, S. L., & O'Brien, M. (2008). Moderate-to-vigorous physical activity from ages 9 to 15 years. *Journal of the American Medical Association, 300*(3), 295–305.

Nagy, Z., Westerberg, H., & Klingberg, T. (2004). Maturation of white matter is associated with the development of cognitive functions during childhood. *Journal of Cognitive Neuroscience, 16*(7), 1227–1233.

Nance, D. M. (1983). The developmental and neural determinants of the effects of estrogen on feed behavior in the rat: A theoretical perspective. *Neuroscience and Biobehavioral Reviews, 7*(2), 189–211.

Navarro, V. M., Fernandéz-Fernandéz, R., Castellano, J. M., Roa, J., Mayen, A., Barreiro, M. L., et al. (2004). Advanced vaginal opening and precocious activation of the reproductive axis by kiss-1 peptide, the endogenous ligand of GPR54. *Journal of Physiology, 561*(2), 379–386.

Nelson, C. A., & DeHann, M. (1997). A neurobehavioral approach to the recognition of facial expression in infancy. In J. A. Russell & J. M. Fernandez-Dols (Eds.), *The psychology of facial expression* (pp. 176–204). New York: Cambridge University Press.

Nelson, E. E., Leibenluft, E., McClure, E., & Pine, D. S. (2005). The social re-orientation of adolescence: A neuroscience perspective on the process and its relation to psychopathology. *Psychological Mediciine, 35,* 163–174.

Nelson, E. E., McClure, E. B., Monk, C. S., Zarahn, E., Leibenluft, E., Pine, D. S., et al. (2003). Developmental differences in neuronal engagement during implicit encoding of emotional faces: An event-related fMRI study. *Journal of Child Psychology and Psychiatry, 44*(7), 1015–1024.

Nesse, R., & Berridge, K. (1997). Psychoactive drug use in evolutionary perspective. *Science, 278,* 63–66.

Nestler, E. J., Barrot, M., DiLeone, R. J., Eisch, A. J., Gold, S. J., & Monteggia, L. M. (2002). Neurobiology of depression. *Neuron, 34,* 13–25.

Neufang, S., Specht, K., Hausmann, M., Güntürkün, O., Herpertz-Dahlmann, B., Fink, G. R., & Konrad, K. (2009). Sex differences and the impact of steroid hormones on the developing human brain. *Cerebral Cortex, 19,* 464–473.

Newlin, D. B., & Thomson, J. B. (1990). Alcohol challenge with sons of alcoholics: A critical review and analysis. *Psychological Bulletin, 108*(3), 383–402.

Noble, E. P. (2003). D2 dopamine receptor gene in psychiatric and neurological disorders and its phenotypes. *American Journal of Medical Genetics, 116B*(Part B), 103–125.

Numan, S., Gall, C. M., & Seroogy, K. B. (2005). Developmental expression of neurotrophins and their receptors in postnatal rat ventral midbrain. *Journal of Molecular Neuroscience, 27,* 245–260.

O'Brien, M. C., McCoy, T. P., Rhodes, S. D., Wagoner, A., & Wolfson, M. (2008). Caffeinated cocktails: Energy drink consumption, high-risk drinking, and alcohol-related consequences among college students. *Academic Emergency Medicine: Official Journal of the Association of American Medical Colleges, 15*(5), 453–460.

O'Dell, L. E., Bruijnzeel, A. W., Smith, R. T., Parsons, L. H., Merves, M. L., Goldberger, B. A., et al. (2006). Diminished nicotine withdrawal in adolescent rats: Implications for vulnerability to addiction. *Psychopharmacology, 186*(4), 612–619.

Odgers, C. L., Caspi, A., Nagin, D. S., Piquero, A. R., Slutske, W. S., Milne, B. J., et al. (2008). Is it important to prevent early exposure to drugs and alcohol among adolescents? *Psychological Science, 19*(10), 1037–1044.

Okazawa, H., Leyton, M., Benkelfat, C., Mzengeza, S., & Diksic, M. (2000). Statistical mapping analysis of serotonin synthesis images generated in

healthy volunteers using positron-emission tomography and a-[¹¹c]
methyl-l-tryptophan. *Journal of Psychiatry and Neuroscience, 25*(4), 359–
370.

Oken, E., & Gillman, M. W. (2003). Fetal origins of obesity. *Obesity Research,
11*(4), 496–506.

Olesen, P. J., Macoveanu, J., Tenger, J., & Klingberg, T. (2006). Brain activity
related to working memory and distraction in children and adults. *Cerebral Cortex, 17*, 1047–1054.

Olesen, P. J., Nagy, Z., Westerberg, H., & Klingberg, T. (2003). Combined
analysis of DTI and fMRI data reveals a joint maturation of white and
grey matter in a fronto-parietal network. *Cognitive Brain Research, 18*,
48–57.

Oppenheim, R. (1981). Ontogenetic adaptations and retrogressive processes
in the development of the nervous system and behavior: A neuroembryological perspective. In K. J. Connolly & H. Prechtl (Eds.), *Maturation
and development: Biological and psychological perspectives* (pp. 73–109).
Philadelphia: Lippincott.

Oppenheim, R. (1991). Cell death during development in the nervous system. *Annual Review of Neuroscience, 14*, 453–501.

Ortiz, J., & Raine, A. (2004). Heart rate level and antisocial behavior in children and adolescents: A meta-analysis. *Journal of the American Academy
of Child and Adolescent Psychiatry, 43*, 154–162.

Ott, S. L., Spinelli, S., Rock, D., Roberts, S., Amminger, G. P., & Erlenmeyer-Kimling, L. (1998). The New York high-risk project: Social and general
intelligence in children at risk for schizophrenia. *Schizophrenia Research, 31*, 1–11.

Pajer, K. A. (2007). Cardiovascular disease risk factors in adolescents: Do
negative emotions and hypothalamic–pituitary–adrenal axis function
play a role? *Current Opinion in Pediatrics, 19*, 559–564.

Pakkenberg, B., & Gundersen, H. J. G. (1997). Neocortical neuron number
in humans: Effect of sex and age. *Journal of Comparative Neurology, 384*,
312–320.

Parent, A.-S., Teilmann, G., Juul, A., Skakkebaek, N., Toppari, J., & Bourguignon, J.-P. (2003). The timing of normal puberty and the age limits of
sexual precocity: Variations around the world, secular trends, and
changes after migration. *Endocrine Reviews, 24*(5), 668–693.

Pariente, J., Cole, S., Henson, R., Clare, L., Kennedy, A., Rossor, M., et al.
(2005). Alzheimer's patients engage an alternative network during a
memory task. *Annals of Neurology, 58*, 870–879.

Paus, T. (2005). Mapping brain maturation and cognitive development during adolescence. *Trends in Cognitive Sciences, 9*(2), 60–68.

Paus, T., Collins, D. L., Evans, A. C., Leonard, G., Pike, B., & Zijdenbos, A. (2001). Maturation of white matter in the human brain: A review of magnetic resonance studies. *Brain Research Bulletin, 54*(3), 255–266.

Pautassi, R. M., Myers, M., Spear, L. P., Molina, J. C., & Spear, N. E. (2008). Adolescent, but not adult, rats exhibit ethanol-mediated appetitive second-order conditioning. *Alcoholism: Clinical and Experimental Research, 32*(11), 1–12.

Pellegrini, A. D. (2006). The development and function of rough-and-tumble play in childhood and adolescence: A sexual selection theory perspective. In A. Goncu & S. Gaskins (Eds.), *Play and development: Evolutionary, sociocultural, and functional perspectives: The Jean Piaget Symposium Series* (Vol. XIV, pp. 310). Mahwah, NJ: Erlbaum.

Pereira, M. E., & Altmann, J. (1985). Development of social behavior in free-living nonhuman primates. In E. S. Watts (Ed.), *Monographs in primatology: Nonhuman primate models for human growth and development* (Vol. 6, pp. 217–309). New York: Liss.

Pérez-Edgar, K., Roberson-Nay, R., Hardin, M. G., Poeth, K., Guyer, A. E., Nelson, E. E., et al. (2007). Attention alters neural responses to evocative faces in behaviorally inhibited adolescents. *NeuroImage, 35,* 1538–1546.

Petersen, A. C. (1998). Adolescence. In E. A. Blechman & K. D. Brownell (Eds.), *Behavioral medicine and women: A comprehensive handbook* (pp. 45–50). New York: Guilford Press.

Petersen, A. C., Silbereisen, R. K., & Sorensen, S. (1996). Adolescent development: A global perspective. In K. Hurrelmann & S. F. Hamilton (Eds.), *Social problems and social contexts in adolescence* (pp. 3–37). New York: Aldine de Gruyter.

Peterson, B. S. (2003). Conceptual, methodological, and statistical challenges in brain imaging studies of developmentally based psychopathologies. *Development and Psychopathology, 15*(3), 811–832.

Pfefferbaum, B., & Wood, P. B. (1994). Self-report study of impulsive and delinquent behavior in college students. *Journal of Adolescent Health, 15,* 295–302.

Phan, K. L., Fitzgerald, D. A., & Tancer, M. E. (2006). Association between amygdala hyperactivity to harsh faces and severity of social anxiety in generalized social phobia. *Biological Psychiatry, 59*(5), 424–429.

Phillips, M. L., Drevets, W. C., Rauch, S. L., & Lane, R. (2003). Neurobiology of emotion perception: I. The neural basis of normal emotion perception. *Biological Psychiatry, 54*, 504–514.

Philpot, R. M., Badanich, K. A., & Kirstein, C. L. (2003). Place conditioning: Age-related changes in the rewarding and aversive effects of alcohol. *Alcoholism: Clinical and Experimental Research, 27*(4), 593–599.

Piaget, J. (1954). *The construction of reality in the child.* New York: Basic Books.

Piazza, P. V., Rougé-Pont, F., Deroche, V., Maccari, S., Simon, H., & Le Moal, M. (1996). Glucocorticoids have state-dependent stimulant effects on the mesencephalic dopaminergic transmission. *Proceedings of the National Academy of Sciences of the United States of America, 93*, 8716–8720.

Piazza, P. V., Deminiere, J. M., Maccari, S., Moal, M. L., Mormede, P., & Simon, H. (1991). *Individual vulnerability to drug self-administration: Action of corticosterone on dopaminergic systems as a possible pathophysiological mechanism.* Chichester, UK: Wiley.

Pilgrim, C., & Reisert, I. (1992). Differences between male and female brains: Developmental mechanisms and implications. *Hormone and Metabolic Research, 24*, 353–359.

Pine, D. S., Grun, J., Zarahn, E., Fyer, A., Koda, V., Li, W., et al. (2001). Cortical brain regions engaged by masked emotional faces in adolescents and adults: An fMRI study. *Emotion, 1*(2), 137–147.

Plomin, R., Fulker, D. W., Corley, R., & DeFries, J. (1997). Nature, nurture, and cognitive development from 1 to 16 years: A parent–offspring adoption study. *Psychological Science, 8*(6), 442-447.

Pohjalainen, T., Rinne, J. O., Nagren, K., Lehikoinen, P., Anttila, K., Syvalahti, E. K. G., et al. (1998). The A1 allele of the human D_2 dopamine receptor gene predicts low D_2 receptor availability in healthy volunteers. *Molecular Psychiatry, 3*, 256–260.

Pohorecky, L. A. (1991). Stress and alcohol interaction: An update of human research. *Alcoholism: Clinical and Experimental Research, 15*, 438–459.

Pollak, S. D., & Kistler, D. J. (2002). Early experience is associated with the development of categorical representations for facial expressions of emotion. *Proceedings of the National Academy of Sciences, 99*(13), 9072–9076.

Pope, H. G., Jr., Gruber, A. J., Hudson, J. I., Cohane, G., Huestis, M. A., & Yurgelun-Todd, D. (2003). Early-onset cannabis use and cognitive deficits: What is the nature of the association? *Drug and Alcohol Dependence, 69*(3), 303–310.

Porges, S. W. (1995). Cardiac vagal tone: A physiological index of stress. *Neuroscience and Biobehavioral Reviews, 19*(2), 225–233.

Porges, S. W. (2001). The polyvagal theory: Phylogenetic substrates of a social nervous system. *International Journal of Psychophysiology, 42*(2), 123–146.

Post, G. B., & Kemper, H. C. G. (1993). Nutrient intake and biological maturation during adolescence: The Amsterdam growth and health longitudinal study. *European Journal of Clinical Nutrition, 47*(6), 400–408.

Post, R., Leverich, G., Weiss, S. R. B., Zhang, L.-X., Xing, G., Li, H., et al. (2003). Psychosocial stressors as predisposing factors to affective illness and PTSD. In D. Chicchette & E. Walker (Eds.), *Neurodevelopmental mechanisms in psychopathology* (pp. 491–525). Cambridge, UK: Cambridge University Press.

Price, C. J., & Friston, K. J. (1999). Scanning patients with tasks they can perform. *Human Brain Mapping, 8*, 102–108.

Price, G., Cercignani, M., Parker, G. J. M., Altmann, D. R., Barnes, T. R. E., Barker, G. J., et al. (2007). Abnormal brain connectivity in first-episode psychosis: A diffusion MRI tractography study of the corpus callosum. *Neuroimage, 35*(2), 458–466.

Primus, R. J., & Kellogg, C. K. (1989). Pubertal-related changes influence the development of environment-related social interaction in the male rat. *Developmental Psychobiology, 22*(6), 633–643.

Pryce, C. R. (2008). Postnatal ontogeny of expression of the corticosteroid receptor genes in mammalian brains: Inter-species and intra-species differences. *Brain Research Reviews, 57*, 596–605.

Quas, J. A., Hong, M., Alkon, A., & Boyce, W. T. (2000). Dissociations between psychobiologic reactivity and emotional expression in children. *Developmental Psychobiology, 37*(3), 153–175.

Quirk, G., & Beer, J. S. (2006). Prefrontal involvement in the regulation of emotion: Convergence of rat and human studies. *Current Opinion in Neurobiology, 16*, 723–727.

Radley, J. J., Arias, C. M., & Sawchenko, P. E. (2006). Regional differentiation of the medial prefrontal cortex in regulating adaptive responses to acute emotional stress. *Journal of Neuroscience, 26*(50), 12967–12976.

Rahman, Q. (2005). The neurodevelopment of human sexual orientation. *Neuroscience Biobehavioral Reviews, 29*(7), 1057–1066.

Rajah, M. N., & D'Esposito, M. (2005). Region-specific changes in prefrontal function with age: A review of PET and fMRI studies on working and episodic memory. *Brain, 128*, 1964–1983.

Rakic, P., Bourgeois, J.-P., & Goldman-Rakic, P. S. (1994). Synaptic development of the cerebral cortex: Implications for learning, memory, and mental illness. In J. van Pelt, M. A. Corner, H. B. M. Uylings, & F. H. Lopes da Silva (Eds.), *The self-organizing brain: From growth cones to functional networks* (Vol. 102, pp. 227–243). Amsterdam: Elsevier Science.

Rao, M. S., & Jacobson, M. (2005). *Developmental neurobiology* (4th ed.). New York: Kluwer Academic/Plenum Press.

Rapoport, J., Addington, A. M., Frangou, S., & Psych, M. R. C. (2005). The neurodevelopmental model of schizophrenia: Update 2005. *Molecular Psychiatry, 10*, 434–449.

Resnick, M. D., Bearman, P. S., Blum, R. W., Bauman, K. E., Harris, K. M., Jones, J., et al. (1997). Protecting adolescents from harm: Findings from the National Longitudinal Study on Adolescent Health. *Journal of the American Medical Association, 278*(10), 823–832.

Reyna, V. F., & Farley, F. (2006). Risk and rationality in adolescent decision making. *Psychological Science, 7*(1), 1–44.

Rice, F., Harold, G. T., & Thapar, A. (2003). Negative life events as an account of age-related differences in the genetic aetiology of depression in childhood and adolescence. *Journal of Child Psychology and Psychiatry, 44*(7), 977–987.

Ristuccia, R. C., & Spear, L. P. (2008). Adolescent and adult heart rate responses to self-administered ethanol. *Alcoholism: Clinical and Experimental Research, 32*(10), 1–9.

Robbins, T. W. (2005). Chemistry of the mind: Neurochemical modulation of prefrontal cortical function. *Journal of Comparative Neurology, 493*, 140–146.

Roberson-Nay, R., McClure, E. B., Monk, C. S., Nelson, E. E., Guyer, A. E., Fromm, S. J., et al. (2006). Increased amygdala activity during successful memory encoding in adolescent major depressive disorder: An fMRI study. *Biological Psychiatry, 60*, 966–973.

Robinson, T. E., & Berridge, K. C. (2003). Addiction. *Annual Review of Psychology, 54*, 25–53.

Rodd-Henricks, Z. A., Bell, R. L., Kuc, K. A., Murphy, J. M., McBride, W. J., Lumeng, L., et al. (2002a). Effects of ethanol exposure on subsequent acquisition and extinction of ethanol self-administration and expression of alcohol-seeking behavior in adult alcohol-preferring (P) rats: I. Periadolescent exposure. *Alcoholism: Clinical and Experimental Research, 26*(11), 1632–1641.

Rodd-Henricks, Z. A., Bell, R. L., Kuc, K. A., Murphy, J. M., McBride, W. J., Lumeng, L., et al. (2002b). Effects of ethanol exposure on subsequent acquisition and extinction of ethanol self-administration and expression of alcohol-seeking behavior in adult alcohol-preferring (P) rats: II. Adult exposure. *Alcoholism: Clinical and Experimental Research, 26*(11), 1642–1652.

Rodriguez de Fonseca, F., Ramos, J. A., Bonnin, A., & Fernandez-Ruiz, J. J. (1993). Presence of cannabinoid binding sites in the brain from early postnatal ages. *NeuroReport, 4*, 135–138.

Roemmich, J. N., Richmond, E. J., & Rogol, A. D. (2001). Consequences of sport training during puberty. *Journal of Endocrinological Investigation, 24*, 708–715.

Rolison, M. R., & Scherman, A. (2002). Factors influencing adolescents' decisions to engage in risk-taking behavior. *Adolescence, 37*(147), 585–596.

Rolison, M. R., & Scherman, A. (2003). College student risk-taking from three perspectives. *Adolescence, 38*(152), 689–704.

Romeo, R. D., & McEwen, B. S. (2006). Stress and the adolescent brain. *Annals of the New York Academy of Sciences, 1094*, 202–214.

Romeo, R. D., Richardson, H. N., & Sisk, C. L. (2002). Puberty and the maturation of the male brain and sexual behavior: Recasting a behavioral potential. *Neuroscience and Biobehavioral Reviews, 26*(3), 381–391.

Romeo, R. D., & Sisk, C. L. (2001). Pubertal and seasonal plasticity in the amygdala. *Brain Research, 889*(1–2), 71–77.

Romer, D., & Hennessy, M. (2007). A biosocial–affect model of adolescent sensation seeking: The role of affect evaluation and peer-group influence in adolescent drug use. *Prevention Science: The Official Journal of the Society for Prevention Research, 8*, 89–101.

Rose, R. J. (1998). A developmental behavior–genetic perspective on alcoholism risk. *Alcohol Health and Research World, 22*(2), 131–145.

Ross, M. G., Desai, M., Khorram, O., McKnight, R. A., Lane, R. H., & Torday, J. (2007). Gestational programming of offspring obesity: A potential contributor to Alzheimer's disease. *Current Alzheimer Research, 4*, 213–217.

Royall, D. R., Lauterbach, E. C., Cummings, J. L., Reeve, A., Rummans, T. A., Kaufer, D. I., et al. (2002). Executive control function: A review of its promise and challenges for clinical research. *Journal of Neuropsychiatry, 14*(4), 377–405.

Rubia, K., Halari, R., Smith, A. B., Mohammed, M., Scott, S., Giampietro, V., et al. (2008). Dissociated functional brain abnormalities of inhibition in boys with pure conduct disorder and in boys with pure attention deficit hyperactivity disorder. *American Journal of Psychiatry, 165*, 889–897.

Rubia, K., Overmeyer, S., Taylor, E., Brammer, M., Williams, S. C. R., Simmons, A., et al. (2000). Functional frontalisation with age: Mapping neurodevelopmental trajectories with fMRI. *Neuroscience and Biobehavioral Reviews, 24*(1), 13–19.

Rubia, K., Smith, A. B., Taylor, E., & Brammer, M. (2007). Linear age-correlated functional development of right inferior fronto–striato–cerebellar networks during response inhibition and anterior cingulate during error-related processes. *Human Brain Mapping, 28*, 1163–1177.

Rubia, K., Smith, A. B., Woolley, J., Nosarti, C., Heyman, I., Taylor, E., et al. (2006). Progressive increase of frontostriatal brain activation from childhood to adulthood during event-related tasks of cognitive control. *Human Brain Mapping, 27*, 973–993.

Rutter, M., Graham, P., Chadwick, O., & W. Y. (1976). Adolescent turmoil: Fact or fiction? *Journal of Child Psychology and Psychiatry, 17*, 35–56.

Ryan, N. D. (1998). Psychoneuroendocrinology of children and adolescents. *Psychoneuroendocrinology, 21*(2), 435–441.

Rypma, B., Berger, J. S., Prabhakaran, V., Bly, B. M., Kimberg, D. Y., Biswal, B. B., et al. (2006). Neural correlates of cognitive efficiency. *Neuroimage, 33*, 969–979.

Saal, D., Dong, Y., Bonci, A., & Malenka, R. (2003). Drugs of abuse and stress trigger a common synaptic adaption in dopamine neurons. *Neuron, 37*(4), 577–582.

Salami, M., Itami, C., Tsumoto, T., & Kimura, F. (2003). Change of conduction velocity by regional myelination yields constant latency irrespective of distance between thalamus and cortex. *Proceedings of the National Academy of Sciences, 100*, 6174–6179.

Sanes, D., Reh, T., & Harris, W. (2000). *Development of the nervous system* (pp. 145–202). San Diego: Academic Press.

Saper, C. (2004). Central autonomic system. In G. Paxinos (Ed.), *The rat nervous system* (3rd ed., pp. 761–796). New York: Elsevier.

Sato, S. M., Schulz, K. M., Sisk, C. L., & Wood, R. I. (2008). Adolescents and androgens, receptors and rewards. *Hormones and Behavior, 53*(5), 647–658.

Saugstad, L. (1994). The maturational theory of brain development and cerebral excitability in the multifactorially inherited manic–depressive psychosis and schizophrenia. *International Journal of Psychophysiology, 18*, 189–203.

359

Savin-Williams, R. C., & Weisfeld, G. E. (1989). An ethological perspective on adolescence. In G. R. Adams, R. Montemayor, & T. P. Gullotta (Eds.), *Biology of adolescent behavior and development* (pp. 249–274). Newbury Park, CA: Sage.

Scheff, S. W., Price, D. A., & Sparks, D. L. (2001). Quantitative assessment of possible age-related change in synaptic numbers in the human frontal cortex. *Neurobiology of Aging, 22*, 355–365.

Scheibel, A. B., & Conrad, A. S. (1993). Hippocampal dysgenesis in mutant mouse and schizophrenic man: Is there a relationship? *Schizophrenia Bulletin, 19*(1), 21–33.

Schepis, T. S., Adinoff, B., & Rao, U. (2008). Neurobiological processes in adolescent addictive disorders. *American Journal on Addictions, 17*(1), 6–23.

Scherf, K. S., Sweeney, J. A., & Luna, B. (2006). Brain basis of developmental change in visuospatial working memory. *Journal of Cognitive Neuroscience, 18*(7), 1045–1058.

Schlaggar, B. L., Brown, T. T., Lugar, H. M., Visscher, K. M., Miezin, F. M., & Petersen, S. E. (2002). Functional neuroanatomical differences between adults and school-age children in the processing of single words. *Science, 296*, 1476–1479.

Schlegel, A. (1995). A cross-cultural approach to adolescence. *Ethos, 23*(1), 15–32.

Schlegel, A., & Barry, H., III, (1991). *Adolescence: An anthropological inquiry.* New York: Free Press.

Schmahmann, J. D., & Sherman, J. C. (1998). The cerebellar cognitive affective syndrome. *Brain, 121*, 561–579.

Schmidt, L. A., Fox, N. A., & Hamer, D. H. (2007). Evidence for a gene–gene interaction in predicting children's behavior problems: Association of serotonin transporter short and dopamine receptor D4 long genotypes with internalizing and externalizing behaviors in typically developing 7-year-olds. *Development and Psychopathology, 19*(4), 1105–1116.

Schmithorst, V. J., Wilke, M., Dardzinski, B. J., & Holland, S. (2005). Cognitive functions correlate with white matter architecture in a normal pediatric population: A diffusion tensor MR imaging study. *Human Brain Mapping, 26*(2), 139–147.

Schneider, M. (2008). Puberty as highly vulnerable developmental period for the consequences of cannabis exposure. *Addiction Biology, 13*, 253–263.

Schramm-Sapyta, N. L., Cha, Y. M., Chaudhry, S., Wilson, W. A., Swartzwelder, H. S., & Kuhn, C. M. (2007). Differential anxiogenic, aversive, and locomotor effects of THC in adolescent and adult rats. *Psychopharmacology, 191*(4), 867–877.

Schramm-Sapyta, N. L., Morris, R. W., & Kuhn, C. M. (2006). Adolescent rats are protected from the conditioned aversive properties of cocaine and lithium chloride. *Pharmacology, Biochemistry, and Behavior, 84*(2), 344–352.

Schuckit, M. A. (1994). Low level of response to alcohol as a predictor of future alcoholism. *American Journal of Psychiatry, 151*(2), 184–189.

Schulz, K. M., Nolenda-Figueira, H. A., & Sisk, C. K. (2009). Back to the future: The organizational-activational hypothesis adapted to puberty and adolescence. *Hormones and Behavior, 55*, 597–604.

Schumann, G., Johann, M., Frank, J., Preuss, U., Dahmen, N., Laucht, M., et al. (2008). Systematic analysis of glutamatergic neurotransmission genes in alcohol dependence and adolescent risky drinking behavior. *Archives of General Psychiatry, 65*(7), 826–838.

Seckl, J. R., & Meaney, M. J. (2004). Glucocorticoid programming. *Annals of the New York Academy of Sciences, 1032*, 63–84.

Seeman, P. (1987). Dopamine receptors and the dopamine hypothesis of schizophrenia. *Synapse, 1*(2), 133–152.

Seeman, P., Bzowej, N. H., Guan, H.-C., Bergeron, C., Becker, L. E., Reynolds, G. P., et al. (1987). Human brain dopamine receptors in children and aging adults. *Synapse, 1*, 399–404.

Segal, M. (2005). Dendritic spines and long-term plasticity. *Nature Reviews Neuroscience, 6*(4), 277–284.

Segalowitz, S. J., & Davies, P. L. (2004). Charting the maturation of the frontal lobe: An electrophysiological strategy. *Brain and Cognition, 55*(1), 116–133.

Shah, P. J., Ebmeier, K. P., Glabus, M. F., & Goodwin, G. M. (1998). Cortical grey matter reductions associated with treatment-resistant chronic unipolar depression. *Molecular Psychiatry, 5*, 262–269.

Shalitin, S., & Phillip, M. (2003). Role of obesity and leptin in the pubertal process and pubertal growth: A review. *International Journal of Obesity, 27*, 869–874.

Shedler, J., & Block, J. (1990). Adolescent drug use and psychological health: A longitudinal inquiry. *American Psychologist, 45*(5), 612–630.

Sheline, Y. I., Wang, P. W., Gado, M. H., Csernansky, J. G., & Vannier, M. W. (1996). Hippocampal atrophy in recurrent major depression. *Proceedings of the National Academy of Sciences, 93*, 3908–3913.

Shifren, J. L., & Avis, N. E. (2007). Surgical menopause: Effects on psychological well-being and sexuality. *Menopause: Journal of the North American Menopause Society, 14*(3), 586–591.

Shoal, G. D., Giancola, P. R., & Kirillovac, G. P. (2003). Salivary cortisol, personality, and aggressive behavior in adolescent boys: A 5-year longitudinal study. *Journal of the American Academy of Child and Adolescent Psychiatry, 42*, 1101–1107.

Short, R. V. (1976). The evolution of human reproduction. *Proceedings of the Royal Society of London Series B, 195*(1118), 3–24.

Shram, M. J., Funk, D., Li, X., & Le, A. D. (2006). Periadolescent and adult rats respond differently in tests measuring the rewarding and aversive efffects of nicotine. *Psychopharmacology, 186*, 201–208.

Siciliano, D., & Smith, R. (2001). Periadolescent alcohol alters adult behavioral characteristics in the rat. *Physiology and Behavior, 74*(4-5), 637–643.

Silbereisen, R., & Noack, P. (1988). On the constructive role of problem behavior in adolescence. In N. Bolger, A. Caspi, G. Downey, & M. Moorehouse (Eds.), *Persons in context: Developmental processes* (pp. 152–180). Cambridge, UK: Cambridge University Press.

Silbereisen, R. K., & Reitzle, M. (1992). On the constructive role of problem behavior in adolescence: Further evidence on alcohol use. In L. P. Lipsitt & L. L. Mitnick (Eds.), *Self-regulatory behavior and risk taking: Causes and consequences* (pp. 199–217). Norwood, NJ: Ablex.

Silberg, J., Pickles, A., Rutter, M., Hewitt, J., Simonoff, E., Maes, H., et al. (1999). The influence of genetic factors and life stress on depression among adolescent girls. *Archives of General Psychiatry, 56*, 225–232.

Silk, J. S., Steinberg, L., & Morris, A. S. (2003). Adolescents' emotion regulation in daily life: Links to depressive symptoms and problem behavior. *Child Development, 74*(6), 1869–1880.

Silveri, M. M., & Spear, L. P. (1998). Decreased sensitivity to the hypnotic effects of ethanol early in ontogeny. *Alcoholism: Clinical and Experimental Research, 22*(3), 670–676.

Sisk, C. L., Schulz, K. M., & Zehr, J. L. (2003). Puberty: A finishing school for male social behavior. *Annals of the New York Academy of Sciences, 1007*, 189–198.

Sisk, C. L., & Zehr, J. L. (2005). Pubertal hormones organize the adolescent brain and behavior. *Frontiers in Neuroendocrinology, 26*(3–4), 163–174.

Slotkin, T. A. (2002). Nicotine and the adolescent brain: Insights from an animal model. *Neurotoxicology and Teratology, 24*(3), 369–384.

Slovic, P., Finucane, M., Peters, E., & MacGregor, D. G. (2004). Risk as analysis and risk as feelings: Some thoughts about affect, reason, risk, and rationality. *Risk Analysis, 24*(2), 311–322.

Slyper, A. H. (2006). The pubertal timing controversy in the USA, and a review of possible causative factors for the advance in timing of onset of puberty. *Clinical Endocrinology, 65,* 1–8.

Smith, C. (1996). The link between childhood maltreatment and teenage pregnancy. *Social Work Research, 20,* 131–141.

Smith, E. A., Udry, J. R., & Morris, N. M. (1985). Pubertal development and friends: A biosocial explanation of adolescent sexual behavior. *Journal of Health and Social Behavior, 26,* 183–192.

Smith, K. S., & Berridge, K. C. (2005). The ventral pallidum and hedonic reward: Neurochemical maps of sucrose "liking" and food intake. *Journal of Neuroscience, 25*(38), 8637–8649.

Smith, P. K. (1982). Does play matter? Functional and evolutionary aspects of animal and human play. *The Behavioral and Brain Sciences, 5,* 139–184.

Smith, R. F. (2003). Animal models of periadolescent substance abuse. *Neurotoxicology and Teratology, 25*(3), 291–301.

Snoek, H., Van Goozen, S. H. M., Matthys, W., Buitelaar, J. K., & Van Engeland, H. (2004). Stress responsivity in children with externalizing behavior disorders. *Development and Psychopathology, 16,* 389–406.

Sowell, E. R., Lu, L. H., O'Hare, E. D., McCourt, S. T., Mattson, S. N., O'Connor, M. J., et al. (2007). Functional magnetic resonance imaging of verbal learning in children with heavy prenatal alcohol exposure. *Neuroreport, 18*(7), 635–639.

Sowell, E. R., Peterson, B. S., Thompson, P. M., Welcome, S. E., Henkenius, A. L., & Toga, A. W. (2003). Mapping cortical change across the human life span. *Nature Neuroscience, 6*(3), 309–315.

Sowell, E. R., Thompson, P. M., Holmes, C. J., Batth, R., Jernigan, T. L., & Toga, A. W. (1999). Localizing age-related changes in brain structure between childhood and adolescence using statistical parametric mapping. *NeuroImage, 9,* 587–597.

Spear, L. P. (1997). Neurobehavioral abnormalities following exposure to drugs of abuse during development. In B. A. Johnson & J. D. Roache (Eds.), *Drug addiction and its treatment: Nexus of neuroscience and behavior* (pp. 233–255). Philadelphia: Lippincott-Raven.

Spear, L. P. (2000a). The adolescent brain and age-related behavioral manifestations. *Neuroscience and Biobehavioral Reviews, 24*(4), 417–463.

Spear, L. P. (2000b). Adolescent period: Biological basis of vulnerability to develop alcoholism and other ethanol-mediated behaviors. In A. Noron-ha, M. Eckardt, & K. Warren (Eds.), *NIAAA research monograph 34: Review of NIAAA's neuroscience and behavioral research portfolio* (Publication No. 00-4520, pp. 315–333).

Spear, L. P. (2003). Neurodevelopment during adolescence. In D. Cicchetti & E. F. Walker (Eds.), *Neurodevelopmental mechanisms in psychopathology* (pp. 62–83). Cambridge, UK: Cambridge University Press.

Spear, L. P. (2007a). Assessment of adolescent neurotoxicity: Rationale and methodological considerations. *Neurotoxicology and Teratology, 29*(1), 1–9.

Spear, L. P. (2007b). The developing brain and adolescent-typical behavior patterns: An evolutionary approach. In E. Walker, J. Bossert, & D. Romer (Eds.), *Adolescent psychopathology and the developing brain: Integrating brain and prevention science* (pp. 9–30). New York: Oxford University Press.

Spear, L. P. (2009). Adolescent responsiveness to stressful and emotional stimuli: Commentary on special section on adolescence. *Development and Psychopathology, 21*(1), 87–97.

Spear, L. P., & Brake, S. C. (1983). Periadolescence: Age-dependent behavior and psychopharmacological responsivity in rats. *Developmental Psychobiology, 16*(2), 83–109.

Spear, L. P., & Varlinskaya, E. I. (2005). Adolescence: Alcohol sensitivity, tolerance, and intake. In M. Galanter (Ed.), *Recent developments in alcoholism: Vol. 17. Alcohol problems in adolescents and young adults* (pp. 143–159). New York: Kluwer Academic/Plenum Press.

Stadler, C., Sterzer, P., Schmeck, K., Krebs, A., Kleinschmidt, A., & Poustka, F. (2007). Reduced anterior cingulate activation in aggressive children and adolescents during affective stimulation: Association with temperament traits. *Journal of Psychiatric Research, 41*(5), 410–417.

Stead, J. D. H., Neal, C., Meng, F., Wang, Y., Evans, S., Vazquez, D. M., et al. (2006). Transcriptional profiling of the developing rat brain reveals that the most dramatic regional differentiation in gene expression occurs portpartum. *Journal of Neuroscience, 26*(1), 345–353.

Steinberg, L. (1987). Impact of puberty on family relations: Effects of pubertal status and pubertal timing. *Developmental Psychology, 23*(3), 451–460.

Steinberg, L. (1988). Reciprocal relation between parent–child distance and pubertal maturation. *Developmental Psychology, 24*(1), 122–128.

Steinberg, L. (1989). Pubertal maturation and parent–adolescent distance: An evolutionary perspective. In G. R. Adams, R. Montemayor, & T. P. Gullotta (Eds.), *Advances in adolescent behavior and development* (pp. 71–97). Newbury Park, CA: Sage.

Steinberg, L. (2004). Risk taking in adolescence. What changes, and why? *Annals of the New York Academy of Sciences, 1021*, 51–58.

Steinberg, L. (2005). Cognitive and affective development in adolescence. *Trends in Cognitive Sciences, 9*(2), 69–74.

Steinberg, L., & Belsky, J. (1996). *An evolutionary perspective on psychopathology in adolescence.* Rochester, NY: University of Rochester Press.

Sterzer, P., Stadler, C., Krebs, A., Kleinschmidt, A., & Poustka, F. (2005). Abnormal neural responses to emotional visual stimuli in adolescents with conduct disorder. *Biological Psychiatry, 57*, 7–15.

Sterzer, P., Stadler, C., Poustka, F., & Kleinschmidt, A. (2007). A structural neural deficit in adolescents with conduct disorder and its association with lack of empathy. *Neuroimage, 37*, 335–342.

Stettler, D. D., Yamahachi, H., Li, W., Denk, W., & Gilbert, C. D. (2006). Axons and synaptic boutons are highly dynamic in adult visual cortex. *Neuron, 49*, 877–887.

Stevens, J. R. (2002). Schizophrenia: Reproductive hormones and the brain. *American Journal of Psychiatry, 159*(5), 713–719.

Stevens, B., Porta, S., Haak, L. L., Gallo, V., & Fields, R. D. (2002). Adenosine: A neuron–glial transmitter promoting myelination in the CNS in response to action potentials. *Neuron, 36*, 855–868.

Stevens, M. C., Kiehl, K. A., Pearlson, G. D., & Calhoun, V. D. (2007). Functional neural networks underlying response inhibition in adolescents and adults. *Behavioural Brain Research, 181*, 12–22.

Stroud, L., Foster, E., Panpandonatos, G. D., Handwerger, K., Granger, D. A., Kivlighan, K. T., et al. (2009). Stress response and the adolescent transition: Performance versus peer rejection stressors. *Development and Psychopathology, 21*(1), 69–85.

Stroud, L., Salovey, P., & Epel, E. S. (2002). Sex differences in stress responses: Social rejection versus achievement stress. *Biological Psychiatry, 52*, 318–327.

Substance Abuse and Mental Health Services Administration (2008). Office of Applied Statistics. The National Survey on Drug Use and Health Report—Quantity and Frequency of Alcohol Use among Underage Drinkers, Rockville, MD (March 31, 2008).

Sullivan, P. F., Kendler, K. S., & Neale, M. C. (2003). Schizophrenia as a complex trait: Evidence from a meta-analysis of twin studies. *Archives of General Psychiatry, 60,* 1187–1192.

Sundet, J. M., Eriksen, W., & Tambs, K. (2008). Intelligence correlations between brothers decrease with increasing age difference. *Psychological Science, 19*(9), 843–847.

Sur, M., & Rubenstein, J. L. R. (2005). Patterning and plasticity of the cerebral cortex. *Science, 310,* 805–810.

Surbey, M. K. (1990). Family composition, stress, and the timing of human menarche. In T. E. Ziegler & F. B. Bercovitch (Eds.), *Socioendocrinology of primate reproduction* (pp. 11–32). New York: Wiley-Liss.

Surbey, M. K. (1998). Parent and offspring: Strategies in the transition at adolescence. *Human Nature, 9,* 67–94.

Surguladze, S., Brammer, M. J., Keedwell, P., Giampietro, V., Young, A. W., Travis, M. J., et al. (2005). A differential pattern of neural response toward sad versus happy facial expressions in major depressive disorder. *Biological Psychiatry, 57,* 201–209.

Susser, E., Neugebauer, R., Hoek, H. W., Brown, A. S., Lin, S., Labovitz, D., et al. (1996). Schizophrenia after prenatal famine: Further evidence. *Archives of General Psychiatry, 53,* 25–31.

Swaab, D. F. (2004). Sexual diffrentiation of the human brain: Relevance for gender identity, transsexualism, and sex- ual orientation. *Gynecological Endrocrinology, 19*(6), 301– 312.

Swaab, D. F., & Hofman, M. A. (1990). An enlarged suprachiasmatic nucleus in homosexual men. *Brain Research, 537,* 141–148.

Swanson, L. W., & Petrovich, G. D. (1998). What is the amygdala? *Trends in the Neurosciences, 21*(8), 323–331.

Szyf, M., Weaver, I., & Meaney, M. J. (2007). Maternal care, the epigenome, and phenotypic differences in behavior. *Reproductive Toxicology, 24,* 9–19.

Tambour, S., Brown, L. L., & Crabbe, J. C. (2008). Gender and age at drinking onset affect voluntary alcohol consumption but neither the alcohol deprivation effect nor the response to stress in mice. *Alcoholism: Clinical and Experimental Research, 32*(12), 2100–2106.

Tamm, L., Menon, V., & Reiss, A. L. (2002). Maturation of brain function associated with response inhibition. *Journal of the American Academy of Child and Adolescent Psychiatry, 41*(10), 1231–1238.

Tapert, S. F., & Schweinsburg, A. D. (2005). The human adolescent brain and alcohol use disorders. In M. Galanter (Ed.), *Recent developments in alcoholism: Vol. 17. Alcohol problems in adolescents and young adults* (pp. 177–197). New York: Kluwer Academic/Plenum Press.

Tarazi, F. I., & Baldessarini, R. J. (2000). Comparative postnatal development of dopamine d_1, d_2, and d_4 receptors in rat forebrain. *International Journal of Developmental Neuroscience, 18*(1), 29–37.

Taylor, J. B. (2008). *My stroke of insight: A brain surgeon's personal journey.* New York: Viking Books.

Taylor, M. J., McCarthy, G., Saliba, E., & Degiovanni, E. (1999). ERP evidence of developmental changes in processing of faces. *Clinical Neurophysiology, 110,* 910–915.

Taylor, P. D., & Poston, L. (2007). Developmental programming of obesity in mammals. *Experimental Physiology, 92*(2), 287–298.

Taylor, S. E., Gonzaga, G. C., Klein, L. C., Hu, P., Greendale, G. A., & Seeman, T. E. (2006). Relation of oxytocin to psychological responses and hypothalamic–pituitary–adrenocortical axis activity in older women. *Psychosomatic Medicine, 68,* 238–245.

Teicher, M. H. (2002). Scars that won't heal: The neurobiology of child abuse. *Scientific American, 286*(3), 68–75.

Teicher, M. H., Barber, N. I., Gelbard, H. A., Gallitano, A. L., Campbell, A., Marsh, E., & Baldessarini, R. J. (1993). Developmental differences in acute nigrostriatal and mesocorticolimbic system response to haloperidol. *Neuropsychopharmacology, 9*(2), 147–156.

Teicher, M. H., Dumont, N. L., Ito, Y., Vaituzis, C. K., Giedd, J. N., & Andersen, S. L. (2004). Childhood neglect is associated with reduced corpus callosum area. *Biological Psychiatry, 56,* 80–85.

Teicher, M. H., Gallitano, A. L., Gelbard, H. A., Evans, H. K., Marsh, E. R., Booth, R. G., et al. (1991). Dopamine D1 autoreceptor function: Possible expression in developing rat prefrontal cortex and striatum. *Brain Research: Developmental Brain Research, 63,* 229–235.

Teicher, M. H., Krenzel, E., Thompson, A. P., & Andersen, S. L. (2003). Dopamine receptor pruning during the peripubertal period is not attenuated by NMDA receptor antagonism in rat. *Neuroscience Letters, 339*(1), 169–171.

Tena-Sempere, M. (2006). The roles of kisspeptins and G protein-coupled receptor-54 in pubertal development. *Current Opinion in Pediatrics, 18*(4), 442–447.

Thomas, K. M., Drevets, W. C., Dahl, R. E., Ryan, N. D., Birmaher, B., Eccard, C. H., et al. (2001a). Amygdala response to fearful faces in anxious and depressed children. *Archives of General Psychiatry, 58,* 1057–1063.

Thomas, K. M., Drevets, W. C., Whalen, P. J., Eccard, C. H., Dahl, R. E., Ryan, N. D., et al. (2001b). Amygdala response to facial expressions in children and adults. *Biological Psychiatry, 49*, 309–316.

Thomas, K. M., Hunt, R. H., Vizueta, N., Sommer, T., Durston, S., Yang, Y., et al. (2004). Evidence of developmental differences in implicit sequence learning: An fMRI study of children and adults. *Journal of Cognitive Neuroscience, 16*(8), 1339–1351.

Thomasson, H. R., Edenberg, H., Crabb, D. W., Mai, X. L., Jerome, R. E., Li, T. K., et al. (1991). Alcohol and aldehyde dehydrogenase genotypes and alcoholism in Chinese men. *American Journal of Human Genetics, 48*(4), 677–681.

Thompson, P. M., Vidal, C., Giedd, J. N., Gochman, P., Blumenthal, J., Nicolson, R., et al. (2001). Mapping adolescent brain change reveals dynamic wave of accelerated gray matter loss in very early-onset schizophrenia. *Proceedings of the National Academy of Sciences, 98*(20), 11650–11655.

Todd, R., & Heath, A. (1996). The genetic architecture of depression and anxiety in youth. *Current Opinion in Psychiatry, 9*(4), 257–261.

Toni, I., Krams, M., Turner, R., & Passingham, R. E. (1998). The time course of changes during motor sequence learning: A whole-brain fMRI study. *Neuroimage, 8*, 50–61.

Tonks, J., Williams, W. H., Frampton, I., Yates, P., & Slater, A. (2007). Assessing emotion recognition in 9–15-year olds: Preliminary analysis of abilities in reading emotion from faces, voices and eyes. *Brain Injury, 21*(6), 623–629.

Torres, O. V., Tejeda, H. A., Natividad, L. A., & O'Dell, L. E. (2008). Enhanced vulnerability to the rewarding effects of nicotine during the adolescent period of development. *Pharmacology, Biochemistry, and Behavior, 90*, 658–663.

Trachtenberg, J. T., Chen, B. E., Knott, G. W., Feng, G., Sanes, J. R., Welker, E., et al. (2002). Long-term in vivo imaging of experience-dependent synaptic plasticity in adult cortex. *Nature, 420*, 788–794.

Trezza, V., Cuomo, V., & Vanderschuren, L. J. M. J. (2008). Cannabis and the developing brain: Insights from behavior. *European Journal of Pharmacology, 585*, 441–452.

Tribollet, E., Charpak, S., Schmidt, A., Dubois-Dauphin, M., & Dreifuss, J. J. (1989). Appearance and transient expression of oxytocin receptors in fetal, infant, and peripubertal rat brain studied by autoradiography and electrophysiology. *Journal of Neuroscience, 9*(5), 1764–1773.

Trimpop, R. M., Kerr, J. H., & Kirkcaldy, B. (1999). Comparing personality constructs of risk-taking behavior. *Personality and Individual Differences, 26*(2), 237–254.

Truitt, W., Sajdyk, T. J., Dietrich, A. D., Oberlin, B., McDougle, C., & Shekhar, A. (2007). From anxiety to autism: Spectrum of abnormal social behaviors modeled by progressive disruption of inhibitory neuronal function in the basolateral amygdala in wistar rats. *Psychopharmacology, 191*, 107–118.

Tschann, J. M., Adler, N. E., Irwin, C. E., Millstein, S. G., Turner, R. A., & Kegeles, S. M. (1994). Initiation of substance use in early adolescence: The roles of pubertal timing and emotional distress. *Health Psychology, 13*(4), 326–333.

Tseng, K. Y., & O'Donnell, P. (2006). Dopamine modulation of prefrontal cortical interneurons changes during adolescence. *Cerebral Cortex, 17*(5), 1235–1240.

Turkeltaub, P. E., Gareau, L., Flowers, D. L., Zeffiro, T. A., & Eden, G. F. (2003). Development of neural mechanisms for reading. *Nature Neuroscience, 6*(6), 767–773.

Turner, R. J., & Lloyd, D. A. (2004). Stress burden and the lifetime incidence of psychiatric disorder in young adults. *Archives of General Psychiatry, 61*, 481–488.

Turrigiano, G. G., & Nelson, S. B. (2004). Homeostatic plasticity in the developing nervous system. *Nature Reviews Neuroscience, 5*, 97–107.

Twiggs, D. G., Popolow, H. B., & Gerall, A. A. (1978). Medial preoptic lesions and male sexual behavior: Age and environmental interactions. *Science, 200*, 1414–1415.

Unkelbach, C., Guastella, A. J., & Forgas, J. P. (2008). Oxytocin selectively facilitates recognition of positive sex and relationship words. *Psychological Science, 19*(11), 1092–1094.

Uvnäs-Moberg, K. (1997). Oxytocin linked antistress effects: The relaxation and growth response. *Acta Physiologica Scandinavica, 640*, 38–42.

Uysal, N., Tugyan, K., Kayatekin, B. M., Acikgoz, O., Bagriyanik, H. A., Gonenc, S., et al. (2005). The effects of regular aerobic exercise in adolescent period on hippocampal neuron density, apoptosis, and spatial memory. *Neuroscience Letters, 383*(3), 241–245.

Vallée, M., Mayo, W., Dellu, F., Le Moal, M., Simon, H., & Maccari, S. (1997). Prenatal stress induces high anxiety and postnatal handling induces low anxiety in adult offspring: Correlation with stress-induced corticosterone secretion. *Journal of Neuroscience, 17*(7), 2626–2636.

van Bokhoven, I., Van Goozen, S. H. M., van Engeland, H., Schaal, B., Arseneault, L., Séguin, J. R., et al. (2005). Salivary cortisol and aggression in a population-based longitudinal study of adolescent males. *Journal of Neural Transmission, 112*(8), 1083–1096.

van de Wiel, N. M. H., Van Goozen, S. H. M., Matthys, W., Snoek, H., & Van Engeland, H. (2004). Cortisol and treatment effect in children with disruptive behavior disorders: A preliminary study. *Journal of the American Academy of Child and Adolescent Psychiatry, 43*, 1011–1018.

van der Zwaluw, C. S., van den Wildenberg, E., Wiers, R. W., Franke, B., Buitelaar, J., Scholte, R. H., et al. (2007). Polymorphisms in the mu-opioid receptor gene (OPRM1) and the implications for alcohol dependence in humans. *Pharmacogenomics, 8*(10), 1427–1436.

van Duijvenvoorde, A. C. K., Zanolie, K., Rombouts, S. A. R. B., Raijmakers, M. E. J., & Crone, E. A. (2008). Evaluating the negative or valuing the positive? Neural mechanisms supporting feedback-based learning across development. *Journal of Neuroscience, 28*(38), 9495–9503.

van Goozen, S. H. M., Fairchild, G., Snoek, H., & Harold, G. T. (2007). The evidence for a neurobiological model of childhood antisocial behavior. *Psychological Bulletin, 133*(1), 149–182.

van Leijenhorst, L., Crone, E. A., & Bunge, S. A. (2006). Neural correlates of developmental differences in risk estimation and feedback processing. *Neuropsychobiologia, 44*, 2158–2170.

Varlinskaya, E. I., & Spear, L. P. (2002). Acute effects of ethanol on social behavior of adolescent and adult rats: Role of familiarity of the test situation. *Alcoholism: Clinical and Experimental Research, 26*(10), 1502–1511.

Varlinskaya, E. I., & Spear, L. P. (2003, November). *Chronic tolerance to ethanol effects on social behavior of adolescent and adult rats.* Society for Neuroscience, New Orleans, LA.

Varlinskaya, E. I., & Spear, L. P. (2007). Chronic tolerance to the social consequences of ethanol in adolescent and adult Sprague–Dawley rats. *Neurotoxicology and Teratology, 29*(1), 23–30.

Varlinskaya, E. I., Spear, L. P., & Spear, N. E. (2001). Acute effects of ethanol on behavior of adolescent rats: Role of social context. *Alcoholism: Clinical and Experimental Research, 25*(3), 377–385.

Vastola, B. J., Douglas, L. A., Varlinskaya, E. I., & Spear, L. P. (2002). Nicotine-induced conditioned place preference in adolescent and adult rats. *Physiology and Behavior, 77*(1), 107–114.

Vázquez, D. M. (1998). Stress and the developing limbic–hypothalamic–pituitary–adrenal axis. *Psychoneuroendocrinology, 23*, 663–700.

Velanova, K., Wheeler, M. E., & Luna, B. (2008). Maturational changes in anterior cingulate and frontoparietal recruitment support the development of error processing and inhibitory control. *Cerebral Cortex, 18*(11), 2505–2522.

Verdejo-García, A., Perez-Garcia, M., & Bechara, A. (2006). Emotion, decision-making and substance dependence: A somatic-marker model of addiction. *Current Neuropharmacology, 4,* 17–31.

Vetter, C. S., Doremus-Fitzwater, T. L., & Spear, L. P. (2007). Time-course of elevated ethanol intake in adolescent relative to adult rats under continuous, voluntary-access conditions. *Alcoholism: Clinical and Experimental Research, 31*(7), 1159–1168.

Vidal, C. N., Rapoport, J. L., Hayashi, K. M., Greaga, J. A., Sui, Y., McLemore, L. E., et al. (2006). Dynamically spreading frontal and cingulate deficits mapped in adolescents with schizophrenia. *Archives of General Psychiatry, 63*(1), 25– 34.

Vik, P., & Brown, S. A. (1998). Life events and substance abuse during adolescence. In T. W. Miller (Ed.), *Children of trauma* (pp. 179–204). Madison, CT: International Universities Press.

Volkow, N. D., Fowler, J. S., Wang, G.-J., Ding, Y., & Gatley, S. J. (2002b). Mechanism of action of methylphenidate: Insights from PET imaging studies. *Journal of Attention Disorders, 6*(Suppl. 1), S31–S43.

Volkow, N. D., Fowler, J. S., Wang, G.-J., & Goldstein, R. Z. (2002a). Role of dopamine, the frontal cortex and memory circuits in drug addiction: Insight from imaging studies. *Neurobiology of Learning and Memory, 78*(3), 610–624.

Volkow, N. D., Wang, G.-J., Telang, F., Fowler, J. S., Logan, J., Jayne, M., et al. (2007). Profound decreases in dopamine release in striatum in detoxified alcoholics: Possible orbitofrontal involvement. *Journal of Neuroscience, 27*(46), 12700–12706.

Vorhold, V., Giessing, C., Wiedemann, P. M., Schütz, H., Gauggel, S., & Fink, G. R. (2007). The neural basis of risk ratings: Evidence from a functional magnetic resonance imaging (fMRI) study. *Neuropsychologia, 45*(14), 3242–3250.

Wager, T. D., Phan, K. L., Liberzon, I., & Taylor, S. F. (2003). Valence, gender, and lateralization of functional brain anatomy in emotion: A meta-analysis of findings from neuroimaging. *Neuroimage, 19,* 513–531.

Wagner, E. F. (1993). Delay of gratification, coping with stress, and substance use in adolescence. *Experimental and Clinical Psychopharmacology, 1,* 27–43.

Walker, B. M., & Ehlers, C. L. (2008). Age-related differences in the blood alcohol levels of wistar rats. *Pharmacology, Biochemistry, and Behavior, 91*(4), 560–565.

Walker, D. L., Toufexis, D. J., & Davis, M. (2003). Role of the bed nucleus of the stria terminalis versus the amygdala in fear, stress, and anxiety. *European Journal of Pharmacology, 463*(1–3), 199–216.

Walker, E. F., Baum, K. M., & Diforio, D. (1998). Developmental changes in the behavioral expression of vulnerability for schizophrenia. In M. Lenzenweger & R. Dworkin (Eds.), *Origins and development of schizophrenia: Advances in experimental psychopathology* (pp. 469–491). Washington, DC: American Psychological Association.

Walker, E. F., & Diforio, D. (1997). Schizophrenia: A neural diathesis–stress model. *Psychological Review, 104*(4), 667–685.

Walker, E. F., Sabuwalla, Z., & Huot, R. (2004). Pubertal neuromaturation, stress sensitivity, and psychopathology. *Development and Psychopathology, 16*(4), 807–824.

Walker, E. F., Savoie, T., & Davis, D. (1994). Neuromuscular precursors of schizophrenia. *Schizophrenia Bulletin, 20*(3), 441–451.

Walker, E. F., & Walder, D. (2003). Neurohormonal aspects of the development of psychotic disorders. In D. Cicchetti & E. Walker (Eds.), *Neurodevelopmental mechanisms in psychopathology* (pp. 526–543). Cambridge, UK: Cambridge University Press.

Walker, E. F., Walder, D. J., & Reynolds, F. (2001). Developmental changes in cortisol secretion in normal and at-risk youth. *Development and Psychopathology, 13*(3), 721–732.

Walker, Q. D., Schramm-Sapyta, N. L., Caster, J. M., Waller, S. T., Brooks, M. P., & Kuhn, C. M. (2009). Novelty-induced locomotion is positively associated with cocaine ingestion in adolescent rats; anxiety is correlated in adults. *Pharmacology, Biochemistry, and Behavior, 91*(3), 398–408.

Wallen, K. (2001). Sex and context: Hormones and primate sexual motivation. *Hormones and Behavior, 40*, 339–357.

Wand, G. (2008). The influence of stress on the transition from drug use to addiction. *Alcohol Research and Health, 31*(2), 119–136.

Wang, Y. (2002). Is obesity associated with early sexual maturation? A comparison of the association in American boys vs. girls. *Pediatrics, 110*(5), 903–910.

Ward, I. L., & Ward, O. (1985). Sexual behavior differentiation: Effects of prenatal manipulations in rats. In N. Adler, D. W. Pfaff, & R. W. Goy

(Eds.), *Handbook of behavioral neurobiology* (Vol. 7, pp. 77–98). New York: Plenum Press.

Waylen, A., & Wolke, D. (2004). Sex 'n' drugs 'n' rock 'n' roll: The meaning and social consequences of pubertal timing. *European Journal of Endocrinology, 151*, 151–159.

Weaver, I. C. G., Cervoni, N., Champagne, F. A., D'Alessio, A. C., Sharma, S., Seckl, J. R., et al. (2004). Epigenetic programming by maternal behavior. *Nature Neuroscience, 7*(8), 847–854.

Weickert, C. S., Webster, M. J., Gondipalli, P., Rothmond, D., Fatula, R. J., Herman, M. M., Kleinman, J. E., & Akil, M. (2007). Postnatal alterations in dopaminergic markers in the human prefrontal cortex. *Neuroscience, 144*, 1109–1119.

Weisfeld, G. E. (1979). An ethological view of human adolescence. *Journal of Nervous and Mental Disease, 167*(1), 38–55.

Weisfeld, G. E. (1999). *Evolutionary principles of human adolescence.* New York: Basic Books.

Weisfeld, G. E., & Berger, J. M. (1983). Some features of human adolescence viewed in evolutionary perspective. *Human Development, 26*, 121–133.

Weisfeld, G. E., & Janisse, C. (2004). Some functional aspects of human adolescence. In B. J. Ellis & D. F. Bjorklund (Eds.), *Origins of the social mind: Evolutionary psychology and child development* (pp. 189–218). New York: Guilford Press.

Welsh, M. C., Pennington, B., & Groisser, D. (1991). A normative-developmental study of executive function: A window on prefrontal function in children. *Developmental Neuropsychology, 7*(2), 131–149.

Werner, E. (2005). Resilience and recovery: Findings from the Kauai longitudinal study. *Focal Point, 19*(1), 11–14.

Whalen, P. J., Shin, L., McInerney, S. C., & Fischer, H. (2001). A functional MRI study of human amygdala responses to facial expressions of fear versus anger. *Emotion, 1*(1), 70–83.

White, A. M., & Swartzwelder, H. S. (2005). Age-related effects of alcohol on memory and memory-related brain function in adolescents and adults. In M. Galanter (Ed.), *Recent developments in alcoholism: Vol. 17. Alcohol problems in adolescents and young adults* (pp. 161–176). New York: Kluwer Academic/Plenum Press.

White, T., Kendi, A. T., Lehericy, S., Kendi, M., Karatekin, C., Guimaraes, A., et al. (2007). Disruption of hippocampal connectivity in children and adolescents with schizophrenia: A voxel-based diffusion tensor imaging study. *Schizophrenia Research, 90*(1–3), 302–307.

Whitefield, C. W., Cziko, A.-M., & Robinson, G. (2003). Gene expression pro-files in the brain predict behavior in individual honey bees. *Science, 302,* 296–299.

Whitelaw, N. C., & Whitelaw, E. (2006). How lifetimes shape epigenotype within and across generations. *Human Molecular Genetics, 15*(2), R131–R137.

Whitfield, J. B. (2005). Alcohol and gene interactions. *Clinical Chemistry and Laboratory Medicine, 43*(5), 480–487.

Whitford, T. J., Grieve, S. M., Farrow, T. F. D., Gomes, L., Brennan, J., Harris, A. W. F., et al. (2007). Volumetric white matter abnormalities in first-episode schizophrenia: A longitudinal, tensor-based morphometry study. *American Journal of Psychiatry, 164*(7), 1082–1089.

Whittle, S., Yap, M. B. H., Yücel, M., Fornito, A., Simmons, J. G., Barrett, A., et al. (2008a). Prefrontal and amygdala volumes are related to adolescent's affective behaviors during parent–adolescent interactions. *Proceedings of the National Academy of Sciences, 105*(9), 3652–3657.

Whittle, S., Yücel, M., Fornito, A., Barrett, A., Wood, S. J., Lubman, D. I., et al. (2008b). Neuroanatomical correlates of temperament in early adolescents. *Journal of the American Academy of Child and Adolescent Psychiatry, 47*(6), 682–693.

Wiesel, T. N., & Hubel, D. H. (1965). Comparison of the effects of unilateral and bilateral eye closure on cortical unit responses in kittens. *Journal of Neurophysiology, 28,* 1029–1040.

Wilkinson, L. S. (1997). The nature of interactions involving prefrontal and striatal dopamine systems. *Journal of Psychopharmacology, 11,* 143–150.

Willey, A. R., Varlinskaya, E. I., & Spear, L. P. (2009). Social interactions and 50 kHz ultrasonic vocalizations in adolescent and adult rats. *Behavioural Brain Research,* in press.

Williams, B. R., Ponesse, J. S., Schachar, R. J., Logan, G. D., & Tannock, R. (1999). Development of inhibitory control across the life span. *Developmental Psychology, 35*(1), 205–213.

Wilmouth, C. E., & Spear, L. P. (2006). Withdrawal from chronic nicotine in adolescent and adult rats. *Pharmacology, Biochemistry, and Behavior, 85*(3), 648–657.

Wilmouth, C. E., & Spear, L. P. (2009). Hedonic sensitivity in adolescent and adult rats: Taste reactivity and voluntary sucrose consumption. *Pharmacology, Biochemistry, and Behavior,* in press.

Wilson, D., & Daly, M. (1993). Lethal confrontational violence among young men. In N. J. Bell & R. W. Bell (Eds.), *Adolescent risk taking* (pp. 84–106). Newbury Park, CA: Sage.

Wilson, D. M., Killen, J. D., Hayward, C., Robinson, T. N., Hammer, L. D., Kraemer, H. C., et al. (1994). Timing and rate of sexual maturation and the onset of cigarette and alcohol use among teenage girls. *Archives of Pediatrics and Adolescent Medicine, 148*, 789–795.

Wilson, M., & Daly, M. (1985). Competitiveness, risk taking, and violence: The young male syndrome. *Ethology and Sociobiology, 6*, 59–73.

Woo, T.-U., Pucak, M. L., Kye, C. H., Matus, C. V., & Lewis, D. A. (1997). Peripubertal refinement of the intrinsic and associational circuitry in monkey prefrontal cortex. *Neuroscience, 80*(4), 1149–1158.

Worthman, C. M. (1999). Epidemiology of human development. In C. Panter-Brick & C. M. Worthman (Eds.), *Hormones, health, and behavior: A socio-ecological and lifespan perspective* (pp. 47–104). New York: Cambridge University Press.

Wright, P., Albarracin, D., Brown, R. D., Li, H., He, G., & Liu, Y. (2008). Dissociated responses in the amygdala and orbitofrontal cortex to bottom-up and top-down components of emotional evaluation. *Neuroimage, 39*(2), 894–902.

Wulfert, E., Block, J. A., Santa Ana, E., Rodriguez, M. L., & Colsman, M. (2002). Delay of gratification: Impulsive choices and problem behaviors in early and late adolescence. *Journal of Personality, 70*(4), 533–552.

Wurtman, R. J., Wurtman, J. J., Regan, M. M., McDermott, J. M., Tsay, R. H., & Breu, J. J. (2003). Effects of normal meals rich in carbohydrates or proteins on plasma tryptophan and tyrosine ratios. *American Journal of Clinical Nutrition, 77*, 128–132.

Yakovlev, P. I., & Lecours, A.-R. (1967). The myelogenetic cycles of regional maturation of the brain. In A. Minkowski (Ed.), *Regional development of the brain in early life* (pp. 3–70). Philadelphia: Davis.

Yang, T., Simmons, A., Matthews, S., Tapert, S. F., Bischoff-Grethe, A., Frank, G. K., et al. (2007). Increased amygdala activation is related to heart rate during emotion processing in adolescent subjects. *Neuroscience Letters, 428*(2–3), 109–114.

Young, E. A. (1998). Sex differences and the HPA axis: Implications for psychiatric disease. *Journal of Gender-Specific Medicine, 1*(1), 21–27.

Young, L. J., & Francis, D. D. (2007). The biochemistry of family commitment and youth competence: Lessons from animal models. In K. K. Kline (Ed.), *Authoritative communities: The scientific case for nurturing the whole child* (pp. 71–85). New York: Springer.

Young, L. J., Lim, M. M., Gingrich, B., & Insel, T. R. (2001). Cellular mechanisms of social attachment. *Hormones and Behavior, 40*, 133–138.

Yurgelun-Todd, D. A., Killgore, W. D. S., & Cintron, C. B. (2003). Cognitive correlates of medial temporal lobe development across adolescence: A magnetic resonance imaging study. *Perceptual and Motor Skills, 96*, 3–17.

Zakharova, E., Leoni, G., Kichko, I., & Izenwasser, S. (2009a). Differential effects of methamphetamine and cocaine on conditioned place preference and locomotor activity in adult and adolescent male rats. *Behavioural Brain Research, 198*(1), 45–50.

Zakharova, E., Wade, D., & Izenwasser, S. (2009b). Sensitivity to cocaine conditioned reward depends on sex and age. *Pharmacology, Biochemistry, and Behavior, 92*(7), 131–134.

Zalc, B., & Field, R. D. (2000). Do action potentials regulate myelination? *The Neuroscientist, 6*(1), 5–13.

Zald, D. (2003). The human amygdala and the emotional evaluation of sensory stimuli: Review. *Brain Research Reviews, 41*(1), 88–123.

Zehr, J. L., Todd, B. J., Schulz, K. M., McCarthy, M. M., & Sisk, C. L. (2006). Dendritic pruning of the medial amygdala during pubertal development of the male Syrian hamster. *Journal of Neurobiology, 66*, 578–590.

Zheng, W., & Knudsen, E. I. (1999). Functional selection of adaptive auditory space map by GABA$_a$-mediated inhibition. *Science, 284*, 962–965.

Zuckerman, M. (1990). The psychophysiology of sensation seeking. *Journal of Personality, 58*(1), 313–345.

Zuckerman, M. (1992). Sensation seeking: The balance between risk and reward. In L. P. Lipsitt & L. L. Mitnick (Eds.), *Self-regulatory behavior and risk taking* (pp. 143–152). Norwood, NJ: Ablex.

Zuckerman, M., Eysenck, S., & Eysenck, H. J. (1978). Sensation seeking in England and America: Cross-cultural, age, and sex comparisons. *Journal of Consulting and Clinical Psychology, 46*(1), 139–149.

Zuo, Y., Chang, P., Lin, A., & Gan, W.-B. (2005a). Development of long-term dendritic spine stability in diverse regions of cerebral cortex. *Neuron, 46*, 181–189.

Zuo, Y., Yang, G., Kwon, E., & Gan, W.-B. (2005b). Long-term sensory deprivation prevents dendritic spine loss in primary somatosensory cortex. *Nature, 436*, 261–265.

Index

action potentials, 63–64
adenosine, 20, 306–7
adrenal gland hormones, 50, 162
adrenocorticotropic hormone, 162
age
  brain activation patterns in emo-
    tional response, 183–84
  definition of adolescence, 5–6
  determinants of puberty onset, 6,
    55–56
  psychosocial outcomes of early
    puberty, 57–58
  sex differences in puberty onset,
    15
  sexual activity patterns, 156
  sociocultural factors in perception
    of adolescence, 10–11
  sociocultural factors in pubertal
    maturation, 9–10
  trends in puberty onset, 56
  see also development, adolescent
    transition
aggressive and violent behaviors
  amygdalar development and, 177
  corticosteroid levels and, 255–56
  sociocultural context, 7–8, 11
alcohol and drug use
  adolescent sensitivity to effects of,
    as risk factor for abuse, 211–
    16

age of puberty onset and risk of,
  57–58
animal studies of adolescent development, 18–19
associated psychological problems, 231
binge drinking, 191–92
brain development and, 226–28
brain regions and neurocircuitry
  activated by, 65, 70, 149, 193,
  203
cannabinoid receptors, 201
cannabis use in schizophrenia,
  251–52
cognitive outcomes, 225–26
delay discounting and, 143
epidemiology, 191–92
evolutionary advantages of moderate experimentation, 135–36
genetic risk factors, 219–22, 223
individual differences, 194
initiation, 219–20
international comparison, 192
long-term effects of adolescent exposure, 222–30
metabolization of alcohol, 213–
  14
multi-drug use, 231
reward system neurobiology and,
  194–99, 207–8, 230–31

diestrostibestrol, 42
diffusion tensor imaging, 93
DNA, 20–21, 22, 25, 31–32, 37–38, 80
dopamine system
 adolescent development, 65–66, 200–203
 drug interactions, 65
 externalizing disorders and, 259
 measurement strategies, 201–2
 neural projections, 65, 68, 70
 receptor polymorphisms, 31–32
 in reward system, 195–99, 200, 218
 schizophrenia and, 247–48, 249, 250
 substance use and, 65, 197, 200, 203, 221
 synaptic input, 83
dorsal striatum, 68, 152, 201
drug use. *see* alcohol and drug use
dysbindin gene, 250

eating disorders, 33, 233
economic context, perception of adolescent development in, 6, 10–12
electroencephalography, 91–92, 127–28
electrophysiology, 91–92, 127–28, 173
emotional functioning
 bilateral organization of brain and, 182–83
 brain areas associated with processing facial expressions, 170–76
 brain areas associated with risk-taking, 147–49, 154
 characteristics of adolescent development, 159
 cognitive interaction, 158
 in externalizing disorders, 256, 260–61
 hormonal changes in adolescence and, 49, 50–51, 160–61

hot cognitions in socioemotional processing, 187–88
hot cognitions leading to risk-taking, 139–40, 154
internalizing disorder risk, 266
neurobiology of depression, 269–71
neurophysiology, 68, 69
physiological manifestations, 160
processing of bodily information in, 147–48, 160, 165–70, 186, 189–90
recognition of emotional states in others, 155, 171–76
research needs, 159–60, 189–90
risk of risk-taking, 142
scope and function, 158
social behavior and, 155, 158
socioemotional brain systems in adolescence, 178–89
empathy, externalizing disorders and, 260
environmental factors
 axonal myelination, 288–90
 behavioral research methodology, 28–32
 in brain development, 78–80, 85–86
 in brain reserve alteration, 300–302
 cognitive functioning in adolescence, 33
 developmental neuroplasticity, 287–93
 in gene transcription and heritability, 22–23, 24–28, 80
 in internalizing disorders, 264–65
 opportunities for developmental programming in adolescence, 297–303
 scope of, in adolescent development, 24–25
 in synaptic pruning in adolescence, 290–93
 trends in age of puberty onset, 56